# Rogue Regimes

## Terrorism and Proliferation

Raymond Tanter

St. Martin's Griffin
New York

ISBN 0-312-21786-2

Library of Congress Cataloging-in-Publication Data
Tanter, Raymond.
Rogue regimes : terrorism and proliferation / Raymond
Tanter. — Rev. and updated ed. p. cm.   St. Martin's Griffin edition.
  Includes bibliographical references and index.
  ISBN 0-312-21786-2 (paper)   1. State-sponsored terrorism. 2. International relations. 3. Nuclear nonproliferation. 4. National security—United States. 5. United States—Foreign relations—20th century. I. Title.
HV6431 .T39
1999   327.1'17—dc21                                    99-11978
                                                           CIP


Design by Acme Art, Inc.
First St. Martin's Griffin edition: February, 1999
10 9 8 7 6 5 4 3 2 1

*To Kirk and Shawn*

# CONTENTS

# ACKNOWLEDGEMENTS

Thanks to those who provided insights for this book. These include Russell Bailey (North Korea); Joseph Gigliotti (politics and policies); Stephen Hessler (Syria); Michael Janson (Libya); Jonathan Mallin (Libya); Aman McLeod (Libya); Kristin McLean (Iran); John Post (Iraq, Syria); Randall Roth (North Korea); Anna Vania Song (North Korea, prospect theory); Charles Spies (American politics); and John Valentine (Libya). Acknowledgements to colleagues at the Council on Foreign Relations; institut français des relations internationales; Royal Institue of International Affairs; American Committees on Foreign Relations; World Affairs Councils of America; Trinity College and St. Antony's College; Oxford University; London School of Economics; Bristol University and the University of Kent for their feedback. Particular thanks to Paula Dobriansky, Bassama Kodmani-Darwish, and Eric Watkins for their interest and encouragement. Thanks to the University of Michigan Faculty Assistance Fund, to Mishkenot Sha'ananim for a peaceful writing place in Jerusalem, to Maya Savarino for companionship, Jan DiRomualdo for assistance, as well as to Alice and John Tanter for inspiration.

# PREFACE

## CONTAIN OR EMBRACE

In deciding whether to contain or embrace foreign countries, Americans love to personalize conflicts between the United States and its enemies. The three leaders in the photographs on the dust jacket of this book are well known to the American people: Osama bin Laden, Muammar Qadhafi, and Saddam Hussein. When *Time* magazine places such "rogue" leaders on its cover, the editors exploit a desire to demonize foreigners who dare to confront Washington. Americans see the rogue leaders of this book, the Ayatollah Khomeni and his colleagues, Saddam, Qadhafi, Hafez al-Assad, and Kim Jong-Il, as candidates for a gallery of adversaries. As the East-West conflict fades in intensity, a rogues' gallery imagery replaces photographs of Cold War notables such as Stalin, Brezhnev, and Mao. Kim, however, represents a leftover from the Cold War days. While the threat of global nuclear war and the prospect of a Soviet invasion of Germany were major dangers during the Cold War, the principal threats in the post–Cold War era stem from the rise of outlaw regimes led by members of our gallery.

As these men go about the unsavory business of terrorism and acquiring weapons of mass destruction, the world has a choice: to contain, embrace, or pursue a mixed policy toward these outlaw regimes. The new international villains are leaders of nations that have large conventional military forces and that condone international terrorism and/or seek weapons of mass destruction, including nuclear, biological, and chemical armaments.[1]

Iran, Iraq, Libya, Syria, and North Korea have large conventional military forces, sponsor or practice international terrorism, and are developing or acquiring weapons of mass destruction. Cuba, however, hardly fits these three criteria. As a result, this paperback edition excludes Cuba. It has been substituted by a chapter entitled, "Rogue Regimes, Contractors, and Freelancers."

While international terrorism alone is a menace to the world community, the joint occurrence of terrorism and weapons proliferation is a double threat. Accordingly, Congress acted in 1994 to expand the term "terrorism" to include efforts by any individual, group, or nonnuclear-weapon state to acquire unsafeguarded, special nuclear material or to use, develop, produce, stockpile, or otherwise acquire any nuclear explosive device.[2] If a state engages in either terrorism or proliferation of weapons of mass destruction, it enters the rogues' gallery; once there, they are candidates for this book.[3]

The remaining five rogue states in this volume have sought to acquire weapons of mass destruction. Regarding nuclear weapons development, Iran, Iraq, and North Korea are on the hunt, while chemical armaments are the main weapons of choice for Libya and Syria. Demonizing the leaders of another nation is one way to justify imposition of sanctions for their pursuit of weapons of mass destruction. In addressing this menace, there are three main approaches: (1) to contain these states with economic sanctions and deter or coerce them with threats of force; (2) to embrace them with promises of rewards; and (3) to embrace as well as contain them with these carrots and sticks. The best option to pursue depends upon whether a defender favors retribution or rehabilitation. If the goal is retribution, the policy is to contain. But if the goal is rehabilitation, the approach may be either to contain or embrace, or to do both.

## RETRIBUTION OR REHABILITATION

In writing this book with the help of a group of research assistants, we formed a computer conference. A flurry of E-mail messages reflected heated debate among the participants. An assistant noticed that our research group of eight students, dubbed "the Rogues," was divided over a core concern. At issue was what to do about ineffective deterrent and coercive policies. This problem goes beyond our study and cuts across different societal domains. Should a parent punish a child who continues to misbehave? Should a state government drop a death penalty that fails to deter murder? Should international coercive policies continue in the face of evidence that they fail to change behavior? To the last of these questions, three of the students, Joseph Gigliotti, Jonathan Mallin, and Randall Roth, immediately answered with a booming "yes." Five others, Rachael Farber, Thekla Fischer, Jeffrey Binder, Danielle Frappier, and Erin Ross, promptly countered with a resounding "no."

The members of the first group would persist with "fruitless" punishment of children, continue "ineffective" death penalties, and retain "futile" international coercive policies. They were ideologues who would punish wrongdoing for retributive purposes, irrespective of rehabilitation. They believed in the intrinsic worth of symbolic action.

The members of the second group would cease "ineffective" child discipline, abolish "pointless" death penalties, and abrogate "unprofitable" international coercive diplomacy. They were pragmatists who could not justify actions that did not produce behavioral change. They were unwilling to inflict pain without the prospect of gain. The entire debate added fuel to the fire over whether nations should retain or abandon coercive policies that fail to rehabilitate.

Retribution involves punishment to right a wrong; rehabilitation consists of punishment to correct misbehavior. This theme is a central concern of the literature on political theory and is a constant in our daily lives. The students who supported retribution advocated unilateral or individual action to ward off international chaos; the rehabilitative students preferred multilateral or collective action because it had the legitimacy of international consensus. Therefore, the research students who advocated retribution suggested an ideologically based unconditional containment, while the students supporting rehabilitation suggested a pragmatically based policy of contain, embrace, or both, depending upon their expected effects.

In developing a rationale for the unilateral imposition of economic sanctions, I sided with the retributive group. We reasoned that it is possible to recognize rogue behavior—that is, unacceptable international conduct. And once you detect rogue deeds, there is an obligation to act against their perpetrators—with sanctions, for example. The rehabilitative students questioned whether the term "rogue" should be used to describe regimes. They agreed that unacceptable behavior did exist in international politics, but differed from the retributive students on how to explain this behavior. Retributive students underestimated present compliant behavior and focused on prior deeds and the nature of the regime. Rehabilitative students, however, overestimated present compliant behavior and discounted prior deeds and the regime's nature. In making a choice between punishment for retribution or rehabilitation, moreover, a distinction must be made between opportunity and fear.

## "WINDOWS OF OPPORTUNITY" OR "BASEMENTS OF FEAR"

Those who favor retribution would punish regardless of challengers' motivations. But defenders who support rehabilitation want to know the motivations of the challengers before deciding to embrace, contain, or both. Those who would punish for retributive justice would do so irrespective of whether an actor's conduct derives from gain or fear. Those who would punish in order to rehabilitate would do so only if behavior stems from net gain; that is, the actor subtracts costs from benefits and is thereby approximately rational.[4]

But the rehabilitative approach assumes that sanctions are valid tools of coercion only if leaders are acting from a "window of opportunity" rather than from a "basement of fear." When people act out of opportunity, they weigh gains and losses about equally and are approximately rational in their behavior. Because opportunistic challengers have the capacity to understand the effects of their behavior, sanctions are appropriate. For supporters of rehabilitation, sanctions would not be considered for paranoids, who are fear-driven challengers and do not have the capacity to comprehend their actions. Fear allows biases to distort threat perception. As such, people motivated by fear are not likely to understand the consequences of sanctions.

When people act out of fear, they tend to be less rational. Opportunists, however, can be held accountable for their behavior, and for them, sanctions are a legitimate response to misbehavior. It is illegitimate to hold paranoids accountable for their irresponsible behavior; sanctions seem inappropriate responses to their desperate actions. Yet, it is legitimate to punish opportunistic individuals. In other words, it is comparatively difficult to penalize persons whose behavior derives from apprehension and easier to justify being tough on those whose misbehavior stems from opportunity.

The research group also debated whether economic sanctions should be imposed if they are instrumental failures but symbolic successes. An explicit purpose of sanctions generally is to change behavior, but an implicit aim may be to punish in order to right a wrong. We concluded that it was justifiable to use sanctions for symbolic aims. Our group discussed retribution as a tacit goal in the imposition of economic penalties and surmised that the persistence of ineffective sanctions was an indicator of their retributive nature.

One of the assistants suggested that when ineffective sanctions continue, it might be due to pressure for continuity by important domestic political constituencies. She explained that even when the original purpose of sanctions is solely for rehabilitation, its goal could shift later to retribution. For example, even if sanctions fail to bring about the desired change, they may nevertheless continue due to domestic pressure for reprisal. And even before succeeding, or failing to achieve, the end goal of rehabilitation, the process of adopting sanctions itself serves to send a retributive message. The group applauded this insight, with only a few low grumbles from dissenters.

In conclusion, decisions about containment and accommodation of rogue states take place in the context of an American tendency to personalize conflicts. Once "demonization" occurs, one is on the slippery slope of choosing sanctions. Depending upon whether challengers' motivations stem more from gain than fear, sanctions are legitimate. But sanctions for retribution are legitimate, irrespective of the challengers' purposes.

## LAYOUT OF THE BOOK

*Rogue Regimes* divides five states as well as formal groups and freelancers along geopolitical and historical lines. The first two chapters pair cases linked by geography but separated by ideology and history—Iran and Iraq. This approach is consistent with the dual containment policy of the United States, which treats Iran and Iraq as twin pariahs. Although both reject being classified as a pair, American policy groups them together. The Clinton White House refrains from the traditional practice of supporting either Iran or Iraq in order to block expansion by the other. The administration tries to work with the world community and regional allies to isolate and contain both rogue states. It has had more success in isolating Iraq than Iran.

In contrast to the Clinton policy of dual containment toward Iran and Iraq, the Reagan and Bush Administrations followed the Nixon tradition of balance of power diplomacy in the Gulf—alternately supporting Iran or Iraq. At times, the rationale was to prevent either state from gaining the upper hand. On other occasions, the United States responded to Iranian pressure, in order to bargain for the release of American hostages, or to Iraqi offers to facilitate the Israeli-Palestinian peace process.

The next two chapters of the book include Libya and Syria. Libya entered the gallery based on its status as a rogue even within the Arab world. It has a tradition of confrontation with neighboring states like Egypt, Tunisia, and Chad, as well as with the West in general and the United States in particular. As an offspring of an era of Arab nationalism and anti-colonialism, Libya is also a rejectionist state that does not accept the American-led peace process with Israel. Syria, in addition to Libya, is in a confrontation with the United States over issues like chemical weapons, state-sponsored terrorism, and the Israeli-Palestinian peace process. Damascus aligns with Iran against Iraq, is in conflict with Turkey over terrorists based there, and is in a no-peace, no-war status with Israel.

The final chapters address two additional cases—North Korea as well as a chapter that compares regimes, groups, and freelancers. As a child of the Cold War, Pyongyang is an orphan that retains an outdated communist system. In its waning days, this relic of a bygone era may be even more dangerous than in earlier times. Because North Korean rulers feel insecure without a Cold War safety net, the danger of political implosion and/or military explosion has increased. In a similar vein as with the regime in Pyongyang, the chapter on regimes, groups, and freelancers also discusses leaders whose insecurity and sense of loss make them a menacing band.

CHAPTER ONE

# PERSONALITY, POLITICS, AND POLICIES

IN THE COLD WAR ERA, the "stars" that dominated the world stage came from the superpowers. In the post–Cold War world, players from less powerful states have surfaced onto the international scene. One way to discuss these new celebrities is to organize their "infamy" by key dates that epitomize their rule. Absent the checks and balances of a democratic order and the bureaucracies of a large totalitarian state, rogue regimes are more subject to the politics of personality. In this respect, the policies of the new rulers are more a reflection of the whims of charismatic individuals than the outcome of bargaining among multiple centers of power.

## TIMES TO RELIVE[1]

*November 4, 1979.* Americans held their collective breath as some 3,000 Iranian students raided the U.S. embassy in Tehran. Our eyes were glued to television sets, waiting to hear the fate of the seventy Americans held inside against their will. Government officials were sweating. Military minds were turning. The public was not only dazed and confused, but angry as well. Who would dare do this to the United States of America, and how was Washington to respond? Six months later, America got its answer.

Washington launched a secret special-operations rescue mission called Desert One, only to see it fly to a fiery crash, leaving eight soldiers dead. After 444 days, the supreme spiritual and political leader of Iran, the Ayatollah Khomeni, released the hostages to President Ronald Reagan. Americans focused hostility and fear on Khomeni, who appeared on television as the personification of evil. Khomeni and everything associated with him invaded the American conscience. Never again could the United States look toward Iran without thinking of Khomeni and the acts of terrorism he seemed to condone.

*August 2, 1990.* The self-described "Knight of the Arab Nation," Saddam Hussein, ordered Iraqi troops to invade the small neighboring country of Kuwait. In response, President Bush ordered a huge military deployment of American troops, created a coalition of Western and Arab states, and subsequently authorized air and ground combat operations against Iraq.

Again, Americans watched on television as Scud missiles flew over the western Iraqi desert over Jerusalem en route to Tel Aviv. Coalition aircraft launched waves of strikes against Iraq. We held our collective breath as the Iraqi military took its first prisoners of war. Television viewers watched in horror as U.S. soldiers and Israeli citizens donned gas masks in anticipation of chemical warfare. Pundits reminded us of Saddam's ruthless use of poison gas against the Iranian military, against innocent civilians, and against the Kurds of his own country. Americans quickly forgot that this man was once a distant ally of the United States, and only saw Saddam Hussein as "the Butcher of Baghdad."

*February 1982.* Saddam is not the only Middle Eastern dictator who tried to annihilate his own citizens. Hafez al-Assad is the calculating, seemingly rational leader of Syria.[2] He is known to be just as ruthless and cruel as his counterpart in Iraq and has frequently shocked the world with violent and bloody displays of cruelty.

Assad ordered an attack on Hama, a city of about 180,000 people: over 10,000 individuals died.[3] The city harbored an organization, the Muslim Brotherhood, that opposed him. After a failed assassination attempt on his life, Assad first retaliated by torturing and executing

600 to 1,000 imprisoned Muslim Brothers. Then, in an effort to extinguish further opposition, he unleashed his military upon Hama.[4]

*December 21, 1988.* Another day that remains seared into America's collective memory—the day of the Pan Am 103 disaster over Lockerbie, Scotland. According to the U.S. State Department, two Libyans planted a bomb set to explode one hour after the commercial flight's departure. After an investigation, the U.S. Department of Justice and Scottish officials uncovered a trail that led to senior Libyan intelligence officers. Evidence also pointed to involvement by the infamous Muammar Qadhafi. As the 1990s close, the two suspects remain at large in Libya. Colonel Qadhafi may be shielding them from the international demands for justice.[5]

Pan Am 103 was neither the first nor the last act of terrorism involving Qadhafi. On October 6, 1981, Egyptian dissenters whom Washington believed were backed by Colonel Qadhafi assassinated Egyptian President Anwar El-Sadat.[6] After that incident, Libya and the United States became locked in a spiral of escalation. The mutual hostility reached a height on April 15, 1986, when President Reagan ordered airstrikes on various Libyan sites. One of them was Qadhafi's personal residence on a military base. The attacks killed his infant daughter and wounded two of his sons. The assault was in immediate response to a bombing of the La Belle discotheque in Berlin, a place known to be frequented by U.S. service men and women. American analysts traced the Berlin disco bombing to the government of Libya.

Perhaps because of Washington's use of force, Qadhafi cut back his sponsorship of terrorist organizations that assault American citizens. Many Americans, nevertheless, retain a knee-jerk image of a Qadhafi-like character. This archetype would be blamed for acts of terrorism, such as the bombing of Centennial Park during the 1996 Summer Olympics in Atlanta.

Despite Qadhafi's trend toward moderate behavior, incidents like Pan Am 103 serve to strengthen stereotypes of Middle Eastern leaders. The image is of an evil, domineering man in a green military suit who masterminds terror targeting the United States. Because of the relative frequency of terrorist incidents that occur in the Middle East, there is a mental picture in American culture that the region is an incubator for terrorists. Witness the wild speculation that Middle Eastern terrorism was responsible for the 1995 bombing of the Federal Building in Oklahoma City and the loss in 1996 of TWA 800 off the coast of New York. Militiamen from the Middle West and "Good-Old Boys" from the South were not the images that came to mind when we learned about these explosions. However, there are other regimes outside the Middle East that have become painful thorns in Washington's side. One case stems from the Cold War era—North Korea. American-North Korean relations have evolved from the days of the Korean War, through a crisis over nuclear weapons development, to crises regarding humanitarian issues.

*October 17, 1994.* Pyongyang and Washington reached an agreement on the text of a framework document on North Korea's nuclear program. Even though most of the international community had made a movement toward nonproliferation, the Democratic People's Republic of Korea pursued nuclear weapons until Pyongyang and Washington struck a deal in 1994. At issue is whether that accord will be sufficient to steer North Korea away from the acquisition of weapons of mass destruction. Hence, a prudent assumption is that Pyongyang will continue its pursuit of nuclear weapons. Global pressures against proliferation are less effective against North Korea because Kim Jong-Il is not as concerned with international censure as other leaders.

As confrontation over nuclear weapons subsided, new crises arose over floods and famine. North Korea has suffered from floods and a devastating rice famine. But Kim Jong-Il has used his country's resources to build a monumental skyscraper. This misallocation of resources suggests that his concern with personal aggrandizement might be at the expense of the people of North Korea. While Pyongyang's long time rival, Seoul, was sending shipments of rice to alleviate the starvation in the North, Kim Jong-Il sent saboteurs to infiltrate the South. He has commented, "No one can figure me out, especially the Americans . . . but it is they who are confused."[7] He is correct. When you bite the hand that feeds you, it appears to be inexplicable.

Not since the Ethiopian famine of the 1980s, has the world seen such horrors as the scenes in North Korea during the 1990s. In a rare, and perhaps desperate move, the Stalinist-like North Korean regime allowed Western reporters to document the suffering and starvation that had rocked its population. Floods and famine have wiped out much of this small country's crops, leaving millions of faces hollow and blank. Photographers panned over live bodies that looked like corpses. Pictures of babies with swollen stomachs circulated around the world, tugging at hearts and consciences.[8] Though this image alone was horrifying, the civilized world suspected that Kim Jong-Il hid even more appalling and gruesome scenes.

In fact, this same man used his starving country to strong-arm the United States into negotiations with neighboring countries Japan and South Korea. Kim Jong-Il's regime pointed fingers at Tokyo and Seoul, which were reluctant to give rice, even though they had warehouses full of rotting crops. True, other countries hesitated to come to North Korea's aid. Their unwillingness may be due to North Korea's million-man army, which exercises along the demilitarized zone. Because Pyongyang siphons off humanitarian assistance for the military before rationing it out to the population, the international community struggles with the following dilemma. Should we save the lives of millions of North Koreans at the risk of strengthening the military regime that threatens 37,000 American soldiers and millions of South Koreans? To anticipate the conclusion of Chapter Six, the regime needs to be contained, but the North Korean population needs to be saved. At issue is how to contain a puzzling leader like Kim Jong-Il and embrace his starving population.

## PERSONALITY AND POLITICS[9]

Because the actions of the rogue leaders appear puzzling, there is a need to answer the question, "Why?" With every rogue act, all eyes turn to the leaders of these international troublemakers. In an attempt to answer this question, it is imperative to look to the stars on the stage of the New World Order for their motives, fears, and beliefs.

*Rogue Regimes* analyzes the luminaries of the post–Cold War era. They include the Ayatollahs Khomeni and Khameni, Presidents Rafsanjani and Khatemi of Iran, Saddam Hussein of Iraq, Muammar

Qadhafi of Libya, Hafez al-Assad of Syria, and Kim Jong-Il of the Democratic People's Republic of Korea. There also are contract terrorists for hire—Abu Abbas, Abu Nidal, Ahmed Jibril, and George Habash. Finally, there are "freelancers" like Ramzi Ahmed Yousef, Sheik Omar Abdul Rahman, and Osama bin Laden.

Personality, politics, and policies form a triangle that describes rogue leaders. These three factors are manifest in an intricate framework of emotions and experiences, a drive for power, and a willingness to use violence to accomplish their goals. Most of these leaders were born around the same time period, and thus they can be considered in the same generation. A pattern of violence is evident in their behavior.

## IRAN'S LEADERS: KHOMENI, KHAMENI, RAFSANJANI, AND KHATEMI

Like most of the rogue leaders and their nations, the Ayatollah Khomeni was the heart and soul of postrevolutionary Iran. Before the revolution, Iran was dominated by foreign powers that exploited the resources of the nation. From the coup that toppled Mossadegh to the revolution that ousted the Shah, the period of 1953-1978 was a time of growing resentment and hostility against the United States.[10]

Khomeni had many reasons to be bitter toward the ruling secular elite of Iran and the West. Assassins sent by an absentee landlord supposedly murdered and hence martyred Khomeni's father in the winter of 1903.[11] Some Iranians believe that a baby brings good or bad luck to its family. In the case of the assassination of Khomeni's father, many took this event to be a sign of bad luck, especially because it was a violent death. Consequently, the villagers called Khomeni "bad-qadam" or "ill-omened." His mother then gradually decreased her visits with him until they stopped altogether. Not willing to withstand the harsh treatment from the villagers, the mother abandoned Khomeni, leaving him with his aunt. When both mother and aunt died, their deaths left Khomeni under the care of his brother. Essentially, Khomeni grew up without ever knowing the love of his parents.[12] He had honored the legacy of his father by giving his first-born son the father's name—Mostafa. But Khomeni suspected that agents of the ruler of Iran, Reza Shah, killed Khomeni's son, Mostafa.[13] And because of the strong ties between the Shah and the West, Khomeni's dislike of the United States grew. During the Eisenhower years, the United States supported Mohammed Reza Shah, whose father's regime Khomeni thought was responsible for Mostafa's death. The Shah's regime lasted until 1978, when Khomeni began his bloody ascent to power. Khomeni had a deep-rooted hatred for the West that he used to fuel his climb to the top. Disgusted with the corruption capitalism had brought to the predominately Islamic Iran, Khomeni vowed to bring death to the "Great Satan."

At the time, Mohammed Reza Shah was under intense attack from Iran's Islamist factions. They criticized him for betraying the teachings of Islam. The Shah, more preoccupied with his international image than the threat of Khomeni and his growing group of Shiite Muslim followers, became increasingly dependent on Washington's advice and support. As increasing numbers of influential Iranians defected to Khomeni's camp, the Shah fled the country. Finally, taking advantage of the power vacuum in Iran after the Shah's flight, Khomeni seized the reins of the country. The overthrow signaled the beginning of a rapidly deteriorating relationship between Tehran and Washington.

Khomeni eventually monopolized secular and sacred power in Iran. His supporters viewed him as the champion of the poor and the working class. His disdain for the monarchy and the capitalist West brought him strong political support, which was evident in the frequent sight on the nightly news of huge crowds screaming, "Death to the Great Satan!" The Ayatollah's reign, characterized by terrorism and war, was marked by three factors: an intense belief in Islam, a great hatred of the West, and aggressive reaction toward perceived threats.

During his reign, he maintained power through executions, expulsions, and torture. The walls of many buildings in Tehran were painted with pictures and messages of hatred aimed at the West, a visual representation of Khomeni's attitude. From 1978 to 1981, Khomeni dominated Iran's politics and religion. One of the most poignant examples of his monopoly of power is his portrait in the center of Tehran. Years after his death, Khomeni's face still broods over the city, watchfully inspecting the daily activities of his people.

Khomeni's facial demeanor was not the only feared aspect of the man. His actions gave the world good reason to fear him. The danger that Khomeni posed became obvious when Iranian "students" seized the United States embassy in Tehran and held its occupants as hostages. Though the Carter Administration made many attempts to persuade or coerce Khomeni into releasing the hostages, the government of Iran did not free them until President Carter left office.

Why did Khomeni continue to defy the United States in spite of the painful losses that were threatened? Evidence suggests that his tightening grip on power was chafing many disgruntled factions within his regime. As the economic situation in Iran began to deteriorate, two opposing views began to develop inside the country; one argued for continuing the fight against Western imperialism and corruption, but the second felt that Iran needed Western assistance to recover from years of war and internal conflict. During the remainder of the Ayatollah's reign, small voices of opposition began to emerge, and Khomeni felt he had to expend more energy in extinguishing them. Influenced by his traumatic upbringing and tapping into his country's collective hatred for the West, he began to lash out more strenuously. Most of Khomeni's rhetoric was laced with themes of overcoming Western decadence and resisting the Great Satan. He continued to rail against the "evils" of the West, for which he felt both hatred and fear.

Upon the death of Khomeni in 1989, two men assumed his role, the Ayatollah Khameni and President Ali Akbar Hashemi Rafsanjani. Although Khomeni would have frowned upon any separation of mosque and state, the sharing of power between the two men hints at such a division. As a result, ideology became less instrumental in governance under them than it was under a single charismatic ruler.

Ayatollah Khomeni's religious successor, Khameni, was a power beyond the mosque precisely because he was from the mosque. Yet, he lacked the one dominating characteristic of Khomeni—charisma. While Khomeni was worshiped and feared, politicians dared to maneuver around Khameni. Such coalition-building would have been unthinkable under Ayatollah Khomeni. Perhaps it should also be noted that not much has been said about Khameni as an individual.

Writing about Ayatollah Khomeni was a tribute to him as a person. The fact that much less was written about Khameni is indicative of his status as one among many ayatollahs.

Toning down Khomeni's anti-Western rhetoric, President Rafsanjani appeared to be something of a moderate. Under him, Iran's focus was largely a secular one. He made efforts to distance himself from both the radical politics of the Ayatollah Khomeni and those who sought to reintroduce Khomeni's policies. His regime was a liberal one by Iranian standards. He paid attention to economic development and private property, calming ethnic minorities, and rebuilding Iran after years of bitter warfare. Under Rafsanjani, Iran legalized foreign loans, merged the religious Revolutionary Guards into the army, welcomed foreign investment in Iran's oil reserves, and moved to privatize industries that had been nationalized after the revolution in 1979.[14]

Within Iran, there was opposition to Rafsanjani's reforms. Some opposed him because they felt he betrayed the egalitarian nature of Islam. In addition, the failure of his economic plans to come to fruition lent support to his hard-line opponents. Both the mullahs and the bazaari merchant class opposed his reforms, and they formed a powerful coalition.[15] Indeed, opposition culminated in an assassination attempt on February 1, 1994. By placing secular goals ahead of religious objectives Rafsanjani exposed himself to criticism from the "Islamists."[16]

It is inaccurate, however, to view Rafsanjani as a true liberal by Western standards simply on the basis of his economic reforms. Though not as adamant about ridding the world of the Great Satan, he nevertheless contributed his share to the tension between Tehran and Washington. Under the rule of Rafsanjani and the influence of Khameni, Iran still supported terrorist groups. Many terrorist suspects had been trained in an Iranian camp that Rafsanjani created. His Iran supported the 1992 bombing of the Israeli embassy in Buenos Aires as well as the assassination of former Iranian Prime Minister Shapur Bakhtiar in Paris that same year.[17] But many Iranians saw Rafsanjani as sacrificing the revolution in favor of the state. He, unlike Khomeni and Khameni, was more preoccupied with the economic rejuvenation of Iran.

In the May 1997 elections, Mohammed Khatemi won the Iranian presidency with about 70 percent of the vote. He defeated Natiq Nouri, the speaker of the Iranian parliament, which has a majority of mullahs as deputies. Nouri was the handpicked successor of the mullahs, like Khameni. Although Khatemi is also a mullah, his colleagues did not favor him. But Khatemi may prove even more pragmatic than Rafsanjani (another mullah) and thus continue to stress economic growth.

Though the most popular description of Khatemi is "pragmatic," this portrayal ignores the social influences that hinder him. As of the late 1990s, Iran had been in dire economic straits for more than fifteen years. Nevertheless, the country's economic need was overshadowed by its strict adherence to Islam. There is a pull between economic growth, which calls for Western technology, and religious "Islamism." This gap could spell disaster for Khatemi. His Iran is one with which Europe, if not America, can strike deals. Yet even as the idea of globalization becomes more enticing to the Iranian population, Khameni, Rafsanjani and Nouri, remain ready to pounce on any misstep Khatemi makes. This intricate web of personalities, politics, and policies may make Tehran amenable to striking a grand bargain with Washington.

## IRAQ'S SADDAM HUSSEIN: THE GODFATHER

While there is bargaining and collective leadership in Iran, Iraq is under the firm hand of Saddam Hussein. In this respect, it is no surprise to learn that his favorite movie is *The Godfather*.[18] What is astonishing in this choice is the many similarities between Saddam and the protagonist of the movie, Don Vito Corleone. Both men grew up without a father in a time of turbulence. Both sought respect and power, and they committed murder when necessary. They also share a sense of paranoia. But where Vito Corleone trusted a few in the extended Mafia family, Saddam only trusts those in his immediate family.

Circumstantial evidence of Saddam's paranoia comes from the wiretaps that have resulted in the execution of many Iraqi citizens. Some of these executions have stemmed from the whispered rumors about one of Saddam's family members. For example, Saddam married his second wife, Samara Shahbandar, after her first husband stepped aside so that Saddam could court her. For giving up his wife, the erstwhile husband not only saved his own life, but he also received a promotion! After the wedding, a member of the Shahbandar clan confided to his wife in the privacy of their bedroom that Samara was not a legitimate member of the family. Little did he know that Saddam had bugged their bedroom. Both the husband *and* the wife were given life sentences in prison.[19]

Another incident occurred when one of Saddam's generals insulted his mother, Subha. General Omar al-Hazzah made the fatal mistake of bragging about a love affair between himself and Subha. Like the Shahbandar clan member, Hazzah had no idea that Saddam had bugged his confidant's room. When Saddam heard this conversation, he first wept and then became enraged. He then ordered the execution of Hazzah and his son.[20]

Again, we see a connection between Saddam's life and *The Godfather*. In the movie, family honor was something that no one could demean. If anybody dared to offend the Corleone family, death was inevitable.[21] Think of Saddam as the Don of the Hussein family. Anyone who dares insult the family name, can be assured of an early end.

In his childhood, Saddam developed a sense of suspicion. He brought this distrust into the political arena.[22] This paranoia and his drive for power became evident when Saddam overthrew President Ahmed Hassan al-Bakr on July 16, 1979. The overthrow of a regime was not enough to satisfy Saddam. He used violence to attain power, and he used violence to maintain power.[23]

One explanation for Iraq's invasion of Kuwait is Saddam's paranoid personality. During the Iran-Iraq war of 1980-1988, he adopted the name "Knight of the Arab Nation" for defending Arab interests. After the war, Iraq was physically ravaged and financially devastated. Saddam was suspicious of the other Arab leaders. Kuwait contributed to Saddam's feeling of betrayal and Iraq's mounting economic difficulty. He felt betrayed because Kuwait refused to forgive Baghdad's debts that Iraq incurred in the Iran-Iraq war. Kuwait also deliberately exceeded the oil production quota of the Organization of Petroleum

Exporting Countries. Accordingly, Saddam felt justified in teaching Kuwait, and the world, a lesson on August 2, 1990.[24]

The bottom line to this explanation is that Saddam's paranoid personality drives him to seek absolute power. This motivation constrains the type of policies that Iraq pursues. While multiple power centers in Iran created room for bargaining and thus moderation, a monopoly of power in Iraq limits bargaining space and promotes extremism. Another Middle Eastern nation, Libya, is more like Iraq than Iran. Ruled by Colonel Muammar Al-Qadhafi, Libya is a virtual unitary actor in the style of Saddam's Iraq.

## LIBYA'S QADHAFI: A ROGUE ELEPHANT

Within the global village, the Islamic world, and the Arab nation, Qadhafi is like a rogue elephant. He wanders away from the mainstream norms of the herds to which he belongs. At issue is whether Qadhafi's actions are cool and calculated, fearful and desperate, or reasonable *and* reckless. His tendency to combine reason and recklessness goes back to his early childhood.

Qadhafi was born in 1942 to a nomadic Berber tribe in Italian-occupied Libya. Like Khomeni, Qadhafi's hatred for Western imperialism began at an early age. His grandfather had been brutally murdered by an Italian colonist in 1911, just as agents of an absentee landlord murdered Khomeni's father. Following the Second World War, the British victors took over Libya from the defeated Italians. One imperial ruler replaced another in the eyes of the Libyans who opposed foreign domination. Libyan tribes continued to resent imperial occupation and were finally granted a reprieve by the international community in 1947, when the UN General Assembly approved Libyan independence. The measure became effective in 1951. Nevertheless, the colonial powers still determined the course of events in Libya for some time. It was not until 1956 that the powers lifted the yoke of foreign occupation, and Libya became autonomous.

During those years of foreign control, Qadhafi became an adult. At the age of sixteen, Egypt's Gamal Abdel Nasser's pan-Arabism greatly influenced him. Young Qadhafi started a revolutionary cell that aspired to take over Libya. By the age of twenty-seven, he and his group of revolutionaries successfully overthrew the regime and took control of every government office and media outlet.[25]

Qadhafi's speeches exhibit a belief that violence is an effective tool for achieving his goals. One interpretation of Qadhafi's anti-American statements is that, "There will be blood in American streets." In pursuit of his goals, Qadhafi protects those accused of international terrorism, such as the suspects linked to the Lockerbie bombing. The international community has demanded that Tripoli deliver the suspects for a trial, yet Qadhafi refuses to release them to the criminal justice system in London and Washington. Failure to do so has increasingly isolated him not only from the international community but from most of the Arab world as well.

It is extremely difficult to understand Qadhafi's continued sponsorship of international terrorism. From a rational choice perspective, the balance of expected benefits and punishments would argue against the sponsorship of terror. But by attributing a degree of irrationality to his actions, we also lessen Qadhafi's responsibilities over such actions.[26]

One act of retaliation by the United States was the April 15, 1986, air raid on Qadhafi's military base, in which he and his family suffered intense emotional and physical trauma. As stated earlier, he lost a daughter and two sons in the attack. Since the airstrike, Qadhafi has constantly moved, rarely sleeping in the same place for two consecutive nights.

Qadhafi may be like a rogue elephant, but he is not demented. Another member of the rogue gallery is Hafez al-Assad. Like Qadhafi, he too is not deranged. And unlike Qadhafi, Assad seems closer to the mainstream of the global village and the Arab Nation. But in fact, this façade is just that—a mask that fronts the true identity of a brutal dictator.

## SYRIA'S ASSAD: THE HAMA RULES

Like Qadhafi and Saddam, Assad uses rough tactics to bully his opponents, international and domestic. The "Hama rules" refer to the brutal slaying of 10,000 residents of the Syrian city of Hama. This massacre gave Assad the reputation of having a ruthless, calculating mind. Indeed, an anecdote about him reflects this rancor. "After a national 'election' in Syria, an aide comes to President Assad and says, 'Mr. President, you won the election with 99.7 percent majority. That means only three-tenths of 1 percent of the people did not vote for you. What more could you ask for?' Assad replies, 'Their names.'"[27]

If President Hafez al-Assad did seek those who would defy him, what would he do? Perhaps the Hama massacre can provide a possible scenario. Survivors of Assad's wrath reported horrific torture techniques involving the removal of fingernails and heated probes.[28]

But what makes Assad tick? Who is he? On the outside, he looks like a distinguished gentleman. With silver hair and a nice smile, he could be anybody's grandfather, or a high school teacher. But it is widely believed that Assad is responsible for the deaths of thousands of people in order to keep his political position.[29]

Like Qadhafi, Assad came from a stable family. His family was warm, large, and a respectable pillar of the community. Assad's father, Ali Sulayman, was one of the very few literate Syrians in the early 1900s, and was highly respected for it. His emphasis on education carried over to his sons. Liberal French teachers educated Assad because France controlled Syria after the First World War. But this liberal education went for naught in transmitting humanitarian values.

At the age of nine, Assad was sent to a school in Latakia, where he lived with his older sister. Tragically, his sister and her husband were forced to move, abandoning Assad in a city that hated him because of his Alawite faith. Though he was homesick, alone, in a place where people despised him, Assad refused to give up and excelled in school. His tough-mindedness may come from the disciplined training he received from his father and grandfather. His grandfather built a family reputation of being physically domineering and morally steadfast. Assad's grandfather supposedly came down from the mountains into a little village and physically challenged potential opponents. When he thoroughly defeated his first opponent, the townspeople cried, "He's a wild man!" From that point on, they viewed Assad's family as courageous and strong. From his father, Assad gained prominence and prestige. He acquired a love for learning and took up literature and art to become a well-rounded, educated man.[30]

Several of the same factors that drive Saddam Hussein also motivate Assad. Both men strive for power, demand respect, and resort to violence in order to sustain their dominance. Also, they insist on absolute power in their respective nations. And they have taken severe actions against opponents to demonstrate their resolve as the embodiment of their nation's identity.[31]

Another example of Assad's ruthlessness was the assassination of a rival Lebanese tribal chief, Kemal, for crossing him.[32] When Kemal's successor, his son Walid Jumblat, made a visit to Syria, Assad asked him to do a small task for him. Jumblat tactfully declined, so Assad answered, "You know, Walid, I look at you sitting there and you remind me exactly of your dear father. What a man he was. What a shame he is not with us."[33] Jumblat understood what Assad was telling him—the son could be killed just as easily as the father had been.

Personality, politics, and policies constitute a triad useful for analyzing the mullahs of Iran, as well as rulers of Iraq, Libya, and Syria. These three factors also apply to the ruler of a nation left over from the Cold War—Kim Jong-Il.

## NORTH KOREA'S KIM JONG-IL: WILL THE SON ALSO RISE?

A relic of the Cold War who seeks to manipulate the American threat for political purposes at home is the would-be dictator of North Korea—Kim Jong-Il. At issue in his ascension to office is whether he will be able to amass as much power as his father, Kim Il-Sung.

Violence and grief marred the son's childhood. In 1949, when Kim was eight, his mother mysteriously died. North Korean "spin doctors" quickly squelched rumors about her death being a suicide. They issued a government announcement that she died of a heart attack.[34]

While his father was alive, Kim Jong-Il blamed him for the loss of his mother. Not only was Kim Jong-Il a difficult son to his parents, he became an even larger problem for soldiers, workers, and teachers in Pyongyang. His destructive rebellion as a child carried over into adulthood. Former teachers, acquaintances, and schoolmates recall Kim's dangerous antics in his Mercedes-Benz, his impolite demeanor, and his obvious pleasure in exploiting his power.[35]

Kim Jong-Il also keeps a group of women to use at his disposal. Approximately two thousand young women are currently "employed" in Kim's "Pleasure Team," "Satisfaction Team," and "Happiness Team."[36] While the pleasure groups are well known in North Korea, the government's propagandists work hard to keep Kim Jong-Il's activities from the light.

Even though his father, Kim Il-Sung, made provisions to ensure a stable succession upon his death in 1993, he ran into difficulties in promoting his son as a successor. In 1982, Kim Jong-Il failed to acquire one of three vice-presidential seats. Yet, because of his birthright, he remained one of the most powerful men in North Korea. However, it took the North Korean government 100 days to declare the intended successor, Kim Jong-Il, Supreme Leader of the Democratic People's Republic of Korea. Trying to downplay the fact that he led a privileged yet tumultuous life, propagandists have tried to create a Weberian image of a charismatic leader.[37] They have even lied about Kim Jong-Il's birthplace, declaring that he was the "Baby General Star" that appeared on the holy Mt. Paekdu. A sacred shrine now marks his birthplace.[38] In reality, this is a ploy to give Kim Jong-Il an image of divinity. He was really born in a Siberian military camp in Watsukoye, Russia.[39] This fabrication was a tool to change his public personality in order to strengthen his control of the politics and policies of Pyongyang.

All of his life, Kim Jong-Il has been running from responsibility. Does this carry over into his political responsibilities to his country? Perhaps so, but an argument can be made that he is still that little frightened boy who is lashing out at the world. At issue is whether he is a greedy, selfish, power-hungry dictator, on the one hand, or a troubled, pampered, socially created, and fear-driven maniac, on the other hand.

## ROGUE PERSONALITIES
## AND THE NEW WORLD ORDER

Idiosyncratic politics are the order of the day in the post–Cold War era. As the discussion above of key dates demonstrates, stars from less powerful states have walked onto the world stage. Without the checks and balances of a democratic system or the constraints of large-scale bureaucracies, rogue regimes are subject to the whims of charismatic individuals. These leaders may hold the future of international stability in their hands. For about fifty years, the world had been preoccupied with two superpowers battling each other for dominance. A few regional powers remained on the periphery of their confrontation. As the twentieth century closes, the United States faces a new world order of regional challengers to its global hegemony. Whether the challengers represent threats or opportunities depends upon the values and perceived interests of status quo powers like the United States and its European allies.

## THREAT VERSUS OPPORTUNITY

In the forest of East-West politics, the West slew a dying Soviet bear. In the aftermath, the United States perceives itself in a woodland teeming with additional beasts—fresh threats to the Washington-dominated post–Cold War world. Viewed through an American prism, they are the rogue elephants of the international system.[40] In dispute is why America's Western allies view these same states as opportunities to be embraced and accommodated rather than as hazards. As threats, rogue states need to be contained or confronted.[41] If they are a combination of both opportunity and threat, the United States could balance accommodation with confrontation.

The Chinese ideogram for "crisis" contains characters that mean both threat and opportunity.[42] In this respect, peril and promise are two faces of a similar problem. But what is a threat to national security for some leaders may be a domestic economic opportunity for others. This peril and promise competition occupies a central role in a great debate during the transition from the Cold War to the post–Cold War era. Two questions characterize the controversy. Are there new threats or additional opportunities in the global village, and, if so, how should the industrialized democracies react to these risks or rewards?

In addressing these questions, two schools of thought divide the Western allies. One theme that cuts across these perspectives is the nature of threat perception. Both camps acknowledge that there are threats in the world. They differ, however, in their perceptions of danger and what to do about the menace. Sometimes threats are overestimated; at other times they are underestimated. Those who misperceive threats do so because they see what they want to see and/ or what they expect to see.

Threat misperception derives from the misleading influences of biases on perception. Biases come in two types—motivated and unmotivated. If you see what you want to see, that is a motivated bias. If you see what you expect to see, that is an unmotivated bias. These two cause threat misperception.[43]

The American school perceives high dangers from rogue states and imposes sanctions in order to deter and coerce them.[44] The European school does not perceive much of a threat from these same states and resists the imposition of trade restraints. Indeed, this school would embrace rather than confront. By embracing America's "rogues," they are less likely to become Europe's problems later. Twin issues addressed here are why certain leaders see outlaws and others perceive opportunities; and conversely, why particular leaders choose to contain the perilous possibilities, while others decide to embrace the promising prospects. Those who select containment via economic sanctions do so despite evidence that this approach often fails to coerce. And those who choose to embrace by means of trade incentives do so in spite of indications that dialogue frequently fails to reduce misbehavior.

As a result of its high threat perception, the United States imposes trade restraints on its newly found beasts. When there is allied consensus, Washington prefers multilateral action; in the absence of accord among the allies, Washington imposes unilateral penalties. Both collective and individual trade restraints reflect the approach of the pro-sanctions school of thought.

Europe, leader of the anti-sanctions school, strongly resists unilateral U.S. sanctions and is even cool to multilateral trade penalties.[45] While Americans perceive outlaws abroad, Europeans foresee lost opportunities at home. Not having businesslike relations with less-than-perfect nations abroad makes little sense. Viewed through the European prism, American-defined rogues are not only areas for business opportunity but are also candidates for democratization through economic development. Due to Europe's propensity for appeasement and engagement over antagonism and confrontation, it tends to avoid the American approach of applying restraints on trade. European nations would rather buy off and engage potential rogues with goods and services, instead of confronting them with threats and sanctions. And even when threat perceptions are similar on both sides of the Atlantic, Europeans prefer cooperation to coercion.

Indeed, the Brussels-based European Union acknowledges concern about the threat to the West from countries like Libya and Iran. But in contrast to Washington, Brussels pursues a multilateral approach to achieve change and strongly objects to unilateral measures imposed by the United States.[46] European countries hold that it makes sense to keep lines of communication open to those states with which there are political, ideological, and religious differences.

Therefore, when Washington chooses to magnify the misbehavior of comparatively small states like Libya and discount the violations of large states like China, Europeans accuse the United States of inconsistency. They charge U.S. presidents with being guilty of selling American foreign policy in bipolar terms. The public then encourages decisionmakers to follow policies that isolate the "good guys" from the "bad." Europeans do not view the world in bipolar terms and hence are inclined to incorporate all states into an overall trade system. The debate is between emotional American idealism and cynical European realism.

Europeans question the U.S. assumption that it can sit in judgment on the moral fitness of other states. They challenge America's self-designated right to instruct Europe as to which countries are suitable for trading relationships. Europeans ask why they should not have business relations with a country like Libya, which has over five million people, most of whom are not politically active, anti-Western, or terrorists. Europeans also reason that it is absurd to imagine a nation inducing another to change its ways unless open communication exists. Moreover, they contest the assumption that negative measures are capable of exerting a positive influence on a rogue state.[47]

And even if an isolationist policy contributes to financial and monetary instability, the question arises as to whether the existence of unstable countries on the European periphery is in the interest of the

West. If, for example, sanctions on Libya destabilize its regime, one result might be a flood of refugees. Such emigration would transfer instability from North Africa across the Mediterranean into Europe.

In other words, Washington perceives threats from miscreant states, while the members of the European Union see ongoing relationships with a potential for expansion. Washington considers these states as rogues, wandering out of control, meriting isolation, and deserving punishment. By not adhering to international standards of conduct, the rogue-elephant state separates itself from the herd of nations and roams alone. But once isolated from the herd, most rogues find that re-admission is a difficult task; because the United States chooses to ostracize them even further, they find themselves prey to a cumulative isolation.

The question for the United States is which nations it will accept as part of the herd, and which it will exclude as rogues. Those that cross an American threshold of perceived threat prompt Washington to push them even further from the pack. Through its own behavior, a rogue state is a vulnerable nation on the verge of isolation; sanctions then reinforce the separation. The question for Europe is whether to accept America's exclusionary approach or to press for an inclusionary policy. But the downside of inclusiveness is that Europe risks dividing the Atlantic alliance. Pragmatic Europe has a higher threshold of threat perception than does ideological America. With a longer history of dealing with states that fit America's rogue image, Europe is more tolerant of deviant behavior than the United States.

European governments and businesses generally speak with one voice when it comes to their preference for engagement over confrontation with potential rogue states.[48] In contrast to Europe, there are differences both within the U.S. government and between it and the American business community. Consider a split within the government among departments and agencies that dealt with Nigeria during the mid-1990s. The military regime in Lagos hanged a writer, Ken Saro-Wiwa, and eight other political activists in 1995. Advocates for strong sanctions included National Security Adviser Anthony Lake, Assistant Secretary of State for Human Rights John Shattuck, and Undersecretary of State for Global Affairs Timothy Wirth. As a pro-sanctions group, these three pressed for even tougher measures than the Clinton Administration already had imposed on Nigeria. They were opposed by representatives from the Department of Commerce and other business-oriented cabinet departments. These officials argued that unilateral sanctions would only succeed in increasing the price of heating oil for Americans.

Regarding the split between a U.S. administration and the American business community on sanctions, the former often chooses sanctions while the latter generally opposes them. Business considers sanctions a blunt tool of last resort. Like their European counterparts, businesses from Wall Street to Main Street belong to the anti-sanctions school of thought. American firms believe that commercial engagement should be used before governments impose sanctions. They assume that sanctions designed to place pressure on the economies of a target nation damage U.S. interests abroad, hurt the people, and fail to punish the elite.[49]

Mobil Oil typifies the attitude of American firms toward international economic sanctions.[50] It allows that unilateral sanctions may be gratifying—punishing an offender's behavior makes Americans feel good. But despite this positive feeling that comes from dispensing "retributive justice," Mobil Oil emphasizes the negative aspects of sanctions, which usually fail to accomplish what they set out to do— deter and rehabilitate. The corporate sector holds that democratic elections may be facilitated more through dialogue with the offending government than through punishment of its citizens by sanctions. American-based firms operating abroad contend that they reinforce American values and oppose sanctions on the grounds that they prevent the firms from spreading the values.

If there are to be sanctions, corporate America prefers the effective rehabilitation of a target nation rather than punishment for retribution. Allowing American firms to operate in rogue states provides an opportunity to demonstrate such values as protection against human rights abuses in the workplace; an assumption here is that values learned on the job will be incorporated into the wider culture.

The American private sector also stresses other negative consequences of sanctions, especially unilateral restraints. Such actions may cause states to view U.S.-based companies as potentially bad risks, a perception that could result in a decrease in sales, investment opportunities, and foreign trade earnings.[51] Commercial engagement should be used instead to rein in nations that wander outside accepted moral boundaries. The bottom line of American business is that engagement offers the chance for a "critical dialogue," which in turn inspires change in what Washington would call a rogue state.

Threat and opportunity are different aspects of comparable situations; politics, moreover, reinforce threat perception or perceived opportunities and provide a setting out of which policies emerge.

## POLITICS AND POLICIES

In contrast to New York's business-oriented Wall Street, Washington's Pennsylvania Avenue views sanctions in a positive light. From Capitol Hill to the White House, government officials are willing to use sanctions. They are midway between doing too much, such as sending in the troops, and doing too little, such as making empty threats.[52] This intermediate position attracts supporters on the Main streets throughout the country.

American political leaders accuse Europeans of opposing U.S. sanctions while offering little in the way of containing the threat posed by the likes of Iran, Iraq, Libya, Syria, Cuba, and North Korea. They charge that these rogue states manipulate the Europeans' critical dialogue approach in order to advance the development of weapons of mass destruction. In a harsh accusation, a former American diplomat explains what he terms "Euroblindness." He defines it as an unwillingness of Europeans to see threats to their own interests and to prefer cooperation over confrontation with rogue states. Why? Because, ". . . Europeans have never lost faith in appeasement as a way of life."[53]

Unlike their counterparts across the Atlantic, American political leaders see sanctions as historically successful. In contrast to business leaders, these politicians want to win elections; hence, they view sanctions as a means of appealing to the values of their domestic political constituencies. The pro-Israel community in New York applauds the Clinton Administration's hard-line approach toward four of Israel's enemies: Iran, Iraq, Libya, and Syria. The anti-Castro community of Cuban-American exiles in Florida praises the Administration's tough stand toward Castro. Preferences of politicians, decisions of diplomats, and lobbying by interest groups converge to produce a policy of sanctions. In other words, the vectors of American politics line up with those of U.S. diplomacy. Politics reinforce the morally motivated grounds for American foreign policy.

But domestic politics, international diplomacy, and human rights idealism may not always converge, as in the case of Nigeria during the mid-1990s. The regime hanged several of its opponents. These hangings led to international pledges for strong punitive measures against the military regime in Lagos. But the campaign for international sanctions stalled. Along with international oil companies, the Nigerian government launched a lobbying effort that took the wind out of the sails of sanctions. But Lagos not only aligned with the international oil industry; the regime also had its local American allies. This alliance defeated the American opposition to Nigeria led by a civil rights coalition.[54]

Following the hangings in Nigeria, the coalition of American human rights, environmental, black, and labor groups had launched a campaign. TransAfrica, an organization devoted to enhancing ties between Africa and the United States, initiated a letter to President Clinton signed by 54 prominent American blacks. It advocated strong sanctions against the military regime in Lagos. As a result of this lobbying effort, Senator Nancy Kassebaum (Rep.-Kansas) and Representative Donald Payne (Dem.-New Jersey) introduced bills in the Senate and House that would have both cut off most investment by American firms in Nigeria and laid the basis for an international oil embargo. But Senator Carol Moseley-Braun (Dem.-Illinois) and the Nation of Islam leader Louis Farrakhan returned from their respective trips to Nigeria with a call for the Clinton Administration to give the regime a chance to enact democratic reforms before imposing sanctions. This split gave the Clinton Administration a pretext for shelving strong action against Nigeria.

The Administration had imposed only modest prohibitions against Nigeria. These consisted of a ban on sales of military equipment, a reduction in humanitarian aid, the recall of the U.S. ambassador, and a broadening of an existing ban on visas for Nigerian officials and their families. And following a review at the State Department, officials said that the United States would take further steps in collaboration with European and African states and did not exclude an embargo on Nigerian oil sales.

But the government of Nigeria countered by purchasing services of nine American public relations and lobbying companies for about $10 million.[55] Mobil Oil, Amoco, Chevron, and firms with involvement in a $3.8 billion liquefied natural gas project in southeast Nigeria joined the effort. A central group in the lobbying on behalf of Lagos was the 107-member Corporate Council on Africa, a private, nonprofit organization dedicated to promoting business relationships between African countries and American corporations. The Corporate Council held that dialogue rather than confrontation was more likely to produce political reforms in Nigeria.[56]

In leading the anti-sanctions school, the business community trumped American ethnic politics and the traditional commitment to idealism. The effect was to stop the momentum for imposing strong sanctions against Nigeria. One of the reasons why the business community triumphed was because human rights concerns did not converge with strategic or intrinsic interests. In the case of Iran and Libya, however, ideals, interests, and politics do intersect. Hence, Washington imposed weak sanctions on Nigeria and strong sanctions against Iran and Libya.

Here is the argument for the pro-sanctions school of thought. Strong measures would place regimes like Nigeria's on the defensive. Sanctions would lessen the ability of rogue regimes to wreak havoc abroad and would demonstrate international outrage with the targeted regime's policies. Meanwhile, sanctions would strengthen the domestic opponents of targeted regimes. Through their experience with Cuba, Iraq, North Korea, and Serbia, American political leaders believe that consistently applied pressure in the form of sanctions weakens rogue regimes and facilitates change. Perhaps as a result of sanctions, Cuba is no longer in a position to destabilize other regimes across the Caribbean and in Central and South America, as it did in the first years under Castro.

Regarding Iraq, the U.S. resolve to maintain sanctions helps to contain Saddam Hussein's regime. Although sanctions against Baghdad have indirectly hurt the Jordanian economy, King Hussein has been impressed by the steadfastness of their implementation. The maintenance of sanctions despite international clamor to lift them may have facilitated the King's shift in his position from passive neutrality to active opposition regarding Saddam.

Faced with unremitting American hostility, including the imposition of sanctions and the use of force, Libya is much less adventuresome in its dealings with neighboring states like Egypt, and appears to be more hesitant in its support of terrorist operations abroad. For Serbia, the Clinton Administration insisted on maintaining sanctions, despite pressure from its European allies to lift them prematurely. According to representatives of the pro-sanctions school, sanctions and a preponderance of military power by NATO forces ultimately brought Serbia's Slobodan Milosevic to the table. While there, Serbia and its allies were in a position to deliver on their international obligations under the Dayton Peace Accords.[57]

## SANCTIONS FOR REHABILITATION

Given the competing claims of the pro-sanctions and anti-sanctions schools, the question arises whether sanctions are effective. The issue is whether sanctions are rehabilitative; that is, do they coerce target states. In addressing the consequences of sanctions, consider a description of which states initiate them, where they occur, and to what effect. The United States initiated more than two-thirds of all sanctions between 1945-1982. Since 1990, there has been a sharp increase in the use of multilateral sanctions.[58]

Here is a breakdown of 63 sanctions and threats issued by the United States from 1945 to 1982: Latin America, 28; Western Europe, 11; Eastern Europe and the USSR, 5; sub Saharan Africa, 6; North Africa and Middle East, 10; South Asia, 8; East Asia, 11. In this respect, American penalties against Cuba, Iran, and Syria have been unilateral, while Washington has joined the international community in imposing multilateral sanctions on Iraq, Libya, and North Korea. Unilateral sanctions are rarely effective, while multilateral penalties have a better record of success.

As the world moves from the certainty of Cold War threat perceptions to the uncertainty of a new world in disorder, sanctions are of increasing importance for implementing coercive and retributive policies. In the stable bipolarity of the Cold War, the focus of the West was on influencing the external behavior of fairly unitary actors like the Soviet Union. Because vital interests were clear, the U.S. strategy of containment bound European, Asian, and other regional allies in a multilateral effort to deter the Soviet bloc and China. Coercive diplomacy during the Cold War made use of sanctions in an effort to compel relatively unitary states to cease undesirable behavior or take an action favored by the United States. Western multilateral sanctions, in the form of export controls, were a defining element of the containment strategy.

In the unstable multipolarity of the post–Cold War era, trade controls are still in vogue. But those subjected to controls offer new dangers. Absent the Communist threat, rogue states continue to cross an American-defined threat-perception threshold and subsequently receive a large proportion of sanctions. The United States uses export and import controls to contain and coerce rogue states. But coercive sanctions are less likely to be effective against rogues as they once were in the Cold War. In the post–Cold War era, there is less of a consensus on the definition of vital interest, the allies have different perceptions of threat, and they differ regarding the nature of the response to a situation. While the United States is still militarily powerful, it is less politically influential. In periods of declining influence, unilateral sanctions reflect a decrease in the ability of a Great Power to lead.[59]

Absent the Soviet threat, the diminished capacity of the United States as a leader makes it difficult to achieve consensus in the West on multilateral sanctioning. And consensus is problematic on the selection of measures to address threats. Not only are group decisions harder to effect than those of a single state, but concerted action requires harmonizing the policies of nations with varying interests, ideals, and prior commitments.[60]

One of the reasons it is difficult to achieve consensus is that the targeted state may develop defensive measures that would affect sanctioning states differently. For example, Italy resists participating in a multilateral regime—a set of international norms—against Libya because Tripoli's reaction to such sanctions would harm Rome more than Washington.

Another reason why consensus formation is difficult to achieve concerns the difference in threat perceptions in relation to the capabilities of the target state to withstand sanctions. Washington perceives threats and is less concerned with the targeted states' capacity to absorb the penalties. Brussels perceives the same situations as only potential threats: they lie dormant unless exacerbated by Western sanctions or military intervention.

A further reason why international consensus is problematic is that defensive measures taken by a targeted nation may result in the establishing of ties to non-sanctioning states. These links may disadvantage sanctioning states. Thus, Germany resists taking part in American-imposed sanctions against Iran, arguing that German firms stand to lose too much Iranian business to Japanese companies if Berlin participates in Washington-initiated sanctions against Tehran. International accord is difficult when countermeasures damage sanctioning states differently.

Additionally, the breakup of empires and emergence of "failed" nations causes the Western coalition of democracies to have less of a coercive effect on the rest of the world. In particular, failed states, for example, the "Somalias" of the world, are less "state-like" in nature. And hence, they are less amenable to strategies of economic threats and actual sanctions. Normal nation-states have capitals on maps and employ standard communications devices that are subject to intelligence means, such as electronic interception. Nations in disarray lack these accoutrements of state. Their leaders are overridden with fear, isolated from the international community, with too much to lose domestically to be concerned about foreign threats. They may fear losing domestic standing as a result of compliance more than the effects of sanctions imposed by an outside power.

In other words, it may be futile to threaten economic sanctions against a warlord who lacks a foreign ministry building and has no fax machines or mobile telephones to receive threats. But the warlord may have enemies at home whom he fears more than the threats of external powers like the United States. Hence, coercion is virtually impossible when dealing with failed states like Somalia. Rehabilitative punishment is difficult to justify when taken against failed states that have degenerated beyond the capacity to cause further mischief.

However, coercion for rehabilitation is more likely to be effective when addressing a developed state that is a product of a disintegrated empire, such as the former Yugoslavia. Serbia—a product of this collapsed empire—is an entity whose leaders are amenable to coercion and deserving of retribution. One reason that states like Serbia are vulnerable to coercion is that its leaders have sought gains from neighbors more than attempting to protect against losses from domestic or international opponents.

## SANCTIONS FOR RETRIBUTION

Irrespective of the instrumental effectiveness of sanctions, there is the retributive punishment aspect to consider. In addition to coercion as a goal, a power may seek retribution—punitive action without regard to behavioral change.[61] Punishment inflicted for retribution deserves some discussion, as it may appear to be a less rational means to achieve a policy goal. Retributive punishment is simply a means to an end. The ultimate goal is to satisfy the desire for payback for previous misconduct, rather than to coerce changes in behavior. Retributive sanctions are a politically safe route to take—success is virtually guaranteed. As soon as the sanctioner inflicts harm, sanctioning as a tool of retribution is immediately effective. For the United States, such punishment is gratifying because of an American belief that sinners should receive their just desserts.[62] Sanctions not only send a symbolic message to the wrongdoer abroad but also to the relevant domestic constituency that wrongs will be righted.

Punishment for the sake of retribution pays scant attention to the future behavior of wayward states. Sanctions against Iraq combine castigation to change future behavior as well as retributive justice; that is, deserved punishment for evil done. Because Iraq committed an evil deed in its invasion of Kuwait in 1990, retributive justice demands castigation beyond that which is necessary to coerce. Even if Iraq were in compliance with international demands to destroy its weapons of mass destruction and to allow inspections (which it didn't allow as of January 1999), retribution might justify continuation of sanctions to right the initial wrong. But if retributive sanctions cause more damage than they are worth, they may not be wise.

When Washington imposes sanctions for retribution and leaders of the target state believe that they are being wronged for no good reason, they may feel compelled to act in the manner that the United States was originally trying to deter. When imposing retributive sanctions, one should weigh the expected benefit of "feeling good" against the prospects and costs of backlash. When retribution derives from ideals, however, it is difficult to employ a cost-benefit standard.

When leaders of states hit by retributive American sanctions feign surprise and shock about their graduation to rogue status, it is a clear sign that they do not understand an America defined by its ideals. The *mythos* of the patriot who goes to war for the ideals of life, liberty, and the pursuit of happiness is a core element of U.S. history. *Democracy in America,* the prescient work of the French political theorist Alexis de Tocqueville, abounds with passages lauding the idealistic motives of the American people.[63]

Alexis de Tocqueville attributes high idealistic standards in the United States to widespread political discourse. Although Americans have usually focused their discussions on matters of religion, such activity has had the net effect of increasing both their awareness and their moral standards. Consequently, when the United States evaluates the conduct of other nations to determine whether economic sanctions should be imposed, ideals jump-start the decision-making process. In contrast to American moralizing, however, European nations are largely devoid of idealistic concerns. To draw again on de Tocqueville, the states of Europe lack that quintessential sense of moral right and wrong he saw so often in the American mindset.

Given such a broad base of moralizing throughout the culture, it is no surprise that American ideals play such a large part in the decision-making process regarding the application of sanctions. But idealism alone lacks consequence; it is the convergence of idealism with other vectors that carries weight and causes a change in behavior.

The convergence of idealism and international politics is most strikingly observed through U.S. relations with Cuba. Despite immense support by the American business community to lift economic sanctions and reenter the Cuban market, every president since

John Kennedy has held the line on restricting economic interaction with Castro's regime. In the spring of 1996 corporate giants, the United States Chamber of Commerce, and the Association of Exporters and Importers clamored for President Clinton not to tighten sanctions. But when business interests go up against the multiplicative effect of politics and idealism, economic interests be damned; as a result of such interaction, President Clinton proposed instead to strengthen United States sanctions. How can one account for such a gap between interests and politics? On a cursory level, it can be argued that Clinton was merely kowtowing to the Cuban-American community, whose support he needed in the 1996 presidential campaign.

But it must be understood that Cuban-Americans are influential when their behavior coincides with American ideals. For a domestic lobby to make an impact, it must line up its vectors in such a fashion that they seem to intersect seamlessly within the larger picture of the Old Glory version of the Red, White, and Blue. When this interaction occurs, the doors to power close on the "greedy hands" of powerful multinational firms, such as Mobil Oil, and the doors open up to local constituencies like Cuban-Americans.

The conflict between ideals and interests may be peculiar to America. A French official would justify a sale to a nation on Washington's hit list of rogues by simply saying, "France wishes to sell technology, roads, and lorries." Whether the customer was a key player in the serious game of state-sponsored terrorism would be a concern to an official from Washington but not from Paris. For example, the French give rhetorical opposition to Iranian involvement in terrorism, but then they continue to cut business deals with Tehran. Meanwhile, they shower the Congress with lengthy letters opposing the Iran and Libya Sanctions Act because of its "extraterritorial application of U.S. jurisdiction."[64] The French serve as a telling example of the difference in perceptions between the United States and its allies regarding the nature of the threat from rogue regimes and application of sanctions on them.

Most Americans do not want to trade with Iran because they consider what that country is doing to be fundamentally wrong. Profits are well and good, but the sight of charred and broken bodies from Iranian-sponsored terrorism remains a powerful image even after the money from oil trading has been spent. Money is fleeting, and while America is a land of staunch capitalists, it is also a land of principled moralists. Americans qualify capitalism; they do not want to have dealings with evil men and women—those who traffic in human suffering. The Founding Fathers created the United States on a principle that all are created equal and deserve a life free from tyranny, which allows for the pursuit of personal endeavors. Iranian-sponsored terrorism threatens those principles, and accordingly, the United States imposes sanctions to counteract that threat.

But the concept of practicing what you preach, a popular American colloquialism, has simply not struck a chord among the French. They would rather build roads for any nation that can pay the bill. They are inadvertently assisting those who not only hold a set of ideals the French claim to oppose, but actually possess the will to apply those ideals—with force against the French. Practicing what you preach is an approach that leads Americans to impose retributive punishments unlinked to interests.

## SANCTIONS AND INTERESTS

In contrast to the imposition of sanctions based on ideals, those levied to further American interests prove far easier for other nations to comprehend. Both European nations and rogue states readily understand such actions because they fall within the normal rules of *Realpolitik*. Yet even within the realm of interests there is confusion. Ideals often coincide with strategic interests, such as the American reputation for being the champion of the Free World. Ideals, however, may not converge with intrinsic interests—tangible assets like trade, natural resources, and financial capital.

Illustrative of the clash between ideals and economic interests is the debate in the Congress about how to treat nations that have poor records for religious freedom but that also are economic powerhouses. China and Saudi Arabia are two such examples. On the one side are human rights advocates who would use trade sanctions in order to induce Beijing and Riyadh to cease their persecution of religious minorities. On the other side are business interests that oppose the use of sanctions to transform China and Saudi Arabia.

The Clinton Administration is torn between these two sides regarding religious oppression abroad. But because fighting religious persecution is a hot-button issue in Washington, the Administration may have to take a stand one way or another. In this respect, there are proposals before the Congress to punish nations that oppress religious minorities.

Senator Arlen Spector and Representative Frank Wolf introduced companion bills in the Senate and the House during 1997.[65] Their bills are part of a concerted effort to fight religious subjugation abroad. The Spector-Wolf Bill would ban all exports to foreign government entities that carry out religious persecution, cut off non- humanitarian assistance to the persecuting nation, and require the United States to consider a country's record on religious oppression in deciding whether to support its membership in the World Trade Organization.[66] Such proposals imply a tradeoff of intrinsic economic interests in favor of ideals.

Subsumed under the category of strategic interests are prior commitments to American friends such as Israel. In this respect, consider the unlikely trio of the United States, Israel, and Iran. As the Arab-Israel conflict winds down, the pro-Israel community in the United States perceives a new threat on the horizon. The fresh menace is an Iran that each year is increasingly capable of delivering nuclear weapons. The community also views Tehran as a fountainhead of terrorism directed at Jews in general and Israel in particular. American citizens are also under attack, and Washington is responsive to the pro-Israel community as a loyal ally of Jerusalem. Consequently, the United States increases the severity of economic sanctions against Tehran. Washington imposes such sanctions even at the cost of intrinsic interests to American oil firms like Conoco and to U.S. strategic interests in the Gulf. America prides itself on committing blood and treasure to the defense of its friends against its foes, so that the light of liberty can survive, to paraphrase President John Kennedy's inaugural address.[67]

Similarly, prior commitments not only refer to international obligations, but pledges also imply domestic political constituencies.

Because the United States is a democracy, assurances to interest groups are often made to secure support. The degree to which these interest groups influence U.S. policy, however, stems from their ability to associate their aims with American strategic interests and ideals. The pro-Israel community is powerful to the extent that its activities reinforce other vectors. In this respect, it is increasingly influential in shaping legislation to counter the Iranian threat to Israel and the United States.

## SANCTIONS IF LEADERS
## ACT FROM WINDOWS OF OPPORTUNITY

When deciding whether to impose sanctions against regimes like the one in Tehran, consider a distinction between windows of opportunity and basements of fear. Underlying the discussion of which states are most likely to be coercible is the mindset of leaders of pariah states and which type of "sanctions regime" might control them.[68]

When rogue actors focus on possible gains, it is as if they were standing in front of windows of opportunity poised to act. Yet, because opportunists concentrate on profiting, they also focus on possible consequences. Rogues encountering windows of opportunity work cautiously in order to avoid punishment. Rehabilitative sanctions are appropriate because such leaders are less willing to accept possible risks to attain gains. Approximately rational actors should think twice about pursuing a goal in the light of possible punishment, such as economic sanctions. Retributive sanctions, however, are suitable, because one can justify punishment when portraying rogues as mercenaries.[69]

In other words, when rogue actors behave in order to maximize gains, they want to attain their goal, but they cautiously proceed in order to avoid possible negative consequences. They need to calculate carefully the risks of action and inaction. Coercive sanctions are relevant measures to confront such opportunists. Sanctions in this context are like "No Trespass" and "Warning" signs to deter crimes of opportunity by individuals from tough neighborhoods who happen to be in the vicinity of wealthy areas.

During the Cuban Missile Crisis, Moscow was an opportunist in Uncle Sam's backyard, seeking to change the strategic nuclear balance of power in favor of the USSR. By attempting to place nuclear-armed missiles in Cuba, Moscow was taking advantage of an opening that could have been closed if Washington had the presence of mind to reinforce deterrence. Rehabilitative threats were in order to cause the Soviets to think twice about their goals of overturning the balance.[70]

## SANCTIONS IF LEADERS ACT FROM BASEMENTS OF FEAR

When rogue actors behave in order to avoid losses in either domestic or international affairs, it is as if they were trapped in a basement of fear. To escape the trap and avoid the loss, leaders are willing to take enormous risks.

Rehabilitative sanctions are less appropriate for fearful individuals because those who concentrate on expected losses tend to engage in risky behavior, regardless of the likely punishment. Retributive sanctions are harder to justify imposing on actors who are misbehaving out of fear. If rogues in front of a window of opportunity are mercenaries, then actors in a basement of fear are paranoids who lack the capabilities to make rational or cost-effective choices. Sanctions may even be counterproductive, leading to additional feelings of frustration and helplessness and to further aggression.[71]

The process of escalation through miscalculation demonstrates the counterproductive aspects of threats when used in the context of interlocking fears. For example, because of a fear of losing the mobilization race prior to World War I, nations were caught up in such a process. Mutual accommodation could have calmed their joint fears and perhaps avoided a war that no nation wanted. The lesson coming out of World War I, however, was learned too well and misapplied to the events prior to the outbreak of World War II.

There were fears of unintended escalation prior to World War II. The Allies incorrectly characterized Hitler's situation as being a basement of fear rather than his window of opportunity. They falsely believed that Hitler's motives and goals were limited and defensive rather than broad and offensive. In order to accommodate and appease him, the Allies sacrificed Poland and Czechoslovakia. Appeasement was inappropriate, for Hitler's goals were not limited only to Poland and Czechoslovakia. As a result of their miscalculation, the Allies found themselves in another world war.

## SANCTIONS IF LEADERS ARE MOTIVATED BY A COMBINATION OF FEARS AND HOPES

In analyzing the decision-making processes of various world leaders, it is necessary to acknowledge that they may be influenced by a combination of fears and wants. Deterrence theory views leaders as either "rational" or "irrational," operating at windows of opportunity or from basements of fear. But rationality is a matter of degree. Both opportunity and fear influence individuals. When it comes to decision making, however, either one or the other will dominate.

Consider the case of rogue leaders motivated by both opportunity and fear. Washington should be confident that its threats will deter the opportunistic side, but not exacerbate the fearful side to the point where threats become counterproductive. To achieve such a balance requires the use of containment and engagement, a combination of both the American and European schools of thought.

Germany at the close of the nineteenth century serves as a prime example of a state with mixed motivations. Berlin possessed a considerable but diminishing military advantage over its continental rivals, France and Russia. In 1891, those two countries had agreed to an alliance, which Berlin feared was a harbinger of a two-front war. Moreover, Berlin saw the alliance as an opportunity for Moscow to gain advantage.[72] Leaders in Berlin believed that by attacking Russia before it could mobilize fully, Germany's strategic disadvantage could be limited.

Berlin was in the peculiar position of being in a basement while faced with an open window. The window of opportunity recognized by the German government was its decisive military advantage over Berlin's rivals. Such advantage had to be used quickly before it disappeared. Hence, the time was ripe to squelch its adversaries.[73]

Simultaneously, however, Berlin was in a basement of fear. The impending change in the regional balance of power caused by the Franco-Russian alliance frightened German leaders. Time worked to Germany's disadvantage, and Berlin recognized the threat of inaction. However, the Germans did not act until forced into war by their Austrian ally. In short, the Kaiser was neither fearful enough nor desirous enough to act.

## CLASSICAL DETERRENCE
## AND PROSPECT THEORY

With respect to the Cold War, an assumption was that leaders stood in front of windows of opportunity. Only by slamming these windows shut on the fingers of would-be intruders could status quo powers deter unacceptable behavior by others. Deterrence by threat and by denial were the order of the day, according to classical deterrence theory. Deterrence by threat of punishment operated on the motivations and intentions of potential challengers. Deterrence by denial acted on their capabilities. In both cases, defenders closed windows to force target states not to take an action.[74]

In the post–Cold War era, classical deterrence assumptions are less valid. Deterrence is more or less likely to be effective, according to the situation of the target. If within leaders' dual motivations, fear of loss influences more than desire for gain, deterrence is not likely to be effective. Consider the case of Cuba. Sanctions are less appropriate tools when initiators act out of fear. And sanctions for rehabilitation are less effective because fearful individuals are willing to accept punishment to avoid other losses.

Classical deterrence theory assumes that leaders of target states are able to perceive threats and act in an approximately rational fashion. If they misperceive threats because of biased information processing, compliance is unlikely. The theory presumes that if a defender has greater capabilities, resolve, and is able to prevent a challenger from controlling and calculating risks, then compliance is a given. But if there is misperception on the part of the target, compliance is not likely.

Classical deterrence also presupposes that challengers act to maximize their gains and that they weigh gains and losses equally. In this regard, defenders can simply increase the expected cost (risk) of noncompliance so that it is greater than the expected gain from noncompliance. Doing so should assure submission. Classical deterrence either assumes that leaders weigh gains and losses equally or that they desire gains more than they fear losses. Leaders of "broken" or failed states are likely to be so bounded in their rationality that they fear losses more than they desire gains. Because deterrence is more likely to be effective if leaders seek gains more than they fear losses, deterrence is less likely to be effective against leaders of failed states.[75]

## ROGUES' GALLERY: TICKET FOR ADMISSION

Iran, Iraq, Libya, Syria, and North Korea are the American- defined renegades in this study. Outlaws include Ayatollah Khomeni and the militant mullahs' successors, Saddam Hussein, Muammar Qadhafi, Hafez al-Assad, and Kim Jong-Il. Theirs are the photographs that would adorn the walls of the world's post offices, like images of common criminals that appear on the walls of the U.S. Postal Service.

The question is why these leaders, and not others, appear in this book. Initially, I considered the term "LISA" as a device for inclusion of cases. During my service in 1981-1982 on the senior staff of the National Security Council at the White House, members of our office used the acronym LISA as a device to recall nations then on the State Department's terrorism list: Libya, Iraq, Syria, and Aden (South Yemen). Using this criterion would have included Aden, which is now a part of a unified Yemen, and excluded Iran and North Korea.

The standard used was the State Department's annual list that appears in *Patterns of Global Terrorism*. It contains a description of those countries where significant terrorist acts occurred and nations about which the Department notified Congress pursuant to the Export Administration Act of 1979. The report details countries that have repeatedly provided state support for international terrorism—premeditated, politically motivated violence perpetrated against noncombatant targets by subnational groups, usually intended to influence an audience.

By 1994, seven nations had made the terrorism list: Cuba, Iran, Iraq, Libya, North Korea, Sudan, and Syria. All of these states, except for Sudan, qualify for *Rogue Regimes*. As a failed state undergoing civil strife, Sudan simply fails to make the cut. Although Lebanon is not on the terrorism list, it makes the narcotics list. Syria, however, is the power behind Lebanon's participation in drug trafficking.[76]

Practicing terrorism, possessing a large-scale conventional force, and seeking weapons of mass destruction qualify a state for admission to the showroom of miscreants. Terrorism conducted by a state with conventional forces and ambitions to join the nuclear club combine to constitute a threat to American citizens abroad and at home. Because of American ideals, interests, and prior commitments, a large conventional force, terrorism, and proliferation are unacceptable and hence deserving of punishment. In effect, these criteria justify inclusion of states into the gallery of rogues.

Foremost among criteria for incorporation into the gallery is a violation of American ideals. Strategic and intrinsic interests in geographical regions of the world form a second broad band of standards. Lastly, prior commitments to allied states and domestic constituencies are a reason to impose sanctions.

Serbia is no longer a rogue, because of its cooperation in the U.S.-led Bosnia peace process. During part of 1996, however, sanctions on Serbia remained. As a result, Slobodan Milosevic warrants mention for his prior misdeeds. But Syria's President Assad merits more than a mention; he deserves his own chapter. His on-again, off-again cooperation in the U.S.-led Israeli-Syrian peace process, moreover, may serve to enhance the perception of him as a threat. American sanctions on Syria are likely to remain as long as Assad allows for continuing conflict in territories under his control.[77] Nevertheless, both men deserve attention here because of their role in activities that led to the imposition of sanctions in the first place. Serbia was responsible, in part, for the violent actions of local Serbs in Bosnia and Croatia, eliciting multilateral sanctions. Washington also placed unilateral sanctions on Damascus, due to Syria's history of international terrorism and drug trafficking.

While most nations accused by the United States of international terrorism are in this book, many states charged with drug trafficking do not qualify for inclusion. On March 1, 1996, the State Department classified 140 countries according to whether they were drug-producing or drug-transit. In addition, the Department classified nations by their relative degree of cooperation in combating the drug trade. State classified Colombia as one of 31 nations identified as major drug-producing or drug-transit countries. President Clinton certified 22 of these states, including Mexico, as working sufficiently to solve drug problems.[78]

Colombia, however, joined Afghanistan, Burma, Iran, Nigeria, and Syria on the State Department list of countries judged to be uncooperative in the fight against international drug trafficking. Because Bogota did not take sufficient steps to curb the illicit drug trade, President Clinton decertified Colombia and subjected it to U.S. sanctions. American firms seeking to invest in Colombia could no longer qualify for credits from the Export-Import Bank or the Overseas Private Investment Corporation. Washington plans to vote against any loans requested by Bogota from six development banks, including the International Monetary Fund.[79]

There is quite a difference between the type of narco-corruption that results in decertification of Colombia and the directed drug activities of Syria. Through purposeful state action, Syria uses Lebanon as a platform for producing and shipping drugs. During 1992- 1993, Syrian-controlled Lebanon produced and refined over 700 tons of marijuana and 15 tons of heroin, yielding some $3-4 billion in annual revenue to Damascus. In response to American pressure, however, President Assad of Syria took strong yet ultimately futile action against growers and distributors based in Lebanon.[80] As a result of Damascus' control over Lebanon, and its continued production and distribution of drugs, Syria qualifies for inclusion in this book, while Colombia does not.[81]

The idea of a world outlaw assumes a code of conduct similar to the rule of law in domestic affairs. However, the international system's enforcement mechanisms are not as extensive as the counterparts in national courts. Concerts of nations, nevertheless, coordinate their international trade policies, and in so doing, they create multilateral regimes to regulate the actions of others.

The Coordinating Committee (COCOM) associated with the North Atlantic Treaty Organization was a Cold War tool to keep strategic Western exports from falling into Soviet-bloc hands. While there was Western consensus about the Soviet menace, there is no such accord on the nature of the post-Soviet threat. Hence, there is no comparable organization in the post–Cold War era to align policies of the West with respect to exports to American-defined outlaws abroad. Moreover, it is difficult to even conceive of a COCOM-like body in the late 1990s, with the lack of international consensus on who's in and who's out of the rogues' gallery. On the basis of the analyses of the six cases in this book, there is a need to coordinate policies of the West against the new threats to world order.

In summary, the United States perceives post–Cold War threats from Iran, Iraq, Libya, Syria, and North Korea and imposes sanctions on them. With the exceptions of Iraq and Libya, the allies see greater future dangers if U.S. sanctions destabilize these American-defined rogue states. Hence, a transatlantic schism in threat perceptions and policies between America and Europe is a problem facing the Alliance.

Four themes cut across *Rogue Regimes:* threat perception, opportunities, politics, and policies. These themes primarily concern terrorism and weapons of mass destruction. Regarding threat perception, the transition from the Cold War to a post–Cold War age has ushered in a grand debate about the nature of threats in the international system. Two issues characterize that debate: different perceptions of threat and opportunity among the industrialized democracies; and policies that are appropriate for the democracies to meet these perceived dangers or opportunities.

CHAPTER TWO

# IRAN: BALANCE OF POWER VERSUS DUAL CONTAINMENT

## OLD FRIENDS AS NEW ENEMIES

THE 1970S CLOSED WITH THE FALL OF THE SHAH, and Iran shifted in American eyes from ally to adversary. With the rise of the Ayatollah Khomeni, Washington went from being Tehran's mentor to being its menace. The Islamic revolution had ousted the Shah, installed Khomeni, and reversed mutual perceptions between Iran and the United States. At issue was how Washington should treat its old friend, Tehran, which had become a new enemy. Two possible approaches surfaced: the United States as "balancer" between Iran and Iraq; or Washington as "container" of both Tehran and Baghdad. These approaches are balance of power and dual containment, respectively.

On the one hand, balancing consists of applying principles like "The enemy of my enemy is my friend."[1] When Iran and Iraq are adversaries, a balancing approach will play one against the other. In order to deter Iran, the United States would make use of Iraq; in order to restrain Baghdad, Washington would use Tehran. Such a sequence of alternating alignments is the core of a balance-of-power approach. On the other hand, dual containment is an effort by Washington to counter the threats of both Baghdad and Tehran at the same time.[2]

Irrespective of whether the United States is containing both rogue states in sequence or in tandem, their leaders perceive themselves locked in security dilemmas. As a result, it is very difficult to choose accommodation over confrontation. Terrorism from Tehran follows on the heels of containment by Washington.

## Security Dilemma: Terrorism and Containment

Tehran and Washington perceive that they are on the horn of a security dilemma.[3] What one side sees as action to increase its security, the other views as a decrement to its own security. There are incentives to take the offensive in a race to obtain a margin of safety. Increases in Iranian terrorism follow escalation in American containment, a policy of isolating Iran through a combination of measures that includes economic sanctions.

After several terrorist incidents, President Clinton signed the Iran and Libya Sanctions Act on August 5, 1996.[4] He called terrorism, "the enemy of our generation" and said that the United States would fight terrorism alone, if necessary.[5] Two days earlier, Secretary of Defense William Perry had laid the national security groundwork for the presidential signing of the act.[6] Perry said that Saudi Arabia was conducting an investigation to find the source of a June 25, 1996 bombing of a U.S. facility in Dhahran that killed nineteen American military personnel. He speculated that Riyadh would find an "international connection" in its search for causes of the bombing. Perry also surmised that the likely connection would be Iran and that the United States would be prepared to take forceful action if the evidence were compelling.

In discussing the possible involvement of Iran in the killing of Americans in Saudi Arabia, Perry made a statement on August 2, 1996 to National Public Radio.[7] He said that the United States would take strong action against any country proved to be involved in the June bombing. He would not say what action would be taken. The secretary, however, backed away from his initial tough stance against Iran. Perry claimed that he welcomed a chance to clarify his initial comments. Perry said that he only had repeated Iran's own threat to support terrorism against the United States. However, if Iran were proven to have committed the bombing, he said that imminent action still might not be taken.[8]

With respect to the link between his initial comments on Iran and terrorist training camps there, at issue was whether Washington might launch a military strike against these sites. Rather than answering the question directly, Perry said that was a classic case of adding two and two and getting twenty-two.[9] On August 15, the Saudi Minister of Interior, Prince Nayef, said that the suspects were Sunnis, born in Saudi Arabia, and veterans of the Afghan war. Nayef seemed to be stressing the internal origin of the suspects in order to refute suggestions by Perry that Saudi evidence might point to an Iranian connection.[10]

The Ayatollah Ali Khameni, Iran's spiritual leader, accused the United States of trying to isolate Iran from the world community.[11] He said that Washington was trying to separate governments and nations from the Islamic Republic of Iran. In other words, Khameni perceived the threat implicit in the U.S. policy of dual containment, the Clinton Administration's isolating Iran and Iraq from the international community. The threat behind that containment approach is the flip side of a Cold War–born interest that first prompted the United States to make contingency plans for the defense of Iran on anti-Soviet grounds.[12]

Even before Tehran entered a rogues' gallery of enemies that sponsor international terrorism and/or engage in trafficking in weapons of mass destruction, there were contingency plans for an assault on Iran in order to save it from the Soviet menace. In the Cold War Pentagon, a defense "of" Iran from Soviet attack could warrant an attack "on" Iran. Whether Iran was friendly or not was irrelevant to whether it should be saved from Soviet attack.

A Soviet invasion of Iran was one of the major Cold War threat contingencies. The Pentagon considered such a Soviet invasion almost comparable to Moscow ordering an invasion of a NATO country. Realignment in Europe without war would be a consequence of a Soviet invasion of the Gulf. Soviet control of the Gulf oil on which Western Europe depended made this contingency very serious, even though it was not very probable. Also, if there were a war on the central front in Europe, there could be a diversionary military move by Moscow in the Gulf. The contingency of a Soviet invasion of Iran produced a worse-case scenario for the Pentagon, especially in the context of war along the central front in Europe.[13]

During a war with NATO, Gulf oil facilities could have been prime targets for Moscow. Simultaneous crises in Europe and the Gulf would have delayed a Gulf buildup by about two weeks. Regarding an invasion of Iran by Soviet combat forces or a combination of Soviet and Iraqi troops, the Pentagon considered the ground and air military balance, the effect of deployments by the United States in a simulated NATO buildup, as well as American-Iranian versus Soviet-Iraqi resupply capabilities.

With respect to Gulf contingencies and Soviet projection forces, the Pentagon was well aware that Soviet troops were closer as the crow flies; that is, they were some 7,000, versus 15,000, nautical miles from the Gulf area. Also, they maintained seven airborne divisions at a high state of readiness. But the United States in the first 30 days of a crisis could have projected by air and sea more capable ground forces than Soviet troops. Only after the sealift began would the Soviets have enjoyed the benefits of proximity. A constraint on the Soviet sealift, moreover, was that it would have been sensitive to the availability of the Turkish Straits and either the Suez or land routes via Syria.

Other Cold War threats included the most important one—a Soviet incursion into the heartland of Western Europe via the Fulda Gap of a divided Germany. Even as American forces anticipated these major threats, Pentagon analysts began to plan for new dangers of an indirect nature. Pro-Soviet regimes in Afghanistan, Cuba, and Libya acted as surrogates for Moscow and thus were fair game for Pentagon planners.

The Reagan doctrine was a rationale for providing military assistance to friendly challengers who sought to shoot their way into closed regimes that carried out Moscow's wishes. In Afghanistan, Reagan analysts dubbed them "freedom fighters," for these Islamic combatants had become surrogate foot soldiers for the United States in its conflict with the USSR over Afghanistan. In addition to backing Islamic fighters against Soviet forces in Afghanistan, the Reagan Administration tilted toward Iraq in 1982. Although Iraq had been a traditional enemy, Washington made an opening to Baghdad as a means to balance Tehran. In other words, the enemy (Iraq) of my enemy (Iran), is my friend.[14]

Iran and the United States have acted as if they were on the threshold of a security dilemma. What Tehran saw as an action to increase its security, Washington viewed as a decrement to its own security. Each had incentives to take the offensive in a contest to obtain a margin of safety. Increases in Iranian terrorism followed escalation in American containment. With the fall of the Shah and the rise of Khomeni, Washington and Tehran inverted their perceptions from friends to enemies. The question arises as to the origins of Washington's changed attitudes.

## ROOTS OF AMERICAN PERCEPTIONS ABOUT IRAN

The principal sources of American threat perception regarding Iran are campaign politics and national security, domestic and bureaucratic politics, intrinsic and strategic interests, alliance politics, as well as idealism.[15]

### Campaign Politics and National Security

At issue is the effect of campaign politics on the formulation of threat perception. As a member of the Republican National Committee (RNC) National Security Advisory Council during 1979 and 1980, I had the occasion to observe the effect of campaign politics on threat perception. I served with officeholders from previous Republican administrations in a virtual shadow government, that is, one poised to take control in Washington after the 1980 presidential election. Indeed, many of those on the council later assumed high-level positions in the Reagan Administration. The council's chair, Richard Allen, had requested nominees from the American Israel Public Affairs Committee (AIPAC) to serve on the RNC Council. Through my years of association with the pro-Israel community, I became acquainted with Kenneth Wollack of AIPAC, who subsequently nominated me to Allen. He, in turn, appointed me to the council. By suggesting members to the council, AIPAC is able to reward loyal supporters; by accepting nominees, the RNC is able to curry favor with a politically active interest group.

With AIPAC's political support, I had an opportunity to witness the politics of national security from the inside of a presidential campaign, and subsequently, from within the government. I had the occasion to join Reagan's foreign policy and defense advisory group. During the Republican primaries, that group had a meeting on March 10, 1980, in Atlanta, Georgia.[16] Because the Soviet Union had invaded Afghanistan in 1979, the invasion was a topic of discussion. And due to the fact that Americans had been seized as hostages in Tehran in 1979, hostages also were on the Atlanta agenda.

Regarding the Soviet invasion of Afghanistan, the Atlanta group discussed the idea that the United States could threaten the Soviets where Washington had the capability to hurt them. The United States should strike in Cuba, where America was strong, rather than in Afghanistan or in the Gulf, where the United States lacked immediate military capability. In effect, some members of the advisory team favored horizontal expansion across geographical regions rather than vertical escalation within a region.[17] Reagan, moreover, mused that if the Soviets threatened to intervene militarily in the Gulf from their perch in Afghanistan, he could initiate a new arms race that the USSR could not afford to match.

With respect to the Iranian hostage crisis, the Atlanta group discussed an "ultimatum to Iran" option.[18] As president, Reagan could issue a secret threat: "Release the hostages, or else." Because he did not have the authority to act in March 1980, there was no need to specify the "or else." Given the militantly anticommunist nature of the Islamic Republic of Iran, the advisory group discounted the likelihood that Tehran would align with Moscow against Washington. Thus, there seemed to be little risk for issuing an ultimatum.

The purpose of the Atlanta meeting of the foreign policy and defense team was to brief Reagan on national security themes for his campaign. At this briefing, he asked about the 1979 Soviet invasion of Afghanistan and the Iranian hostage crisis. Both events had preoccupied the Carter Administration's national security planning, and the hostage crisis may have doomed the Carter presidency.

Because of a concern that the Carter Administration would effect a release of the Americans held hostage in Iran before the November 1980 presidential election, the Reagan-Bush campaign also set up a group of ten national security experts under Allen's direction, dubbed the "October Surprise Committee." Allen designated former American ambassador to Saudi Arabia and Afghanistan Robert Neumann to be the official "Iran-watcher" for the committee.[19]

After the March 1980 foreign policy briefing, Reagan was to give a speech to the Council on Foreign Relations. As a theme for the speech, the advisory group suggested "peace through strength." Reagan adopted this slogan as his national security theme throughout the campaign and during his first term. He pledged presidential leadership to reverse the downhill slide in American prestige that had occurred during the Carter Administration. Reagan's vision was of a future based upon pride in America's past greatness. The advisory group wanted Reagan to convert the Carter window of vulnerability into a Reagan window of opportunity.

A second meeting of the foreign policy advisory group occurred after Reagan had secured the presidential nomination at the Republican convention in Detroit. On October 4, 1980, the group met with him in Virginia at Wexford—ironically, a former Kennedy estate near Middleburg. Reagan was to receive a briefing about the Iran-Iraq War from Admiral Stansfield Turner, then Director of Central Intelligence in the Carter Administration.[20] Reagan was to receive a "prebrief" in order to prepare him for the Turner briefing.[21] Several members of the advisory team had prior or current high security clearances through government service; hence, Reagan received a briefing of the highest order.[22]

As a result of the hostage crisis and the outbreak of the Iran-Iraq War on September 22, 1980, the October briefing at Wexford focused on the Gulf. The meeting discussed the hostage crisis, oil supplies transiting the Gulf, as well as implications of the war for the Arab-Israel conflict zone.

Henry Kissinger said that the strategic importance of the Gulf area was so great that the United States could not afford to remain hostile for long with any of the countries there. He took the position that there was no reason why a Reagan Administration could not work with Iran once the hostages were freed. Iran was such a vital country that hostility between Tehran and Washington should not be permanent. Admiral Thomas Moorer explained that Iran was the most populous of the oil-rich Gulf states and that it stood in the path of the search by the Soviet Union for warm-water ports to the south.

Kissinger added that the continuation of fighting between Iran and Iraq was in the American interest. As long as it did not facilitate enhanced ties between Moscow and either Baghdad or Tehran, the war served United States goals. The Iran-Iraq War prevented both countries from dominating one another or Gulf states like Saudi Arabia. In effect, Kissinger believed that the United States should capitalize on the continued hostilities.[23]

Kissinger not only blamed the Soviets for taking advantage of the Iran-Iraq War, he also implied that Moscow's activities may have been one of the causes of the war. Sensing a nod from Allen to take Kissinger to task, I challenged him regarding Soviet involvement in the fighting: "Document the intelligence to show that Moscow was the source of the initial conflict or cause for continuation of the war." Moreover, I argued that there were incentives for the Soviets to seek a role as interlocutor between Iran and Iraq. Just as Moscow had sought a mediator role in the hostilities between India and Pakistan, likewise the Soviets had a vested interest to be a peacemaker between Iran and Iraq. Kissinger strongly disagreed with my analysis. And then Reagan said, "I've never heard anyone defend the Russians!" The room erupted with laughter.

After the laughter subsided, we returned to the serious subject at hand: whether Moscow was behind the Iran-Iraq War or simply taking advantage of the fighting. Looking straight at me, Reagan portrayed the Russians as "burglars running down the halls of a hotel, searching for unlocked doors to enter." He turned to Alexander Haig, switched the metaphor, and cast Soviet leaders as "fishermen in troubled waters." Communists were always on the lookout for political instability that would provide an opening into strategically important countries like Iran. A nation that had just undergone a civil war and was experiencing an international conflict was ripe for Soviet intervention.

Pointedly ignoring Kissinger and focusing his eyes directly at Reagan, Haig weighed in with cogent remarks: Baghdad's successes in the Iran-Iraq War were driving Damascus closer to Moscow. In light of the historic enmity between Iraq and Syria, Damascus was aligned with Tehran. Baghdad's victories over Tehran drove Syria in the direction of the USSR for security and political support. Haig's bottom line was that the Soviets could gain a foothold in the Gulf not by subterfuge but by location and by prior support to radical regimes in Baghdad and Damascus. By siding with me against Kissinger, Haig may have bailed me out with Reagan.

Sensing that he was losing the support of Haig, Kissinger appealed to him directly, stating "I am sure that General Haig will agree with me that the Soviets were up to no good in the Gulf, and that they also were poised to exploit the instability there." Kissinger and Haig stared at each other in a standoff that surprised no one who knew their hostility toward one another. Finding no support in that corner, Kissinger appealed to Moorer. And the former chairman of the Joints Chiefs of Staff cheerfully clobbered the Communists for the sake of his old friend, Henry.

To persuade Reagan that, although the Soviets were seeking to take advantage of the fighting, they were not the source of it, I reminded the group of Kissinger's role as a mediator between Egypt and Israel in the 1970s. Then, Washington was not a source of the fighting but sought to gain strategic advantage by facilitating a peace process. I compared Kissinger's activities in the Middle East with the Soviet role in helping to settle the Indian-Pakistan War of 1971.[24] Regarding both cases, the United States and the USSR enhanced their influence with regional belligerents by furthering a peace process between them. In the context of a movement toward peace, neither the United States nor the Soviet Union had to choose between two strategically important states. Moscow could have good relations with Islamabad and New Delhi, while Washington could maintain close ties with Cairo and Jerusalem.

Appealing to his ego, I called Kissinger "the great peacemaker" whom the Soviets sought to emulate. Such flattery temporarily threw him off guard and caused him to grant the validity of a portion of my argument. With his usual self-deprecating humor, he said that he was forced to agree with at least one thing I had said—my characterization of him as "great." Whereupon Bush said, "Golly, this debate reminds me of a Yale seminar." Kissinger then commented that Harvard was a more apt reference, and I countered that, "This is a Michigan seminar conducted by a University of Michigan professor!"

After the laughter waned, Reagan raised the possibility of an arms-for-hostages trade. He asked about a potential trade of Iranian assets in the United States in exchange for American hostages in Tehran. This subject became politically explosive in his second term. Because Haig sat on the Board of United Technologies, his colleagues there asked about the possibility of sending military supply parts to Iran. And Moorer added that Vietnam had begun to sell Iran spare parts for American-origin F-4 aircraft. These parts had been left at the United States base in Danang after the hurried evacuation of American forces from Vietnam in 1975. Not one of the participants spoke out against the idea of arms for hostages, but the proposal did not seem so outrageous at that time. However, in view of the failed Iran-contra deal six years later, arms for hostages should have been a cause for alarm at the Wexford briefing.

Using Kissinger's remarks as a point of departure, Moorer discussed the likelihood of oil interruptions as a result of Gulf War fighting. He said that it was logistically impossible to close the Strait of Hormuz. The Wexford team then discussed sea lines of communications—the Strait of Hormuz as the "choke point" in the Gulf between Oman and Iran. Few believed that Tehran had the capacity to close down the Gulf to Western shipping. Whereupon, Kissinger quipped that President Carter was seeking political credit for keeping open what no one could close. He explained, "Carter has a tendency to discover what is not going to happen and then to act strongly to prevent it from occurring. And in resisting the unlikely, Carter creates an artificial crisis that provides a pretext for arguing that this is not the time to change presidents."

The attack on Carter took the immediate pressure off of me and provided a segue into the Arab-Israel conflict zone. I led the discussion on the 1973 war (Israel versus Egypt and Syria). Using the need to balance force and diplomacy as a theme, I began to compare the Iran-Iraq War with the 1973 war. But Kissinger cut in with the remark that in 1973, the United States had both force and diplomacy; in the 1980 war in the Gulf, the United States had less force and no diplomacy. Heads nodded in agreement, offering me another opening to complete the analysis. I pointed out that a year after the 1973 war, there were both oil-production cutbacks and a Saudi oil embargo of the United States, which led to a fourfold increase in the price of oil. When the Shah fell and Khomeni rose to power in 1978-1979, the price of oil only doubled. We surmised that the Iran-Iraq War could result in an increase in the price of oil. In fact, oil prices did go up by about 25 percent, but in nine months fell back to prewar prices.[25]

Former Ambassador Neumann also weighed in on the linkage between the Iran-Iraq War and the Arab-Israel conflict zone. He said the unresolved Palestinian issue was a barrier to good relations between the United States and Arab Gulf states. Kissinger, however, added that the Saudis were more afraid of Iraq and a radicalized Palestine Liberation Organization (PLO) than Israel. Kissinger thought that an Arab-Israel solution had to be a result of an American peace initiative, not the consequence of Arab radical military action like an Iraqi victory over Iran. Such a victory over Tehran could gain allies for Baghdad in its struggle against Jerusalem.

Kissinger also suggested an American military buildup in the region and an arms transfer policy that would restore the balance of power in Washington's favor. A favorable balance of military power would provide Riyadh with confidence to play both the Arab nationalist game of alignment with the radicals and the pro-Western game of aligning with Washington against Moscow and regional threats. Along the same lines, I said that Saudi Arabia provided funds to Arab radicals and oil at low prices to the United States as a form of risk insurance. Riyadh thought that paying off the PLO insured Saudi Arabia against terrorist attack. Selling oil to the United States and permitting Washington to defend them insured the Saudis against Soviet and Iraqi assault.

The Wexford team was also concerned about the long-term stability of Iran, irrespective of its capabilities and short-term intentions. Because of our emphasis on the Cold War, Reagan advisors saw Iran as a strategic asset. Despite animosity from Tehran, we still considered Iran to be on the U.S. side of the East-West divide. If Iraq succeeded in its goal of a de facto partitioning of Iran, that contingency could provide an opening for Moscow to intervene on the side of Tehran.[26]

Two schools of thought emerged at the October 1980 Wexford briefing. One mainly feared the contingency of an Iranian triumph; the other mostly feared an Iraqi victory. If Iran were winning the war, that would be an opening for the Soviet "burglars" on behalf of Iraq. That is, Baghdad would call on Moscow for military assistance, or even intervention. If Iraq were winning the war, this would not provide an opening for Soviet intervention on behalf of Iran. We believed that the Islamic Republic of Iran would not call upon Moscow. Tehran's anticommunist stance follows the principle, "Better green [Islamic] and dead than alive and red [Communist]." But the group also believed that Baghdad had accepted and would continue to accept assistance from both Moscow and Washington.

If Iran were winning the war, some former officials in the Wexford group expected that Baghdad would call upon Moscow and Washington for assistance. In order to prevent Soviet deployments from arriving first, the United States would need rapid deployment forces for Gulf duty. But, severe transit problems inhibited the movement of heavy American armor across the Atlantic, through the Mediterranean via the Suez Canal to the Arabian Sea, and through the narrow Strait of Hormuz into the Gulf. If called upon to defend Iraq without a conventional ground combat presence in the Gulf region, the United States would be in a difficult position. The group preferred that Washington defend Gulf states without relying on nuclear weapons. In short, the United States needed to have sea- and airlift capabilities for rapid deployment of conventional forces before the Soviets became entrenched.

Those in our group who feared an Iraqi victory more than an Iranian triumph were concerned with the Arab-Israel conflict zone. Former officials in the advisory group who favored a tilt toward Iraq wanted Baghdad to emerge victorious with American assistance.[27] Their eyes were on the effects of the Iran-Iraq War on the East-West struggle. I had the principal action to articulate the consequences of the war on the Arab-Israel zone. At that session, Allen had asked me to speculate on the impact of that war on Israel in particular. I said that Israelis preferred that no single power should exercise hegemony within the Arab world. Jerusalem did not want Baghdad to win a war against Tehran and then to dominate the Arab nation with what would have been a well-deserved high status. In this respect, I disagreed with those briefers who preferred an Iraqi victory with American assistance. Kissinger and I finally found common ground: an Iraqi triumph would not be in the American interest.

While elaborating on the negative consequences of an Iraqi success, I took the position at Wexford that the likelihood of an eastern front war against Israel declined to the degree that Iraq was preoccupied with its war with Iran. But if Iraq were successful against Iran, Baghdad might be in a position to mobilize rejectionists in the Arab world against Israel. Although there were major political problems between Baghdad and Damascus, Jerusalem considered both as threats on an eastern front. This front included the Palestine Liberation Organization, Syria, Jordan, Iraq, Saudi Arabia, and other Gulf states.[28]

I said that Jerusalem followed the principle, "The enemy of my enemy is my friend." Tehran and Istanbul as adversaries of Baghdad and Damascus should be friends of Jerusalem. Iran and Turkey were two states on the outside of the immediate confrontation arena of the Arab-Israel conflict. Israel historically has sought to maintain good relations with both as a counter to hostile Arab states on its borders. In this doctrine of the periphery, Israel tried to have good relations with non-Arab Muslim states on the perimeter of the Arab-Israel conflict zone. Israel's doctrine required that it cultivate an arms supply relationship with radical Iran, without jeopardizing its alignment with the United States.[29]

In the context of the discussion of collusion between Iran and Israel, Henry Kissinger discussed how he had directed the American tilt toward the Kurds of Iraq. The Nixon Administration, along with Israel and Iran, had supported the Kurds of Iraq as a way to pressure Baghdad, beginning in May 1972.[30] But Kissinger failed to say that in March 1975, as secretary of state in the Ford Administration, he had given blessings to a reduction in the tacit alignment that the coalition had with the Kurds. At that time, Saddam Hussein had met with the Shah of Iran in Algiers in order to sign a border accord. It called for Baghdad and Tehran to refrain from any further interference in the other's domestic affairs. Such an agreement meant that the American-Israel alignment with the Kurds of Iraq had ended. As a result, Iraqi Kurdish resistance to Baghdad collapsed on March 22, 1975. Thousands of Kurds who had trusted the American commitment died at the hands of Saddam as a result of the flip-flop in U. S. support.

The 1980 presidential campaign provided Kissinger with a forum to give his spin on history, perhaps in a bid to enter the Reagan Administration. The bottom line of his exposure to candidate Reagan at the briefings was that the president-elect asked Haig to be Secretary of State, and Kissinger did not receive an offer to join the new administration. In order to bolster his anticommunist bona fides, however, Kissinger may have magnified the Soviet threat, toned down the danger from Iran, and made a persuasive case for a balance-of-power approach to the Gulf.

Campaign politics had a definite effect on the formulation of threat perception. During the 1980 campaign, the American sense of threat from the Middle East was even higher because dramatic events abroad coincided with the presidential political season. The electoral clock coincided with the aftermath of the Soviet invasion of Afghanistan, the fall of the Shah and rise of Khomeni, Americans held hostage in Iran, the Iran-Iraq War, East-West tensions, and stalemate in the Arab-Israel conflict. As an anti-Soviet campaigner who also seemed to take a harder line against Iran, in contrast to Carter, Reagan was able to take political advantage of the increased threat perception of the American people.

## Domestic Politics Prevail Over Economic Profits

Executive-legislative branch conflicts are par for the course in the formulation of American foreign policy. But in the case of Iran, there is remarkably little disagreement between these two branches of government. As a result, the Iran and Libya Sanctions Act became law in a unanimous vote in the Congress, with only minor dissent after the vote. One voice was that of the Chairman of the Subcommittee on International Economic Policy and Trade of the House of Representatives.[31] He acknowledged that Iran was a rogue state; but he doubted if economic sanctions against foreign firms that invest in Iran were the best means to change its behavior. The Chairman claimed that sanctions intended to hurt Iran should not have the effect of targeting America's allies. Without their support and cooperation, sanctions would not be effective and might provoke allied retaliation. But he failed to realize that allied support is necessary in the context of sanctions for instrumental, not symbolic, goals. Insofar as symbolic objectives are paramount, the test is whether sanctions please domestic constituencies. And there was no doubt that they were satisfied by U.S. sanctions against Iran.

With respect to the role of interest groups in American foreign policy, ethnic and business groups clash in the formulation of policy toward Iran. The pro-Israel community and the American business sector represent the pro-sanctions and anti-sanctions schools of thought, respectively.

In the aftermath of the fall of the Shah and the rise of Khomeni, the pro-Israel community pressured successive presidents to magnify what might be called Israel's "enemy of the year." At various times, the main antagonist was Iraq, the PLO, Syria, Libya, or Iran. The Iranian threat was not a constant because Israel has had an on-again, off-again relationship with Iran. Even after the fall of the Shah and the takeover by militant anti-Zionist mullahs in Tehran, Jerusalem has formed occasional tacit alliances of convenience with Iran. Because the pro-Israel community is not as engaged in the nuances of a balance of power strategy as the government of Israel, that community has been more consistently and strongly anti-Iran than Jerusalem.

The bottom line is that the pro-Israel community perceives Tehran and Jerusalem as each other's enemies.[32] During the height of the Arab-Israel conflict, the main mission of the pro-Israel community was twofold: first, to facilitate the flow of economic and military assistance to Israel; second, to restrain the stream of aid to Arab regimes hostile to Israel. With the decline in intensity of the Arab-Israel conflict, there is less of a need to lobby for foreign aid just for Israel. Indeed, one task that interest groups friendly to Israel have initiated is to lobby Congress for aid to Arab states and the Palestinian Authority. As former enemies are being transformed into friends, so the pro-Israel community has become an advocate on Capitol Hill of assistance to an emerging "peace bloc."

In the post–Cold War era and as the Arab-Israel conflict winds down, U.S. foreign economic aid and military assistance budgets are becoming harder to justify. With Israel's comparative wealth, it has less of a need for American economic assistance.[33] To the extent that the threat from Arab confrontation states decreases with successes in the peace process, it is increasingly difficult to make a case for American military assistance to Israel.[34] Two developments occur as the Arab-Israel peace process reduces the traditional threat facing Israel. First, Jerusalem suggests Iran is its new "threat of the year."

Second, taking the lead from Jerusalem, the pro-Israel community in the United States pushes Capitol Hill to focus on the Iranian threat to both America and Israel.

The most influential representative of the pro-Israel community on Capitol Hill is AIPAC. In a paradoxical fashion, AIPAC uses crisis as an opportunity for increasing its clout. During 1981, it lost a major fight with the Reagan Administration over the transfer to Saudi Arabia of Airborne Warning and Control System (AWACS) aircraft. The loss on AWACS jolted AIPAC to become a superlobby. Its budget went up by a factor of eight in nine years, while its membership multiplied from 9,000 households during 1978 to 55,000 in 1987. AIPAC's leadership steered $4 million in campaign contributions to candidates friendly to Israel.[35] In other words, AIPAC's loss on AWACS was an opportunity for growth.

AIPAC used a second crisis as an occasion for change: the success of the peace process with the Palestinians. With the Oslo Accord of 1993, the Israeli government and the PLO began an exchange of autonomy for the Palestinians in return for peace to Israel. Following on the heels of Oslo was a peace treaty between Israel and Jordan. During the transition from the Arab-Israel conflict to a comprehensive peace settlement, AIPAC assists Jordan in obtaining foreign economic aid and military assistance from the Congress. AIPAC sought a new mission. Enter Iran. Although different from the traditional Arab-Israel threat, Tehran nevertheless is a useful tool for AIPAC's survival.

The Iran and Libya Sanctions Act sailed through Congress in 1996 because of AIPAC's lobbying and its new image as an "Iran-basher." AIPAC used the following argument in lobbying for the act. The organization claimed that Iran needed to be contained until Tehran moderated its behavior and ceased behaving like an international outlaw. American sanctions would impose a cost on the rogue behavior of Iran. The Tehran regime would be less able to devote resources to the export of international terrorism and would have less capital available for the development of weapons of mass destruction. Quarantined by the world, Iran would lack international legitimacy. The regime then would have to explain to the Iranian people how its policies have resulted in such adverse world reaction.

In addition, AIPAC argued that sanctions on Iran would escalate dissatisfaction with the Iranian regime. Economic problems had already contributed to growing discontent. Sanctions also would diminish the regime's ability to buy off or placate its internal opponents. Export and import controls would undermine support for the government by the military. A military deprived of contemporary equipment and technology might diminish support for the Islamic regime. Iran would have fewer resources for terrorism, the export of its Islamic revolution, building up its military forces, developing weapons of mass destruction, and opposing the Arab-Israel peace process.

Consider the relationship between AIPAC and the oil industry in regard to Iran. A noted private oil consultant, Christine Helms, director of country analysis for the Petroleum Finance Company, described the conflict between AIPAC and the industry over Iran. After President Clinton's Executive Order of May 1995, which banned most trade with Iran, she stated "U.S. companies—sensing that Clinton was strumming American chords in the countdown to elections—merely hunkered down in their trenches."[36]

Oil industry sources admitted to Helms that in light of AIPAC's role in formulating anti-Iran legislation, business groups were reluctant to join the battle. "Given AIPAC's involvement in stirring political waters," she wrote, "oil industry sources acknowledge they are reluctant to wade in too deep."[37] Why would businesses be afraid to take on an ethnic lobby? Perhaps the reluctance stems from fear of being accused of anti-Semitism and/or being on the wrong side of counterterrorism.

Shying away from a frontal assault on the pro-Israel community, oil analysts attack the Administration's policy of containment of Iran. The main line of argument is that in order to lower the price, more oil has to flow from as many sources and through as many different routes as possible. They reason that because of the American embargo of Iran, there is too great a dependence on oil from Arab Gulf states like Saudi Arabia and Kuwait. With flat production and increasing demand, prices are on the rise. Hence, there is a need to free the Iranian market from the constraints of the U.S. embargo. And regarding transportation of oil, the embargo makes it difficult for the West to tap the large oil reserves in the Central Asian states of Azerbaijan, Kazakhstan, and Turkmenistan. This oil would have to be shipped across the Caspian Sea, through Iran, then via the Gulf to emerging markets in Asia.[38] Despite the lobbying efforts of American firms and industry consultants, however, ethnic politics triumph over business economics. But the business community has had an impact on policy making.

Before the adoption of the Iran and Libya Sanctions Act, Undersecretary of State Peter Tarnoff repeated an argument of American business. He said on March 17, 1995, that the State Department was concerned about the effect of unilateral restrictions on Iran for American firms. He felt that such controls "could hurt Americans more than the government of Iran."[39] In other words, because the sanctions are unilateral, they are ineffective against the target but considerably risky for American firms. U.S. businesses believe that unilateral sanctions diminish their market opportunities and place them at a competitive disadvantage.

While AIPAC is a formidable foe of Iran in the war for Washington, there are business associations willing to work against anti-Iran legislation. Mobil Oil exemplifies the prevailing views of American firms toward international economic sanctions.[40] Mobil opposes sanctions because it contends that they fail to achieve their goals. The Petroleum Industry Research Foundation and the Middle East Institute are organizations in Washington that also were on the losing side of the Iran sanctions legislation. In discussing the oil market and economic sanctions, John Lichtblau, the chairman of the foundation, echoes the Mobil Oil argument concerning the ineffectiveness of punitive, unilateral American legislation regarding Iran.[41]

The business community concerned with American sanctions against Iran held a conference sponsored by the Petro-Hunt Corporation during May 1996 in Dallas, Texas. Several former Bush Administration cabinet officials were very critical of the Clinton Administration's approach of containing Iran because of the unilateral nature of the policy.[42] In addition to the tepid effort by the American business community, a convergence of domestic and bureaucratic politics reinforces the likelihood that politics prevail over profits. But politics also converge with counterterrorism ideals in the battle over whether to impose sanctions on rogue states and foreign firms dealing with them. Not surprisingly, politicians seek the moral high ground on rogue regimes, even if they leave American businesses "high and dry."

## Bureaucratic Politics Prevail Over Economic Profits

To illustrate the political roots of American attitudes about Iran, consider an anecdote told by President Reagan. During a visit to the Department of Interior, he came across a bureaucrat from the Bureau of Indian Affairs who was crying. "Why are you crying?" asked Reagan. "My Indian died," answered the bureaucrat, "and now what am I to do with my life?" Imagine a Pentagon bureaucrat crying. Why? The threat from Moscow has waned. The USSR died, Russia was reborn, and the former constituent Soviet republics emerged as independent states. What does this official do in the absence of the Soviet threat? Enter Iran. Although less than a Cold War threat, Tehran nevertheless is a useful tool in bureaucratic battles over budget allocations.

The question arises whether the Pentagon engages in a deliberate and systematic overestimation of the Iranian threat for budget purposes. Under the psychological principle that motivated biases cause leaders to see what they want to see, that process would explain why American defense officials would magnify the Iranian threat.

According to the reasoning of those who accuse the Pentagon of threat magnification, the military needs a pretext to defend its budget. It is nonsense, however, to imagine that the Pentagon created an Iranian threat out of thin air just to serve its bureaucratic needs. Nevertheless, Michael Klare makes the case that the Pentagon virtually invented the Iranian threat, among others.[43] In discussing the nature of American post–Cold War strategy, Klare argues that the Pentagon manufactured a rogue state threat. He assumes that the policy of containment against the USSR shifted to containment of rogue states simply to maintain the approximate levels of defense spending of the Cold War years.

Without much evidence, Klare presumes that the Pentagon magnifies the rogue state threat for its own bureaucratic purposes. He holds that some officials seek "to invent a new *raison d'être* for the military establishment."[44] Congress and the public no longer support a Soviet-oriented military posture at a time of decreasing Russian capabilities. Therefore, Pentagon officials have developed an alternative strategic outlook based on non-Soviet threats to American security. He acknowledges that some rogue states do threaten global peace because of the proliferation of weapons of mass destruction and terrorism. But they were, in fact, engaged in these activities even before the rise of rogue state terminology. Consequently, he is on weak ground in suggesting that the Pentagon invented the rogue state threat and on even weaker ground in suggesting that rogue regimes only seek weapons of mass destruction and partake in terrorism because the United States singles them out.

Klare labels deliberate overestimation of threat, coupled with the desire to disrupt a peaceful status quo, as a rogue state doctrine. An alternative policy he prefers is "rogue state marginalization," a policy that would diminish the perceived importance of rogue states. In so doing, the United States would deny them the ability to serve as role models for potential rogue states. In order to induce outlaws to change their ways, Klare favors a policy of holding out increased rewards—economic assistance, trade, and investments.[45]

Because of Washington's practice of "demonizing the alien Other," says Klare, the United States overestimates the rogue state threat.[46] He may be correct that the Pentagon overestimates the Iranian threat somewhat and gains some budgetary advantage; he goes too far in stating that the Pentagon "invents" that threat. In any event, the psychological concept of motivated bias would explain threat magnification: you see what you want to see. Pentagon officials saw what they wanted to see—a threat that would fit the size of their budgetary needs.

## RETRIBUTION TRUMPS REHABILITATION

In addition to bureaucratic and domestic politics as sources of decisions to impose sanctions, consider the rehabilitative and retributive goals of an embargo policy. Besides politics, idealism adds to the tendency of presidents to choose sanctions. Ideals provide an incentive for rehabilitation: American presidents believe they have a virtual fiduciary responsibility to change the behavior of foreign leaders, that is, to rehabilitate them. This tradition derives from the idea that occupants of the Oval Office have a right to sit in judgment over, and change the behavior of, their counterparts abroad. Presidents from Carter to Clinton have believed they were entrusted with the charge of transforming Iran's behavior. At least, however, they have not sought to remake the Iranian regime the way they intended for Cuba.[47] Presidents have accepted the Islamic nature of the Republic of Iran, but opposed the export of its revolution.

Regarding idealism and retribution, American presidents think they have the moral obligation to punish wrongdoing. In addition to using coercive sanctions against Iran, the United States has sought retribution—punitive action without regard to changing Tehran's behavior. In terms of domestic politics, retributive sanctions against Iran are gainful and risk-free: as soon as Washington inflicts harm on Tehran, sanctioning as a tool of retribution is effective. Such punishment has proved immediately gratifying to the presidents as well as to the pro-Israel community. But with regard to international politics, retributive sanctioning jeopardizes alliance unity.

In short, the U.S. embargo not only had an instrumental rehabilitative function—to change Iran's behavior—but also a symbolic retributive purpose—to signal Tehran and the pro-Israel community that wrongs were being righted. The only legitimate basis for imposing rehabilitative sanctions on Iran would be if it were acting "opportunistically," that is, because of a window of opportunity; rehabilitative sanctions would then be appropriate. But if Tehran were motivated by fear, then rehabilitation would be inappropriate. The only legitimate basis for punishing a person acting out of fear is retribution.

In the context of symbolic goals like retribution, it is unnecessary to evaluate the effectiveness of economic sanctions in changing a regime's behavior. They are effective because sanctions make interested domestic groups "feel good." While it is not mandatory to invoke a rehabilitative test, if one were to do so, the issue would be whether a policy that makes the American people feel good makes the regime in Tehran feel bad enough to alter its ways. Congress designed the Iran and Libyan Sanctions Act to achieve both retributive and rehabilitative objectives.

When leaders act because of a "window of opportunity," that is a metaphor for assuming that their conduct approaches the standards of "bounded rationality."[48] The window signifies freedom of choice for an actor to pursue expected gains. And when leaders act from a "basement of fear," that is a metaphor for assuming that their conduct is less rational. The basement psychology suggests restricted choice and minimization of expected losses. If leaders emphasize loss avoidance over gain, tools like economic sanctions may have counterproductive effects.

With this overview of retribution and rehabilitation, consider now an analysis of historical sanctions.

President Carter imposed sanctions on Iran during the hostage crisis of 1979.[49] His goal was to coerce Iran, that is, force the government to crack down on the so-called students who held U.S. citizens hostage in the American embassy in Tehran. Carter's sanctions were intended to be rehabilitative: they sought to change Iran's behavior. But because of the Iranian revolution, there was no "Iran" to coerce: the Shah was on the run, the government was in disarray, and mullahs were assassinating pro-Western military officers.[50] Because Iran lacked the quality of a unitary actor, American economic sanctions for rehabilitative purposes were irrelevant. Retribution for holding American hostages was the only legitimate basis for economic sanctions.

President Reagan imposed sanctions on Iran in 1987 during the Iran-Iraq War.[51] He wanted to compel Tehran to end its attacks on Gulf-bound Kuwaiti ships that had been reflagged as American vessels. In contrast to the disorganized Iran of the Carter years, Tehran then was more or less a unitary actor seizing a window of opportunity. As a result, Reagan's rehabilitative sanctions were an appropriate means to change Iran's aggressive behavior toward Kuwait. But once Iranian behavior became less offensive, the rehabilitative aim withered, leaving only the retributive goal of righting a wrong. Even after that first Gulf War ended in 1988, the Reagan sanctions remained. When controls stayed in effect after the attacks against Kuwaiti shipping ceased, these sanctions retained a retributive purpose. The persistence of sanctions when a threat has diminished suggests that retributive purposes are given greater weight than rehabilitative goals. In effect, retribution trumps rehabilitation.[52]

As a result of state-sponsored terrorism by Iran and its accelerated acquisition of weapons of mass destruction, President Clinton tightened the Reagan sanctions. Clinton issued two executive orders in the spring of 1995. And on August 5, 1996, he signed the Iran and Libya Sanctions Act, which institutionalized his 1995 executive orders into legislation and also expanded the sanctions to include firms from third countries.[53] Clinton prohibited American oil firms like Conoco from engaging in commercial transactions with Iran without an export license. In this regard, he designed these prohibitions as a deterrent to American investment in the oil and gas sectors of Iran. And the Iran and Libyan Sanctions Act of 1996 served as a deterrent to investment by foreign firms.

In addition to goals of retribution and rehabilitation, another aim is to weaken a rogue state challenger so that it is less able to carry out behavior deemed undesirable by a defender. Weakening an actor is equivalent to deterrence by denial, a method of diminishing the capabilities of a challenger in order to enhance the prospect for compliance.[54] There is little doubt that Iran is less capable of threatening its neighbors as a result of American sanctions.[55] In this respect, one of the achievements of the sanctions against Iran has been to force it to curtail its ambitious 1989 plan for the acquisition of a large-scale modern military. Tehran had proposed to purchase $10 billion in armaments during 1989-1994, mainly from the USSR. Hard currency military expenditures had to be cut in half during 1992-1994, when sanctions imposed by Washington hurt Tehran in the world capital markets. A reduction in military expenditures slowed down Iran's program to develop weapons of mass destruction, including ballistic missiles. Indeed, writes Iran expert Patrick Clawson, " . . . cash constraints explain why Iran was not able to take delivery on a submarine for two years, as well as the delays in acquiring more missile launching boats and modern mines."[56]

Designed to coerce Iran into ceasing its sponsorship of terrorism and stopping the development of nuclear, biological, and chemical armaments, the Clinton sanctions also had a domestic political bonus for him: they sent a signal to the pro-Israel community that wrongs were being righted. While the Reagan sanctions were retributive, Tehran provided Clinton with a rationale for a return to rehabilitative sanctions.

Clinton signed the Iran and Libya Sanctions Act less than a month after the midair explosion of TWA Flight 800 over waters near New York. Although there was no evidence at the time to link Iran to the downing of the aircraft, the conventional wisdom on Capitol Hill was to assume an Iranian connection. A bias toward inferring Iranian involvement suggests that retribution influenced decision making. Because the predisposition was to presume the worst of Iran, members of Congress blamed Tehran without waiting for proof. Furthermore, these politicians received domestic political kudos from the general American public and especially the pro-Israel community for tightening the sanctions on Iran.

## Interests Under Siege: Intrinsic and Strategic

*Intrinsic Interests at Stake.* Contrary to the assumption that the pro-Israel community "invented" the Iranian threat, there indeed is a perceived danger from Iran as seen from within the United States government. American leaders believe that Iran threatens both intrinsic and strategic interests, which are two sides of the same coin under assault.[57] The Iranian menace threatens American civilians and military personnel in the Gulf—intrinsic interests. Iran also is a risk to other inherently valuable targets like Western petroleum products transiting the Gulf and other sea-lanes of communications.

An incident in Saudi Arabia exemplifies the Iranian threat to civilians as well as U.S. military personnel and installations. A fuel truck exploded on June 25, 1996, outside the northern fence of an apartment complex near an air facility at Dhahran, close to the eastern Saudi coast. The explosion killed 19 people and injured about 160 others. The facility housed F-15 and F-16 aircraft belonging to the anti-Iraq coalition's Joint Task Force, Southwest Asia, which includes American, British, French, and Saudi Arabian combatants. Besides U.S. Air Force personnel in the housing area, there were Army technicians who operated a Patriot missile air defense unit.

About 2,000 Americans were stationed at the Dhahran air facility.[58] They helped enforce the UN No-Fly-Zone over southern Iraq. Operation Southern Watch is intended to protect Shiite Muslims against Saddam's Sunni Muslim air force.[59] After the Gulf War, the

Shiite Muslims of southern Iraq challenged Saddam's rule, and he cracked down on the insurgents. Consequently, Washington designed Southern Watch in order to deter any further move by Baghdad against the south. Iranian agents working with Saudi dissidents have intrinsic motives for attacking Americans in Saudi Arabia. U.S. civilian and military personnel are innately valuable to Washington. Hence, Tehran's motive could be to destroy what is of such inherent importance. But the same event can be of both intrinsic and strategic value. In this respect, a strategic aim is what would be gained from publicizing the bombing of U.S. military facilities in Saudi Arabia. Attacking such a facility calls attention to the American presence in the Kingdom and places pressure on the United States to reduce its postwar "occupation forces."

But the paradox of the Gulf War victory is a requirement for a semipermanent American combat presence in Saudi Arabia to monitor the No-Fly-Zone in southern Iraq. While triumph in the Cold War reduced the need for an American combat presence to contain the Soviet Union from penetrating the Gulf region, victory in the Gulf's "hot war" reinforced the need for deployment in Saudi Arabia.

*Strategic Interests at Stake.* Irrespective of the termination of the Cold War, the U.S. strategic interest in the Gulf is about the same—preserving the uninterrupted flow of petroleum to the world market at prices that are compatible with the economic growth of the industrialized democracies. The post–Cold War era only changed the source of danger; the strategic interests at stake remain constant. The external threat of the Soviet Union gave way to a regional threat from Iran and Iraq.

While there is a threat to intrinsic interests, there is also an Iranian danger to U.S. strategic interests. These include the credibility of America's threat to use military force; its resolve to remain engaged in the world; as well as the commitment to defend its friends against its foes.[60] To the extent that Tehran stands up to Washington, it challenges U.S. credibility, resolve, and commitment. One means by which Tehran confronts Washington is through state-sponsored terrorism. Not only does Iran target American citizens, it also directs terrorism against the Iranian political opposition at home and abroad. Insofar as the domestic opposition derives from Iranians who were associated with the Shah's regime and thus tarred by the American brush, Tehran's attacks are assaults on U.S. strategic interests.

After the rise of Khomeni and the seizure of American citizens as hostages in Tehran, occupants of the Oval Office perceived Iran as an "evil" nation of international terrorists. This perception constitutes an unmotivated bias that associates Iran with malice, irrespective of its behavior. Thus, any president perceives Iran's current conduct as malicious without evaluating that behavior on its own merits. Such misperception is an overestimation of the threat posed by Iran's behavior.

Threat magnification notwithstanding, Iran deserves its status as a repeat offender on the annual Department of State list of nations that sponsor global terrorism.[61] In order to export terror throughout the global village, the regime formed the Supreme Council for Coordination of the Islamic Revolution. Activities of such an Islamic council may have been discussed during a meeting in Paris during mid-June 1996.[62]

There were reports from Paris that Egyptian President Hosni Mubarak presented a confidential file to French President Jacques Chirac. The file supposedly contained information on a secret conference in Tehran between leaders of terrorist organizations and Iranian intelligence. Reports indicated that the participants discussed plans to carry out systematic attacks directed mainly at American targets. Hezbollah's senior leadership used the conference to establish an organized international terrorist association that would incorporate all of its branches in approximately 15 countries.[63]

Iran's Supreme Council may have been behind several incidents abroad that endangered American strategic interests. With respect to the threat to Iranian opposition forces, several defectors have been assassinated in countries throughout the region, such as Pakistan.[64] And concerning the threat against American allies, Iranian-sponsored Hezbollah combatants in southern Lebanon periodically launch rocket assaults on northern Israel. Iran provides arms, training, and money to the Lebanese Hezbollah, which, in turn tries to derail the Middle East peace process.[65] In addition to being the leading suspect in the October 1983 bombing of the American Marine barracks in Beirut, and the 1994 bombing of a building housing Jewish organizations in

Buenos Aires, Argentina, Hezbollah may have been involved in the bombing of Iranian dissidents in Pakistan.[66]

Iran, furthermore, encourages Palestinian groups that reject the peace process with Israel, such as Hamas.[67] Additionally, there is the Popular Front for the Liberation of Palestine-General Command (PFLP-GC).[68] U.S. intelligence officials reported on a June 1996 meeting in Tehran of suspects in airline bombings, at which representatives of the PFLP-GC reportedly requested permission to carry out terrorist attacks against U.S. interests. This meeting occurred one month prior to the July 17 midair explosion of TWA Flight 800 departing from New York for Paris.[69] Because of Iran's role in slowing down the Arab-Israel peace process, Tehran poses a threat to United States strategic interests in furthering it.

In addition to supporting the PFLP-GC, Tehran provided a safe haven to the Kurdistan Workers' Party (PKK) after various attacks against Turkey and Westerners traveling there. The Islamic Republic of Iran also supported Turkish Islamic groups suspected of assaults against secular Turks and Turkish Jews. And the State Department surmises that Tehran is guilty of using terrorism to destabilize friendly regimes in Algeria, Egypt, and Tunisia.[70] To the degree that Washington is unable to provide security for its allies and friends from the Iranian threat of terrorism, Tehran poses a threat to United States strategic interests in the Middle East.

In addition to the worldwide confrontation between Iran and the United States over international terrorism, there is a direct confrontation in the area lying between Bosnia and Baghdad. A strategic aim of both Iran and the United States is to extend their separate authorities in this geopolitical sphere. This "region" is the only part of the world where American military forces are on the increase. The U.S. military has conducted operations in support of Bosnian and Afghani Muslims. Tehran has interpreted the American military presence on behalf of the Muslims under siege as a direct threat to its own authority. As the presumed leader of a supposedly emerging Islamic empire, Tehran believes that it, not Washington, has the responsibility to protect Muslims. Rather than acknowledging the American contribution to Muslim security, Tehran berates Washington as the "Great Satan," who acts on behalf of "Little Satan," Israel.

Yet, in two Muslim wars, Washington and Tehran had a tacit
alignment. Both sponsored the Islamic Mujahadeen in Afghanistan
against the Soviet occupation. Both Iran and the United States supported the Bosnian Muslim regime against Christian Orthodox Serbia
and the Bosnian Serbs. In Afghanistan, the CIA provided covert
assistance to Islamic rebels fighting against the Soviets. So did Iran. In
the former Yugoslavia, the United States supported the Bosnian
Muslims. So did Iran.[71] Washington gave a green light for Zagreb to
receive arms from Tehran en route to Sarajevo.[72] Despite rejecting the
American role in Afghanistan and Bosnia, Iranian Revolutionary
Guards and their Saudi brethren fought in Muslim wars against the
Soviets in Afghanistan and against the Serbs in Bosnia.

But Iran was not only at war with the USSR via proxies in
Afghanistan. During February 1982, there also was growing cooperation between Tehran and Moscow in the field of arms trade. When
Western nations showed a reluctance to deal with the religious
extremists of Iran, the Soviets began to make inroads. Unable to find a
secure source of Western arms, Tehran sought arms wherever it could
find them. In addition to approaching American arms merchants on a
regular basis, Iranian representatives also made the rounds of arms
bazaars in Eastern Europe. And there were some 2,000 Soviet advisers
in Iran, as well as about 75 Cubans. Iranians were increasingly
confident that they could handle such Soviet ties and still export their
own revolution to places like Riyadh and Mecca.

Upon returning to Saudi Arabia from the Afghanistan war against
the Soviets and from the Bosnian crusades, the Saudi fighters became
dissidents. They used the presence of non-Muslims in Saudi Arabia as
a means to challenge the Saud family dynasty. The Saudi dissidents
opposed both Saudi Arabia's close ties with non-Muslim countries and
its failure to observe Islamic tenets. The primary non-Muslims under
fire in Saudi Arabia are American military personnel. The dissidents
are ardent readers of the London-based Saudi, Mohammed al-Masari,
who publishes reports documenting human-rights abuses and
excesses of the Saudi ruling family.

Initially, Riyadh accused Saudi dissidents of being responsible for
a prior bombing of the Saudi National Guard installation in Riyadh on
November 13, 1995. In the next year, Saudi Arabia pointed fingers at

both Iran and Syria as sources of assistance for the Saudi dissidents. That assault was the first political attack against the American military in Saudi Arabia. The Kingdom "convicted" four dissidents and beheaded them. One motive for the June 25, 1996, attack was to avenge these beheadings.

In addition to protecting friends against the threat of Iranian terrorism, American strategic interests include coercing Iran to cease its development of weapons of mass destruction, including nuclear, biological, and chemical armaments. A purpose of such weapons is to enable Iran to deter attacks from states like Iraq. The two neighbors fought a war of the cities from 1980 to 1988, in which they both employed weapons of mass destruction. Additionally, possession of nuclear, biological, or chemical armaments would allow Tehran to coerce neighbors like Saudi Arabia. The two explicitly negotiate or tacitly bargain over issues like Iranian pilgrims visiting Saudi holy sites, oil production quotas, as well as the presence of U.S. combat personnel in the Kingdom.

Tehran seeks to import sophisticated weapons systems and expand its own internal capabilities. Iran has the ability to obtain a nuclear device from a former Soviet republic, such as Muslim Kazakhstan, which possessed nuclear weapons. But to acquire such a device on its own could take some five years.[73] Whether with outside assistance or not, there are Central Intelligence Agency reports to indicate that Iran may have a nuclear weapon by the year 2000.

Iran has a larger stockpile of chemical weapons than nuclear or biological armaments. Chemical weapons, however, are not as lethal as either the nuclear or biological hazard. Tehran began acquiring chemical arms in its war with Baghdad. The Islamic Republic stockpiled mustard gas as well as blood and nerve agents. But Tehran has also initiated limited production of biological weapons. It is creating an infrastructure to sustain biological arms at places ostensibly engaged in pharmaceutical research.[74]

Regarding systems to deliver weapons of mass destruction, Beijing and Pyongyang are selling ballistic missiles to Tehran. While the Islamic Republic has the ability to produce its own ballistic missiles, it prefers to import them from sources like China and North Korea. Iran's inventory consists of about 450 Scud-B and Scud-C missiles. Not satisfied to rely on these limited-range systems, Tehran is obtaining longer-range, solid-fuel missiles. Intelligence analysts expect Iran in 1996-1997 to take delivery on North Korea's Rodong ballistic missile, which has a range of about 800 miles, thus bringing most of the Middle East into Tehran's missile envelope. This range, coupled with the capacity to deliver weapons of mass destruction, will enable Tehran to emerge as a world-class strategic threat to the United States.

In short, in order to counter the coercive potential of Iranian armaments, Washington has a strategic interest in preventing Tehran from acquiring weapons of mass destruction. Presidents have acted upon this strategic interest, whether directed at Iran, Iraq, or other rogue regimes. In the history of American-Iranian relations, several presidents have formulated what might be called doctrines regarding the Gulf in general and Iran in particular. A discussion of these approaches should assist in the process of understanding the use of economic sanctions as a tool of choice by American presidents in their relations with the Islamic Republic of Iran.

## A Tale of Presidential Doctrines

Although presidents do not label their policies as doctrines, it is possible to outline the defining characteristics and label them as such. Here is a brief overview of these policies toward the Gulf, with special emphasis on Iran.

Presidential doctrines vary according to the extent to which American regional allies act as proxies, the degree of U.S. resolve, and the overall balance of military power in the area. As Cold War Presidents, Nixon and Carter focused on the external threat from the Soviet Union. During the transition to the post–Cold War era, Presidents Reagan, Bush, and Clinton emphasized the internal threat from the Gulf region.[75]

*Nixon Doctrine—Containment of the USSR with the Twin Pillars.* In view of the 1971 British military withdrawal from the area east of Suez, the Nixon aim was to reinforce American strategic nuclear deterrence of the Soviet Union. The method was to strengthen U.S. regional proxies—Iran and Saudi Arabia.[76] A twin pillars policy provided justification for supplying arms to Tehran and Riyadh so that each could act as props to hold up Western interests in the Gulf. In 1969, Nixon acknowledged the declining ability of the United States to take unilateral action in defense of its regional allies. Consequently, he put them on notice that they would have to shoulder more of the burden. Military assistance was the tool of choice in order to facilitate allied defense initiatives. Faced with fighting the Vietnam War, Nixon formulated a policy that would encourage U.S. allies to participate in their own defense and minimize the American role.

*Carter Doctrine—Containment of the USSR Via American Resolve and Rapid Deployment Force.* President Carter issued a statement of intent to intervene in the event of a Soviet military move in the Gulf. With the withdrawal of the British and the Soviet invasion of Afghanistan in 1979, the USSR had an imbalance of power in its favor in the Gulf region. Moscow could stage combat aircraft from airfields in Afghanistan. In the contingency of a Backfire bomber attack on U.S. naval forces in the Arabian Sea, Soviet use of Afghanistan would extend the range of fighter protection for that aircraft.[77]

Consequently, Carter said that he would act to prevent a takeover of that region by any hostile outside power.[78] The President's aim was to show resolve in order to deter a Soviet move into Iran from the Caucasus or Afghanistan.[79] The problem was, however, that the United States lacked the capability in the Gulf region to implement the Carter Doctrine.

During the summer of 1980, tensions increased between Iran and Iraq. But the United States focused on the possibility of a Soviet military intervention of the Gulf area. Washington downplayed the likelihood of an Iran-Iraq War. In effect, Carter held that he would not allow the Soviets to do to Iran what they had done to Afghanistan.

*Reagan Corollary—Balance of Power Between Iran and Iraq to Preserve Stability of Saudi Arabia.* The fall of the Shah of Iran in 1978 and the subsequent rise of the Ayatollah gave Reagan an occasion to issue what analysts later dubbed the Reagan Corollary of the Carter Doctrine. The United States would use military force in the Gulf region not only to make sure that oil flowed freely but also to ensure that the regime in

Saudi Arabia would be safe from internal and external threats. It was important that American-supplied armaments, such as the Airborne Warning and Control System (AWACS), not fall into unfriendly hands. The Iranian scenario should not be repeated. When the Shah fell, American military equipment came into the hands of anti-American Iranian radicals. Reagan vowed to use military force if necessary to foreclose the Iranian scenario.

In short, the Reagan Corollary stated that President Reagan would not allow the Iranian revolution to spread to Saudi Arabia. He would not permit Riyadh to move away from Washington because of a change of regime.[80] Reagan would not allow Saudi Arabia to go down the same path as Iran, e.g., for a revolution to overthrow a friendly regime and for the successors to oust the United States from a position of influence.

But just as President Carter asserted the Carter Doctrine to protect the Gulf area without the military forces to back it up, President Reagan asserted a commitment to Saudi Arabia without having the political or military capabilities to back up that undertaking. Although the Saudi monarchy is more stable than the Shah's regime, the forces that assassinated Sadat of Egypt during October 1981 were operating in Saudi Arabia two decades later. If there were a coup in Saudi Arabia and the new rulers wanted to slow down oil production and accommodate Islamist opponents, there would be little justification for United States military action to save the regime. Additionally, a commitment to the Saud regime commits Washington to shore up a family whose future is bleak in light of the social and economic forces that are on the rise there. And the United States lacks the capability to stop a coup from opposition groups, including a military coup of competing elites within the Royal family.

One way to protect Saudi Arabia from Iran or Iraq was for the United States to act as a "balancer" between the two. The United States provided tacit support to either so that neither could dominate the Gulf. However, once Iran became hostile to the United States and Iraq invaded Iran in 1980, Washington acted as the "holder of the balance" in the Gulf. It initially tilted toward Iraq.[81] But when Reagan sent U.S. arms to Iran in exchange for American hostages held in Lebanon by terrorist allies of Tehran, Washington tipped toward Tehran.

*Bush Doctrine—Balance of Power between Iran and Iraq to Preserve Security of Saudi Arabia.* In the post–Cold War era, the Bush Administration continued the Reagan policy of acting as holder of the balance between the two enemies. Bush first leaned toward Iraq by selling it dual-use equipment, removing it from the terrorist list, providing import subsidies, and encouraging the country to play a major role in the Arab-Israel peace process.[82] With the Iraqi invasion of Kuwait, Bush "drew a line in the sand," with the deployment of American ground combat forces to the Arabian peninsula.[83]

Bush, in effect, stated that he would not allow the Iraqis to do to Saudi Arabia what they had done to Kuwait. Following the defeat of Iraq, American ground troops remained in order to deter Baghdad and monitor the terms of the cease-fire. Although the purpose was deterrence, American combat forces created a predominance of military power that could be used to contain either Baghdad or Tehran.

*Clinton Doctrine—From Balance of Power to Dual Containment.* The United States will refrain from the Reagan-Bush balance of power approach of tacitly supporting either Iran or Iraq in an attempt to thwart expansion by the other.[84] The basic purpose of dual containment is to counter the threats of both Baghdad and Tehran. The Administration has sought to fashion an approach specific to each country, as separate threats.[85]

A balance of power assumption is that the "holder" should keep its options open regarding whether to have political relations with states in a region. Depending upon the balance in the area at any particular time, the balancer may intervene to prevent either state from dominating third parties. Iran's traditional aspirations to become a regional hegemon have in the past been kept in check by a rough balance of power with Iraq. Baghdad could count on the support of its Arab neighbors in any conflict involving Arabs and Persians.[86] U.S. policy under Reagan and Bush was in the British balance of power tradition of preventing the emergence of any hegemonic power in the Gulf capable of controlling the production and pricing policies of the oil-producing states.

Contrary to the Reagan-Bush balance of power policy is an approach that rules out political relations on ideological grounds. The Clinton doctrine of dual containment rejects the balancing assumptions in favor of an ideological approach to Iran and Iraq. This ideological rigidity contrasts sharply with the flexibility of the balancing approach. But the principal flaw of dual containment is the assumption that it is possible to contain both Iran and Iraq at the same time, without making use of the hostility of the one against the other.[87]

Isolation of Tehran assumes a comparatively powerful and united Iraq on the Islamic Republic's extensive western frontier; if not, Iraq becomes a tempting location from which Tehran can seek to escape containment. Likewise, isolation of Iraq assumes Iranian complicity. In this respect, multilateral economic sanctions on Baghdad would not be very effective if Tehran refused to enforce the embargo. Indeed, during the summer of 1996, these two states had a de facto economic alignment that allowed some Iraqi oil to be shipped across Iranian borders contrary to United Nations restrictions against such shipments.

Additionally, dual containment encourages Iran and Iraq into a de facto political alignment against the United States. But a rogue state alliance is precisely not the goal of American policy; the Clinton Administration's aim is to separate and isolate Iran and Iraq not only from the rest of the world, but from each other. Paradoxically, the Clinton policy pushes Tehran and Baghdad together. Fortunately for the Administration, local forces work to separate these two states.

With respect to local populations, Iran and Iraq compete for allegiance of the Kurds along their borders. But the Kurds in northern Iraq divide into two competing groups. The Patriotic Union of Kurdistan and the Kurdistan Democratic Party have appealed for assistance from Iran and Iraq, respectively. As a result of Iranian intervention on the side of the Patriotic Union in the Iraqi city of Irbil, Saddam's ground troops attacked that city on the weekend beginning August 30, 1996. In launching this assault, however, Iraqi forces violated the Western-protected safehaven above the 36th parallel. The United States responded with a cruise missile attack.[88]

In light of the dual containment policy, it would be hypocritical for the United States to intervene on behalf of Iranian-supported Kurds in Iraq. This approach does not permit Washington to align temporarily with Tehran in order to thwart Baghdad. Because of dual containment, the Administration is on the horn of a dilemma. On the one hand, acceptance of Baghdad's violations would leave Iraqi forces in control of a portion of a haven that was supposed to be safe from them. On the other hand, American attacks against Iraqi forces in the safehaven would aid Kurds aligned with Tehran, contrary to dual containment's requirement to isolate Iran.

In order to avoid these unacceptable options, the Administration chose to launch cruise missile strikes against Iraqi defense installations in the south. In doing so, Washington sought to avoid either rewarding Baghdad or aligning with Tehran. But in fact, the attacks only weakened Iraqi capabilities in the south and left Saddam's forces in control of the safehaven. Despite Clinton's claim that the cruise missiles were a success, they did not resolve the dilemma.

Dual containment also places a disproportionate political problem on Saudi Arabia. By housing the American forces that implement the military aspects of the containment policy for both states, Riyadh assumes the burden of retaliation from both neighbors. The number of troops required to enforce the No-Fly-Zone in southern Iraq is fewer than the number needed to monitor it and to deter Tehran. And if there were an Iranian connection to the June 1996 bombing of an American military installation in Saudi Arabia, that could be payback for Riyadh's collusion with Washington.

Dual containment is a flawed policy. It is indicative of the failure of the Clinton Administration to come to grips with regional and local factors that sustain conflicts in the Gulf, absent the external threat from the Soviet Union. As Cold War presidents, Nixon and Carter successfully dealt with the external threat posed by the USSR. And during the transition to the post–Cold War era, Presidents Reagan and Bush managed the internal threat from the region. A return to the flexibility inherent in the balance of power policy of the Reagan and Bush years would allow Washington to make use of changing circumstances in the Gulf. Dual containment does not permit external actors to take advantage of future political instability in the region. A balance of power approach would permit the United States to make flexible adjustments in policy by temporarily siding with either Iran or Iraq.

While the United States sought to build consensus within the international community and regional allies to contain both rogue states, it succeeded only in the case of Iraq. Containment of post–Gulf

War Iraq is an international strategy based upon UN resolutions. Containment applied to Iran, however, is problematic because the allies are reluctant to isolate Tehran.

In short, another assumption of the Clinton doctrine of dual containment is that the allies would help enforce it. Failure to persuade the allies to boycott Iran has led to a situation in which they must accept the American approach or be in public dispute with the United States. By punishing foreign firms that invest in Iran above a threshold determined in Washington, the United States seeks in vain to compel its allies to accept dual containment.

## American Politics and Idealism Trump Alliance Obligations

There is a convergence of bureaucratic and domestic politics with idealism and perceived interests. As a result, alliance obligations have less influence on American policy regarding terrorism and weapons of mass destruction. In this respect, the Pentagon's threat perceptions, the pro-Israel community, counterterrorism ideals, and principles against proliferation prevail.

Even though the allies oppose designating countries as rogues, opposition was comparatively mild when Secretary of State George Shultz placed Iran on the list of states that sponsor international terrorism on January 13, 1984.[89] He thereby subjected Tehran to a set of antiterrorism laws, which included the Anti-Terrorism and Effective Death Penalty Act of 1996. In a prohibition of assistance to terrorist states, this Act imposes penalties upon U.S. "persons" (individuals or firms) who engage in financial transactions with a country knowing, or having reason to know, that it has been designated under the Export Administration Act as a country supporting international terrorism.[90]

Because Americans are the subjects of the 1996 antiterrorism law, the allies have little problem with its prohibitions. What is at issue for them in the Iran and Libya Sanctions Act is that Washington applies its laws to "any person," for example, either people or foreign firms trading or investing with Iran or Libya.[91] In response to the act, the European Union voiced its strong opposition. It claimed that the Iran/

Libya legislation was a case of extraterritorial application.[92] The Union criticized the act under the assumption that it would allow a president to impose sanctions, even if the relevant parties were located outside of the United States and the transactions involved no American financial instruments or technology.

The act is a secondary boycott, a ban against firms that fail to comply with a primary sanction like the United States boycott of Iran.[93] But the Iran and Libya Sanctions Act may be more like the Arab League boycott of Israel than it is like the Cuban Liberty and Democratic Solidarity Act against Cuba.[94] It gives U.S. citizens the right to sue foreign companies that traffic in Cuban property formerly owned by Americans. Because foreigners who acquire confiscated property are liable to prosecution under American laws, the act is an illustration of extraterritoriality.[95] Therefore, the Cuban Liberty and Democratic Solidarity Act may be a more extreme application of extraterritoriality than the Iran and Libya legislation, due to the involvement of U.S. courts.[96]

In connection with the imposition of penalties against foreign persons, there are previous cases in American laws. Here is legislation that contains precedents for the application of sanctions against foreign persons: the Foreign Relations Authorization Act of 1994 and the Arms Export Control Act of 1967. The Missile Technology Control Regime (MTCR) provisions in the Arms Export Control Act apply to foreign persons. The penalties deny future U.S. government contracts to persons in violation of the MTCR. In addition, they lose the right to export goods and services to the United States.[97]

Other precedents for imposing sanctions against foreign persons include the Anti-Economic Discrimination Act of 1994 and the National Defense Authorization Act for 1993. They penalize foreign persons who support the Arab boycott of Israel.[98] These two acts restrict the departments of State and Defense from doing business with foreign persons who are in compliance with the Arab boycott of Israel.

Because of the U.S. assertion of legal precedents for its secondary boycott regarding Iran and Libya, the European Union passed its own regulations, which make it difficult for its member states to comply with the American boycott. In addition, the Union threatened to mount a legal challenge to the United States through the General

Agreement on Tariffs and Trade (GATT) and the World Trade Organization (WTO). The European Union Council of Foreign Ministers called for a WTO dispute settlement panel that would deal with the issue of extraterritoriality.[99] But the American view is that because the GATT permits a signatory state to adopt measures to protect its national security, the GATT allows economic sanctions by member states.[100]

Legal issues notwithstanding, the European Union, " . . . fails to see why the United States needs to hit out at its friends while targeting its adversaries."[101] It is because of a convergence of politics, idealism, and perceived interests that Washington hurts its friends while targeting its enemies. Despite Iran's attempt to divide America from its allies, however, the battle is still mainly between Washington and Tehran.

## SCENARIOS

Three broad scenarios are relevant to an understanding of the future of American-Iranian relations: limited war based on dual containment, differentiated containment, and a grand bargain.

### Limited War: Dual Containment

Washington could find Tehran to be responsible for the bombing of American citizens in Saudi Arabia. The president might order retaliatory air strikes against terrorist bases in Iran. Tehran might answer with naval attacks against U.S. assets in the Gulf, American citizens abroad, and installations within the United States. Because of the constraint on American policy due to dual containment, Washington would be unable to play off Baghdad against Tehran. But Iraq might take advantage of a limited conflict between its two adversaries to move against the Kurds in the north or the Shiites in the south. Also, Iran and Iraq might confront each other over Iranian dissidents in southern Iraq. Violations of the No-Fly-Zone in the south could result in Coalition attacks against Iraqi aircraft and U.S. strikes against Iran. The cost of even a limited war is so great, however, that both Tehran and Washington are likely to take steps to limit escalation and expansion. While the likelihood of a war scenario is low, skirmishes over the No-Fly-Zone are likely.

## Differentiated Containment: Balance of Power?

In addition to limited war, differentiated containment also is plausible. There is a growing dissatisfaction with dual containment and a reluctance to accept an explicit return to balance of power. How is it possible to achieve the national security benefits of balance of power without incurring its domestic political costs? The answer: differentiated containment.[102]

Leaders in the move away from dual containment include two former national security advisors and a former assistant secretary.[103] Their argument in favor of differentiated containment is simple: contain Saddam, but take actions regarding Iran in order to keep the anti-Saddam coalition united. The nuanced approach would acknowledge that Washington's efforts at unilateral isolation of Iran are costly and ineffective. Differentiated containment concerning Iran would include tradeoffs.[104] Those who advocate differentiated containment, however, divide into two camps. One approach would be to deny Iran an unconventional weapons capability. The other approach would relax opposition to Iran's nuclear program. The second school would pay less attention to the Iranian nuclear threat in exchange for Tehran's agreement to comprehensive international inspection and control procedures. The possibility of a tradeoff in the nuclear area suggests prospects for a grand bargain across the entire spectrum of American-Iranian relations.

## A Grand Bargain:
## Capital for Terror and Arms Control

Both Washington and Tehran use weapons of choice in confrontations with one another. Export controls on investments are tools of the capital-rich to take advantage of the susceptibility of the capital-poor; the export of international terrorism is a weapon of the weak to exploit the vulnerability of the strong. Because the United States is a primary source of global capital, it employs economic sanctions to constrain international investment in Iran. Tehran is a regional power with a capacity for exporting its revolution worldwide; it engages in state-sponsored terrorism against the United States. Exporting terrorism is an Iranian tool of choice befitting its aspirations to become a fountainhead for the Islamic revolution.

While exporting terrorism is a way by which Iran can spread the ideology of its revolution, importing equipment for the development of weapons of mass destruction is a means for the country to catapult its way into Great Power status. The acquisition of nuclear, biological, and chemical armaments is a method to achieve an equality of deterrent and coercive potential with the United States, at least in the Gulf region. Just as revolutionary ideologues are reluctant to give up the option of resorting to state-sponsored terrorism, so the more secular-oriented officials may be hesitant to give up what Iranians may perceive as a great equalizer—weapons of mass destruction.[105]

The currency for Washington is capital for investment and relief from its embargo; the currency for Tehran is cessation of its campaign of terrorism and weapons proliferation as well as a commitment to keep its oil production and pricing free from politics. At issue is whether there can be a currency exchange—a grand bargain between the two confrontation states. Is there a potential for an accord that would trade a piece of capital for a piece of peace? Doubtful. As long as each state derives both national security and domestic political benefits from confronting the other, there is little prospect for such a bargain. Idealism motivates both Tehran and Washington. Hence, there is scant potential that these new enemies can resume their old friendship. And within Iran, revolutionary ideologues may have reached an accommodation with their secular competitors: the religious faithful can export the revolution; the secular military can have its weapons systems.

The Iran and Libya Sanctions Act, moreover, also contains seeds for an exchange. For a cessation of Iranian terrorism, conventional military buildup, and acquisition of weapons of mass destruction, there is an implicit promise of a removal of American sanctions. In the currency exchange proposed here, there would be an explicit pledge of sanctions removal. More important, there would be a promise of capital investment. For its part, Iran would have to cease the practice of terrorism, reduce its conventional armaments, and dismantle its rudimentary nuclear, biological, and chemical components. On the one hand, the allies would be somewhat optimistic regarding the prospects for a currency exchange between Tehran and Washington. Iran projects a moderate image of itself to the allies in order to enhance the prospects of business relations with them. The State Department views this quest for respectability as an explanation why Tehran reduced its attacks in Europe during 1995: "Tehran wants to ensure Western capital and markets."[106] The Europeans claim that their "critical dialogue" with Iran yields dividends. They take a critical posture toward Iran's misbehavior, while they maintain normal commercial and political relations. The allies would argue that if Iran decreases its terrorist assaults in order to gain access to European and Japanese capital and markets, perhaps Tehran would be willing to do the same with respect to Washington.

On the other hand, the United States would be pessimistic concerning the possibility of a bargain. For Washington, there is no question that Iran is disingenuous regarding its moderate posture and should not be trusted. American officials believe that Tehran is making a tactical, short-term reduction in its practice of terror in order to gain capital and market access.[107] Iran still retains its long-term use of terror as a strategic weapon, while making a tactical accommodation for the moment. Washington assumes that Tehran's moderate posture is a ploy to gain short-term advantage with the European Union, Japan, and Canada in their disputes with the United States over Iran.

Because of Iran's subterfuge, critics may view the idea of a currency exchange as appeasement. In contrast to the appeasement policy implicit in the arms-for-hostages tradeoff, the exchange of investment capital for a cessation of terrorism and proliferation is more demanding on Tehran. The arms/hostages arrangement gave Iran an incentive to seize hostages in order to gain additional armaments. A capital-for-terrorism/proliferation arrangement would place the ball in Tehran's court: only in the context of a reduction in terrorism and arms acquisition would there be a corresponding cutback in economic sanctions. The pain would remain before Iran received the gain.

In the arms-for-hostages swap, there was no new pain for Iran but a high prospect for a weapons gain. In the capital-for-terrorism/proliferation bargain, the gain would only come after the terror ceased and the pain ended. In short, an incremental reduction in terrorism and proliferation would be a necessary condition for a gradual decrease in sanctions; success of this tit-for-tat process would mean an end to the Iranian terrorism threat and weapons buildup. Only then could investment capital flow freely to Iran from capital-rich Europe, Japan, and North America.

As the emerging markets of Asia require more oil to fuel explosive growth, Iranian oil could help meet the demand and keep prices low. Such an achievement could allow new enemies to rekindle their old friendships. Furthermore, the inflexible policy of dual containment should revert back to the flexible balance of power approach. America can act as a balancer between Iran and Iraq and contain both better than it can contain one or the other at the same time.

Recall the four themes that cut across *Rogue Regimes:* threat perception, opportunities, politics, and policies. For Iran, bureaucratic and domestic politics reinforced by idealism are the key factors that explain Washington's sanction policies toward Tehran. With respect to the debate about the nature of threats in the international system, a rogue regime does occupy Tehran. It is a fitting substitute for the Soviet threat. But given the different perceptions of threat and opportunity that divide the United States from its allies about Iran, it is difficult to fashion policies to change the regime's behavior or to punish it for misbehavior. A continuation of punishment is justified only on retributive grounds.

# CHAPTER THREE

# IRAQ: RECONCILE, CONTAIN, OR OVERTHROW?

## OPTIONS AND SCENARIOS

In the late 1990s, three options dominated the debate about Iraq in the United States. At issue is whether Washington should reconcile with the regime in Baghdad, seek to contain it, or endeavor to overthrow it. "Reconciliation" is a policy of rewarding an adversary, hoping to effect compliance. "Containment" is a strategy of threatening a party in order to gain acquiescence. "Overthrow" takes into account current noncompliant behavior and favors brute force, rather than rewards or threats; indeed, rather than altering the behavior of a regime, an aim is to overturn the government itself.

Although reconciling with Iraq is a political nonstarter for the United States, it needs to be discussed as a potential option. Reconciliation merits consideration if for no other reason than to rule it out on analytic rather than political grounds. The three policy options have three corresponding scenarios that range on a continuum from optimistic to pessimistic: compliance, neither compliance nor defiance, and confrontation.

"Compliance" assumes that Baghdad conforms to UN–mandated requirements to dismantle, destroy, or otherwise account for Iraq's weapons of mass destruction (WMD). "Neither compliance nor defiance" presumes that Iraq alternates between these two. "Confrontation" presupposes that Baghdad is in noncompliance with the United Nations, cracks down on the Kurdish opposition in the north or the Muslim Shiite dissidents in the south, or restarts a war against one of its neighbors, such as Iran or Kuwait.

"Reconciliation" assumes either adherence—a sunny scenario that Iraq is approaching compliance—or that the country would conform, once Baghdad receives its rewards. Whether before or after rewards, reconciliation intends to effect a return of Iraq to the family of nations.

There is a precedent for an American policy of reconciling with Iraq. At the end of the Reagan Administration and the beginning the Bush tenure in office, Washington provided diplomatic and economic inducements to encourage acceptable behavior on the part of Baghdad. The Bush overture to Iraq during 1989–1990 included credit guarantees for the import of American grain. But Saddam responded by accusing Washington of conspiring against him. Nevertheless, the Bush Administration maintained its policy of seeking to engage Iraq, an approach that dominated until Iraq invaded Kuwait in August 1990.[1]

If the Clinton Administration were to embrace Iraq, Washington would have to take the lead in working for removal of multinational economic sanctions, discontinuation of international inspections, and incorporation of Iraq into a web of political and economic ties. The restraining effect of this mesh of positive reinforcements would keep Iraq in check, according to this approach.

Containment assumes a more pessimistic or cloudy scenario than reconciliation—neither full compliance nor complete defiance. Containment presupposes that Baghdad would accede to demands only when faced with economic sanctions accompanied by credible threats of overwhelming force. Containment continues economic sanctions, isolates Iraq diplomatically, and employs brute force should Iraq take a significant act, such as another invasion of Kuwait. At issue in a policy of containment, however, is how to handle the paradox involving international inspection.

Containment with inspection is unlikely to be successful. When the inspectors get too close to the weapons of terror, Baghdad plays a game of delay, denial, and defiance. Containment without inspection, however, is hazardous. The regime would be able to reconstitute its capability to create nuclear, biological, and chemical weapons.

Because of the paradox of containment, the Clinton Administration has been inconsistent in handling the issue of inspection. In November 1997, the Administration raised the value of inspection to a very high level. After Baghdad's announcement that it would expel Americans from the UN inspection team, Washington held that this move was unacceptable and a challenge to the international community and countered that it would pursue the Iraqi declaration in "a very determined way." In February 1998, Baghdad again blocked the weapons inspectors. Washington then called attention to the dangers of Iraq's weapons, and said that it would go to war to protect the inspectors' "full and unfettered access."

Contrary to its earlier approaches, the Administration prepared to reverse itself in October 1998. It attempted to forsake inspection as an effective instrument of policy toward Iraq.[2] Rather, Washington reemphasized other forms of containment, such as continued economic sanctions and the periodic use of force. Because the United States thought that Saddam would not cooperate with the inspectors, in early November 1998 it moved to discount the importance of inspection. As long as Baghdad did not block the inspectors, Washington could downplay the significance of inspection. But when Saddam created another crisis by not permitting inspectors to have access to suspect weapons sites, inspection again became the focus of American policy.

By mid–November, the Clinton Administration weighed the benefit of military action against the cost of attacking. On the gain side, military action would have significantly degraded Iraq's capability to develop WMD and to deliver them on targets. On the loss side, military force would have marked the end of the UN weapons inspection team in Iraq. With these possible results in mind, the Administration declined to launch military strikes in November: it feared the cost of losing the ability to inspect more than it desired the benefit of degrading Iraq's weapons of terror.

By December 1998, the Administration reversed course: it traded off inspection for military action. Washington launched four days of airstrikes against military, political, and economic targets in Iraq when the regime failed to abide by an agreement that foreclosed military action in November. Baghdad absorbed that bombing and announced the termination of inspection.

At the beginning of 1999, the Administration sought to contain Iraq with a policy of sanctions without inspections. Focusing on inspection had given Iraq's supporters on the UN Security Council an occasion to make the inspectors the issue. Doing so diverted attention from the real issue, which is the Iraqi government itself.

Besides shifting the focus away from the regime, there was another downside to making inspection a core concern of Washington's policy toward Baghdad. Because evacuation of inspectors would precede an authorization to commence bombing, Iraq would have advance warning of military action against it. The presence of international inspectors on the ground in Iraq assures the regime at least a day's warning of an armed assault ordered by London and Washington.

Also, an emphasis on inspection left Saddam with the upper hand. At any time, he can create a crisis by expelling the inspectors from Iraq and daring the international community to use force or accept this action as a fait accompli.

The pattern is for Saddam to create a crisis over inspection. He links inspections to sanctions and then seeks a reduction in the length of time Iraq will be the target of international restrictions. He bargains about the nature of inspections—how many, where the inspectors might go, and what they might see. Just before the bombs are to fall on Iraq, an endgame and dénouement appear on the horizon. At that moment, Saddam agrees to readmit inspectors under ambiguous rules of the game. Every time inspectors are not present, Saddam has the opportunity to move equipment, hide contraband, and act in other ways that defeat the purpose of inspection.

A containment policy that includes ineffective inspection contains hidden hazards. An imperfect inspection policy falsely conveys the impression that arms inspectors might complete their goals of discovery, dismantlement, and destruction of all of Iraq's WMD. Because Saddam creates a crisis when the inspectors get too close to his chemical and biological agents, however, it is doubtful if they will ever be able to finish their tasks.

Despite the downside of inspection, containment without inspection is also risky. Without inspection, Iraq would be able to reconstitute its WMD capability—in about five years for nuclear weapons and "almost immediately" for chemical and biological armaments.[3] Because of the regime's pattern of cheat and retreat, containment with inspection is hardly feasible; without inspection, however, containment is too dangerous. In the absence of inspection, overthrow emerges as a serious alternative.

Overthrow presumes a stormy scenario and has the most pessimistic script. Neither rewards nor threats of punishment are sufficient to coerce Saddam. Faced with a realization that the United States would never permit lifting of economic sanctions and that he is able to make last–minute concessions to avert American military force, Saddam is simply not coercible. Hence, brute force is the option of choice.

There are at least three aspects of the overthrow option: supporting a guerrilla war by opposition forces, helping them hold territory from which the renegades might come to power, and employing Western airpower to assist the dissidents in a direct challenge to the regime. These three alternatives range from least to most risky. Because all of them are too hazardous for the United States, however, containment plus regime change is an option favored in Washington at the close of the century.

Following the December 1998 bombings, the Clinton Administration adopted a policy of containment with overthrow as a long–term goal. Blatant advocacy by one nation to remove another government from power, however, flies in the face of international norms. According to one overthrow variant, someone in his immediate circle might assassinate Saddam. For example, a disgruntled leader from the Iraqi military might be willing to execute Saddam in order to seize power for himself.

In contrast to the palace coup plot, London and Washington might be able to encourage Iraqi opposition forces in locations around Mosul in the north and Basra in the south of Iraq. From these sites, the opponents of the regime might be able to launch a guerrilla war campaign or seize additional territory with the assistance of their Western allies.

In order to choose from among policy options in view of the future scenarios, consider explanations of the behavior of the principal actors—the United States and Iraq.

## WASHINGTON MOVES THE GOAL POST, SADDAM CHEATS ON COMPLIANCE

Why does Washington fail to accept Iraq's claims that it is in compliance? The simple and valid answer is that Baghdad is not in acquiescence. The more complex answer, however, is that not only does Iraq engage in massive cheating, but the United States shifts criteria for adherence.

The main criterion for compliance is UN Security Council Resolution 687, and Iraq simply is not in compliance with it.[4] In addition, however, Washington endeavors to overturn the regime in Baghdad. Holding out for a change in government is equivalent to moving the goal post in the middle of the game.[5]

A nightmare scenario is that Saddam might fully accede to the requirements of Resolution 687 and allow the inspectors to verify his compliance. So long as inspection is a central part of a containment strategy and overturning the regime is not pursued with zeal, there is some likelihood that the bad dream may become a reality.

Why does Iraq fail to dismantle its weapons of mass destruction and allow international verification of their eradication? Baghdad is not willing to adhere fully to the international sanctions regime because Saddam has not given up his vision of uniting Kuwait with Iraq and becoming the all–powerful ruler of the Gulf region.

Those who think that Saddam acts on the basis of fear also believe that the United States "pockets" Iraqi concessions, rarely reciprocates with conciliatory gestures, and fails to recognize Iraq's genuine acquiescence. This approach assumes that Saddam takes the risk of defying the United States in order to avoid other losses. As he is deprived, he will accept some risk. Saddam resists the United States because he feels he has already lost a great deal and is immune to further threats. Because Clinton is intent on changing the regime in Baghdad, Saddam has nothing to gain by compliance. Adherents of this approach would reconcile with and accommodate him. They would engage him in a "critical dialogue" in order to rehabilitate him. Also, they would refrain from retributive punishment, avoid forcing Saddam into a corner, and assure him that the West is not out to topple his regime.[6]

The conciliate Saddam idea assumes that he is not deterrable but may be amenable to assurance and persuasion. Because he believes that the United States is determined to undermine his regime no matter what he does, Saddam is relatively immune even to reassuring statements. According to this school, he is a vulnerable leader motivated by need rather than an opportunity–driven aggressor motivated by greed. Irrespective of Saddam's actual behavior, reassurance would have to take into account his acute sense of vulnerability.[7]

Few rewards have been promised for compliance with American demands. Deterrence is unlikely to be effective against Saddam; therefore assurance, while also problematic, is the more feasible option.[8] Indeed, at the close of 1998 there was consensus in Washington that Saddam and his inner circle had concluded that the United States would never permit economic sanctions against Iraq to be lifted. As a result, Baghdad's strategy was to stage a series of confrontations that stop short of provoking a military strike.[9]

In addition to believing that the United States would never allow economic sanctions to end, Saddam also believes that his Arab brethren had slighted him. He feels that his accomplishments as the "Knight of the Arab Nation" have not been appreciated.[10] Kuwait added to his feelings of persecution by refusing to forgive war debts Baghdad incurred in the Iran–Iraq War. By siphoning a disproportionate amount of oil from a shared field and by overproducing contrary to oil production quotas, Kuwait added to Iraq's mounting economic difficulties. Because Saddam saw Kuwait as a threat to his status and power base, he chose the military option in 1990.

## AT THE BRINK, SADDAM BLINKS

Why would Saddam Hussein risk so many lives, so much capital, and his political legacy by challenging a coalition that has greater military capabilities than Iraq? In terms of classical strategy, it is puzzling for a weaker actor to contest stronger parties. In comparison with Iraq, the combined arsenals of the United States and its allies is overwhelming.

One solution to this puzzle derives from deterrence theory and focuses on threat credibility. Deterrence theorists would explain

Saddam's challenge to result from his perception that his adversaries lack resolve and their threats are not credible. The right combination of capability and resolve should produce credible threats, which in turn should effect compliance. Until Saddam believes that an overwhelming capability is about to be used against targets of value to him, he will continue to challenge.

While classical deterrence ideas take into account capability differentials, resolve, and threat credibility, deterrence discounts the psychological character of Saddam and the political culture of Iraq. Going beyond deterrence, another solution to the puzzle may be found in prospect theory and in history.

Regarding why Saddam takes the world to the brink of war and then decides to blink, consider this explanation. When he is in a domain of deprivation, he is risk–acceptant and creates a crisis. When Saddam is in a domain of gain, he is risk–averse and deescalates the crisis. In a 14–month period, Iraq took the world community to the edge of war four times. Baghdad backed down in October 1997, February 1998, and October 1998. In December, however, the United States attacked Iraq before it could retreat.

*October 29, 1997.* The first of three crises began in the fall of 1997. At that time, Iraq said it would only continue to allow inspectors to perform their work if the United Nations Special Commission (UNSCOM) excluded its Americans from the group and if talks began about lifting economic sanctions on Iraq.

On November 2, Iraq announced that it would not allow three American UNSCOM inspectors into the country. Saddam was trying to use the threat to deny access as a bargaining tool to effect repeal of UN economic sanctions on Iraq. On November 5–7, regularly scheduled American U–2 overflights of Iraq were to occur, flights that were a point of contention. Baghdad stated that Washington should cancel the flights. Expecting military action led by the United States, the Iraqi ambassador to the United Nations stated that entry of an American "spy plane cannot be accepted." [11]

Although Iraq expected military strikes and there was domestic consensus within the United States, Baghdad still failed to comply.[12] Noncompliance in the face of perceived credible threat is puzzling.

According to strategic deterrence theory, Baghdad should have acceded to the demand to cease interference with UNSCOM. Prospect theory explains Iraq's failure to conform: Baghdad risks noncompliance because the regime has lost so much that it is not susceptible to further threats. In a domain of deprivation, actors are risk–acceptant.

On November 13, 1997, Iraq further escalated the situation by expelling six more U.S. inspectors. In response, the United Nations removed the entire team. The Security Council condemned the expulsion and demanded that Baghdad rescind its decision. A senior Clinton Administration official said that a massive attack against Iraq might be required to achieve results.

The United States began to build up its military presence in the region on November 20. In the face of overwhelming capabilities, Iraq backed down and announced that UNSCOM inspectors, including Americans, could return. Iraq said that it would agree unconditionally to cooperate.

*February 1998.* The second case began in the winter of 1998. Again Saddam decided to block the weapons inspection team. The crisis that the Clinton Administration had been battling for months was now further entrenched. Despite a January 14, 1998 condemnation of the Iraqi regime by the UN Security Council, Baghdad continued to obstruct the inspection agreement.

The U.S. Senate approved a bipartisan resolution calling for the President "to take all necessary and appropriate actions." Secretary of State Madeline Albright attempted to convince the allies from the Gulf War to join in a concerted effort to weaken the Iraqi leader. Albright was unsuccessful in persuading the Gulf state Arab rulers. Instead, they tended to supported Saddam, which gave him more reason to continue the crisis.

Washington's efforts to change the minds of Arab leaders eventually succeeded. Perhaps because of economic concerns, Gulf allies as well as Egypt condemned Saddam for increasing tensions in the region. With an increase in American forces in the region and a decrease in Iraqi allies in the Arab world, Baghdad initiated a February 11, 1998 proposal for limited and conditional inspections.

In the context of a military buildup and increased tensions, UN Secretary General Kofi Anan departed for Iraq to serve as an interlocutor for the two sides. President Clinton emphasized American resolve to act and use force. Polls demonstrated that Americans were in favor of an attack, despite a showdown at a university town hall meeting where students criticized American officials.

Anan finally succeeded on February 23, when he announced an accord with the Iraqi regime, which Washington reluctantly accepted. The agreement allowed for a diplomatic settlement. Baghdad permitted the inspectors to return in exchange for no military attack.

*October 1998.* The third case began in the fall of 1998. On October 1, Saddam Hussein called for an end to trade and military restrictions on Iraq. He then halted all work by UN inspectors. A week later the United Nations pulled 15 inspectors out of Iraq, the first in a series of planned staff pullbacks in the face of Baghdad's decision to halt cooperation. Clinton declared that the United States would be prepared to act forcefully to end Iraq's defiance of the United Nations and authorized a new buildup of military forces in the Gulf.

The United States accelerated deployment of a second aircraft carrier and a Marine amphibious group to the Gulf region. The crisis deescalated on November 15. After aborting a massive missile attack against Iraq, the United States rebuffed a conditional offer by Iraq to allow UN weapons inspectors to resume their work. Washington insisted that military strikes were still on the table if Iraq fails to comply unconditionally with UN demands. Although Saddam defied a request from UNSCOM for documents relating to its prohibited weapons programs, by November 18 the inspection team began routine checks of the weapons monitoring gear and got ready to test Iraqi cooperation anew.

*November 1998.* The fourth case opened where the third closed. On November 15 President Clinton stated that Iraq had avoided punishing military strikes by dropping its defiance of the United Nations, and that Saddam Hussein must cooperate with UN weapons inspectors without conditions. On November 20, however, Iraqi deputy foreign minister, Riyadh al–Qaisi, told Richard Butler, chief UN weapons inspector, that Iraq had destroyed documents Butler had demanded regarding the production of nuclear, biological, and chemical armaments and missiles. Alternatively, Baghdad supposedly had already turned over the documents or they never existed.

In the face of Iraqi noncompliance, on December 8 the White House declared that the United States planned to work step-by-step with foes of Saddam Hussein to bring down the Iraqi president. And two days later, the Pentagon stated that the refusal to allow inspectors access to Iraq's ruling party offices created a "very serious situation" that could prompt a no–notice military attack. The trigger for military action was a December 15 report from Butler that Iraq had not met promises made a month ago to cooperate fully with UN inspectors and that Baghdad had imposed new restrictions on the inspection process. As a result, on December 16 President Clinton and British Prime Minister Tony Blair ordered a series of airstrikes against Iraq that lasted four days.

These four cases pitted Iraq against a multinational coalition led by the United States and the United Kingdom. Baghdad confronted the inspection regime of the United Nations to get economic sanctions lifted. Iraq created crises in order to avoid further losses that derive from economic sanctions. In other words, Baghdad invents emergencies over weapons inspection to effect an end to economic sanctions. Saddam confronts the inspectors, gathers allies, and then backs down only when credible American and British military forces array against him. Other causes besides credible military force account for Iraqi compliance.

One reason concerns Saddam's perception of his diplomatic situation. The extent to which he views himself as having allies, the less likely Saddam is to comply. The more he sees himself as isolated, the more likely he is to submit.

When there is a stalemate in Arab–Israel diplomacy, Saddam has allies in the Arab world. With such diplomatic support, Saddam confronts the inspection regime. Progress on the Palestinian–Israeli front isolates Saddam from the Arab nation as a whole. When Yasser Arafat and Benjamin Netanyahu are shaking hands, Saddam stands alone with folded hands. When Hafez al–Assad is next in line for his own handshake with Netanyahu, Saddam stands even further away from the Arab mainstream.

When Washington warms up to Tehran, Baghdad feels a chill. Recall the principle that "The enemy of my enemy is my friend." If two adversaries of Iraq become friendlier, Baghdad is liable to come under their joint pressure rather than each one's separate hostility. If Washington and Tehran are increasingly hostile toward each other, they have less time and energy to be against Baghdad. If the United States improves relations with Iran, Tehran may seize upon closer relations with Washington to make trouble for Baghdad.

As stated in Chapter Two, Washington shifts back and forth between balance of power and dual containment vis-à-vis Tehran and Baghdad. A détente in American–Iranian relations signals a shift toward balance of power or at least a differentiated containment that tilts toward Tehran over Baghdad. Saddam is likely to confront the inspection regime when Iran and the United States are at odds.

According to prospect theory, Saddam chooses the risky option of noncompliance when he is in a dominion of deprivation. But once he confronts the prospect of diplomatic isolation and credible military power, he "renormalizes" his status quo so that he is in a domain of gain.

In contrast to a fear–based explanation, another account of Iraq's behavior assumes that Saddam is an aggressor in a domain of gain. Although he probably is a mixture of an opportunity–driven Machiavelli and a need–based paranoid, the Machiavellian part dominates. If Saddam's personality contains both loss-aversion and gain-seeking attributes, he should be risk–acceptant when in the domain of loss and risk–averse while in the domain of gain. He should cheat dramatically and then retreat dramatically. He should go to the brink until he blinks.

Saddam's decision to go to war with Iran was partly a matter of being provoked, but mostly his own opportunism explains his choice to invade.[13] In this respect, he does not act just on the basis of short–term issues that divide him from others; rather, his actions stem from long–term goals.

With respect to long–range aims, consider Saddam's ascension to power. At the age of 26, he returned to Baghdad after four years of exile to take part in a revolution that began his successful climb to power. For 11 years Saddam waited patiently and schemed behind the scenes.

Then, in July 1979, he succeeded in seizing ultimate power—the presidency of Iraq. Saddam's violent rise to power is evidence of his long–term aggressive tendencies. On his way up the ladder of opportunity, nothing could stop him. He kept his eye on the prize—to be recognized as the absolute ruler of Iraq.[14]

Regarding Iraq's invasion of Kuwait, Saddam saw an occasion to assert his long–standing claim to Kuwait and to control oil pricing. These short–term needs were not that important for the opportunity–driven Saddam. He used them only as a point of departure for achieving the long–term goal of exercising suzerainty over the Gulf, solving the border dispute with Kuwait as a first step.

Saddam saw the contemporary borders of Iraq and Kuwait, which were drawn up in 1922 by British High Commissioner Sir Percy Cox, as an injustice brought about by outsiders.[15] Believing that Kuwait was rightfully Iraq's, Saddam saw an opportunity to right a wrong.[16] He invaded Kuwait and, on August 28, 1990, renamed Kuwait City al–Kadhima, a province of Iraq.[17]

Besides dramatic moves, such as the invasion of Kuwait, Saddam also practices the politics of incrementalism. Indeed, when confronted with opposing power, Saddam achieves his opportunity–driven goals by engaging in "salami tactics." By taking a slice at a time, Saddam may believe that he can get away with individual actions and eventually erode the overall international commitment to sanction Iraq. Each step is too small to cause the coalition that defeated him in the Gulf War to come together again. In total, however, the steps constitute a massive challenge to the resolve of the victors by the vanquished. Hence, Saddam makes incremental challenges to the sanctions regime.

To ignore gradual Iraqi challenges would be an invitation for Saddam to move once more against the Iraqi Kurds, Kuwait, and perhaps Saudi Arabia as well. On balance, Saddam acts on the basis of a window of opportunity, and he seeks to gain advantage from noncompliance. Proponents of this view would contain and confront Iraq, and if possible, destabilize his country in order to depose Saddam.

Examining American–Iraqi relations over time is one means of highlighting the interplay of fear–based and opportunity–driven explanations as well as changes in images and behavior.

## BAGHDAD AND WASHINGTON:
## FRIENDS IN THE 1980s, ENEMIES IN THE 1990s

American–Iraqi relations have been on a roller coaster of ups and downs. While the two countries were on friendly terms, the dominant explanation for Saddam's rogue behavior was that he was afraid of losses and in need of Western understanding. In the 1980s, it was believed that Saddam could be a friend. Sanctions can be lifted on a rogue who is paranoid; although they may be retained for reasons of retribution, such punishment is hard to justify.

When problems arose in the relationship, Washington explained Saddam's outlaw behavior as a consequence of his Machiavellian desire for gain. If true, he would not deserve Western empathy. Indeed, sanctions as punishment could rehabilitate him. Rehabilitation notwithstanding, sanctions could be justified on the basis of retribution. As an aggressor in the 1990s, the image of Saddam was that he was an enemy. He was a thug who deserved to be mugged.

Empathy coincided with an upswing in American–Iraqi relations in the 1980s; intolerance accompanied a downswing in the 1990s. In response to one specific downturn, Washington ordered a cruise missile attack against Iraq on September 3, 1996.[18] The assault was in retaliation for Iraqi military attacks against the Kurds in the north. American warships and B–52 bombers launched missiles against air defense sites and military command and communications facilities in southern Iraq.

U.S. officials had warned that Iraqi President Saddam Hussein must pay for ignoring American warnings not to attack the Kurdish population north of the 36th parallel of Iraq. U.S. aircraft had been policing No–Fly–Zones north of the 36th parallel in northern Iraq and south of the 32nd parallel in southern Iraq. The goal was to keep Saddam's forces from attacking the Kurds in the north and the Shiite Muslims in the south. Saddam had sent three tank divisions composed of 30,000 to 40,000 elite Republican Guard troops into northern Iraq to help one Kurdish faction involved in a bloody power struggle with another.

The downward spiral in relations represented by the airstrikes was typical of the way Washington treated Baghdad in the mid–1990s. There was a general expectation that Saddam was driven by a desire for gain, that he constituted a severe threat, and that had to be met with American force.[19] Not only should sanctions be maintained, but also military force was needed to supplement economic warfare.

There are four main reasons why Saddam seized a window created by external circumstances. First, there was an internally focused United States, with its 1996 American presidential campaign in full swing. Second, there was a sympathetic government in Turkey with an Islamic prime minister. Third, there existed a divided Kurdish region where Iran had been interfering. Finally, the Arab–Israel peace process was on the rocks, and a new right–wing Israeli government seemed to be responsible for the diplomatic stalemate.

With respect to the American presidential campaign, Saddam may have surmised that he could strike against the Kurds when no one was looking. But someone was looking. Indeed, Republican presidential nominee Bob Dole said he hoped President Clinton's missile assault against Iraq marked the start of decisive action to curtail Saddam's power and end his atrocities against the Kurdish minority in the north. Dole said the goal of the U.S. action should be the withdrawal of Saddam's troops from the Kurdish–populated north, release of Kurdish prisoners, and a halt to interference in the Kurdish civil war by both Iran and Iraq.

In addition, Dole called for a reestablishment of UN weapons inspection efforts and an end to Saddam's support of international terrorism.[20] In short, because of consensus in Washington, American airstrikes failed to cause a domestic political stir during the 1996 presidential campaign. The use of force against Iraq was received with a virtual "ho–hum" response.

In connection with Turkey, Saddam may have calculated that Ankara would have been less likely to authorize allied air attacks against his forces than the previous, Western–oriented government had authorized. Again, he was wrong. The government in Ankara was displeased about the allies' use of Turkey's southern airbase at Incirlik to protect Iraqi Kurds from Baghdad. Nevertheless, the United States continued to use Turkish bases to monitor the No–Fly–Zone over northern Iraq, even though allied unity was under strain.[21]

Taking advantage of the traditional disunity among the Kurdish population of northern Iraq, Saddam saw a window of opportunity through which to move against one Kurdish faction that was supported by America's enemy, Iran. If the Kurds in Iraq had been in accord, Saddam would have been less likely to make a military move. With respect to the Arab–Israel talks, Saddam moved against the Kurds in northern Iraq when the peace process had hit a roadblock. The international community held the new government of Prime Minister Benjamin Netanyahu in Israel responsible for the deadlock in talks with the Palestinians and Syrians. With stalemate in the Arab–Israel peace process, Saddam may have calculated that the time was right to pounce on the Kurds.

While there was a consensus in Washington that Saddam acted on the basis of opportunity, a case may be made that he also acted out of fear. The move against the Kurds could have been the gasp of a desperate and failing ruler. Confronted with dissent in his military, Saddam Hussein decided that this was the time to move. Analysts and Iraqi dissidents agreed that one of the most significant factors pushing Saddam to act was his discovery in June 1996 of a network of key midlevel officers in Baghdad supplying his opponents abroad with information; they were preparing to overthrow his regime.

Saddam's intelligence organization had discovered a Central Intelligence Agency (CIA) supported coup attempt directed from Irbil in northern Iraq. He wished to destroy the CIA presence and their collaborators. The U.S. preoccupation with the presidential elections and the small possibility of serious military intervention made this low–cost action attractive to the Iraqi regime. Having arrested hundreds and executed scores of conspirators, Saddam wanted a show of strength both to discourage other would–be plotters and to create a cause for celebration in the ranks of the Iraqi military. The move on Irbil, which is in principle under allied protection in the northern No–Fly–Zone, offered a chance for a weak leader to boost his prestige.[22]

But routine mutual hostility in American–Iraqi relations during the 1990s was quite different from the situation two decades earlier. As stated in Chapter Two, the 1970s closed with a crescendo of multiple crises that converged on the Middle East. Their effects ricocheted against the padded walls of the White House Situation Room and caused a reassessment of the U.S. policy of sanctions against Iraq. These crises enhanced the perception of dangers from the Gulf area, and they provided an incentive for the United States to acquire a new friend—Iraq—to compensate for new a enemy—Iran. On one hand, Washington interpreted Saddam as a fearful leader in need of U.S. aid. On the other hand, U.S. leaders perceived that a show of American power was necessary to confront Iran's Ayatollah Khomeni.

The crises included the fall of the Shah in 1978 and the rise of Khomeni the following year. Additionally, there was the 1979 Soviet invasion of Afghanistan and the Iran–Iraq War in 1980. After entering Afghanistan, Soviet military forces in the USSR Southern Theater of Military Operations conducted in 1980 a command post exercise (CPX) simulating an invasion of Iran. The simulation set off alarm bells in the White House, transforming President Jimmy Carter from a dove to a hawk. Although he had sought accommodation with Moscow, Carter accepted the possibility of a Soviet–American confrontation over Iran. The Soviet CPX for an invasion of Iran also drew attention to a need to keep Iraq out of Soviet hands. In this respect, the Carter Administration sought to widen the gap between Baghdad and Moscow.

These multiple crises in the Gulf had a potential for spilling over into the Arab–Israel conflict zone. In addition, Ethiopia and Syria began to emerge as large recipients of Soviet arms. The U. S. threat perception rose as Washington bureaucrats viewed Soviet arms transfers to the Middle East as a danger to American friends and allies in the region.

After the Soviet invasion of Afghanistan, Gulf Arab states, such as Saudi Arabia, became less concerned about too close an identification with the United States. They had been reluctant to align publicly with Washington because of a lack of resolution of the Palestinian issue and the vulnerability the Arab elites felt in regard to their domestic political foes. Nevertheless, Saudi Arabia still wanted the United States to be out of sight—just over the horizon, but available in case the Arab states needed help against external threats.

Following the Islamic revolution in Iran, Riyadh perceived neighboring Tehran to be more of a threat to the Arab states than Moscow. Muslim, non–Arab Iran intervened in the Arab world and tried to destabilize conservative Arab states. Tehran gave an Islamic dimension to the Palestinian fight and thus maintained pressure on the reactionary Arab states for militant action against Israel on behalf of the Palestinians.

Baghdad and the Palestine Liberation Organization (PLO) shared a joint dependence on Moscow, but the PLO had strained relations with Iraq. The Iran–Iraq War also heightened tensions between Baghdad and the Palestinian mainstream leadership. Contrary to the PLO's preferences, Baghdad had tried to destabilize Tehran by encouraging the Arabs of the Khuzestan Province of Iran to revolt. But these efforts failed because the so–called Persian Arabs considered themselves more Iranian than Arab.

The first Gulf War (1980–1988) provided Washington with an opening to Baghdad. The explicit issue between Baghdad and Tehran was the location of the Iran–Iraq border along the Shatt–al–Arab waterway. An implicit problem between these two neighbors, though, was Iran's political instability and hence its vulnerability to Iraqi attack. In Tehran, the fall of the Shah and rise of the Ayatollah gave Baghdad an occasion to force a favorable revision of the border. Iran's vulnerability also gave Iraq a chance to assert its suzerainty over the Gulf area. Because of Khomeni's Islamic revolution and Saddam's attack on Iran, Washington had to decide whether or not to contain or accommodate Baghdad.

Those who explained Saddam's assault on Iran as being driven by his fears favored accommodation with Iraq. Others who explained the attack as a consequence of his innate aggressive drive preferred containment and confrontation of Baghdad.

The Islamic revolution in Iran reversed mutual perceptions between Tehran and Washington.[23] The revolution also presented the United States with a need to retain a foothold in the strategically important region of the Gulf. Hence, as relations with Iran deteriorated, the United States had an incentive to improve its relationship with Iraq. Historically, the Cold War had been an impetus for Washington to maintain good ties with both Baghdad and Tehran. Iranian hostility forced Washington policymakers concerned with Iraq to choose between East–West interests and stakes in the Arab–Israel zone.

At issue was Washington's treatment of its old enemy Baghdad in light of a new adversarial relationship with Tehran, continued conflict with Moscow, and the Israeli perception of the Iraqi threat. During the Cold War, there was consensus within the U.S. bureaucracy over the need to contain the USSR. But such an understanding failed to carry over from the global East–West arena to a regional policy in the Gulf that sought to contain Iraq.

The Iran–Iraq War highlighted a split between domestic political groups versus economic associations and the national security bureaucracy over whether to contain or accommodate Baghdad. A pro–Israel community favored containment, but the business and bureaucratic preference was for accommodation.

## SOURCES OF AMERICAN THREAT PERCEPTIONS ABOUT IRAQ

Sources of American threat perception of Baghdad underlie the issue of accommodation or containment of Iraq. They include politics versus business and the bureaucracy. The preferences of American decision makers are sources of motivated biases that affect their estimation of the Iraqi threat.[24]

### Ethnic Politics versus Business Interests

Interest groups clash in the formulation of policy. One traditional lineup for the Middle East is the conflict between the pro–Israel community and firms that profit from doing business in the area. Ethnic groups with ties to an area may overestimate the threat, in order to protect the country with which they have links; business associations with economic interests in a region tend to underestimate the threat, in order to do business there.

Regarding the Middle East, the pro–Israel community had more of an impact in the Reagan Administration than did the business sector. The reverse was the case for the Bush Administration. The composition of these presidents' campaign staffs might explain the different threat perception.

In the 1980 campaign, candidate Reagan had a pro–Israel reputation, and he had excellent ties with the pro–Israel community; so did those around him. Richard Allen chaired the campaign's Foreign Policy and National Security Advisory Council, and I served as cochair of the Middle East Task Force, having been recommended by the American Israel Public Affairs Committee (AIPAC) to Allen. After the election, White House National Security Advisor Allen was able to make good use of his well–deserved reputation of being staunchly pro–Israel. This reputation enabled him to minimize the political costs to the Reagan Administration of arms sales to Arab states.

But in the 1988 campaign, candidate Bush did not display a pro–Israel stance, nor did he attract a staff with the views of the Reagan team. Allen's counterpart on the Bush team was the distinguished General Brent Scowcroft (U.S. Air Force, retired). Although he had a sterling reputation, he had no known standing in the pro–Israel community comparable to that of Allen.

And who was my counterpart in the Bush campaign? Richard Fairbanks, a paid registered lobbyist on behalf of the government of Iraq, who headed up the Middle East Policy Task Force for Bush. While I had the support of AIPAC, Fairbanks served on the board of the U.S.–Iraq Business Forum, a pro–Baghdad lobbying group that had quite an impact on Washington policymaking as a result of having former national security personnel on its board. [25]

Although Fairbanks had served earlier in the Reagan Administration as one of the Secretary of State's Middle East envoys, it would have been inconceivable for him to be on the staff of the Reagan campaign or the National Security Council. His pro–Iraq views would not have been compatible with the dominant pro–Israel mindset. Although no pro–Iraq American citizens were as influential in the Bush campaign as the pro–Israel community was in the Reagan campaign, business groups did have the ear of pro–Iraq American national security professionals, such as Fairbanks.

Despite the views of the Reagan campaign staff, once the Administration began to govern, it came under the sway of the bureaucracy and began to lean toward Iraq. The clout of the business community and bureaucracy rose. There was little domestic political opposition to the embrace of Baghdad. With the hostage crisis still foremost in the mind of the American populace, there was much hostility toward Iran. Unlike Iran, Iraq had not seized Americans and held them hostage.

Moreover, the profit motive from the prospective sale of grain and dual–use technology provided incentives for a policy of accommodation with Iraq. American business interests, however, had to contend with the influence of an ethnic lobby—the pro–Israel community, which was anti–Iraq.

Led by AIPAC, the pro–Israel community favored Iraq's containment. While it worked to retain Iraq on the State Department's list of nations that sponsor international terrorism, the effort was not very strenuous.[26] Thus, when anti–Iraq sanctions came before the Congress in 1988, AIPAC did not work against that legislation as much as it worked on the Iran and Libya Sanctions Act.[27] Perhaps as a result, the anti–Iraq legislation of the 1980s failed.

One reason AIPAC gave a less–than–maximum effort against Iraq is that Iran had gained major military advantages in the 1980–1988 war. As a result, there was a growing consensus within the bureaucracy for a tilt toward Iraq. The pro–Israel community was reluctant to suggest to Washington that it sacrifice influence with Baghdad against both Moscow and Tehran. Despite the fact that counterterrorism against Iraq was one of the community's major concerns, its top priority at that time was economic and military assistance for Israel.

With progress in the Arab–Israel peace process in the 1990s, AIPAC has turned its attention to the threat from non–Arab Iran against Israel. In the 1980s, the community's tepid opposition to transfers of dual–use equipment to Iraq was insufficient to turn the tide of the American business community and national security professionals. Although the community still also gave attention to efforts by Iraq to acquire weapons of mass destruction and applauded Israel's successful airstrike against Iraqi nuclear facilities, AIPAC did not organize political opposition against Baghdad.

AIPAC also paid little attention to Tehran in the 1980s. The organization was aware of Israel's covert program of arms transfers to Iran. This program led to a similar arms sales policy by the Reagan Administration, which in turn culminated in the arms–for–hostages fiasco.[28] Although a debacle, the policy of American arms for Iran was consistent with the balance-of-power approach of the Reagan–Bush era, and it was compatible with Israel's policy of supplying arms to Iran.

## Politics and National Security

Not only did Reagan attract professionals who had good ties with ethnic interest groups; he also recruited analysts with excellent links to the national security community. As a result, these professionals had access to intelligence that proved of use in the 1980 presidential campaign.

In addition to being cochair of the Reagan–Bush Task Force, I also was on the Chief of Naval Operations (CNO) Civilian Executive Panel, an advisory committee to the chief. Membership on his panel provided access to information that was useful for briefing the candidate. With respect to Iraq and the Gulf, a celebrated strategist, Albert Wohlstetter, headed the strategy subpanel. He also was a Reagan advisor. His company, Pan Heuristics, had just completed a major study of the Gulf for the Pentagon.[29]

The impetus for the Wohlstetter study came from a concern at the Department of Defense that a growing preponderance of Soviet power in the Gulf area coincided with comparative weakness of the West. Wohlstetter highlighted a paradoxical reassurance that dominated conventional wisdom of the early 1980s: the Soviets would never attack in so vital an area where the West was at a disadvantage. To do so would mean World War III, the prospect of which would deter Moscow. Wohlstetter, critical of this sunny scenario, extended it to show its absurdity. If the Soviets would not strike at vital points where the West was weak, they also would not attack where the West was strong. And regarding nonvital areas, the Soviets would be irrational to risk attacking for marginal gains.[30] Thus, according to the wishful thinkers, a Soviet invasion of the Gulf area was inconceivable.

In conjunction with analysts at Pan Heuristics, the Pentagon had conducted its own study of Gulf security.[31] It dealt with topics, such as American strategic stakes in the area, allied interests, Soviet objectives, Great Power rivalry, sources of instability in the Gulf and the Arabian Peninsula, Soviet military options, and military threats to U.S. interests. American objectives included protecting Western oil supplies, restoring the flow of oil in the event of an interruption, and minimizing Soviet influence over the policies of oil–producing states.

In connection with deterring attacks on oil facilities, topics debated in the Pentagon included oil facility vulnerability to air attack, threat to oil sea–lanes of communications outside the Gulf, and mining of the Strait of Hormuz. Regarding lesser Gulf contingencies, analysts considered local wars as well as superpower and third–country interventions. Finally, concerning an invasion of Iran by Soviet or a combination of Soviet and Iraqi forces, analysts discussed the ground and air military balance, the effect of deployments by the United States in a simulated North Atlantic Treaty Organization (NATO) buildup, and American–Iranian versus Soviet resupply capabilities. [32]

In the Pentagon study, U.S. goals were to contain radical Arab states, such as Iraq, and to prevent them from using military power to coerce moderate Arab nations, such as Kuwait and Saudi Arabia. Iraqi control of the Arab Gulf states would have placed too much power into Saddam's hands. Also, radical Arab domination of the Middle East could lead to another Arab–Israel war, oil embargo, and superpower confrontation.

To place defense policy planning of the 1990s into historical perspective, consider the debate about the Gulf at the Department of Defense during the early 1980s. The Iraqi threat to Kuwait was neither the most probable nor the worst contingency facing the Pentagon. Nevertheless, that threat, consisting of a direct invasion of Kuwait and the use of implicit Iraqi power to coerce Kuwait and the Arab Gulf states, was a consideration in defense planning.

Regarding non–Soviet Gulf contingencies of concern to American defense planners, Baghdad's threat to Tehran was the most serious and probable. Iraq and prerevolutionary Iran were in approximate balance. But the postrevolutionary situation found Iraq militarily preeminent in the Gulf. Iraq's role was critical for a successful Soviet invasion of Iran. In a scenario with Iraq and Soviet forces against Saudi Arabia and forces from the United States, overall force ratios would have been very unfavorable to the United States.

To address the problem of unfavorable force ratios and thus meet non–Soviet Gulf contingencies, Baghdad had to be weaned from Moscow. One American policymaker in the Carter Administration who sought to move Iraq from the Soviet to the American camp was National Security Advisor Zbigniew Brzezinski. [33] In his view, Washington should seek to moderate Iraq's policies regarding Iran while balancing Baghdad's power. In addition, the threat in the Gulf had to be met on its own terms.[34]

Alternatives to meeting this threat include reducing the American need for imported oil, creating a regional security pact, and threatening to escalate or expand fighting outside of the Gulf. Even if the United States could reduce its dependence on Gulf oil, Europe would remain dependent and thus subject to Soviet–Iraqi coercion.

In connection with a regional security organization, instabilities were too great and Soviet power too strong for a regional security system to be effective. Regarding escalation, moreover, threatening to go nuclear in light of a Soviet–Iraqi attack on Iran would not be a credible response. And a threat to expand a Gulf war, for example, to the northern flank of NATO, would frighten allies, such as Norway, even more than it would deter a Soviet invasion of Iran.

Meeting the threat on its own terms would have required joint consultations with the allies. At issue was how to create an allied force to confront a combined Soviet–Iraqi threat without compromising the Western capability needed outside of the Gulf and without destabilizing host countries, such as Saudi Arabia.

These goals required the achievement of the following tasks: an upgrading of the American forces in the Indian Ocean and deployment of U.S. and allied forces throughout the Indian Ocean and, insofar as was politically feasible, into the Gulf. Other tasks included the conduct of military exercises separately and jointly with local forces; a year–round presence of at least one carrier task force group, and pre–positioning of equipment and supplies to facilities that could handle a rapid buildup of ground forces and tactical aircraft. Such a combat presence had to be politically acceptable, able to defend itself against land–based attacks, and capable of projecting enough firepower ashore to deter an Iraqi–Soviet military move in the upper Gulf.

During an October 8, 1980 meeting with the Chief of Naval Operations, our panel discussed general global challenges and threats to the Gulf. At issue was Moscow's overall aim for the area, given the Soviet presence in Afghanistan, the Iran–Iraq War, and possible Soviet military moves in Poland to quell labor unrest. The chief, Admiral Tom Hayward, spoke about the opportunity that the Iran–Iraq War created for the United States: enhanced prospects for deploying American military forces in Saudi Arabia. He reasoned that because Iranian advances against Iraq threatened Riyadh, the Saudis would be more amenable to an American force deployment in the kingdom. But he also expressed great concern that an unraveling Iran might be a pretext for a Soviet military move into that troubled country.

But if Soviet forces did deploy in Iran, Hayward suggested that such an action would be a constraint on Moscow's prospective crackdown against striking Solidarity union members in Poland.[35] From our discussion about threats to the Gulf, it was clear that we saw the global Soviet danger there to be more important than the threat from regional powers, such as Iran or Iraq. While we focused more on that external Soviet threat, Saudi Arabia paid more attention to the indigenous menace—Iran. Indeed, American intelligence felt Saudi Arabia believed it might ensure its security against the threat from Iran through close ties with Baghdad.[36]

While both Saudi Arabia and Iraq worried about the Iranian threat, Baghdad also was concerned about the threat from Moscow via Afghanistan. Alarmed about CIA reports regarding the Soviet need for oil in the near future, Saddam interpreted those requirements to mean a potential Soviet military move against Iraq to secure oil. In this respect, he felt that the main source of uncertainty and instability in the Gulf were the two superpowers .

Saddam opposed plans for an American rapid deployment force because it provided the Soviets with an incentive to match that force. The Saudis also expressed a similar fear. Both Iraq and Saudi Arabia did not perceive the supposed benefit of American protection of the Gulf to be worth the potential price of an increased Soviet presence.

Intelligence reports in the summer of 1980 indicated that Iraq wanted to maintain its independence from the USSR, but not enough to throw itself into the hands of the West. Saddam strongly disapproved of Moscow's decision to invade Afghanistan and was equally opposed to Washington's use of the Soviet presence there as a rationale for bringing in U.S. military forces. Until that invasion, Saddam had taken it for granted that the Soviets were nonexpansionist in the Middle East. After it, however, Saddam increased the distance that he had begun to impose in Iraq's relations with the USSR. While maneuvering was taking place in the Middle East, moreover, another balancing act was occurring in Washington.

The battle between ethnic politics and business interests was a war for the White House and Capitol Hill. In the case of Iraq in the 1980s, economic views triumphed. Businesses with ties to Iraq lined up their vectors with those of national security bureaucrats. While firms wanted to make money on Iraq, national security professionals desired to leverage Baghdad against both Moscow and Tehran. They sought an opening to Iraq in order to balance Soviet forces in Afghanistan and against Iranian combat units across the waterway.

While Baghdad was winning the war for Washington, Iraq was losing its war with Iran. Thus, professionals in the U.S. national security community had a great incentive to reconcile the United States with Iraq. Yet full–scale accommodation with Iraq, a state that sponsored terrorism, was politically risky. Here the business community proved helpful. Industry brought its influence to bear on behalf of Iraq, downplaying the Iraqi threat to the American public while profiting from the sale of dual–use equipment to Saddam's military. Economics provided a cover for security professionals to slide away from a policy of isolating Iraq. Ordinarily, moving closer to a rogue regime would have been a controversial policy and not advisable in an election year.

In the run–up to an election, containment of a rogue state is less risky than accommodation. Pressures to continue containment often rise in even years and fall in odd years, while the reverse is true for reconciliation. Ethnic groups reinforce the politics of containment during an election, while business groups buttress the politics of accommodation in off–election years.

During the 1980 presidential primary campaign, the pro–Israel community bolstered the politics of containing Iraq. After the election, however, the business community dominated the policymaking process regarding Iraq. Momentum for the Reagan Administration to take Iraq off the list of states that support international terrorism began during late 1981, an off–election year, and culminated the following year in Baghdad's removal from the list.

## BUREAUCRATIC POLITICS AND
## THREAT PERCEPTION

Washington's accommodation with Baghdad began on February 26, 1982, when the Reagan Administration deleted Iraq from the list of states that sponsor international terrorism. The Administration's public explanation for this was because of Iraq's supposed improved record on state–sponsored terrorism. But the implicit reason was to assist Baghdad in its war against Tehran.[37] Nations on the terrorism list are subject to export controls on the sale of arms and high–technology equipment. And because Iraq was losing the Iran–Iraq War, Baghdad had an incentive to obtain American arms and dual–use technology.

The tilt toward Iraq was also a part of a general shift away from the Arab–Israel region to the Gulf zone. In March 1984, President Reagan's Special Envoy to the Middle East, Donald Rumsfeld, began to refocus Washington's attention. Because of Iranian successes in the Iran–Iraq War, he was able to persuade Saudi Arabia and other Arab Gulf states to initiate joint contingency planning and pre–positioning of supplies and equipment at their military facilities.

Besides deleting Iraq from the list of states that sponsored terrorism, the Reagan Administration took other actions that favored Baghdad. During 1984, the President signed a directive that authorized a limited intelligence–sharing program with Iraq. Another directive specified the goal of countering Soviet influence as a rationale for expanding ties with Iraq. Washington might be able to take advantage of strained relations between Baghdad and Moscow. Iraq had denounced the Soviet invasion of Afghanistan, and the USSR had been an inconsistent arms supplier for Iraq.

Even before the Iran–Iraq War began in September 1980, Iraqi–Soviet relations were strained. That war heightened tensions between Moscow and Baghdad and thus provided an opening for Washington. This war also furnished an occasion for advocates of Iraq to lobby within the American national security bureaucracy on behalf of Baghdad.

The Iran–Iraq War of 1980 to 1988 highlights a globalist versus regionalist split in the American bureaucracy across the Carter and

Reagan administrations. Despite their political differences, both administrations contained globalists, who saw conflicts in East–West terms, and regionalists, who perceived the same conflicts through the lens of the area in which they occurred.

Globalists preferred an alignment between the United States and Arab states on the periphery of the Soviet Union. Regionalists favored leaving some distance between these states and Washington, for fear that too close an identification would be a source of instability for their fragile regimes. Globalists wanted to move closer to Iraq and the Arab Gulf states, while regionalists were concerned that such an alignment would be destabilizing to those regimes. Bureaucrats with a regional inclination also had reservations about too great a focus on the Gulf at the expense of the Arab–Israel zone in general and Egypt in particular.

Regarding the bureaucratic politics of containment versus accommodation, two approaches toward Iraq surfaced within the Carter, Reagan, and Bush administrations. The Arab–Israel first perspective suggested discontinuation of a policy of containment of Iraq in order to use Baghdad as a facilitator in the Arab–Israel peace process.

A Gulf–first group advocated détente with either Iran or Iraq, for the sake of containing the Soviet Union. Given that the Iranian option was unrealistic, the group gravitated toward Iraq. Bureaus at the State Department found common ground with economic units in Treasury and Commerce, both of which preferred a conciliatory American policy toward Iraq as a part of their probusiness perspective.

Some officials in the State Department's European and Canadian Affairs (EU) and Politico–Military Affairs (PM) bureaus perceived American options in East–West terms. The Bureau of Near Eastern and South Asian Affairs (NEA) tended to view the Iran–Iraq War according to its implications for the Arab–Israel conflict and the balance of power between a hostile Iran and friendly Arab Gulf states.[38] NEA wanted to use the good offices of Baghdad in order to move the Arab–Israel peace process forward. Although PM took a harder line on Iraq, the outcome of bargaining between the two bureaus favored Baghdad.

The slant toward Iraq became manifest in National Security Directive 26, signed by President Bush on October 3, 1989. It states that: "Normal relations between the U.S. and Iraq would serve our long–term interests and promote stability in both the Gulf and the Middle East. The U.S. Government should propose both economic and political incentives for Iraq to moderate its behavior and to increase our influence with Iraq."[39] Clearly, the Bush Administration as a whole had made a strategic commitment to accommodate Iraq.

But there were dissenters within the Administration. It may be useful to trace the interest expressed by the Department of Defense in the Gulf area in order to place the Bush Pentagon within an historical setting. Not until the fall of the Shah and Soviet invasion of Afghanistan did the Department of Defense manifest a major interest in the Middle East. Before then, the American military paid more attention to European and Asian threats. The Department of Defense had focused on containing Moscow and Beijing, in order to restrain them from attacks on Berlin and Tokyo. "Palestine" had been on the periphery of Pentagon policymaking.

As the Cold War spread to the Middle East, that region became an important part of national security planning. With the extension of the anti–Soviet policy of containment eastward—the Eisenhower Doctrine—there was a need to sign up countries on the periphery of the East–West divide. In this connection, Iraq, Iran, Pakistan, and Turkey were in demand as allies.[40] Indeed, the 1955 Baghdad Pact aligned the United Kingdom and the United States with states on the perimeter of the USSR.

In the mid–1980s, officials at the White House and the State Department who wished to focus on the Gulf prevailed over "Egypt–firsters" at the Central Intelligence Agency who worried whether Cairo would drift toward Moscow if Washington did not pay enough attention to Egypt. Department of Defense officials reinforced the bureaucratic consensus toward Iraq. Those in the Secretary of Defense's Office of the International Security Affairs (ISA) leaned toward Iraq in order to balance Iran.[41] One assistant secretary in that department, Bing West, was adamantly in favor of accommodation with Iraq. However, a successor, Richard Armitage, was less inclined than West to support reconciliation.

On balance, Armitage favored compromise with Iraq. But his counterpart at Defense, Richard Perle, opposed the embrace of Saddam Hussein. In March 1985, Perle tried without success to require a nonnuclear–use assurance agreement from Baghdad as a condition for exporting two advanced computers. Perle lost the battle to a coalition that included his colleague Armitage and officials from the White House and the Department of State.[42]

Other dissenters to the rush to embrace Saddam Hussein were in the Office of the Joint Chiefs of Staff. Many military officers were wary of Iraq's military buildup. Indeed, during the early 1980s, a growing number began to see Iraq as a threat to the United States, even while other government agencies perceived Baghdad as a candidate for membership in an American alignment. Because Iraq had been an ally against the USSR until the Iraqi revolution in 1958, Reagan and Bush national security bureaucrats hoped to restore this alignment in the 1980s.

Saddam and his ilk in Baghdad saw a White House leaning in their favor, a split State Department, a divided Pentagon, and a tilt on their behalf from Treasury and Commerce. The net policy effect of the differences among the departments was for the United States to pursue accommodation with Iraq and to continue containment of Iran. From the point of view of American planning for possible war with Iraq, the Defense Department's views were on the rise; from the perspective of planning for peace in the Arab–Israel conflict, the White House and the State Department seemed to be in control.[43] And with respect to economic planning, Treasury and Commerce were in ascendancy.

Because of a tendency to see what you want to see, Saddam interpreted the friendly signals from the White House as the valid representation of American foreign policy and discounted the Pentagon's hostile signals. Saddam also expected that the White House view would be dominant, just as the executive branch was the sole factor in the governance of Iraq. Because Saddam did not want to see a deterrent threat, he paid more attention to the White House and the State Department than to the Pentagon. Indeed, officials at the White House and at State communicated their reassuring views to Baghdad on a regular basis, while the military officials at the Pentagon kept their secret planning documents to themselves.

Civilians at the White House and at the State Department were biased toward perceiving Iraq as a potential ally, while military officials at the Pentagon had a motivated bias to perceive Iraq as an adversary. In terms of threat perception, the Pentagon tended to overestimate the Iraqi threat, while the White House and State Department tended to underestimate it.

Because of the perceived threat of Iraq, a minority within the American bureaucracy favored containment of that country. I belonged to that small group of officials during the early 1980s. We perceived Baghdad to be a threat to Israel and a major competitor of Egypt. Iraq was a leader of the rejectionist front against Jerusalem, a rival of Cairo and Damascus over leadership within the Arab world, and a threat to the United States because of international terrorism and proliferation of weapons of mass destruction.[44]

Hence, we vainly sought to contain Iraq within its own borders. Because successive regimes in Baghdad had made a cottage industry of being anti–Israel and anti–American, it was simple to justify a continuation of a containment policy to the American people. Opposition to Iraq was an easier sale on Capitol Hill than within the national security bureaucracy. The argument that Baghdad was an enemy of Israel and an adversary of the United States appealed more to politicians than to bureaucrats.

On one hand, politicians on the Hill were sensitive to ethnic interest group pressures and ideals regarding the Arab–Israel zone; they thus favored containment of Iraq. On the other hand, professionals at State, Treasury, Defense, and Commerce emphasized American interests in the Cold War and Gulf oil; consequently, this consensus view wanted accommodation with Iraq. The bureaucrats reasoned that Iraqi setbacks in the 1980 to 1988 war against Iran required Washington to lean toward Baghdad so that neither Tehran nor Moscow would reign supreme in the Gulf area.

With its Cold War orientation, the Gulf–first school split into two groups: one focused on Iran, the other on Iraq. Both shared an antipathy toward the Soviet Union. This anti–Soviet attitude was a common lens through which to perceive the Middle East. The Iran camp in the United States saw Tehran as the key to preventing a Soviet invasion of the Arab Gulf. Although Iran was anti–American, its long border with the USSR made it a gateway through which the Soviet Union could make inroads into the Arab Gulf.

Within the Reagan Administration, National Security Advisor Robert McFarlane was reluctant to give up on Iran, even though Tehran had seized American citizens and held them as hostages. He wrote during 1982, in his first official memo to the President: "Our position on the Iran–Iraq War is also extremely sensitive. I do not think we should undertake actions [that] could be seen as a clear tilt toward Iraq, unless Iraq is on the losing end of the fight. As hostile as the current government of Iran is, that country remains a strategically decisive one; we do not therefore want to burn all of our bridges, particularly to those elements which will be of interest to United States in any post–Khomeni succession struggle."[45]

From a balance-of-power perspective, Iraq bordered on hostile, threatening states: Iran, Syria, and Turkey. Pro–Iraq officials at the White House and State Department were inclined to follow a balance-of-power approach rather than a containment policy; Pentagon officials tended toward a containment approach, and they prepared for a worst–case scenario—war with Iraq.

The Iraq camp of the Gulf–first school in the U.S. bureaucracy was motivated less by the USSR and more by the Arab–Israel conflict. It wanted to solve the Palestinian problem and secure economic profits for American corporations and farmers. This faction assumed that Saddam could be accommodated with both American–origin dual–use equipment, such as trucks, machine tools, and computers, and midwestern wheat. A satisfied Saddam then would be active in Palestinian diplomacy and less belligerent toward Israel and would serve as a bulwark in the conflict with Iran.

Regarding the peace process, the aim of the Iraq camp of American bureaucrats was to enhance diplomatic, military, and economic ties with Baghdad. They wanted to bring the PLO into direct negotiations with Israel. But because of the Iraqi threat to Israel, this camp sought to deny Baghdad sophisticated American–origin military equipment while providing it with the capability to quell domestic unrest and deter Iran. With respect to economic motivations, Iraq sought the assistance of congressional allies, and it lobbied the U.S. national security bureaucracy to gain American technology.

## Interests under Siege: Intrinsic and Strategic

*Intrinsic Interests at Stake.* During the 1990s, American leaders believe that Iraq threatens both intrinsic and strategic interests, which are two sides of the same coin under assault.[46] The Iraqi menace endangers American civilians and military personnel in the Gulf—intrinsic interests. And before its defeat in the Gulf War, Iraq also was a risk to other inherently valuable targets, such as Western petroleum products transiting the Gulf.[47] But in the mid–1990s, Iraq still had 2,000 tanks and 300 combat aircraft, making it the largest military force in the region.[48] Hence, while Saddam's military was diminished by the Gulf War and UN sanctions, it nevertheless still is a threat.

Baghdad is also a danger to American citizens in general via its support for international terrorism.[49] According to the State Department, Saddam probably ordered the assassination of former President Bush in Kuwait during April 1993. The group arrested for the assassination attempt was also planning a bombing campaign to destabilize Kuwait in general.

Iraqi–sponsored terrorism has become a routine fact of life in northern Iraq. Baghdad probably has been responsible for attacks on UN and other international relief agency staff as well as on humanitarian aid convoys.[50] Iraq has not recovered its capability to launch terrorist attacks outside its borders after several Arab states deported Iraqi intelligence agents during the Gulf War. Nevertheless, Baghdad has begun to deploy agents in search of Saddam's adversaries who reside abroad.

Although the Iraqi government agreed in 1992 to comply with UN Security Council Resolution 687, which requires that Iraq not allow any terrorist organization to operate within its territory, Baghdad still maintains contacts with or provides sanctuary to several groups and individuals that have practiced terrorism. For example, the Kurdish Workers Party, which has killed hundreds of people in attacks inside Turkey and has mounted two separate terrorist campaigns against Turkish interests in Europe in 1993, has training camps in Iraq. Baghdad supports an opposition group that carried out several violent attacks in Iran from bases in Iraq. It also harbors members of several extremist Palestinian groups, including the Arab Liberation Front and the Palestine Liberation Front.[51]

*Strategic Interests at Stake.* U.S. strategic interests regarding Iraq are related to objectives for the Gulf as a whole. Washington has an interest in continuing the flow of oil to the world market at prices that are consistent with the economic growth of the industrialized democracies. With the end of the Cold War, the regional menace from Iraq (and Iran) replaced the Soviet threat.

The Iraqi threats to American strategic interests include Baghdad's challenge to U.S. threat credibility, the American resolve to remain involved in global affairs, and the U.S. commitment to defend its allies against its adversaries. One means by which Baghdad confronts Washington is Iraq's failure to comply with United Nations Security Council Resolutions 686 (March 2, 1991) and 687 (April 3, 1991), which specify the terms of reference for the end of the Gulf War.

Resolution 687 intends to prevent Iraq from once again becoming a threat to the Gulf region. It mandates the destruction, removal, or dismantlement under international monitoring of Iraq's nuclear, biological, and chemical armaments, as well as ballistic missiles with a range over 150 kilometers. The United Nations formed a special commission to implement Resolution 686, which demanded that Iraq execute its acceptance of all 12 previous resolutions and specified the necessary measures to be undertaken to end hostilities.[52] To the extent that Iraq fails to comply with these two resolutions, Baghdad is a threat to international credibility in general and American credibility in particular.

Another strategic threat concerns nuclear weapons. Iraq remains a potential nuclear proliferation threat despite its lack of fissile material and production facilities in the post–Gulf War era. Baghdad had constructed a large nuclear weapons program with the assistance of Western suppliers and may seek to do so again. Although Operation Desert Storm damaged those facilities and UN sanctions make reconstructing them difficult, Saddam has not abandoned his nuclear weapons goals. And he has taken steps to thwart the process of international inspections.[53]

## MILITARY FORCE VERSUS
## ECONOMIC DIPLOMACY

Once Baghdad ordered the invasion of Kuwait in August 1990, there was no doubt that Iraq constituted a threat to American interests. There was a spirited debate within the bureaucracy, however, over how to meet that threat. As tensions mounted after the Iraqi invasion, at issue was whether an impending war involving the United States was to be an instrument of first or last resort.

The Bush Administration split into two camps. One proposed the use of airpower even before there was a ground war capacity in place.[54] This camp would have used airpower prior to exhausting other remedies, such as sanctions, and before the capacity was deployed to conduct combined combat operations.

The chairman of the Joint Chiefs of Staff during the Gulf War, General Colin Powell, represented the second camp, and his position became American policy. He advocated economic sanctions while building up for possible offensive action. If and when the President decided to liberate Kuwait, Powell proposed using combined air, naval, and ground forces to oust the Iraqi army.[55]

Powell's views are consistent with a doctrine of just war, which says warfare is legitimate to the extent that leaders can show that other solutions, such as economic sanctions, are found to be inadequate. In this respect, Secretary of Defense Caspar Weinberger provided a series of "tests" in a 1984 speech on the use of military power at the National Press Club. One principle was that the commitment of U.S. forces to combat should be a last resort.[56] The American policy during the Gulf War reflected the Weinberger–Powell principle. Other aspects of the Powell view include the hope that economic sanctions work, the preparation for war by assembling an overwhelming amount of firepower, and the delay of ground war until there is a force in place that guarantees victory.

Powell denies that he was an advocate of either sanctions or war options. His goal was to make sure that the President had the opportunity to consider both "fully and fairly." Even before the air war began in mid–January 1991, Powell told President Bush that sanctions had serious disadvantages: "Sanctions left the initiative with the Iraqis to decide when they had had enough. And sanctions take time, if they work at all."[57]

The issue posed by Powell is not either military force or economic warfare; it is how to combine force and diplomacy in ways that secure compliance at minimum costs. To have used airpower prior to exhausting other remedies, such as sanctions and before the capacity was deployed to conduct combined combat operations, would have both lessened the legitimacy of the coalition war effort and diminished allied effectiveness once war began. As the Gulf nations maintained an uneasy cease–fire, economic warfare continued during the mid–1990s.

As Washington sought to balance force and diplomacy, the balance of power on the ground began to change. Consider the history. As the 1970s closed, the Arab Gulf states were increasingly fearful of a growing threat from Iran. Similarly, as the decade of the 1990s ends, the Arab Gulf states are worried again about Iran. In the earlier era, Arab states in the Gulf region doubted that the Carter Administration had the resolve to defend them against either a Soviet or an Iranian threat. Likewise, these Gulf states believe that dual containment punishes Iraq more than Iran. Consequently, they wonder if the Clinton Administration has the resolve to defend them against Iran.[58]

Perceptions of threat differ among Arab Gulf states that are members of the anti–Saddam coalition. Consider in this regard the threat perceptions of the Gulf Cooperation Council members.[59] Leaders in the Arab Gulf both support and oppose Washington's dual containment policy toward Iran and Iraq among the leadership levels. But there is much less support among the informed elites and on the Arab street—that is, the general public. And there are differences in threat perception between Saudi Arabia and Kuwait. Elites and the Arab street in Riyadh perceived an Iraqi mobilization along the Saudi border during October 1994 as less of a threat than did their counterparts in Kuwait City and in Washington. Saudi Arabia saw Saddam's military move as a diplomatic means to highlight Iraq's economic plight brought about because of UN sanctions. In this respect, Saudi elites and the Arab public believed that the United States overreacted with its military response.

While there is support for dual containment, there also is quiet opposition. Some Arab Gulf states view dual containment in a dubious light because of its equal treatment of Baghdad and Tehran. On one hand, Iraq is more of a short–term menace due to Saddam's continued reign. Hence, UN sanctions provide an unintended prop for Saddam to use in order to maintain his power in Iraq: The sanctions bolster him and prolong his rule while turning the population against those Arab Gulf states that support the sanctions.

On the other hand, Iran is the long–term threat to the Arab Gulf states. Even though these nations perceive a threat from Iran, however, there also is reluctance to antagonize Iranian leaders. U.S. measures, such as trade sanctions, cause anxiety about the prospects for a potential military confrontation between Tehran and Washington. The Gulf Arab states prefer a balance-of-power approach instead of dual containment because the former has the potential for accommodating both Iran and Iraq.[60]

As at the turn of the century, the 1980s found moderate Arab states pressuring the United States to move closer to Baghdad as a counter to Tehran; and Washington followed that advice. As the twenty–first century approaches, the same pressure may provide the seeds for a change in American policy toward Iraq.[61] A weakened Iraq seems less of a threat to some Arab states than a growing Iran. Also, there exist Iranian efforts to destabilize the Arab–Israel zone with increased levels of arms transfers to Hezbollah combatants in Lebanon.

The increased Iranian threat to Israel may forge an unholy alliance of moderate Arab states and Israel in tacit alignment with Iraq against Iran. And because Syria is aligned with Iran, Damascus serves as a convenient transshipment point for Iranian weapons for Hezbollah in Lebanon. As the 1990s close, we must consider scenarios for the future of the Gulf region, which will determine in part whether the United States continues to pursue a posture of containing and confronting Iraq.

## FUTURE SCENARIOS

The policy options—reconcile, contain, and overthrow—have corresponding scenarios. They range on a continuum from optimistic to pessimistic: compliance, neither compliance nor defiance, and confrontation. Because containment includes regime change, contain and overthrow options are actually one alternative.

So far the chapter discussed the containment policy in relation to the scenario labeled neither compliance nor defiance. The focus here is on reconciliation with Iraq in the context of its compliance as well as containment and regime change in conjunction with Iraq's defiance.

## Reconciliation–Compliance:
## Iran Attacks or Subverts Arab States

Consider the contingency of an assault by Iran against one or more of the Arab Gulf states. If Iran attacked, a policy of reconciliation with Iraq may be feasible, and Baghdad might adhere to UN demands. It is conceivable that Saudi Arabia and the Gulf Arab states would implore Iraq to reconcile with the international community in order to join an Arab coalition against Iran.

A second set of contingencies consists of Iranian attempts to destabilize Arab states, such as Saudi Arabia, Kuwait, the United Arab Emirates, Bahrain, and Oman. In this event, Washington also might consider whether to embrace Baghdad as a counter to Tehran. Here the danger from Iran might serve as an integrating mechanism that brings Iraq back into the Arab mainstream.

Iran's aircraft poses a moderate threat to high–value targets in the Gulf region. These warplanes have the capacity to launch small–scale surprise attacks of vast destruction and with even greater psychological impact. Ships and transshipment facilities in Kuwait and the United Arab Emirates might be fruitful targets for Iranian assault. But an attack on Saudi Arabia is the least likely because of the deterrent threat of retaliation. Regardless of damage, such an assault would raise the threat of concerted American and Arab Gulf state retaliation on key Iranian facilities.

As a result of enhanced capabilities acquired during and after Desert Storm, Saudi Arabia is better able to engage in self–defense than in times past. But even with American–supplied radar surveillance aircraft, the Saudi airforce and ground–based air defense system might not be able to counter a surprise Iranian airstrike on its oil installations. The time and distances are just too short. Iranian fighter–bombers could strike oil fields anywhere in the eastern provinces of Saudi Arabia from bases in Bandar–e–Abbas Iran in just a few minutes. Nevertheless, Riyadh considers diplomatic and subversive activity on the part of Iran to be the more likely threat.

Another contingency of concern to Riyadh is for Iraq to be under American and British assault while Iran strengthens its diplomatic ties in the region. The Saudis would worry about Iranian diplomatic moves to improve relations with Turkey and Pakistan. Such overtures would be designed to protect Iran's flanks.

Tehran also might expand its relations with other third–world countries near the Gulf. A shield of compliant rulers from friendly neighboring states would help secure the Islamic revolution at home, lower U.S. influence in the region, and allow for a more vigorous challenge to the Gulf states. Hence, Riyadh would be very concerned about contingencies, such as Iraq under siege from allied warplanes, while Iran was on the upswing in military capabilities.

Iranian–sponsored subversion would be directed at the Gulf nations in order to foment popular uprisings among their Shiite Muslim population. Had the Iran–Iraq War ignited a broad–based Shiite revolt in Iraq, that instability might have created smaller–scale flare–ups in Bahrain and perhaps even in Saudi Arabia and Kuwait.

Regarding other contingencies that include Saudi Arabia, there might be a recurrence of the July 1987 Iranian–inspired riots in the kingdom, in which about 400 people died. At the time Shiite pilgrims from Iran clashed with Saudi security forces near the Grand Mosque in Mecca.[62]

In addition, Saudi Arabia accused Tehran and Damascus of masterminding attacks on American–Saudi military facilities in Riyadh and Dhahran during 1995 and 1996. Such riots and bombings might escalate tensions between Tehran and Riyadh to the point of involving American airstrikes against Iran in defense of the kingdom.

Due to Kuwait's proximity to Iraq, Iran, and Saudi Arabia, any conflicts involving Saudi Arabia and Iran would threaten Kuwait as well. Consider the contingency of a conflict between Saudi Arabia and Kuwait versus Iran. Washington might deter or defend against such a contingency better if there existed an alignment of convenience between Iraq and the United States.

Besides Saudi Arabia, tensions exist between Iran and smaller Arab Gulf states.[63] In December 1982 during the Iran–Iraq War, Iran undertook to induce the United Arab Emirates to be more responsive to Tehran and less sensitive to Riyadh. The UAE responded by seeking a balance between the two. So long as Iran did not defeat Iraq, Iranian efforts to tip the balance in its favor failed. Iran's approach, however, was disingenuous. It was designed to win support from the Arab Gulf states and pave the way for a reassertion of Iranian influence in the postwar era.

During the mid–1990s, the UAE has been the most outspoken Gulf state critic of the Clinton Administration's dual containment policy. It feels that Iran would have adopted a more aggressive posture toward the UAE if the comparatively pragmatic Iranian President Ali Akbar Hashemi Rafsanjani had yielded to the more radical Speaker of the Majlis—the Iranian assembly—Natiq–Nouri. But, in fact, Mohammad Khatemi won the Iranian presidency with about 70 percent of the vote. And his reputation is similar to Rafsanjani's, so there is little reason to expect that Iran would adopt a more assertive posture toward the Emirates.

During September 1993, the UAE's regime of Sheik Zayed ibn Sultan al–Nahayan was involved in a long–standing dispute with Iran over the administration of the island of Abu Musa. The conflict had escalated during April 1992, when Iran declined to permit hundreds of expatriates back onto the island. Under a 1991 accord, Iran and the UAE jointly administer it. To make matters even more difficult, the UAE has had other conflicts with Iran over the two Tunb islands in the Gulf. In the context of enhanced tensions over the three islands, this contingency of escalating tension might be met more effectively if there were cooperation between Iraq and the United States.

Bahrain is another Arab Gulf state in fear of Iran. After the Iranian Shiite revolution in 1979, Tehran stimulated instability among Bahrain's Shiite Muslims and revived its claim to islands in dispute between Bahrain and Iran. And during 1981, Bahrain thwarted an Iranian–inspired plot to foment revolution in the emirate. Similar plots occurred in 1985. Again, détente between Baghdad and Washington might help deter Iranian moves against Bahrain and facilitate the defense of that state in the event of deterrence failure.

Oman has been worried about its security, especially after the Iranian revolution and the Soviet invasion of Afghanistan. And during the Iran–Iraq War, Oman signed defense agreements with neighboring Arab states against the Iranian threat. In order to block first the rise of Soviet and then Iranian influence around the entrance to the Gulf, the Sultan of Oman signed a 1980 accord with Washington. The arrangement provided for American military assistance in exchange for American access to Omani bases. Because Oman is located at the southern end of the Gulf, its defense suggests accommodation between Iraq and the United States for its defense.

As a result of contingencies involving hostilities between Arab Gulf states and Iran or Iranian–inspired efforts to destabilize these regimes, the Arab states would like to see an Arab counterweight to Iran, and that could only be Iraq.[64] These contingencies argue for Washington to have a tacit alignment with Baghdad as a counter to Tehran.

American attacks in the Gulf on Iranian shipping and U.S. cruise missile attacks on military positions within Iran would provide Baghdad and Washington with incentives to cooperate against a common adversary—Tehran. And Saddam's fall from power might be a pretext for an incremental reintroduction of Iraq back into the mainstream. With Saddam out, Iraq's tacit alignment with the United States would be a distinct possibility. In fact, Saddam's demise might allow for an explicit coalition between Western countries and Iraq.

On one hand, if Iraq's Arab neighbors come under threat from Iran, Baghdad may adhere to UN demands. On the other hand, Iraq may go beyond the weapons inspection crisis pattern to a more confrontational posture if the Kurdish population in the north and the Shiite population in the south were to challenge Baghdad.

*Containment/Regime Change–Defiance: Baghdad Attacks Kurds and Shiites.* In the context of a defiant Iraq, there was a move in the late 1990s to go beyond containment in order to overthrow the regime. Such an approach trades off the benefit of an inspection policy for the value of military strikes as well as covert and overt support to the Iraqi opposition.

The airstrikes would degrade the capacity of Iraq to create WMD. Although unlikely, covert operations might precipitate a palace coup against Saddam. More likely, overt support for the opposition might destabilize the regime but also may create instability throughout Iraq.

In the event of American financial and military support for the Iraqi opposition, it is likely that a Kurdish civil war would resume. The rebellion in the south also might escalate and expand. In order to place maximum pressure on the regime in Baghdad, the No–Fly–Zone might be expanded and modified. The zone in the north might extend hundred of miles north of the 36th parallel, as the zone in the south has expanded to the outskirts of Baghdad. Additionally, modification of the zones would ban flights by Iraqi helicopters, which Baghdad used successfully to attack Kurdish rebels in 1996.

The United States also might move to reinforce the combat aircraft, including F–14 Tomcats and F/A–18C Hornets, which monitor the northern zone from facilities in Incirlik, Turkey. In the absence of a revision of the terms of reference and rules of engagement for the operation of Iraqi aircraft, Baghdad's fixed–wing air attacks in the north and south would violate the original terms of the No–Fly–Zones in both regions. This breach might result in tit–for–tat escalation and expansion of fighting between Iraq and outside forces in both northern and southern Iraq. [65]

A basis for American assistance to Saddam's opposition is the Iraq Liberation Act. Prodded by the Congress, President Clinton signed the act on October 31, 1998. It appropriates $97 million that might enable opponents of the regime in Baghdad to seize and hold territory, which would no longer be subject to UN economic sanctions. But such a strategy might not bear fruit unless airpower protects the Iraqi opposition from Baghdad's armored forces. Hence, London and Washington might establish and enforce "no–drive zones" in northern and southern areas, from which Iraqi armor and artillery would be excluded.

One result of the effort to destabilize Iraq might be the fall of the regime and the disintegration of the country. Historical tensions exist between the minority Sunni center near Baghdad and the Kurdish north as well as the majority Shiite Muslim south. When Britain formed modern–day Iraq out of its League of Nations Mandate following World War I, it pieced together these three regions. An argument against the Iraq Liberation Act is that a weak, fragmented, chaotic Iraq would be more dangerous than Saddam's reign over a strong, unified, and stable nation.

Several countries would stand to benefit from Iraq's disintegration, including Turkey, Iran, Israel, and Syria.[66] The scenario, however, considers implications for Turkey and Iran only.

With respect to economic motivation, Turkey has major interests in the breakup of Iraq. If Iraq were to dissolve, its oilfields and natural gas refineries in the north might provide Ankara with much–needed revenues. Before the start of the 1991 Gulf War, Turkey and Iraq shared profits from a pipeline that began at oilfields in the northern Iraqi province of Mosul and extended through Turkey to various ports on the Mediterranean Sea. There would be little need to worry about sharing profits with a disintegrating Iraq. The value of such a pipeline, however, decreases if Iraq is unstable.

Regarding military and diplomatic factors for Turkey, Ankara might seize upon Iraq's instability to attack Kurdish bases in the mountainous region of that country. A goal would be to eliminate the Kurdish threat. Indeed, Ankara has undertaken this objective every spring since 1994 and particularly in April of 1998, when it deployed about 10,000 troops as well as heavy artillery and helicopter gunships to Iraq.

The Patriotic Union of Kurdistan (PUK) and the Kurdistan Workers Party (PKK) have fought against each other and against Turkey. Although each often establishes alignments of convenience with the countries of the region, the PKK has found sanctuary in northern Iraq and has had the support of Tehran.[67]

Iran is another state that stands to benefit from the dissolution of Iraq. Should fighting resume in Iraq's north and south, the United States might need to obtain the tacit cooperation of Iran. Such collaboration might result in a relaxation of unilateral American sanctions against Iran. Following the 1991 Gulf War, Iran assisted rebels in southern Iraq against the regime in Baghdad, a move that may have implied some tacit collusion between Tehran and Washington.

With the ouster of Saddam Hussein, Iran might seek to take advantage of the power vacuum to seize the southern province of Basra, which it has a major incentive to absorb, as Basra is a launching pad for National Liberation Army (NLA) terrorist activity against Iran.

Known as the Mujahadeen Khalq (People's Holy Warriors), the NLA conducts its activities from military facilities around that province. [68]

## A GRAND BARGAIN

Reconciliation with Iraq in the context of its compliance seems to be a far–fetched idea. This scenario requires unlikely assumptions, such as an Iranian invasion or subversion of Arab Gulf states. Rather, the scenario containment and regime change in conjunction with Iraq's defiance appears to be a likely policy and perhaps a script for the future.

Nevertheless, in the event of escalating hostilities instigated by Iran against the Arab Gulf states as well as the ouster of Saddam, conditions might be ripe for a deal between Baghdad and Washington. Indeed, a grand bargain is explicit in the sanctions regime imposed on Iraq by the United Nations. Iraq would have to comply fully with UN Security Council Resolution 687. Its main purpose is to prevent Iraq from becoming once again a military threat to its neighbors or to the Gulf region as a whole. And Baghdad would have to demonstrate that it would not seek to acquire or develop nuclear, chemical, and biological weapons.

In exchange for full Iraqi compliance, economic warfare against Baghdad might be terminated. In the meantime, Iraq's partial compliance resulted in a temporary arrangement: UN Security Council Resolution 986. It and subsequent resolutions permit Iraq to sell billions of barrels of oil at regular intervals to pay for humanitarian relief supplies, reparations, and operating expenses of UN monitoring units in the country.[69]

For Washington to agree to a complete lifting of international sanctions, Saddam would have to leave office. With another leader in power, the goal of the United States might change from retribution to rehabilitation. There would no longer be any need to move the goal post as Baghdad approaches compliance.

The likelihood of a grand bargain between Washington and Baghdad is low. It is unlikely that Saddam will be ousted and even less likely that Tehran will act militarily against Saudi Arabia, Kuwait, and the Arab Gulf states. Meanwhile, the United States has to remain alert to the danger imposed by both rogue states, Iran and Iraq, while it keeps open the option of tacitly cooperating with either one against the other.

Consider the four themes that cut across *Rogue Regimes*—threat perception, opportunities, politics, and policies. For Iraq, politics with the added element of personality are core factors that explain American policy. Chapter Two finds that Washington deals with Iran as a nation–state irrespective of who is at the helm in Tehran. By contrast, Washington deals with Saddam as the personification of Iraq. Containment of Iraq with the eventual goal of overthrowing Saddam would allow the United States to treat Iraq again as a nation–state.

In connection with the debate about the nature of threats to the international system, Iraq is a fitting substitute for the Soviet menace. Among the allies, London and Washington share similar perceptions of threat and opportunity with respect to Iraq. Hence, it is easier for the United Kingdom and the United States to fashion a joint policy of sanctions against Saddam than against Iran. At issue, however, is how to bring the other allies on board the American–British consensus. Although punishment of Iraq can be justified because it appeals to domestic political constituencies and is in line with idealism, there is erosion of international support for such punishment with the passage of time.

CHAPTER FOUR

# LIBYA: CONTAIN OR EMBRACE

## THE IRAN AND LIBYA SANCTIONS ACT OF 1996

IN A UNANIMOUS VOTE Congress passed legislation that imposed a secondary trade boycott on the firms of America's closest allies.[1] If they dared to invest substantial sums in the energy sectors of Iran or Libya, the businesses could be subjected to stiff penalties. The unanimity of the vote is an indication of the overwhelming public sentiment against both countries. As the vote suggests, there were no advocates of the option of embracing Colonel Muammar Qadhafi of Libya in order to change his errant ways. Rather, the opinion of the American public was clear: contain Qadhafi so that he cannot engage in subversion, terrorism, or chemical weapons proliferation.

In order to understand why the Sanctions Act passed with no dissent, one must consider the geopolitical situation in the Mediterranean, the American-Libyan relationship over time, American objectives and interests regarding Libya, as well as sources of U.S. threat perceptions. This chapter pays particular attention to bureaucratic political maneuvering during the Reagan years, when the die was cast concerning the hard-line approach toward Libya. With this overview in mind, it is possible to understand the effects of unilateral American as well as United Nations sanctions against

Libya. In addition, the overview provides historical context for the battle being waged by Qadhafi for the "American Street." Finally, there is a discussion for scenarios relevant to the future of American-Libyan relations.

## PREPONDERANCE OF POWER IN THE MEDITERRANEAN

While Iran and Iraq are rogues of the Gulf region, Libya is a geopolitical outlaw of the Mediterranean. The question for Washington regarding Tehran and Baghdad is whether to embrace or contain them, and the answer is less than clear-cut. It requires a determination whether the United States wants to balance Tehran against Baghdad, or vice versa; if so, then accommodation with at least one of these states is conceivable and advisable.[2]

If the leadership of Tehran and Baghdad were waiting to seize windows of opportunity, then containment would be preferable. And, because of indications that these leaders are acting more for gain than to stave off pain, containment is the order of the day. Although there is evidence that fear is a motivating factor, opportunity appears to dominate. And with both rehabilitation and retribution as motivating factors underlying American national security policy toward Iran and Iraq, containment of one or the other can be readily justified.

When Iraq and the United States are on friendly terms, the dominant explanation for Saddam's rogue behavior is that he is a paranoid afraid of losses and in need of Western understanding. As a paranoid in the 1980s, the image of Saddam was that he was capable of being a friend. When problems arose in the relationship, Washington explained Saddam's outlaw behavior as a consequence of his Machiavellian desire for gain, as a result of which he did not deserve Western empathy.

Regarding Qadhafi, his relationship with American presidents has been downhill all the way, in contrast to the ups and downs with Saddam. The explanation is more consistent for Qadhafi's behavior than for Saddam's: Qadhafi has always been a Machiavellian leader out for gain, deserving of United States sanctions, and undeserving of American empathy.

With respect to Libya, therefore, the answer to the question whether to contain or embrace is straightforward: containment and perhaps confrontation are the options to pursue. Hence, the U.S. geopolitical strategy is to surround Libya with a ring of states aligned with Washington and to supplement this with a preponderance of credible American power within striking distance. In this respect, the Gulf of Sidra, an international waterway that borders on Libya, is a flash point of confrontation between Tripoli and Washington.

Unlike the comparatively clear threat posed by Libya and the consensus about how to meet it, there is more ambiguity regarding Iran and Iraq. Because Washington has alternated between a balance of power and a dual containment approach in the Gulf, neither Iran nor Iraq has been the permanent enemy Libya has been.[3] When Presidents Reagan and Bush conducted a balancing approach, there was a move to accommodate Iran and/or Iraq. Upon the adoption of dual containment as Clinton's policy of choice, both regimes were considered rogues. Iran and Iraq were to be isolated until they changed their ways or the offending regimes fell from power.

Balance of power and dual containment are national security policies that focus on the nature of danger from abroad. But what is the menace? Threats depend on perceptions. And perceptions derive from values as interpreted by bureaucratic organizations and political interest groups. A threat to one organization or group may be an opportunity to others.

Economic and ethnic groups clash in the determination of what is a threat and thus in the formulation of policy. In the event of economic interest-group domination of the policy process, there is an inclination for the United States to move closer to Iran or Iraq. When national security and economic vectors line up, they reinforce one another. Hence, a policy of accommodation and even appeasement of rogue states is possible, but often not advisable. But when ethnic-group lobbying magnifies national security threats, this convergence facilitates a policy of containment and confrontation.

Balance of power ideas, however, are not as relevant to the Mediterranean as to the Gulf. It makes no sense to balance Libya and

Syria. There is, however, a perceived need to strengthen countries on all sides of Libya—Morocco, Tunisia, Chad, the Sudan, and Egypt. But such a buildup via economic and military assistance is for the purpose of encircling Libya with antagonist states that are friendly to the United States. Also, there is the belief in Washington that these countries would like the United States to isolate, contain, and confront Libya. Republican and Democratic presidents have imposed varying degrees of sanctions on Libya. Washington imposed a unilateral arms embargo on Tripoli in the mid-1970s, closed the American embassy in Tripoli in 1980, and closed the Libyan mission in Washington in 1981. Because of Libya's aggressive activities toward America's friends in the Mediterranean, there is bipartisan consensus in favor of a containment policy against Tripoli.

In October 1980, during the Carter Administration, Qadhafi sent Libyan ground combat forces as well as helicopters and aircraft into neighboring Chad, a country due south of Libya. With explicit Soviet approval, Cuban and East German military advisors facilitated Libya's invasion. Long-range, Soviet-built aircraft also carried out bombing raids against Chad. As armored and mechanized units proceeded on the ground within that country, Qadhafi also sent his military across the border into the Sudan, just southeast of Libya.

The Libyan invasion of Chad and its raids into the Sudan were accompanied by subversion of regimes throughout Africa: Cameroon, Gabon, Gambia, Ghana, Liberia, Mali, Niger, Nigeria, Senegal, Sierra Leone, and Uganda. As a result, leaders of these states perceived a growing threat from Libya.

One specific manifestation of Libya's troublemaking involves Egypt in the late 1970s. After a military confrontation in its Western Desert, President Sadat had asked the Carter Administration to cooperate with him against Qadhafi. He wanted to develop a preponderance of power to deter and confront Libyan aggression. Washington, however, refrained from conducting coordinated military planning with Cairo for an attack against Libya. Sadat believed that President Carter lacked the determination to stand up against Colonel Qadhafi. This perception on the part of Sadat would cast a shadow on the credibility of the American commitment to Egypt, which felt endangered by the threat of radical Arab states like Libya.

Egypt is not alone in its aversion toward radical Arab regimes. Despite their differences, Egypt and Israel share a common threat perception of extreme Arab states. Like President Sadat, General Ariel Sharon of Israel was also concerned with the radical threat posed by regimes like Libya, Iraq, Syria, and South Yemen. During 1981, he stated that these regimes had a political/military strategy for the liquidation of Israel. Their approach included Soviet political support, a military buildup via arms transfers from Moscow, and the use of the oil weapon. Sharon also saw the PLO as an element in a Soviet strategy to foster subversion against moderate Arab regimes like Egypt's and build up fanatical Arab regimes like Libya's.[4]

According to Sharon, Soviet goals included attaining a sea-control capability in the Mediterranean, the Indian Ocean, the Gulf, and the Red Sea. Moscow wanted to penetrate key countries in the Middle East and the Gulf from the direction of Afghanistan, Iraq, South Yemen, and Syria. The Soviets wanted to outflank NATO's eastern tier through Iran, Iraq, Syria, and Lebanon. In addition, the USSR desired to get around its southern tier in the Mediterranean by aligning with Libya, Syria, and Algeria. Moscow also wanted to gain control over critical states in Africa from the direction of Libya, Algeria, South Yemen, Ethiopia, Mozambique, Angola, and the Congo-Brazzaville. Finally, Sharon defined these areas of Soviet interests as "the strategic hinterland of Israel."[5] Although Libya is not an active confrontation state on the front line against Israel, Tripoli constitutes a serious threat to Jerusalem.

While Sharon expressed his threat perception of Soviet-inspired Arab radicalism in the winter of 1981, Sadat had already expressed similar concerns the summer before his death in October 1981.[6] Following Libya's invasion of Chad, Sadat thought that the Sudan would be Qadhafi's next target. And with Soviet assistance, Egypt could be on Libya's hit list after the Sudan. Sadat suspected that Moscow was behind Libya's efforts to envelop Egypt. Because Egypt and the Sudan share a long border, Cairo has a vital interest in its neighbor. Sadat could not afford to let the Sudan fall prey to Libyan and Soviet domination. Radicals then would control one of Egypt's major strategic assets—the Nile River, where over 90 percent of the Egyptian population resides.

Furthermore, Libya also could gain a foothold along the Red Sea because of its alliance with Ethiopia and Aden (South Yemen). During the late 1970s and early 1980s, leaders of Somalia and the Sudan perceived that a tripartite alignment of Aden, Ethiopia, and Libya was directed primarily toward Somalia, Sana (North Yemen), and the Sudan. And the ultimate objective of this collusion was to undermine moderate regimes in Egypt and Saudi Arabia. As a result, Sudanese President Nimeiri welcomed the Reagan Administration's resolve to deter Qadhafi. He wanted the United States to make Qadhafi powerless to deliver on promised assistance to Ethiopia—assistance that was conditional on active Ethiopian opposition to the Nimeiri regime in Khartoum.[7]

An informal league of extreme states composed of Iran, Libya, and Syria began to worry the Arab moderates that the radicals were out to destabilize their mainstream regimes. Tehran had upgraded its links to Damascus and Tripoli in order to acquire additional military supplies during the Iran-Iraq War. Iran was pursuing an overall strategy with three phases: create an Islamic revolution, starting in Tehran; subvert Arab regimes, beginning with Saudi Arabia and the Arab Gulf states; and spread the Islamic revolution to Turkey, Pakistan, and the Arab states of the Fertile Crescent and the Nile Valley.

One of Iran's moderate Gulf targets was the United Arab Emirates, which wanted to mediate between Libya and the United States in order to split Libya off from Iran. The UAE reasoned that the best way to neutralize Qadhafi was to reconcile him with Washington. The Emirates feared Iranian expansionism. Besides Syria, Libya was the only ally Iran had in the Arab world. The rulers of the Emirates understood that the only protection against an Iranian attack was the United States.

Unless there was advance coordination between the moderate Arab states and the United States, protection would have arrived too late to prevent an Iranian takeover. But the fight between Washington and Tripoli made coordination with the United States on security against an Iranian attack all the more difficult. Note that it was not the Palestinian issue that hindered strategic planning with the United

States, but rather Washington's disagreements with Tripoli. And the USSR stood to gain from lack of strategic cooperation between the United States and the Arab Gulf states.

The consensus in the Reagan Administration during 1981, its first year of office, was that Moscow was attempting to exploit tensions between Tripoli and Washington in order to forge closer links with Libya. The USSR was stepping up arms sales to Libya in exchange for hard currency. The accord among Libya, the People's Democratic Republic of Yemen, and Ethiopia was a way for the Soviet Union to strengthen its presence in the region. Hence, Soviet arms to Libya would have allowed it to arm Yemen and Ethiopia.

Libya also supplied oil for Eastern European states when the Soviets were cutting back on oil shipments. Enhanced access to Tripoli ports and other facilities provided Moscow with the best strategic position it had had since being ousted from Egypt in 1972. Although somewhat close, however, Moscow and Tripoli were still quite a distance apart regarding policy coordination. The October 1981 Soviet deployment preceded one in July of that year. They represented a substantial plus for Moscow's naval interests in the Mediterranean. Since Cairo expelled Moscow's naval air element in 1972, no Soviet naval aviation shore-based aircraft had flown missions for reconnaissance over the Mediterranean until the July and October 1981 deployments. These were a significant step toward Moscow's aim of establishing a permanent naval air presence on the Mediterranean littoral.

While Soviet-supported Libya was invading Chad and the Sudan, as well as subverting regimes to its south, it was less active in the Arab-Israel conflict zone. Tripoli was even out of step with the main confrontation state against Israel—Syria. Despite the fact that they shared a history of acute confrontation with Israel, virulent anti-imperialism, and unwavering Arab nationalism, Libya and Syria differed with respect to their commitment to the Arab-Israel peace process. As stated in the following chapter on Syria, there is evidence that Damascus has made a strategic commitment to make peace with Israel. Libya has not made such a commitment. Indeed, Tripoli stands outside of the peace process, just as it stands outside of the mainstream of African states, the Arab nation, and the Islamic world.

# TRIPOLI AND WASHINGTON:
# FRIENDS IN THE 1960s, ENEMIES THEREAFTER

American relations with Iraq and Iran have been on a roller coaster of ups and downs over time. U.S. relations with Libya, however, were friendly before 1969 and hostile thereafter, when a coup removed a pro-American king from power and replaced him with a group of anti-American leaders. On September 1, 1969, a group of young army officers overthrew the royal government and established a republic.

Dominated by Colonel Muammar Qadhafi, the revolutionary government displayed a strong resolve to play a major role in the Middle East theater. Tripoli negotiated with Cairo and Khartoum to coordinate their political, economic, and military policies. And during September 1971, Libya succeeded in forming a political federation with Egypt and Syria. Designed to be an alliance against Israel, this federation was a nonstarter. It lasted only until 1974, because of internal rivalries.[8]

Despite the failure of the federation, Libya's appetite for coordination was still strong. Tripoli sought to coordinate the oil weapon in the struggle against Israel. After Israel's 1973 war with Egypt and Syria, Libya joined an embargo. Tripoli raised its oil prices in order to take advantage of the panic associated with the war.

One of the reasons for Libya's tensions with Egypt concerns the Arab-Israel peace process. While there is some doubt about the commitment that Damascus has made for peace with Israel, there is less doubt about Egypt's commitment. Tripoli opposed Sadat's peace initiatives toward Israel and played a leading part with Syria in the rejectionist front. Tripoli provided strong political and financial support for the PLO in the late 1970s. In addition, during the early 1980s, Tripoli began a campaign of state-sponsored terrorism and assassinations of Libyan dissidents who lived abroad.

Accelerating the descent from friend to enemy, Libya's relations with the United States deteriorated with the coming of the Reagan Administration to power. I had the privilege of serving on candidate Reagan's political campaign and then on President Reagan's National Security Council staff. At the White House, I shared the action on Middle East matters with these colleagues: Geoffrey Kemp and Douglas Feith, and later, with Oliver North and Howard Teicher. Based on the division of labor at the White House from March 1981 to September 1982, I had the principal action on Libya and Lebanon, but shared it with Teicher once he came on board in the summer of 1982.

Teicher was one of the national security professionals who was a holdover from the Carter Administration's Pentagon and State Department. Although during the transition he was a relatively low-level civil servant, he rose rapidly through the ranks with the incoming Reagan team. He represented the holdovers who were delighted with President Reagan's hard-line stance again the Soviet Union and its radical Arab allies like Libya. Indeed, with the invasion of Chad in mind, Teicher and his allies agreed with our description of Libya as the "cat's paw" of Soviet expansionism.

Unlike the Carter Administration, we Reagan officials not only believed that the United States had a strategic interest in arresting Soviet inroads into the Middle East, but were prepared to combine economic diplomacy with military force to achieve that objective in the case of Libya. That is, we wanted the United States to act in accord with its great-power status in the world at large as well as in the Mediterranean vis-à-vis Libya.

## AMERICAN OBJECTIVES AND INTERESTS

Washington's aims with respect to Tripoli concern antisubversion, counterterrorism, and nonproliferation. Specific American objectives are to coerce Tripoli to cease its subversive behavior toward neighboring countries that are friendly to Washington, to terminate its sponsorship of international terrorist organizations, and to end the pursuit of weapons of mass destruction, with particular reference to chemical armaments. Underlying these specific aims are strategic interests. They are both more general and more important than the specific purposes just mentioned.

### Strategic Interests

As a superpower, the United States has a strategic interest in making sure that it is unchallenged. A perception of invincibility is the glue that holds together the American deterrent system. To the extent that Tripoli stands up to Washington, it challenges U.S. credibility, resolve, and commitments. When a nation like Libya challenges Washington's resolve, the likelihood of deterrence failure elsewhere increases. And if that nation is aligned with another superpower, as Libya was associated with the USSR in the 1980s, then the United States should not tolerate challenges to its will.

Consider the coalition designed to multiply the influence of the radicals and to counter American alliances in the Middle East: the tripartite pact among Libya, the Peoples Democratic Republic of Yemen, and Ethiopia. Signed in August 1981, it was a direct political challenge to the United States and its friends like Egypt, Jordan, and Israel. Also imagine a situation in which Washington took action against Libya and neither Moscow nor its surrogates supported their ally. Such a scenario would constitute a major strategic victory for Uncle Sam over the Russian Bear.

The strategy for achieving American objectives regarding Libya are to challenge Tripoli's claim to territorial waters beyond the normal 12 mile limit, to confront Libya's state sponsorship of international terrorism, and to coerce Libya to cease the development of chemical weapons. Freedom of the seas is not only a strategic interest of the United States, it also is a value that stems from the American principle of free market capitalism. And when ideals reinforce strategic interests, that is a potent brew indeed.

## Freedom of the Seas

Libya posed a threat to freedom of the seas when it asserted an extension of its territorial waters beyond the recognized limits of international law. In light of great-power status, Cold War perceptions, international law ideals, as well as antiterrorism attitudes, it is no surprise that Tripoli and Washington were on a collision course in the spring and summer of 1981.

Consistent with its strategic interest in asserting its principles concerning freedom of the seas, Washington initiated a freedom of navigation challenge in international waters in the Gulf of Sidra, an area of the Mediterranean claimed by Libya as being in its territory.

Although the global standard for national territorial waters is 12 miles, Qadhafi claimed that Libyan waters extended 200 miles. Hence, during March 1981, the U.S. Sixth Fleet began to conduct air and sea exercises in the Gulf of Sidra.

With respect to the use of the Gulf of Sidra for military exercises, the Organization of the Joint Chiefs of Staff was neutral concerning the idea of sending a strategic signal to Qadhafi. They did feel, however, that if there were to be military exercises, there ought to be a military benefit. The Pentagon planned to conduct an exercise to fire a missile from an American warship. The Gulf of Sidra was a good location because it was not along the main sea-and-air-lanes of commerce.

On August 19, 1981, the U.S. Navy conducted a military exercise in the Gulf of Sidra. Upon being challenged by Libyan planes, two U.S. F-14 aircraft shot down two Libyan warplanes. The shoot-down occurred after the Libyan pilots had prepared to attack and activated the target-acquisition radars and guidance systems of their air-to-air missiles.

Qadhafi could not accept the downing of Libyan warplanes, because Libya has a strategic interest in not being seen as a compliant nation. He used the shootdown as a point of departure for rallying domestic political support for his faltering regime and for rallying Arab support against the United States. He was more successful in using the raids to bolster his standing at home than abroad, receiving virtually no support in his calls for Arab leaders to retaliate against Washington in the Gulf of Sidra.

## Counterterrorism

In addition to interests like reputation, resolve, and freedom of the seas, Libya threatens other American interests. One means by which Libya confronts Washington is through state-sponsored terrorism. American intelligence detected Libyan assassination planning. The notorious "Carlos" may have been involved in plans to conduct terror strikes in the United States, and an Amal hit team had been formed in Libya for operations in the United States.[9] There was to be an attack against the President sometime between December 1 and 15, 1981. And later, on January 21, 1982, there were reports that Libyan assassination teams fled to Mexico and remained there.

Regarding terrorism, Tripoli threatens American civilians and military personnel. Although these lives in and of themselves are of great intrinsic value, the reason for their being targeted by Tripoli is not because of who they are as individuals but that they symbolize the United States as a nation. Consequently, intrinsic and strategic interests coincide in the case of international terrorism.[10]

During November 1991, courts in the United States and the United Kingdom indicted two Libyan intelligence agents implicated in the bombing of Pan Am Flight 103 in 1988 over Lockerbie, Scotland. The United Nations Security Council passed three resolutions demanding that the Government of Libya take steps to end its participation in state-sponsored terrorism, and to extradite the two suspects. Resolution 731 of January 1992 demanded that Libya accept responsibility for the bombing, disclose all evidence related to it, and pay appropriate compensation to the families of the victims.[11]

In April 1992, the Security Council adopted Resolution 748.[12] It imposed an arms and civil aviation embargo on Libya, demanded that Libyan Arab Airlines offices shut down, and required that all states reduce Tripoli's diplomatic appearance abroad. Libya's continued challenge to the resolutions led the Security Council to approve Resolution 883, in November 1993, which tightened existing sanctions, imposed a limited-assets freeze, and placed an oil technology embargo on Libya.[13]

The State Department contends that Tripoli made some minor changes to its terrorism infrastructure after the adoption of Resolutions 731 and 748. But Libya made no further changes to its terrorism network. Although there has been a decline in the regime's sponsorship of terrorism, its apparatus for conducting such actions remains intact. Qadhafi repeated his anti-Western ideas throughout 1994 and 1995, and he offered support to radical Palestinian groups opposed to the PLO's Gaza-Jericho accord with Israel.

Also, Qadhafi threatened to support extremist Islamic groups in the neighboring states of Algeria and Tunisia as penalty for not supporting Libya against the UN sanctions effort. Qadhafi's speeches in the fall of 1993, after a mid-October uprising and subsequent crackdown in Libya, became more hostile. He pledged to retaliate against Libyan oppositionists, those who enforced sanctions against Libya, and individuals who cooperated with Washington.

Not only does Libya target American citizens, it also directs terrorism against its own political opposition at home and abroad. The Department of State accuses Tripoli of the 1993 abduction, and continued detention, of a prominent Libyan dissident and human rights activist, Mansur Kikhia.[14] And throughout 1995, moreover, Libya continued to support groups violently opposed to the Middle East peace process. These groups often express their opposition with acts of international terrorism.[15] In addition to international terrorism, Libya fails to comply with Washington's attempts to discourage the proliferation of weapons of mass destruction.

## Anti-Proliferation

While Libya's subversion and terrorism were on the decline, its proliferation of weapons of mass destruction was on the rise. During the late 1980s, Western intelligence agencies held that Libya engaged in chemical weapons development. In this respect, proliferation of chemical weapons in the Middle East became a core concern of United States national security policy during 1988. At that time, three events converged: construction of the Libyan poison gas facility at Rabta, deadly use of chemical weapons by both sides during the Iran-Iraq War, and Baghdad's use of poison gas against its own Kurdish population.[16] As a result of this coincidence of chemical weapons use, the United States called for an international conference. Held in Paris, its purpose was to raise the world's consciousness about these mass destruction devices.[17]

Washington had four main goals for the Paris Conference. The first was to urge the signers of the 1925 Geneva Protocol to restate their commitment to that document.[18] The second was to take multinational steps to discourage chemical weapons use. A third purpose was to conclude a new international treaty prohibiting the production and stockpiling of these weapons. Finally, the United States wanted to apply economic sanctions to those engaging in the use of chemical weapons, but Washington was not able to achieve consensus for their implementation.

Franco-American cooperation was the key to bringing about the chemical weapons conference. Although France did not agree with the United States that Libya indeed was building a chemical weapons facility, Paris joined with Washington in highlighting the dangers of these tools of mass destruction. Contrary to the French and American understanding, Arab nations were dissatisfied with the proposed emphasis on chemical weapons proliferation in the Middle East. From the perspective of Arab states in attendance, they felt that any enforcement actions that might come from the conference could be perceived as pointed at the Middle Eastern nations in general, and Iran, Iraq, and Libya in particular.[19]

Libya was both an attendee of the conference and a target of American accusations. Libya came as a signatory of the 1925 Geneva Protocol. Under the principle that a best defense is an offense, Qadhafi suggested that the conference turn its attention to chemical plants in America, Europe, and Israel. Though few believed him, Qadhafi explicitly declared that Libya was against producing chemical weapons.[20]

As of the late 1990s, the jury was still out as to whether Libya was indeed building a facility that housed chemical weapons. But there is evidence that Tripoli is constructing a facility. Western intelligence agencies believe that Libya is building such a factory at Tarhunah, 40 miles southeast of Tripoli. The plant is reportedly being built into a mountain, which would make it difficult to destroy in a military strike using conventional weapons. Tripoli designed the Tarhunah facility in order to replace the plant at Rabta, which is 55 miles southwest of Tripoli. The Rabta facility was reopened in the fall of 1995, five years after a suspicious fire.[21] Libya insisted that the plant only made material for pharmaceuticals. Western intelligence agencies, however, believed that Libya was constructing it for the purpose of producing chemical weapons.

In retaliation for such accusations, Libya accused the United States of hypocrisy on the issue. Tripoli hoped that Western export controls on Libya would not prohibit the export of technology necessary for the so-called peaceful means of the development of his society. Because of his protests, American national security policy-makers were even more intent than before to contain Qadhafi. But

United States economic decisionmakers were just as intent on not letting national security considerations dominate without a fight.

## SOURCES OF AMERICAN THREAT PERCEPTION

### Politics of Policy Making

Principal sources of threat perception regarding Tehran and Baghdad are ethnic politics, economic interests of the business community, and bureaucratic differences. For Libya, the battle between politics and business interests also applies. While ethnic politics are more important in the cases of Iran and Iraq, they are of less consequence for Libya. Accordingly, this policy-making section for Libya discusses bureaucratic politics at the expense of ethnic politics.

One split in the bureaucracy is between foreign policy and national security—between State, the CIA, and the National Security Council staff and Treasury, Commerce, and the United States Trade Representative. A second divide is between military and civilians from the Department of Defense versus civilians from the White House and the State Department.[22]

And a third gap is within State, between the hard-line functional bureaus—Policy Planning and Politico-Military Affairs—and the softer-line geographical bureaus—Near Eastern and South Asian Affairs as well as European and Canadian Affairs.[23] A fourth division is between foreign policy/national security and criminal justice agencies.

Momentum for the imposition of sanctions picked up on October 1, 1981, when the State Department chaired a meeting of the Libyan Task Force. On the table was the nature of the threat from Libya to Belgium, Greece, and Italy. European countries tolerated a higher level of threat from Libya than did the United States. Nevertheless, there was considerable evidence presented about a growing perception on the part of these nations for the need to take action to counter the threat from Libya.

There was also a discussion of American objectives toward Libya. These aims included the deterrence-by-denial strategy of diminishing

Qadhafi's ability to carry out terror attacks. In addition, there was the political purpose of enhancing his isolation in the Arab world while minimizing risks to American citizens on the ground. A general objective was to carry out the president's policy of bringing swift and effective retribution against those who engaged in terrorism against the United States.

Specific goals included: demonstrating to Qadhafi that Washington would not tolerate acts of terrorism against U.S. interests, and raising the price sufficiently to deter him from future acts of terrorism—a deterrence by threat of punishment strategy. Items of concern to Qadhafi were Libyan military capabilities, economic interests, his personal prestige, domestic political support, and his image within the nonaligned movement.

Egyptian Vice President Mubarak was in Washington during the October 1981 meeting and said Sadat was concerned as to whether the United States would stand tough against Libya. Sadat had good reason to doubt the American resolve, given the unwillingness of the Carter Administration to take forceful action against Libya or to engage in military planning for the destabilization of Qadhafi's regime. While calling for tougher measures against the likes of a Qadhafi, however, Sadat paid the ultimate price for making peace—he was assassinated six days into the month of October.

The 1981 assassination of Sadat gave a new sense of urgency to the planning process regarding Libya. If there were Libyan foreknowledge of the Sadat assassination, this knowledge would have been reflected in the alert sequence of the Libyan armed forces.[24] They did not go on alert prior to the assassination, and thus Tripoli may not have been aware of it. Notwithstanding the time pressure, there also was a need for caution. In this respect, constraints on contingency planning gave rise to cautious risk-averse planning, which was exceedingly slow. As a result, critics seized upon the delays as evidence that the Administration lacked will.[25]

The aversion to risk highlighted a need to assure the safety of American citizens, and those from countries friendly to the United States, who happened to work in Libya. There also was a requirement to avoid measures that would rally support for Qadhafi on the Arab street and in the nonaligned movement. We officials at the White

House were concerned that the United States not push him into a corner where he felt there was no other option except to escalate. In the language of classical deterrence theory, we surmised that he had to believe that the benefits of Libyan escalation were not as important to him as the costs of further retaliation from the United States.

In view of these goals, there was a consideration of diplomatic, economic, and military responses to Libya. On the diplomatic side, options included an embargo on the purchase of Libyan oil, a prohibition on U.S. companies for operating in Libya, and mandatory withdrawal of American citizens. Additionally, there was a ban on U.S. travel to Libya, a freeze on Libyan financial assets, elimination of Export-Import Bank financing for Libya, a ban on U.S. exports to Libya, and a cessation of U.S. visas for Libyan nationals.

Despite the tendency for there to be splits within State, there was a general accord between the functional and geographical bureaus. The Staff for Policy Planning and Politico-Military Affairs, on the one hand, and the Bureau of Near Eastern and South Asian Affairs, on the other hand, agreed on a joint recommendation to Secretary of State Alexander Haig. The consensus was that authorization be given to warn Qadhafi that the United States would respond to a Libyan attack on American assets. Once American citizens had been ordered out of Libya or had departed on their own, military options would include the following: open assistance to anti-Libyan elements in Chad and suggestions that Egypt consider military action against Libya.

Although there was agreement at State, there was less accord between it and the Pentagon. At an October 2, 1981, meeting of the Libyan Task Force, the representative of the Joint Chiefs of Staff first requested, then demanded, a list of political goals.[26] The Chiefs wanted this list of aims to use as a basis for military contingency planning, in the event of anti-U.S. terrorism by Libya. Pentagon officials did not believe that the political aims had been specified clearly enough. Hence, they withheld their support for tough measures against Libya until such time as they felt that there was sufficient specificity.

Another illustration of the battles between State and Defense concerned the clearance process for terms of reference to impose sanctions on Libya. In the process of coalition formation, on December

16, 1981, State Department Counselor Robert McFarlane called me to discuss the procedure for clearing on an interagency basis a terms-of-reference memorandum for cabinet members. Because of tensions between State and Defense, McFarlane wanted to use the National Security Council as the authority for carrying out the State Department's objectives. That is, he wanted the National Security Council, not the Department of State, to be listed as the authorizing agency in the clearance process.

Deputy National Security Advisor John Poindexter told me that he was unsure of what McFarlane was trying to achieve. I replied that it was clear he wanted to cover his flanks by having the White House provide a shield for State against Defense. I suggested that we work closely with McFarlane, while being careful that we were not being used to our disadvantage.[27]

McFarlane's deputy at State, Howard Teicher, called me during December 1981 to inquire about who should receive the inputs for a paper on sanctions regarding Libya and who should compile them. McFarlane's view was that the State Department or the National Security Council staff should receive inputs, but that State should pull the paper together. Poindexter and I agreed that the reports should go to the co-chairs, Bud Nance and McFarlane. State should pull the reports together, I would have an informal role in the process, and then the National Security Council staff should officially receive the paper. State's goal was to forge a coalition with the National Security Council staff as a way to gain additional leverage over the Department of Defense.

And there are other examples of effective policy coordination between the White House and the State Department. With respect to American citizens working in Libya, the Deputy Assistant Secretary of State in the Bureau of Near Eastern and South Asian Affairs called me to inquire where the White House stood in regard to replacement of American workers with those from allied countries. Most Americans in Libya were involved in the exploration for, but not the production of, oil and gas. In this respect, Italy had queried the American embassy in Rome as to the American reaction if Italian workers were to replace Americans who had left. We agreed that State should reply that the United States was neutral to positive, in order to discourage Tripoli from replacing American citizens with Eastern European or Russian workers. State followed the White House line, the outcome was acceptable to Rome, and Russian workers going to Libya were kept to a minimum.

In the process of coalition formation, there are times when advocates of an option in one department will seek allies in another organization in order to affect the decision-making outcome in their own department. During April 1982, a few American citizens wanted to reenter Libya in order to collect on debts due to them prior to the imposition of economic restrictions on travel to Libya. The bureaucratic lineup at the State Department was as follows regarding the reentry option: The Bureau of Near Eastern and South Asian Affairs favored it, its staff for Policy Planning was neutral, and the bureaus of Consular Affairs and Legal Affairs opposed reentry.

Those favoring reentry asked me to weigh in on their side. McFarlane advised me to say that the National Security Council staff had no problem with reentry, but that those who favored it should be aware that the Secretary of State might not look kindly on the National Security Council staff being used to determine the outcome of a bureaucratic dispute at State. I took the position that I had no difficulty weighing in on the decision-making process in favor of reentry, as long as my name was not used in memoranda going to the Secretary of State.

While the bureaus at State were trying to use the White House to gain advantage, there were incidents that reflected just plain confusion and ignorance at Defense. Consider an anecdote about policy coordination that highlights the state of affairs regarding Libya. A military officer on detail with the Office of the Secretary of Defense (OSD)/ International Security Affairs called me to ask whether OSD had coordinated internally on the Libyan study. My answer was, "Why are you calling the White House to find out what your own department has or has not done?" The officer then said that State had suggested that he call the White House to find out if the Department of Defense had coordinated. I told the officer that he should find out within Defense itself whether it had coordinated.

Another policy coordination issue concerned the likelihood of a Soviet response to potential United States military intervention in

Libya. I told an analyst with the CIA to contact her counterpart with the OSD and share names of those working on the Libyan study. She said, "This makes sense. But do you mean that we're going to have a coordinated product?" I replied, "Sorry if it disappoints you, but yes." In other words, there was bureaucratic warfare and policy coordination difficulties among State, Defense, and the CIA. Additionally, there were turf fights within the National Security Council staff over who had the action on Libya. At issue was who would be the point of contact at the White House for Libyan contingency planning. I sparred with General Robert Schweitzer over who would represent the White House on the Libyan Task Force. Schweitzer demanded that a meeting of the military subgroup of the interagency group be canceled, because he had not been invited and I was representing the White House. We did not cancel the meeting, and the general and I worked out a compromise for future meetings.

One of the reasons why generals at the White House and at the Pentagon were on edge about military planning was that the possibility of a regional conflict between Tripoli and Washington could escalate and expand to involve Moscow. On December 14, 1981, McFarlane requested that I write terms of reference for the study of Soviet reactions to potential U.S. military action against Libya. As a result, I chaired a working group on Libya. We met in the White House Situation Room. At our first meeting, I thanked Howard Teicher, who worked for McFarlane, for his good interagency group coordination. And at this meeting, I stressed the benefit of a discussion of points at issue as seen from different perspectives. Once our differences were on the table, I would synthesize them into a coherent paper. Even before drafting the paper, there was consensus that Washington should send a message to Moscow about actions to be taken against Libya only at the time of that action, and not beforehand.

Teicher asked about the Eastern European angle: how should the Soviet Union's European allies be factored into a Soviet response to the Libyan sanctions study? Regarding military action, there was concern about bombing Libyan air defenses, because of the likelihood that Soviets manning the facilities would be killed. But the interagency consensus was that because the Soviets were bogged down in possible military action in Poland and in an actual shooting war in Afghanistan, they would be less likely to challenge American action against Libya. In any event, there was little expectation that the Soviets would interpose their forces on behalf of Libya. At issue was the American response if the Soviets moved a combat unit into Libya. There were no advocates for Washington to match Soviet moves, despite the fact that Moscow had very few viable options regarding intervention on behalf of Libya.

During mid-January 1982, the Libyan working group discussed what to do about American citizens in Libya if export controls were imposed and military force used. There were about 400 Americans in Libya during January 1982, and the goal was to evacuate those who chose to depart by mid-February. There were some 300 additional American citizens not working for U.S. companies, some of whom may have been spouses.

In our discussions, the representative of the Office of the Secretary of Defense took a hard-line position against American citizens who might choose to remain in Libya. He said that the purpose of the drawdown was to avoid a hostage situation. The State Department had to inform those who wished to remain that they were on their own. Defense preferred a mandatory order to compel American citizens to depart. An overall purpose of the withdrawal was to provide flexibility of decision making.[28]

In addition to a drawdown of American citizens from Libya, another option considered was the mining of Libyan harbors and waters. But because of the downside of mining—it would take too long to put into effect—it was not a serious option. Defense also expressed an interest in the use of covert operations to destabilize Libya, rather than direct use of American military force. Coupled with an ultimatum listing particulars, covert operations would get the attention of Qadhafi and could have been instrumental in rehabilitating him. A lack of American intelligence assets in Libya, however, made the option of destabilization difficult to achieve. Other forums existed for a discussion of clandestine activities against Libya. Hence, the working group did not discuss the possibility of conducting covert actions against Tripoli.

The State Department was concerned about the presence of about 5,000 Libyans in the United States. State reported how difficult it was to get a handle on them, who was here, and for how long. The Immigration and Naturalization Service was unable to locate people because of inadequate computerization. Of course, that agency then seized upon the Libya crisis as an opportunity to increase the size of their budgetary requests for computers.

Within the White House staff, there were indications of a struggle for power. The setting for it was a draft I prepared on December 10, 1981, for National Security Decision Directive 16 on Libya. It drew upon National Security Council meetings on December 7 and 8 and a checklist initialed by the president. I coauthored the checklist with Admirals Nance and Poindexter on December 7, and the president approved it on December 9. On that day, I met with several officials who had the action: Nance, Poindexter, McFarlane, and Judge William Clark, Acting Secretary of State.

We were to iron out the details on actions toward Libya in the White House Situation Room. There was a morning meeting of principals in the office of Chief of Staff James Baker. The meeting included Baker, Michael Deaver, Clark, Nance, McFarlane, Communications Director David Gergen, and Richard Darman (deputy to Baker). Ed Meese was absent. Meese's deputy, Craig Fuller, and I were in the hallway outside the meeting. Poindexter said to Nance that I should attend, but Nance said no, because Baker had not explicitly invited me. Although I had prepared the draft, shepherded it through the interagency process, and obtained presidential approval, I remained in the hallway, chomping at the bit.

Consider an indication of how bureaucratic power accrues to those who have it, are willing to use it, and courageous enough to deny it to others. On December 9, 1981, Poindexter asked me to send talking points about Libya to Assistant Secretary of Defense for International Security Affairs Bing West for approval. I said that West does not clear his talkers with the National Security Council staff, so why should we clear with him? Poindexter agreed. By not clearing the talking points with the Pentagon, the White House officials retained and perhaps expanded their power.

Here is yet another example of power plays at the White House concerning Libya. Nance told Poindexter to ask me to send a memo to the president via White House Chief of Staff James Baker. It was clear to me that to have done so would have undercut the independent authority of Nance as Acting National Security Advisor. I counseled against doing so because it would downgrade Nance if his memos to the president went via Baker. Poindexter agreed with me, asked me to remove Baker's name, and Nance would then simply show it to Baker. A power play well executed.

Another principle of bureaucratic politics is that power accrues to those in a position to act during a crisis, not necessarily to those who are in a formal channel of authority. Although I was not in the European part of the National Security Council staff, the planning for Libyan contingencies frequently brought me into contact with West Wing principals. That is, I tended to spend a great deal of time in the West Wing of the White House, rather than in my own office in the Executive Office Building, which adjoins the White House proper. Consequently, I happened to be nearby when the Soviets ordered a crackdown by the government of Poland on its own workers. Just being there allowed me to weigh in on the options being considered. Acting National Security Advisor Nance relied on me to assist him on matters relating to Poland, in part because some of the issues regarding the application of sanctions overlapped the cases of Libya and the USSR.

With respect to the intersection of cases, there was a meeting scheduled for February 4, 1982. I wrote the memo for National Security Advisor William Clark on Libya in relation to Poland. The memo asked whether sterner measures could be taken against Libya. Because those American citizens who wished to leave had departed, there was a window open for intense actions against Tripoli. At issue was whether there was adequate legislative authority and political justification to act against Libya in the absence of an overt Libyan provocation. I answered in the affirmative.

The basic paper for the meeting considered Libyan behavior, U.S. objectives, and changes in the international system, including Poland, the world oil market, relations with regional states, Soviet posture, and public opinion. In the context of competing bureaucracies, two executive summaries appeared at the meeting: one from the State Department and mine from the National Security Council.

Contrary to State's summary, which downplayed disagreement within the bureaucracy, I highlighted the consensus as well as the dissent. Treasury had expressed grave doubts about the proposed course of action set out in the State discussion paper on Libya, which had been written as if the only cost of imposing economic sanctions would be friction with the allies. But there also would be substantial economic costs to the United States. Treasury also took the position that Washington should take all effective measures, but also believed that court rulings concerning extraterritoriality in allied nations could make export controls unenforceable.

At issue at the February 1982 meeting regarding Poland was whether expanded export controls on oil and gas equipment for the USSR should be interpreted to include United States subsidiaries and/ or equipment manufactured by U.S. licensees abroad. In June 1982, the United States government decided this issue in the affirmative.

On the one hand, Defense, Commerce, the CIA, and the U.S. Permanent Representative to the United Nations took a position contrary to that of an opposing coalition led by State. They held that economic sanctions should be interpreted to include subsidiaries and licensees. Their reasoning was as follows. Sanctions might be effective in slowing or stopping the development of the Siberian pipeline. If the sanctions were not interpreted to include subsidiaries and licensees, these controls would only harm United States exports and American workers. Even if litigation resulted from the imposition of sanctions, the uncertainty might damage the pipeline project. And not interpreting the sanctions to include subsidiaries and licensees would be perceived as undercutting American sanctions.

On the other hand, the State Department held that sanctions should not be interpreted to include subsidiaries and licensees. Sanctions might be divisive to the alliance at a time when the United States was attempting to obtain allied cooperation. The allies did not accept use of the crisis in Poland to block the Siberian pipeline. And the legal authority to impose sanctions was questionable over technology transferred prior to December 30, 1981.

The interagency consensus was that if a decision were made to expand export controls to include subsidiaries and licensees, this should be done after the United States requested the allies to apply controls themselves on U.S. subsidiaries and licensees in implementation of their promise not to undercut American sanctions.[29] In the midst of the crisis in Poland, some serious humor surfaced. One official said he believed that the "U.S. business community was even willing to sacrifice the Solidarity Labor Union in Poland rather than impose sanctions on the USSR and Poland." Another cracked, "The American business community did not like labor unions anyway."

Because of the crisis in Poland, the Deputy National Security Advisor and Military Advisor to the President, Admiral Poindexter, was overwhelmed and could not supervise me in regard to the Libyan situation. As a result, I assumed additional responsibility in the decision making. I drafted the terms of reference for the interagency process. And in the middle of the crisis over Poland and contingency planning for Libya, Israel made a move to apply its laws to the Golan Heights, seized from Syria during the 1967 war. The actions were moving in a rapid-fire fashion, to say the least.

The White House is not the only building in Washington where power is the currency of exchange. The Pentagon has its share of would-be power brokers. Regarding military planning for Libya, the Joint Chiefs of Staff had resisted conducting civilian-inspired contingency planning. Until there was a specific provocation for which military force might be an option, the Chiefs declined to do the bidding of the White House or the interagency groups that had the action on Libya. A military officer explained to me why. He said, "Preplanning does not get United States assets there any faster." And without a near-term provocation, officials of his ilk were even less inclined to plan.

Despite reservations about contingency planning in advance of a provocation, we were able to persuade the Chiefs to develop a spectrum of options for the application of force against Libya. But there was a precondition on which they insisted. They demanded a good-faith effort for a drawdown of the number of American citizens from Libya to its lowest possible level. As long as those who wanted to leave were required to leave, the Pentagon then was prepared to use force against Libya.

In the midst of bureaucratic warfare over politico-military contingency planning, there also can be some light moments. One occurred in the middle of a discussion regarding whether an American strike against Libya would heat up the border between Libya and Egypt. If the strike provided an incentive for President Mubarak to attack Libya, the United States might have had a full-scale war on its hands. In the middle of this weighty discourse on war, McFarlane leaned over to whisper something of grave import to me. With a twinkle in his eye, he said, "I don't have any Christmas presents, and it is so close to Christmas!" I nodded, knowingly, as generals and colonels imagined that we were commenting on their brilliant briefing about Libyan military contingencies.

In addition to turf battles, there were legal issues surrounding possible military action against Libya. The international legal authority for taking military action was Article 51 of the United Nations Charter, which allows for individual and collective self-defense. With respect to collective self-defense, the State Department's staff for Policy Planning took the position that the original justification for sanctions against Libya came from Egyptian and Sudanese complaints about Qadhafi's efforts to destabilize them. In addition to the defense of friendly countries like Egypt and the Sudan, there were direct threats from Libya to American citizens. The consensus was that any threats to American citizens or efforts to interfere with their departure from Libya would be regarded as grave provocations and would justify equally grave responses—a proportionality criterion. Additionally, the target should relate directly to the threat. Hence, targeting terror camps in Libya was a reasonable response to Libyan support for terrorism against American citizens.

With respect to the proportionality principle, if Libya launched a terror attack that did not cause loss of life, then economic sanctions would be a legitimate response; if terrorism resulted in a loss of life, then military force would be relevant. Although the State Department had pushed for proportionality, the Department of Defense expressed serious doubts about it. Defense also had reservations about State's suggestions to target oil-production facilities.

Another set of legal issues arose as to what kind of legal authority to use in reacting to Libya. Those who wished to impose broad-scale sanctions favored a maximalist legal authority. In a February 1, 1982, meeting on Libya, the topic for discussion, according to representatives from the White House and State Department, was how to punish Tripoli. Officials from Treasury and

Commerce, however, framed the topic differently. They assumed that the purpose of the meeting was not only to consider whether to punish Libya, but also whether there was a Libyan provocation sufficient to warrant use of certain legal instruments.

In terms of bureaucratic politics, the Commerce Department representative took strong exception to the pace at which decisions were being made. He said that a paper prepared for the meeting was couched as if decisions had already been taken. But without Libya engaging in a provocative incident, those decisions had no legal basis. He also charged that the paper assumed that once American citizens were out, economic sanctions were to be implemented, because the decision had already been made to do so. In fact, however, there had been no such decision. He demanded to know what act by Libya would have to take place that would justify invoking the International Emergency Economic Powers Act (IEEPA).[30]

One of the principles of the politics of policy making is that if you think opponents are going to slow down the momentum toward a preferred option of the group, be sure to exclude them from the meeting. Agencies that were involved with the economy tended to oppose sanctions on Libya, and some were excluded from interagency discussions because of their pro-trade, anti-export control position. The United States Trade Representative was not even on the list to receive one of the main papers that contained options for presidential decision on trade controls. Treasury and Commerce could not be excluded, however, but Justice could be cut out, even though the discussion involved legal interpretations.

A principle of bureaucratic politics is to seek to slow down the process of decision making when it is not going in the direction you favor. One method of delay is to cite laws that require consultation with allies. Those opposed to the rapid pace of decision making in regard to imposition of sanctions on Libya also favored the use of authorizing legislation that required consultation.

Because the Export Administration Act required consultation with allies, the Department of Justice was very concerned that consultation, in fact, be carried out. Regarding consultation over the imposition of sanctions on Libya, the question was whether to consult with intent to impose sanctions or impose sanctions with a plan to consult. We made a decision to act with the intention of consulting the allies. Irrespective of whether they were consulted to find out their views before or after making a decision, Treasury held that we needed to be very clear about what the United States was doing. For example, Treasury wanted the allies to know that Washington was not planning any measures of an extraterritorial nature.

The Commerce Department wanted to invite the Department of Justice to conduct a legal analysis of the issues prior to imposing sanctions. Regarding the favored instrument of choice by the foreign policy and national security community, IEEPA, an official from the Commerce Department compared it with a nuclear weapon. He said that if you only intended to use it partially, it should not be used at all. And if IEEPA had been employed when Libya began its state-sponsored terrorism, such use would have been more valid than introducing it after the fact.

Indeed, a Justice Department official, who had not been invited to a planning meeting about export controls for Libya, told me that in the absence of a clear provocation, it would be hard to justify the use of IEEPA. Because it is a drastic measure rather than selective controls, this act requires a provocation before use. Sanctions against the USSR, for example, were in the category of selective controls, and indeed Lyle Brady from Commerce wanted to place Libya in the same category as the USSR regarding high technology equipment. This position would mean proceeding under general licensing and imposing controls regarding oil and gas licensing. The Export Administration Act was the authority for controlling exports to the USSR, and that act could be used also against Libya.[31] Because there was little experience in the use of IEEPA—it might have been used only once before, in the Iran sanctions case—lawyers should have been present when discussing whether to invoke such a law.

Although IEEPA provided a firm legal basis for a broad range of economic measures, there were significant political disadvantages. The president had to find that policies and actions of the government of Libya constituted an extraordinary threat to national security, and he had to declare a national emergency regarding that threat. There was, however, interagency group agreement that IEEPA could have been invoked, given the broad threat Libyan policies pose to United

States interests: international terrorism, subversion of friendly states, and specific threats to target American assets and personnel.

McFarlane acknowledged that confirming the correct legal authority could have strengthened the interagency draft. But that concession did not result in a decision to postpone the move toward adopting drastic measures. And he also insisted on including in the paper that the government of Libya had to change its behavior. McFarlane held that the American public must be brought along to accept the hard-line action he was proposing. Cutting off oil early could set the stage for tougher measures later. He not only concerned himself with influencing the American public. He also focused on bureaucratic politics in Tripoli.

McFarlane thought that U.S. sanctions were necessary in order to influence political change in Libya. He surmised that an oil cutoff would encourage political opposition against a regime that had engaged in terrorism.

McFarlane recognized that there was bureaucratic opposition to the imposition of sanctions against Libya. Hence, he tried to act as if the President had already made a decision in principle to levy sanctions. Leland of the Department of Treasury strongly disagreed and asked what the legal justification was for invoking IEEPA. He questioned Libya's continued support for international terrorism generally or specifically the hit teams that Qadhafi had sent to the United States. That is, Leland wondered if these teams were still in America.[32]

In addition to this discussion of legal authorities, there was another set of legal issues that concerned the application of sanctions on Libya. The issues highlight the split in the bureaucracy between foreign policy and national security, on the one hand, and the criminal justice system, on the other hand. There were fights in the Reagan Administration in areas ranging from arms control to the Middle East.[33] Despite these fights, there was a conscious effort for an interagency group to work out trade-offs and priorities between foreign policy and national security as well as law enforcement. Although there were serious differences among the departments, there was almost a team approach to international terrorism.

By contrast, the Clinton Administration's procedures for managing international terrorism imply a less than unitary government. In the Clinton years, criminal justice agencies have come to the forefront of the decision-making process on international terrorism. There are troubling legal issues surrounding the growth of "globaloney" issues, such as terrorism, proliferation, and drugs. Consequently, there is a good chance that legal concerns may receive increasing weight in regard to sanctions.

Another set of legal issues concerning Libya arose in 1982. At that time, Edwin Wilson, a former CIA employee with sensitive technological information, defected and lived in Libya.[34] His situation illustrates the interplay of legal and foreign policy/national security concerns. The management of Wilson's defection by an interagency team in the Reagan years contrasts with the Clinton Administration's response to the bombing of American military installations in Saudi Arabia.[35] Both cases are at the intersection of national security and criminal justice. As part of my role on the National Security Council staff, I served as a White House liaison to the Department of Justice in the Wilson matter.

Wilson operated under the guise of being an exporter of civilian goods, but in actuality, he was an arms merchant trading in controlled, clandestine goods. He thus became a fugitive from the American legal system. He found refuge in Libya, where he may have been responsible for providing to Libyan agents the same kind of C-4 plastique that was used in the destruction of Pan Am 103 over Lockerbie, Scotland.[36]

The Department of Justice, FBI, and CIA negotiated terms of reference, from a criminal justice perspective, on how to apprehend Wilson. Once they agreed upon the terms, the Deputy General Counsel for Counterinsurgency briefed me. As the point man at the White House on the Libyan Task Force, I was charged with the responsibility to make sure that those in pursuit of Wilson take into account national security issues in the process of apprehending him.

The government of Libya took Wilson into custody on March 3, 1982, and kept him under virtual house arrest.[37] But when the FBI contacted Wilson in Libya, he was unaware that he was under house arrest there or even under restricted movement. In any event, a decision had to be made whether extradition of Wilson by Libya meant that it was following standard norms for criminal prosecution, or whether Qadhafi was trying to send a signal to Washington of a conciliatory nature. The American assumption was that good-faith extradition of a suspect to a third country like Germany would have implied little in the way of a political concession by the government of Libya.

But from the Libyan perspective, the same act of extradition could be seen as a signal that Qadhafi was in the mood to bargain. If he understood that Bonn intended to extradite Wilson to the United States, then Qadhafi thought he was being conciliatory. Tripoli had good reason to pursue a conciliatory policy during the spring of 1982: the United States was in the process of deciding the nature and scope of export controls that could have hurt the Libyan economy. Conciliation on the part of Qadhafi might have carried with it the expectation of reciprocity by the United States.

The Deputy Director for Intelligence at the CIA surmised that Qadhafi was attempting to be conciliatory by sacrificing Wilson. Libya, in fact, had sent its own deputy intelligence chief to the United States in order to sell Wilson down the river. The fact that Libya was willing to turn Wilson over to American authorities indicated that Qadhafi himself was frightened by the prospect of export controls and possible military escalation later. Indeed, the feeling around Libya was that the American marines were coming again to the shores of Tripoli. Although no officials in the Washington had given any indication that extraditing Wilson would result in any softening of U.S. hostility toward Libya, Qadhafi was, nevertheless, ready to make a deal.[38]

One question was whether Tripoli would extradite without a signal from Washington that a conciliatory gesture would in turn engender cooperation. The Deputy Director for Operations at the CIA interpreted Libyan willingness to sell out Wilson as a sign that Qadhafi was afraid and desperate. Justice and the FBI surmised that Libya expected a quid pro quo. In fact, extraditing Wilson may have been a move by Qadhafi to preempt the imposition of sanctions, for right in the middle of the spring 1982 consultations with the allies about Libyan sanctions, Qadhafi brought the Wilson case to a head.

Washington had to decide whether or not seizing Edwin Wilson was worth the risk of opening up a dialogue with Libya. If that entailed the implicit concession of legitimizing Tripoli's engagement in international terrorism, perhaps extraditing Wilson was not worth the price. Another downside of a dialogue would be to slow the momentum for imposing sanctions when the American-Libyan talks leaked to the press.

Justice wanted to open a dialogue with Libyan intelligence officials about getting Wilson, but deferred to State regarding the foreign policy considerations of such a colloquy. The General Counsel on the National Security Council staff told me that law enforcement did not entail diplomatic concessions. Hence, the United States government could cooperate with Libyan authorities to enforce American laws without implying any diplomatic concession to Libya.

But to avoid a foreign policy snafu, Justice contacted Wilson directly and offered to meet with him on neutral ground. Wilson had met with FBI agents before on impartial territory, but it had come to nothing. Wilson had negotiated with Justice about surrendering and entering into a plea-bargaining arrangement, but no agreement was reached.

The bureaucratic state of play in Washington over the Wilson case initially found the CIA and the FBI at odds over jurisdiction, but to its credit the CIA pulled out of the struggle. Just as the sanctions against Libya were about to kick in, the CIA deferred to the FBI.

Because of the legalities and sensitivities involved in the Wilson matter, the legal attaché at the American embassy in Bonn initially had the action, independent of the American ambassador, Arthur Burns. But this procedure conflicted with the established principle that the ambassador was *the* chief of the mission abroad. Because the legal attaché reported to the Department of Justice, State was cut out of the information loop and foreign policy considerations were not allowed to be weighed alongside criminal justice requirements. Subsequently, however, the legal attaché coordinated with the ambassador.

As a result of the need to weigh national security and criminal justice considerations at the same time, an interagency group in Washington was the coordinating mechanism. This procedure minimized bureaucratic warfare without hindering the process of apprehending a fugitive at large.[39] The management of the Wilson case suggests that bureaucratic politics need not hinder rational decision making and that there are, in fact, situations in which bureaucracy can function in the national interest.

In contrast to the Reagan Administration, the response by the Clinton Administration to the bombing of installations used by American military personnel in Saudi Arabia was one wrought with interagency confusion. The Department of Justice and the FBI took the lead in the investigation. But they did so at the expense of both the State Department and an orderly interagency process, either of which could have made sure that foreign policy and national security considerations were taken into account in the search for clues to the bombings. In this connection, in 1997 a newly appointed Secretary of State, Madeline Albright, found herself caught up in a bureaucratic snafu along with Attorney General Janet Reno and FBI Director Louis Freeh.

Reno and Freeh accused the Saudis of failure to cooperate in investigations regarding the terrorist bombings. Not only was it highly unusual for American officials to make public accusations against the main U.S. ally in the Gulf, but there is some doubt that the two Justice Department officials even spoke with the full authority of the administration. Kenneth Bacon, the Pentagon spokesman, and Nicholas Burns, the State Department spokesman, issued statements to the effect that the Justice Department represented the administration's thinking. But Michael McCurry, the White House spokesman, distanced President Clinton from the Attorney General and the FBI Director.[40] The fact that there were no agreed-upon points among press spokesmen from the White House, Justice, and State was an indication of the lack of an orderly interagency process.

## NATIONAL SECURITY VERSUS ECONOMIC PROFITS

In addition to the legal aspects of policy making, there are national security and economic battles. The primary fault line is between the White House and the State Department versus Treasury and Commerce. Because of the technical nature of decisions to impose sanctions, the economic departments possess influence well beyond their formal status in the cabinet. Treasury has an impact on the nature of the sanctions because of its knowledge of the sanctions procedures. Treasury officials can use persuasion in the sense that they know the details of the law of sanctions and can suggest unanticipated risks that might accrue from pursuing a course of action they oppose.

Likewise, Commerce can be persuasive to the extent that its officials can make informed estimates of the economic effects of sanctions and can cite industry attitudes on export controls. As with Treasury, officials from the Commerce Department are well acquainted with the technical portions of sanctions regimes, are aware of prior precedents in their application, and are a part of the permanent bureaucracy where rewards accrue to those in the know about arcane matters of fact. It was amusing to see prestigious practitioners of the "high policy" of national security being outfoxed by officials from departments that engage in the "low policy" of economic analysis. What looks like "administrivia" to a national security official may be perceived as a core concern to a person from the Commerce Department.

In the context of the battle between security and economics, return to our discussion on whether to impose export controls on Libyan oil and gas equipment. Treasury held that only in the context of a freeze on Libyan assets was a ban appropriate. Upon understanding this assertion, national security officials quickly agreed to a freeze on assets to go along with the proposal. But then, Treasury officials countered with the observation that freezing assets has two negative implications. First, it creates uncertainty that the United States is a reliable place for investments. And second, it creates problems regarding extraterritoriality with respect to American banks abroad.

Treasury also held that the only way to hurt Libya via economic sanctions was to regulate deliveries by wholly owned and subsidiaries of American companies. The trade-off, however, was that the allies were opposed to a U.S. claim of extraterritoriality, as well as any steps Washington might take that would endanger their oil supplies from Libya to European countries like Germany.

Treasury took the position that the American business community could not figure out what was different now as opposed to before regarding Libya. And Commerce officials favored an effort to persuade the allies to come on board. Without allied support, they were reluctant to move unilaterally against Libya. Commerce also held that whatever the United States decided to do against the allies regarding Libya should be consistent with earlier decisions concerning the Soviets' pipeline and the crackdown against Solidarity by Poland.[41]

But critics of the consensus viewpoint said that the use of embargoes for political purposes presupposed there had been a precise specification of what behavior should be changed before deciding to use force. They charged that the United States had not yet made clear what specific behavior Libya should change. Qadhafi had already yielded to pressure to withdraw troops from Chad, and the assassination team that was supposedly in the United States did not seem to be active when Washington imposed the embargo.

The critics decried the slippery slope of sanctions that would have the paradoxical effect of generating additional revenues for Libya. They charged that taking public action against Qadhafi would strengthen him within the Middle East region. How to proceed boiled down to whether to do so incrementally with limited actions in the absence of an explicit provocation, or to move quickly with comprehensive measures without clear provocation. Less extreme measures were not likely to have inflicted pain on Libya and might have provided Qadhafi with a pretext to expropriate property owned by American citizens. In any event, there was no evidence that any of the measures contemplated would inflict enough pain on Libya to warrant a change in its behavior.

The decision to impose unilateral sanctions on Libya by the Reagan Administration recognized that whether they were effective or not in changing behavior, they had to be imposed. There was a grand debate between foreign policy and national security officials on the one hand, and economic departments on the other. This debate reflected an interagency process that operated well as a means to vet differences and build consensus. While some players tried to suppress dissent about the imposition of unilateral sanctions, others made sure that dissenting opinions went forth to the highest levels of decision making.

## EFFECTS OF SANCTIONS AGAINST LIBYA

Rehabilitative aims of American unilateral sanctions against Libya are to compel Tripoli to stop its subversive behavior, terminate support for international terrorism, and cease efforts to procure or develop weapons of mass destruction, especially chemical weapons. Washington has renewed United States sanctions every six months since 1987.[42] These include a ban on the importation of Libyan crude oil into the United States, the freezing of almost $1 billion of Libyan assets, a prohibition on all hydrocarbon imports from Libya, a ban on U.S. oil companies from operating in Libya, and other measures.

Unilateral American sanctions have provided incentives for Tripoli to cease its efforts to subvert other governments. But Qadhafi began to withdraw his military forces from Chad even before Washington imposed sanctions on Tripoli. Nevertheless, the unilateral sanctions did reinforce Libya's decision to withdraw, and there have been fewer efforts on the part of Tripoli to subvert other regimes than before the sanctions. With respect to Libya's support for international terrorism, unilateral American sanctions have raised the cost to Tripoli for sponsoring groups like that of Abu Nidal, who leads a terrorist group that has received funding, logistical support, and instructions from Tripoli.[43] Also, there has been a decline in Libyan state-sponsorship of international terrorism. But that decrease may be attributed more to multilateral United Nations sanctions than to American export and import controls. In regard to Libya's efforts to acquire chemical weapons, American sanctions have been irrelevant at best and perhaps counterproductive at worst.

But sanctions for retribution are always effective. If they make important domestic political constituencies feel good, they achieve their purpose. Embargoes on Libya fulfill a basic American distaste for despotism. Tyrants such as Qadhafi are natural targets for sanctions. Americans feel genuinely satisfied with their detrimental effects on Libya, being staunch moral capitalists who love to retaliate against those who have committed acts of evil. American ideals permit nothing less than counteraction. The manner in which Libya became a part of the Iran Sanctions bill illustrates the role of retribution in the policy-making process.

At the behest of the survivors of the Pan Am 103 bombing, Senator Edward Kennedy inserted Libya into the Iran Sanctions bill while it was on the Senate floor. It later became the Iran and Libya Sanctions Act of 1996. The families of the victims of the Lockerbie crash are the most important political constituency concerning retributive justice in regard to Libya. As a concession to them, Senator

Alfonse D'Amato agreed to include Libya in the Iran legislation. The president invited the families to the signing ceremony in August 1996. This gesture is indicative of the act's political significance.[44]

In addition to retribution, sanctions are designed to have negative economic consequences. But the unilateral trade embargo imposed by the United States has had no major economic effects on Libya. One reason is that the items sanctioned by the United States can be purchased from other nations or sold to other countries.[45] Indeed, American economic sanctions may have had the unintended effect of enhancing the long-term economic performance of the Libyan economy. Since the American trade embargo went into effect, Qadhafi's regime has launched a successful campaign to attract financial investments from companies based in Europe.

Tripoli has provided incentives for European-based oil firms to make massive investments in Libya. After the American sanctions on Libya, Tripoli signed new oil and gas exploration, production, as well as oil development agreements with European oil companies. In addition, the Oil Investments International Company, owned by the government of Libya, purchased a majority interest in several refineries in Europe. As of the mid-1990s, it controlled over 300,000 barrels per day of capacity and owned some 3,300 service stations. A consequence of such control and ownership has been to allow Libya to influence part of its oil market, Europe, which is Tripoli's only importer.[46]

The passage of the Iran and Libya Sanctions Act of 1996 would deny export licenses, loans, and credit guarantees to European and other oil companies investing over a threshold amount—$40 million per year—in the Libyan energy sector. This act is a secondary boycott. It not only punishes firms that invest in Libya, but is also bound to have a great, long-term, negative effect on the Libyan economy. By drying up investment funds from European oil and gas companies, the act will eventually cause erosion in the productivity of the Libyan energy sector.

In addition to unilateral United States sanctions, there are also multilateral United Nations sanctions. These controls are designed to induce the government of Libya to hand over the suspects implicated in the airline bombing over Lockerbie. They have been renewed about every three months. Because the suspects are charged with bombing an airliner, the punishment includes prohibitions on Libyan civil aviation. With respect to the effectiveness of multilateral sanctions, they have had no apparent success in coercing compliance. And regarding their effects on the economic status of Libya, one has to take with a grain of salt the many complaints that began coming out of Tripoli after the United Nations sanctions were imposed. At any one time, Tripoli has had a tendency to announce that it has been severely hurt by whatever penalties happen to be in effect.

Tripoli claims that multilateral sanctions have cost the Libyan economy over $19 billion in trade and more than 21,000 lives due to denied foreign medical treatment. It is difficult to believe these figures because Tripoli has an incentive to inflate the negative effects of sanctions. Because trade continues, mainly with Germany and Italy, sanctions against Libya are, according to one authority, an "inconvenience rather than a serious hindrance."[47]

Regarding the rehabilitative effects of the American sanctions, there have not been any major changes in Libya's behavior. If what has been sanctioned by one country can be purchased from another, unilateral sanctions are bound to be ineffective. If anything, the sanctions have both beneficial long-term economic and political effects for Libya. Implementing a containment policy on Libya has stimulated a self-defense effort. Tripoli has succeeded in attracting foreign investments that have strengthened the regime.

But the Iran and Libya Sanctions Act has a greater negative potential effect on Libya than prior unilateral sanctions. By denying loans, export licenses, and letters of credits to European oil companies that make large investments in Libya, non-American companies have begun to invest less in Libya. Given the overwhelming sentiment of the American business community and European nations, the question arises as to why the act passed the U.S. Congress in a unanimous vote.

## Politics and Idealism
### Trump Profits and Alliance Obligations

In the clash between foreign policy and national security versus economic interests there is no contest. Foreign policy and national security interests found powerful allies in the bureaucracy who were able and willing to fight in defense of high policy over low policy. But business interests reinforced by the actions of the allies caused Libyan policy to be compromised and/or delayed. The overall direction of a policy of containment via sanctions, however, could not be turned around by an alignment of Libya lovers.

The order of battle in the war for Washington had two sides. On one side was a coalition of business firms interested in making profits from trade with Libya, bureaucrats from governmental agencies concerned with trade, and allied governments. On the other was an alignment of the survivors of victims of Pan Am 103, the pro-Israel community, and idealists who would act retributively to punish the tyrant from Tripoli.

In addition to traditional politics practiced by ethnic interest groups, business organizations also are players in American politics. By contributing to political campaigns, businesses hope that they are purchasing a seat at the foreign policy table. Consider the case of the Occidental Petroleum Corporation.[48] During 1997, this firm sought to negotiate a portion of a $930 million oil-exploration project with the Sudan. But Khartoum is an ally of Tehran and politically close to Tripoli. In addition, the Sudan is on the State Department's list of nations that sponsor international terrorism. Antiterrorism legislation bars American companies from doing business with countries on that list. It names seven countries as sponsors of international terrorism, but only five are subject to comprehensive embargoes—Iran, Iraq, Libya, Cuba, and North Korea. Two states escaped sweeping trade embargo status: Syria and the Sudan.

The Anti-Terrorism Act of 1996 permits financial dealings with Syria and the Sudan if these transactions are found not to have an impact on any potential act of terrorism. Syria was subject to less restrictive terms in the 1996 Anti-Terrorism Act because the United States wanted to encourage that country's participation in the Arab-Israel peace process. There has not been any explanation why these same terms applied to the Sudan, which is not a participant in the peace process. Here is where politics may enter the picture. Occidental is an active player in national politics. The U.S. Federal Election Commission indicates that Occidental donated about $600,000 to the two major political parties in 1995 and 1996, including $100,000 to the Democrats during March 1996. President Clinton signed the Anti-Terrorism Act a month later.

Irrespective of the political influence of the business community, however, ethnic political groups have lined up their vectors with those of American idealism and constitute an effective lobby on behalf of sanctions. Thus, Representatives Bill McCollum (Rep.-Florida) and Charles Shumer (Dem.-New York) introduced early in 1997 a bill to close the loophole that favored Occidental and the Sudan. These two members of the House are politically close to the pro-Israel community, and they acted within the context of traditional American idealism against international terrorism. In this respect, McCollum stated, "The only way we are going to eliminate the governmental support terrorist organizations need is to take a firm stance against economic relationships with these countries."[49]

Foreign policy and national security triumph because they converge with ideals and domestic politics. Strategic interests of antisubversion, counterterrorism, and nonproliferation are not only interests; they are ideals as well. Americans do not support regimes that have little regard for human rights. Despots who murder people, blow up civilian aircraft, and espouse revolutionary violence are ripe for the imposition of sanctions. American ideology revolves around the sanctity of human life. Americans do not tolerate barbarians who scorn these ideals. And when domestic groups buttress ideals and strategic interests, these factors constitute a formidable joint effect on American foreign policy and national security affairs.

One reason politics and idealism are so influential in the Libyan case is the unexpected convergence of two dissimilar interest groups: the pro-Israel community and the families of the victims of Pan Am 103. Libya has allies on Wall Street, who seek to profit from trading with an enemy of the United States. But Libya has few allies on Main Street. Hence, in the war for Main Street, Colonel Qadhafi seeks allies.

## THE WAR FOR THE AMERICAN STREET

There are wars in the Middle East and wars in the Middle West. The wars in the Middle East, in part, aim to sway Arab public opinion toward the agenda of ruling elites. Mass opinion is often called the "Arab street." Likewise, there is a war in the United States for public opinion, as Libya fights for the hearts and minds of Muslim-Americans in general and the African-American community in particular. In the section above on the politics of policy making, there is a discussion of the war for Washington, where there are battles between national security officials and those in economic organizations. In addition, the section concludes that bureaucratic politics and idealism are more important than economic profits and alliance obligations in explaining Washington's decisions to impose sanctions on Libya.

Despite American and United Nations sanctions, Qadhafi remains noncompliant. He tries in vain to reassert himself as a major force in the mainstream Islamic community. But due to his notoriety, even among fellow Arab leaders, Qadhafi has been shut out of the many circles of influence. Attempted assassinations and abortive conflicts with neighbors like Egypt and Chad have rightly cast him as a pariah. As such, Qadhafi has turned to nonconventional means of remaining in the spotlight. He knowingly harbors the two suspects in the bombing of Pan Am 103. These two Libyan intelligence agents top the FBI's most wanted list. They are optimal prizes to keep sequestered within Libya's borders.

In addition to harboring suspects from the international community, Qadhafi engages in a search for allies within the American community. He has a history of lending rhetorical and financial support to various dissident groups in the United States. He gave over $300,000 to the Black Panthers during the 1970s.[50] Furthermore, Qadhafi has made contact with the Nation of Islam, headed by Minister Louis Farrakhan.

Farrakhan is an American Muslim to whom Qadhafi has offered $1 billion. Ostensibly, the money is for the purpose for helping the Nation of Islam to work in poor African-American communities. But because of U.S. sanctions against Libya, the Department of Justice ruled that Farrakhan could not accept the offer. The Department monitored his visits to Libya, Iraq, and other rogue regimes while on a tour of pariah countries. Farrakhan visited sixteen nations on a so-called World Friendship Tour.

In entering Libya during his tour, Farrakhan broke the American sanctions regulations. By law, all transportation-related transactions involving Libya by American citizens are prohibited. These consist of the sale in the United States of any transportation by air that includes any stop in Libya. For Farrakhan, the junket had been one to foster unity among Muslims on a global scale. By simply allowing the American "leader" into Libya, Qadhafi purchased political unrest in American domestic politics.

The response to Farrakhan's visit was outrage in Washington. Members of Congress referred to it as a "thugfest tour."[51] White House spokesman McCurry said, "He met with some of the most brutal dictators and leaders of nations that the United States considers pariah states." According to the State Department, Farrakhan was "cavorting with dictators" who had "American blood on their hands."[52]

Allegations abounded that Qadhafi was looking to disrupt American politics. Representative Bob Barr (Rep.-Georgia) said it all when he stated, "Muammar Qadhafi pledged $1 billion to Mr. Farrakhan's Nation of Islam to be used here in this country to . . . improperly influence the American political systems."[53] The Justice Department responded by sending Farrakhan a letter asking him if he planned to register as an agent of Qadhafi as defined by the Foreign Agent Registration Act.

In response, Louis Farrakhan played exactly the role Qadhafi intended by taking a defiant, disruptive stance. He replied to government statements and inquiries by daring the United States to stop him from taking the money. He asserted that he would use the money to build homes and schools, yet there have been no definitive instructions as to how the money would be used. If he is expected to perform any services in return for this "gift," those have not been reported either. As seen above, there is suspicion that Farrakhan will use the money in support of Libyan policies in the United States. But Farrakhan denies any charges that the money is not legal. In open challenge to the U.S. government, he stated, "We're using the money to clean up the mess that you made. Whatever Qadhafi gives me, I'm going to ask you to match it." Farrakhan also paraphrased the Prophet Muhammad in his own defense, "He [Qadhafi] is my friend. He is my brother. Your enemy ain't mine unless I'm your slave."[54]

Farrakhan's aims and objectives are to further Muslim unity and prosperity. In and of themselves, these objectives seem legitimate. But to use the assistance of a Libyan regime dedicated to the use of terrorism against the United States is illegitimate. By choosing to associate himself with Qadhafi, he undercuts his own legitimacy with the American people. He acts as a "useful fool" for Qadhafi, disrupting domestic American politics in a manner that puts the legal responsibility on Farrakhan while giving Qadhafi much needed attention.

The U.S. government may not be able to prevent Qadhafi from giving Farrakhan $1 billion. Qadhafi knows this constraint and so offers the money to a man who calls Judaism a "gutter religion."[55] The offer forces the United States to choose whether or not to violate its own sanctions. Should the government uphold the sanctions, Farrakhan can claim racism and gain political capital and the moral high ground in the American Muslim community. If the government allows the donation, Colonel Qadhafi wins the high ground of having successfully evaded the sanctions. His political agenda is served by Farrakhan's collaboration.

In the war for the American street, Qadhafi seeks to separate the black American Muslim community from other Americans. What he does not understand, however, is that American society is based on a vision of the future that acknowledges religious and racial differences yet transcends them in the pursuit of the American dream. From our origins as observed by de Tocqueville to the contemporary beliefs of Martin Luther King, Jr., Americans judge one another on many different levels. As such, the hateful rhetoric of Farrakhan and Qadhafi falls short. The future of the American street will remain American as long as Qadhafi and his ilk are kept at bay.

## A SCENARIO

### Historical Precedents for Renewal of Military Action

Consider prior confrontations between Tripoli and Washington as a basis for creating scenarios for the future. The Colonel is in "good company" in trying to deter the United States from taking military action. That crowd includes the likes of Saddam Hussein. He promised the world a "mother of all battles" as a means to frighten away challengers from across the seas.[56] And Qadhafi drew a mythical line in the water—the "Line of Death"—across which American warships would pass only at great risk.[57] Neither Saddam Hussein's battle nor Muammar Qadhafi's line proved to be so frightening as their rhetoric implied.

With respect to Libya, the American navy successfully challenged the international waters of the Gulf of Sidra in August 1981. And in January 1986, the United States initiated another challenge based on the 1981 model when the navy began a series of escalating military exercises in the Gulf of Sidra. The goal was to increase pressure on Libya. And on March 24, 1986, the enhanced compulsion took the form of a freedom of navigation challenge. Libya responded with force. But the Pentagon's rules of engagement allowed American commanders on the scene to make a disproportionate retaliation. This encounter in the Gulf of Sidra in March 1986 resulted in the destruction of two Libyan ships by U.S. navy vessels.

On Saturday, April 5, 1986, a bomb exploded in La Belle disco in Berlin, a club frequented by American troops. My former colleagues in the White House, Howard Teicher and Oliver North, reviewed a transcript of two electronic intercepts from the People's Bureau [Libyan Embassy] in East Berlin to Libyan intelligence headquarters.[58] As a result of this evidence of Libyan complicity, President Reagan gave the order to retaliate against Libya. And on April 15, 1986, United States warplanes bombed sites in Libya declared by the President to be "terrorist centers." The planes damaged one of Qadhafi's homes at one of the barracks and unfortunately killed his infant daughter. But they inflicted major damage on other sites that were military in nature.

If Qadhafi were deterrable, Washington's 1986 air strikes could have served to deter him from further adventures. He would have tempered his desire for anti-American actions, his sponsorship of international terrorism, and his development of weapons of mass destruction. The world would have seen a reformed, quieted Qadhafi.

Though the air strike crippled his morale, Qadhafi's anti-Western fear and hatred still served to strengthen his political base. In 1986, there was growing opposition against Qadhafi, but the American air strikes rallied the Libyan people around their symbol against imperialism. His personal defiance tapped into the collective national experience of being dominated by outside forces. Qadhafi learned to hate the West through watching the imperialist powers "pillage" his country. By personally defying Washington, Qadhafi is trying to bolster national unity behind him. In this respect, Washington's sanctions paradoxically encourage the Colonel to resist the United States at any cost.

Just as the Colonel is isolated in the world community, he is slowly being shut out of the Arab world.[59] If Qadhafi were shunned by other Arab nations, then his goal of pan-Arabism would be unrealized. In this regard, Qadhafi may be motivated by fear of loss. His fear of losing prominence may cause him to act in defiance of the West in a pathetic attempt to increase his importance on the world stage.

Before launching assaults against Libya, the United States interagency process analyzed at least two options. As described by Howard Teicher, a senior player at the White House in that confrontation, here is what took place.[60] By early 1985, Vincent Cannistrato, a CIA officer detailed to the National Security Council staff as head of the Intelligence Directorate, had the action on devising new methods to increase pressure on Qadhafi. He had been head of the CIA Libya task force and wrote a paper on U.S. vulnerabilities and opportunities in attempt to influence Qadhafi via covert actions.

Option one of the Cannistrato paper called for a limited, phased strategy to resume air and naval challenges in the Gulf of Sidra. This option assumed that there would be increased restrictions on American citizens doing business in Libya. The paper did not rule out joint planning with Egypt, but focused on how to respond to Libyan actions. Option two intended to oust Qadhafi from power and assumed military planning with Egypt and Algeria as well as covert support that included assistance to Libyan dissidents.

Vice President Bush, Secretary of State Shultz, Director of Central Intelligence Casey, and National Security Advisor McFarlane supported option two. Secretary of Defense Weinberger and the Joint Chiefs of Staff opposed any strategy that would entail the use of force. Their reasoning was that the purposes were too unclear and that not enough attention had been given to a likely Soviet response to American attempts to destabilize Libya.

Washington adopted option one—working with Cairo to destabilize Libya and unseat Colonel Qadhafi. But President Mubarak of Egypt vetoed this option in a meeting during 1985 between him and Poindexter. Libya had given support for the Abu Nidal terrorists who skyjacked an Egyptian airliner in 1985 and had conducted massacres in the Rome and Vienna airports. On the basis of this evidence, President Reagan decided to retaliate, but Mubarak declined to join the initiative.

During the late 1970s, there was a military confrontation between Libya and Egypt. President Sadat had asked the Carter Administration to cooperate with him to unseat Qadhafi. Carter, however, vetoed the option of conducting coordinated military planning with Cairo for an attack against Libya. Because Mubarak was Sadat's Vice President, he should have known that an American president had backed down from a joint Cairo-Washington military initiative against Tripoli. The early 1980s found Mubarak in a position to thwart an American initiative against Libya. Despite the lack of Egyptian support, U.S. military planning moved forward.

With respect to the bureaucratic politics of the 1985 contingency planning, State and Defense were in disagreement. State was in favor of air strikes against Libya, and Defense was not. Secretary of Defense Weinberger opposed retaliation and warned the president that air strikes would endanger the large number of American citizens in Libya and create a hostage-taking situation.

American oil companies continued to operate in Libya. The firms pumped hundreds of thousands of barrels of oil per day. The Department of Defense also expressed doubts about the complicity of Libya in the attacks against the Rome and Vienna airports. In spite of the Pentagon's opposition, the president decided to retaliate.[61]

## Renewal of Hostilities

Over a decade later, in the late 1990s, the likelihood of another confrontation is increasing between Tripoli and Washington. In contrast to the 1986 air strikes, hostilities at the close of the century are likely to be on the land and seas. In an implicit threat to use military force, Defense Secretary William Perry said on April 3, 1996, that the United States would not allow Libya to complete an underground chemical weapons facility. Perry made the remark to reporters after discussing the factory with Egyptian President Mubarak.

As opposed to his position a decade earlier, Mubarak was on board the American contingency planning team. Perry said that he had discussed a variety of evidence with Mubarak. "I showed him photographs," Perry said. "They demonstrate that the Libyans are not now producing chemical weapons, but they have an extensive program under way to develop a chemical weapons production facility." In order for serious military contingency planning to go forward, it is crucial for Mubarak to stay on board.

Western intelligence agencies hold that Libya is building a chemical weapons factory at Tarhunah, 40 miles southeast of Tripoli, the Libyan capital. The plant is reportedly being built into a mountain, which would make it difficult to destroy in a military strike. Asked if the United States would allow completion, Perry simply replied: "No."[62] The Tarhunah facility is designed to replace a plant at Rabta, 55 miles southwest of Tripoli. The Rabta facility was reopened in the fall of 1996, five years after damage from a suspicious fire. Libya insists that it only manufactures pharmaceutical agents there.

Renewal of military action might come from an incremental escalation in the Gulf of Sidra or a decision to prevent the completion of the chemical weapons facility. In this regard, it is very likely that there will be a resumption in hostilities between Tripoli and Washington before the end of the century.[63]

In summary, the U.S. perceives post–Cold War threats from Libya and has imposed sanctions on Tripoli. Because the allies see greater future dangers if American sanctions destabilize Libya, there is a transatlantic schism in threat perceptions and policies between America and Europe. Despite the gap between the allies, the United States appears destined to resume military confrontation with Libya.

In light of the high likelihood in the resumption of hostilities, recall the four themes that cut across *Rogue Regimes*: threat perception, opportunities, politics, and policies. On the basis of high threat perception, the United States is willing to trade off economic opportunities concerning Libya. In addition, domestic politics provide incentives for American presidents to devise confrontational policies toward Libya. As was the case for Iran and Iraq, bureaucratic and domestic politics are keys to the American policy process regarding Libya.

And with respect to threats in the international system, Libya is a rogue elephant that is a fitting substitute for the Soviet bear. But given the different perceptions of threat and opportunity between the United States and its allies about Libya, it is difficult to fashion policies that are effective in changing that regime's behavior. Because of the low likelihood that rehabilitative goals can be easily achieved, punishment may be based on the idea of deterrence by denial. That is, Washington takes military steps that weaken Tripoli's capacity to practice international terrorism and develop weapons of mass destruction. Finally, retribution also provides ample grounds for continuing a policy of containment rather than accommodation.

## CHAPTER FIVE

# SYRIA: CONTAIN OR EMBRACE

## PERSONALITY, POLITICS, AND POLICIES

AS THE 1970S CAME TO A CLOSE, multiple crises converged in the Middle East, and their effects rained down upon the padded walls of the White House Situation Room. These crises enhanced the American perception of dangers from the Middle East. The fall of the Shah and rise of the Ayatollah Khomeni in Iran, the Soviet invasion of Afghanistan, and the Iran-Iraq War threatened Western oil supplies in the Gulf zone. These events also had a potential for spilling over into the Arab-Israel conflict zone. One nation that serves as a link across these two subregions of the Middle East is Syria. It is aligned with Iran against Iraq, is in conflict with Turkey over terrorists based in Damascus, and remains in a no-peace, no-war status with Israel. Hence, it is a state with ties from the Mediterranean to the Gulf. And Syria has an absolute ruler whose forceful personality has a major effect on the foreign policy of his country—President Hafez al-Assad, who took power in 1970.

Besides Israel and Turkey, most of the Arab states of the Middle East are in the grips of absolute rulers. Whether secular like Assad, or religious like the ayatollahs of Iran, these states are personified by their rulers. As president of Syria, Assad is a compelling character. Because the government is for the most part under his sole control, any examination of U.S.-Syrian relations should begin with Assad, the man.[1]

Conventional wisdom about Assad is that he is a rational, patient, and cunning head of state. He rarely makes a move unless he is fairly certain that the outcome is in his best interest. And while his judgments are not always correct in retrospect, the assumption is that he manifests a strong tendency to err on the side of caution. Unlike his main contemporary Arab competitor, Saddam Hussein, Assad is thought to be averse to gambles. According to this interpretation, it would be hard to imagine Assad playing a lottery with its low likelihood of success. Unlike Saddam Hussein, it would be difficult to conceive of Assad ordering the invasion of Kuwait, thereby risking the formation of a Western coalition that could oust his invasion forces and destroy most of them in the process.

But the conditional wisdom fails to take account of Assad's risk-taking propensity in regard to the peace process. Consider the contrasting perspective adopted here. Assad is a leader fearful that the world will accept Israel's occupation of the Golan Heights as permanent; as a result, he may be willing to take risks in the peace process in order to effect the return of the Golan. While the traditional view lets Assad off the hook on making concessions, the alternative assumes that he is able to take chances for peace. The question is whether he is willing to take chances for peace, in light of his aspiration to lead the Arab Nation.

Obsessed with his legacy, Assad yearns to be viewed as the primary leader of the Arab world. Such a role would be a means to the end of restoring the grandeur and respect evoked by the term Greater Syria of past centuries, the exemplar of the pan-Arab ideal.[2] But Assad's vision of himself does not quite jibe with reality. While he may very well be the linchpin in the Arab-Israel peace process, he is hardly its lead voice. But it would be difficult to conceive of a comprehensive settlement between Israel and Syria without Assad's consent in its formulation and implementation, though few expect him to take the lead in the peace process. He is more likely to let the game come to him than to try to take over the game, to borrow a sports metaphor. Assad is no Anwar Sadat, the late president of Egypt who took over the entire peace process with his trip to Jerusalem. In contrast to Assad, who reacts to the initiatives of others, Sadat stimulated an ongoing peace process that led to an accord between Egypt and Israel.[3]

Assad has an impact on policies by dominating the political process. The ayatollahs of Iran, Saddam of Iraq, and Qadhafi of Libya are all ruthless characters who cast a long shadow over their political systems. Because of their ability to operate command systems, they could shift policy almost with a snap of a finger. But even their individual strengths have to overcome domestic political constraints.

A dictator like Assad readily fits in the ranks of rogue rulers who have the ability to make major changes in foreign policy. But he also has domestic political costs to pay for the exercise of power.[4] Assad belongs to the Alawite minority within Syria.[5] Middle East expert Daniel Pipes contends, "An Alawite ruler in Damascus is repugnant to most Syrians."[6] As a result, Assad is constrained from taking bold steps necessary to make a genuine peace with Israel, according to the view of Assad as a risk-averse leader. Other constraints that limit his actions concern the economic dimension. Syria has suffered greatly from the removal of Soviet patronage.[7] And because of the economic cost to Syria due to the collapse of the USSR, Assad should be less willing to take chances in the peace process.

In deciding whether Assad is risk-averse or risk-acceptant, consider his actions in the Arab-Israel peace process. During the decade of 1979-1989, Damascus initially criticized Cairo's peace with Israel. Then Syria abruptly moved back into an alignment with Egypt: following the Gulf War in 1991, Damascus decided to take part in the American-sponsored Arab-Israel peace conference in Madrid.[8] Although there were political protests within Syria about Assad's anti-Saddam policy, he overcame these objections and joined the peace process.

With his reluctance both to take chances and make bold moves, two questions about Assad arise. First, has he made a strategic commitment to the Arab-Israel peace process with its explicit recognition of Israel's right to exist as an independent state in the Middle East? And, second, has he made only a tactical adjustment in a long-term process to weaken Israel as a prelude to its destruction?

On the one hand, if Assad has made a strategic commitment to the peace process, then the United States could build on this shift, accommodate Damascus, and embrace Syria as a partner in the process. On the other hand, if Assad has made a tactical move en route to wearing down and destroying Israel, a policy of containment and even confrontation would be advisable for Washington. Appeasement would occur if Assad were to make a tactical move to weaken Israel and the United States made concessions to him in order to reverse his course of action. Two schools of thought dominate the debate about Assad's intentions. Both assume that his personality has a great impact on the foreign policy of Syria.

The first camp assumes an action-reaction sequence. Syrian policy is more a result of the external environment than its internal milieu. The second camp makes the opposite assumption. The first perspective presumes that changes in the balance of power allow for a shift in Syrian foreign policy toward a political settlement with Israel. The second viewpoint presupposes that domestic politics and economic factors constrain Assad's freedom of action and prohibit him from making concessions necessary for peace.[9] The first camp focuses on international factors as incentives for Assad's risk-acceptant personality. The second camp emphasizes national, political, and economic attributes as incentives for his risk-aversion.

A representative of the first approach is an Israeli scholar, Moshe Maoz.[10] He holds that Assad has made a strategic commitment to make peace with Israel. An emissary of the second approach is an American specialist, Daniel Pipes. He believes that Assad has made only a tactical adjustment in policy as a means to regain the Golan Heights from Israel.[11]

Maoz contends that President Assad has accepted the principle of a political settlement to the conflict with Israel, albeit on his own terms. During late 1973, Syria adopted UN Security Council Resolution 338. It incorporated Resolution 242, which called for peace with Israel in return for withdrawal from occupied territories. But Resolution 338 goes beyond 242 and calls for direct talks among the parties. Since 1988, moreover, Assad has given priority to a political solution instead of a military option.

Assad made a strategic decision in favor of a diplomatic solution because of economic difficulties and changes in Soviet policy that occurred even before the collapse of the USSR in 1991.[12] In addition to changes at the global level, there were regional transitions that prompted a shift in Syrian policy. The elections in Israel were one such change within the region.

Following the 1992 election of Yitzhak Rabin as prime minister of Israel, Assad noted a flexible policy by Israel toward Syria in general and the Golan Heights in particular. With respect to threat perception, Assad may have had an unmotivated bias to see what he expected to see. For example, he expected that the transition in Israel from the Likud to the Labor Party would bring with it a softening of conditions under which Israel would withdraw from the Golan. Because Labor has a reputation of being more flexible in the peace process, Assad may have expected flexibility in the Israeli negotiating stand. Whatever biases operated, Assad acted to decrease the threat from Israel rather than to increase it. As a result of a lower threat perception, Assad has been ready to sign a full peace agreement with Israel, provided it withdrew from the entire Golan Heights and southern Lebanon.

If there is not a political accord reached between Israel and Syria, Damascus is likely to sustain its ideological motivation and military preparation to fight Israel over the Golan Heights. Syria also is likely to enhance its political support for Hezbollah's war of attrition against Israel in southern Lebanon. While strengthening its strategic alignment with Iran, Syria would seek to sabotage Israel's rapprochement with the Palestinians and with Arab states that are contemplating a political settlement.

In contrast, an accord with Israel might reduce the militant intentions of Damascus, weaken its military ties with Iran, and expand Syria's economic development. Additionally, an agreement would foster progress toward peace between Israel and the Palestinians and encourage other Arab states to establish normal relations with the Jewish state.[13]

The Maoz school assumes that Assad not only has made a commitment to make peace with Israel, but that he also has the power and resolve to force an accord upon an unwilling populace. This approach presumes that Assad desires to avoid losing the Golan to permanent Israeli control so much that he would risk his hold on absolute power.[14] This school assumes that Assad focuses more on what he would lose from failure to take part in the peace process than from what he would gain by taking tactical advantage of Israel. Alternatively, he may be willing to run high risks in the peace process in order to avoid domestic political losses: turning his back on the prospect for a peaceful return of the Golan Heights could significantly damage his hold on power.[15]

The Pipes school holds that existence of an enemy, Israel, is a main basis for Assad's rule. If peace with Israel were established, Assad would find himself without a major external threat. The majority anti-Israel Sunni population could turn its hostilities upon the ruling minority Alawites, from which Assad comes. Syria has been in a state of emergency, justified by its war with Israel, since 1963. As a result of the threat perceived from Israel, Assad can justify his oppressive security apparatus. The Pipes approach implies that Assad would magnify the threat from Israel in order to bolster his domestic political position. In this regard, there are motivated biases for threat magnification. Assad stands to gain from overestimation of threat. He sees what he wants to see—a threat from Israel that allows him to sustain his power base.

Remove the potential of war in the Middle East, and it would be nearly impossible, even for Assad, not to lift the state of emergency and refrain from political crackdowns on potential opponents to his rule. If Assad feared domestic pressures as much as losing his chance to regain the Golan Heights, he would not be as cautious in his decisions to make peace, according to the Pipes approach.

But the Pipes approach overlooks the role that Assad's ruthlessness plays in maintaining his power. Just as Assad ordered the killing of thousands of Islamist rebels in the city of Hama during February 1982, he should be willing to enforce a peace accord with Israel. But Pipes would contend that Assad does not want to regain the Golan Heights so much that he would risk his hold on absolute power.

The Maoz versus Pipes debate raises the issue of Assad's priorities—whether he fears permanent loss of the Golan Heights or the possibility of losing office.[16] But Assad may frame the problem in such a fashion that he denies a need to make a trade-off between the peace process to acquire the Golan and continuation of his reign in Syria.[17] For example, Assad may assume that he can engage in a peace process to acquire the Golan Heights and remain in power in Damascus.

This rationale derives from three factors. The dissolution of the Soviet Union, the absence of Moscow as a patron of Damascus, and the presence of Syria in the American-led Gulf War coalition are three reasons Maoz puts forth to explain Assad's strategic commitment to peace. The Pipes approach, however, would downplay the significance of these external events. Rather, for him, the main forces driving Syrian foreign policy are internal political constraints on Assad. When Syria encountered terrorist bombings in December 1996, Pipes would hold that this instability reflected domestic political dissent that would, in turn, explain why Assad would not make peace with Israel.

Consistent with Pipes' reasoning, instead of blaming the opposition, however, Damascus accused Jerusalem of fomenting unrest.[18] These domestic factors are incentives to maintain a state of no-peace, no-war with Israel. Consequently, Assad has not made a commitment to make peace with Israel, according to the Pipes perspective. The United States should refrain from accommodating Syria and should avoid embracing Assad. Therefore, containment and perhaps confrontation would be the best course of action, based on Assad's personality and political constraints under which he operates in Syria.

Pipes also asserts that the Golan Heights is not a key issue for Syria in the peace process with Israel. Rather, maintaining Israel as an enemy is of utmost importance in cementing Assad's hold on power. Maoz, in contrast, claims that the reacquisition of the Golan Heights and southern Lebanon has consistently been demanded in negotiations with Israel. While Pipes contends that it is Assad's fear of losing power in Syria that influences him not to make concessions in the peace process, Maoz suggests that the fear of forever losing the Golan Heights is what influences Assad to negotiate. Despite the anti-Israel majority in Syria and risk of domestic repercussions, Assad is willing to take the chance for a peaceful return of the Golan.

In short, Maoz contends that it is a fear of never regaining the Golan Heights that propels Assad's risk-acceptant attitude in favor of peace; Pipes claims that it is Assad's fear of domestic political losses that encourages him to be risk-averse in the peace process. The Pipes approach is the conventional wisdom about Assad: he is a rational, patient, and cunning politician. In other words, that wisdom assumes that Assad is cautious to a fault, that he is averse to gambles. In fact, however, Assad has been a risk-taker in aligning with the United States against Saddam Hussein and in joining the Madrid peace process with Israel.[19]

Both schools attribute Assad's actions to fears—but different ones. While the Maoz approach is able to justify Assad's risky behavior in the basement of fear, the Pipes approach is less able to explain why he is acting cautiously. The Maoz school is able to provide reasons why Assad is willing to jeopardize political stability in Syria through involvement in the Arab-Israel peace process. The Pipes school, in turn, cannot do so as well.

## CONTAIN OR EMBRACE

Given these two contending sets of beliefs regarding Assad's intentions and power to make peace, a dilemma faces the United States in its approach to Syria. On the one hand, Syria supports groups that engage in international terrorism against the United States and Israel, acquires weapons of mass destruction, and has good relations with Iran—an American adversary. On the other hand, Damascus is a potential partner of Washington in the Arab-Israel peace process, has been less of a practitioner of international terrorism since the end of the Cold War, and is an enemy of Baghdad, another of Washington's opponents. Given this conflicting set of problems, at issue has been whether to embrace or contain Syria since the period of the 1980s.

As a member of the National Security Council staff in the Reagan Administration during 1981-1982, I had the occasion to witness from the inside the struggle to resolve the dilemma over Syria. Successive crises over the Golan Heights and Lebanon were laboratories for observing advocates of accommodation and containment of Syria.[20]

## DOMESTIC POLITICS OR CONTAINMENT

Washington insiders who wished to contain Syria had the support of domestic political allies in the pro-Israel community. There was a meeting at the White House that I attended on November 19, 1981.

President Reagan met with a conference of presidents of major Jewish organizations to discuss American relations with Israel. At issue was Reagan's commitment to maintaining Israel's qualitative arms advantage, in particular its superiority over Syria.

The president wanted to impress on his audience how committed he was to maintain Israel's security with American arms shipments. Reagan told a story about how during the 1973 war, while he was governor of California, he had called Henry Kissinger at the White House to urge the rapid resupply of aircraft for Israel, which was then fighting against Egypt and Syria. Kissinger said that there was little need for the new aircraft in light of Israel's own figures about losses during the war. Reagan told Kissinger of the press reports based on Egyptian figures; these data showed that Israel had absorbed great losses. Reagan asked, "Why don't you just use the Egyptian figures as a basis for resupplying Israel?" According to Reagan, Kissinger then responded to the governor, "You Machiavellian son-of-a-bitch!"[21]

The president told the story to make clear to the pro-Israel community that he was committed to sustaining Israel's qualitative edge in its conflict with the Arab states, especially Syria. The leadership of the community reasonably inferred from the president's statements that he sided with it in containing rather than embracing Syria.[22]

For Iran and Libya, principal sources of American threat perception are ethnic and bureaucratic politics. These two forms of domestic politics, together with idealism, are more important than alliance preferences. In the clash between ethnic and business interest groups in the formulation of policy toward both states, ethnic preferences have dominated. In particular, the pro-Israel community has triumphed over the business sector in the push for sanctions against Tehran and Tripoli.

For Syria, moreover, American domestic politics reinforce bureaucratic preferences but play less of a role in U.S. threat perception. The pro-Israel community has some effect on perceptions about Syria but does not have to take the lead in seeking to contain Damascus. The business community has virtually no impact on Washington policy making toward Syria, perhaps because of the absence of American business in Syria in comparison to strong and historic economic ties with Iran, Iraq, and Libya.

## BUREAUCRATIC POLITICS AND
## THE GOLAN HEIGHTS CRISIS[23]

On December 15, 1981, Israel applied its domestic laws to the Golan Heights, which it had seized from Syria in the 1967 war.[24] Those in Washington who wished to embrace Syria used Israel's de facto annexation of the Golan Heights as a pretext for moving closer to Damascus. Secretary of Defense Caspar Weinberger, a leader of the accommodation school, wanted to use the crisis in order to punish Israel for annexing the Golan, while Secretary of State Alexander Haig, a bureaucratic opponent of Weinberger, wished to use it as leverage on Israel, in order to move the Middle East peace process forward. The compromise policy that emerged was for continued sanctions against Syria and mild punishment of Israel.[25] But that middle course neither moved Syria to make concessions to Israel, nor influenced Damascus to soften its hard line toward Jerusalem.[26]

The State Department's position on the Golan Heights crisis was to caution both Israel and Syria to refrain from hasty or emotional actions or statements. Such would only make it more difficult for the parties to act in their own best interests. The department wanted to keep Damascus from repudiating in the heat of the crisis the cease-fire of 1973 between Israel and Syria, their 1974 disengagement agreement, as well as a United Nations mandate to monitor their activities regarding the Golan Heights.

Syria considered Israel's actions concerning the Golan as a move to cancel the 1973 cease-fire, although the assumption seemed to be that Syria canceled the cease-fire accord with Israel. Damascus had stated that by adopting the decision to annex the Golan Heights, Israel had canceled the basis for the cease-fire between the two, United Nations Security Council Resolution 338.

The American embassy in Damascus also belonged to the embrace Syria school. Embassy staffers believed that Syria was playing its hand in a calm manner by opting for UN action. The embassy supported the successful pattern of action used in June 1981, after the Israeli raid on Iraq's nuclear reactor: Washington and Damascus had worked together on a resolution that both could support. The embassy felt that the U.S.

ambassador to the United Nations should not be out front seeking a delay in the United Nations Security Council meeting.

Secretary of State Haig, however, adopted a policy of delay. Notwithstanding the entreaties of the American embassy in Damascus, the position of the State Department was that the U.S. ambassador to the United Nations should take the following stand: declare that formal consideration of the Golan issue ought to await full clarification of the facts. The department's official statement on the Golan was that the United States would be concerned over any unilateral effort to change the status quo of the Golan and would oppose them. The U.S. view was that any unilateral shift in the status of the Golan or any of the territories occupied by Israel in the 1967 war would be contrary to United Nations Security Council Resolutions 242 and 338. The Camp David Accords and all Middle East peace negotiations since 1967 had been based on these two resolutions. Furthermore, any unilateral change in the status quo of the Golan would violate international law relating to belligerent occupation.

Because Haig belonged to the containment school, he sought to soften the impact of Israel's de facto annexation rather than to seek a reversal. He believed that if some means were not found to ease the significance of Israel's law, it could alienate constructive Arab governments and seriously undermine the peace process. Haig wanted Israel to mitigate, explain, or limit the effect of the law regarding the Golan in a public fashion. He stressed to the Israelis the effect that their precipitate action had on the prospects of American-Israel cooperation and coordination and said that it was an affront to a relationship of mutual trust. The secretary's strategy was to play for time while seeking to limit the crisis.

The embracement school in the Reagan Administration held that Israel's annexation of the Golan had taken advantage of developments along two fronts. First, there was the Soviet military intervention in Poland that occurred about the same time. A second front that allowed Israel to act was the need for Egypt to refrain from taking any actions that would lower the likelihood of Israel's withdrawal from the last occupied part of the Sinai Desert. The government of Egypt was not going to take any action in late 1981 that would jeopardize Israel's planned withdrawal on April 26, 1982. The timing of Israel's de facto annexation of the Golan suggested that Prime Minister Begin had made the decision sometime in the past but had awaited an opportune moment. He wanted to implement the decision before Israel's final withdrawal from the Sinai Desert and while the world's attention was on the Polish crisis.

Israel's motives were a blend of strategic considerations related to the peace process and domestic political pressures on the Begin government. Strategically, Israel wanted to accomplish the annexation without jeopardizing the Egypt-Israel peace process. Annexing the Golan in 1981 secured implicit Egyptian acquiescence irrespective of Cairo's denunciations. Domestically, the Golan move simultaneously solved several problems. It countered the political difficulty of evicting Jewish settlers from the town of Yamit in the Sinai. The Golan move also reassured settlers in the West Bank and Gaza that territorial withdrawals would end in April 1982, at the Egypt-Israel border. The Golan action reconfirmed Prime Minister Begin as a decisive leader who would not compromise on issues of vital importance.

Meanwhile, Washington decisionmakers discussed the nature of a statement deploring Israel's actions concerning the Golan. In a fight between Secretaries Haig and Weinberger over whether to sanction or ignore Israel's annexation, Admiral James Nance, Acting National Security Advisor, sent a lighthearted note to White House Chief of Staff James Baker saying, "I'm going to stay out of this one." Baker sent a tongue-in-cheek note in reply, "It is a job of the Assistant of the President of National Security to straighten out these disputes!" Haig had tried but failed to convince the president to avoid harsh criticism of Israel. The Secretary of State had wanted to use the crisis as leverage to move the peace process forward. But after a tough letter from Israel arrived at the White House, the American line stiffened and Haig lost out to advocates of punishing Israel and accommodating Syria.[27]

Meanwhile, the Deputy Chief of Mission of the Israeli embassy in Washington called me to express concern over rumors that unpleasant things were brewing at the White House. He suggested that Washington not blow things out of proportion. Keep in mind that we're talking about Syria, which was the number one enemy of the West in the Middle East. He said that there had only been an application of Israeli law to an area that was devoid of Syrian inhabitants, so that Syrian law did not then apply in the Golan Heights. Clearly, the Israeli representative wanted to reinforce the strength of that part of the U.S. bureaucracy that wanted to ignore the annexation and focus on how to move the peace process forward.

## EMBRACE SYRIA; SANCTION ISRAEL

Syria had wanted a United Nations Security Council Resolution against Israel to include the phrase "appropriate measures" in the event of noncompliance, because it would have implied the application of economic sanctions. But Washington held that it could not accept this phrase and would have vetoed any such resolution.

At issue between the United States and Israel with respect to the Golan Heights crisis was the effect of Israel's actions on negotiations for a memorandum of understanding (MOU) between Washington and Jerusalem. The group wishing to embrace Syria called for punishment of Israel for its misdeeds. This meant there would be a suspension of the implementation of the MOU, and that, in fact, did become American policy. But Jerusalem considered suspension of the MOU to be an abandonment of legal obligations.

The U.S. position was that the MOU had not yet entered into force. The two parties had not notified each other of the completion of their respective internal processes, as is required by entry into force of the MOUs provisions. The American statement was that the United States would not be able to proceed with implementation of the MOU. Israel's position was that the MOU related solely to external, Soviet-inspired threats and not to Israel's relations with its neighbors.

Haig's letter to Israel referred to the spirit in which the MOU was concluded. The Reagan Administration had considered that over the past few months, an understanding or spirit had been developed between the United States and Israel that obliged each side to take into consideration in its actions the broad policy concerns of the other. The MOU was one specific formal manifestation of this spirit. It was not intended to limit broader understandings in any way. Israel considered suspending the MOU a serious psychological blow. Jerusalem was trying to put Washington on the defensive. Prime Minister Begin's style in a crisis was to go on the offensive rather than admit error.[28]

During the Golan crisis, the Israel Defense Forces in northern Israel and on the Golan went on high-alert status. But some troops received leave for the Sabbath, from Friday evening to Saturday evening, and tourists once again traveled to the area. Israel had about 25,000 troops in the northern part of the country and on the Golan, as compared to 12,000 before the de facto annexation. Israeli officials had rejected a United Nations Security Council Resolution declaring Israel's annexation of the occupied Golan Heights "null and void," saying no world body can change the decision of a sovereign state or its legislature. The officials said there would no reaction to President Reagan's remarks at a news conference in which he deplored the Israeli move and expressed hope that the actions would be "ameliorated," a term that I wrote into the President's briefing materials.

## ALLIANCE POLITICS:
## SYRIA BREAKS OUT OF ISOLATION

Those in Washington who wished to isolate Syria were in for a surprise. An unintended consequence of the Golan Heights crisis was to stimulate realignments among Arab states that decreased Syria's isolation. Israel's de facto annexation had the inadvertent effect of reducing Syria's diplomatic isolation within the Arab world.[29] On December 31, 1981, Libya and Saudi Arabia announced that they were restoring diplomatic relations. After Israel applied its laws to the Golan Heights, Damascus and Riyadh decided to restore ties, stop the Iran-Iraq War, and heal divisions between radical Arab states that supported Iran and conservative Arab states that backed Baghdad. Libya and Syria had criticized Iraq for turning away from the struggle with Israel.

Saudi Arabia had broken ties with Syria in October 1981, after Tripoli blamed the Kingdom for allowing four American radar surveillance planes to deploy in Saudi Arabia. Riyadh requested the aircraft for protection in the event the Iran-Iraq War spilled over into Saudi Arabia. Iraq had broken relations with Libya and Syria shortly after the

Iran-Iraq War began. Baghdad accused Tripoli and Damascus of supporting Tehran.[30]

Tehran's military, political, and economic contacts with Damascus had expanded since the Iran-Iraq War began in September 1980. Iranian-Syrian economic ties strengthened with a tentative trade accord worth over $2 billion. Iran agreed to provide Syria oil in exchange for which Syria would supply Iran with refined oil products or proceeds from the resale of crude phosphates, grain, and textiles, as well as Soviet military supplies.

The oil deal was to yield 180,000 barrels of oil per day to Syria, end its need for Iraqi oil, and reduce Iraq's leverage over Damascus in matters affecting the use of pipelines that ran from Iraq through Syria to the Mediterranean at Banyas and at Tripoli in Lebanon. In the spring of 1982, Iraq had shipped about half its crude oil via the pipeline. Because Baghdad earned some $6 billion per year from these shipments, the link to the Mediterranean via Syria was an important one.

On April 8, 1982, Syria sealed two pipelines that carried Iraqi oil, while closing its border with Iraq. Iraq had been exporting 900,000 barrels per day, 400,000 through the two pipelines across Syria. The pipelines had not been closed for political reasons since 1976. Because of the closing of the Syrian outlets, only by shipping via Turkey could Iraq get its oil to the market safely. The Turkish pipeline had a maximum capacity of about 700,000 barrels per day. As a result of the cutoff of pipelines between Iraq and Syria, Baghdad called for economic sanctions against Damascus. Although Turkey stood to gain from the closing of the Syrian routes for Iraqi oil, Ankara also expressed concern about the religious impact of Iranian victories in the Iran-Iraq War. In particular, Ankara worried that Tehran's successes against Baghdad could result in the spread of the Islamic revolution to Turkey via Iraq.

But Syria did not wish to trade total dependence on Iraq for similar dependence on Iran. As the war dragged on, Iran's reliance on Syria increased. Despite the enmity between Damascus and Baghdad, Riyadh wanted Syria to mediate the Iran-Iraq War. In return, Saudi Arabia would help end the dispute between Iraq and Syria. Algeria served as mediator. But the Saudis fretted over the Iranian view that ideological objectives could be achieved by military means. Such a belief frustrated mediation by Algiers, the Organization of the Islamic Conference, and the nonaligned movement.

By concluding an economic deal with Iran in March 1982, Syria had traded off good relations with Arab Gulf states and aligned itself with Iran. One reason for the alignment between Damascus and Tehran was the regional situation facing Assad. Assured of Iranian support, Damascus increased its action against both Iraq and Jordan, two states that were enemies of Syria. Relations between Damascus and Riyadh suffered when Syria improved its relations with Iran. When the Syrian deputy foreign minister called for the overthrow of Saddam in the spring of 1982, it suggested that Damascus had made a long-term commitment to its alignment with Tehran.

While the intention of Israel was to shore up its security with the de facto annexation of the Golan Heights in December 1981, an unintended effect was to reduce the diplomatic isolation of Damascus within the Arab world and hence to strengthen Syria. Israel's actions against Syria also enhanced the influence of advocates within the U.S. bureaucracy of embracing Syria over supporters of containment.

The decade after Syria began to emerge from isolation found it not only back within the Arab world but also at the center of a coalition of moderate Arab regimes and Western allies arrayed against Saddam of Iraq. It was in 1991 that Syria made its most important policy move by participating in the Gulf War coalition. By joining most of the other Arab states in the alliance, Syria sought mainstream status and hence signaled its desire to conform to international standards of diplomatic intercourse. Although not parading its policy intentions, Damascus hinted at potential peace negotiations with Israel and an end to terrorism. The Gulf War coalition marked restoration of economic and diplomatic ties with fellow Arab states and peace talks on the Golan Heights issue, both of which augmented Syria's primary goal of national security. In just five years, Syria had accomplished what it could not achieve after twenty years of state-supported terrorism.

Assad may have changed Syrian foreign policy because the old approach was failing to achieve both Arab influence and reacquisition of the Golan Heights. He demonstrated an ability to learn from his experiences, adapt policy to meet new situations, and correct past failures. Assad additionally chose his political moves for logical reasons—achieving his foreign policy goals—and ended a low-return policy in exchange for a more efficient and effective one.

## U.S. POLICY TOWARD SYRIA

Although there are advocates of containment within the U.S. government, there is no official policy to contain Damascus as there is with Tehran, Baghdad, and Tripoli. While Syrian ideology expresses a desire for creation of a Greater Syria that would include Israel, the intelligence estimate in Washington is that Damascus does not have operational plans to carry out this goal. Syria absorbed defeats by Israel in both 1967 and 1973. Then there was the loss of its Soviet patron due to the breakup of the USSR. The end of the Cold War and the hot war in the Gulf left the United States and Syria on the same victorious side. Thus, Syria has the option of playing the American game called "peace process." Whatever ambitions Syria had of destroying Israel are passé. While there is no need to contain Syria per se, there is a wish in Washington to influence Damascus with quiet diplomacy to cease its support for international terrorism.

With respect to another criterion for membership in the rogues' gallery—spread of weapons of mass destruction—there is little evidence that the United States has made much of a public issue about Syria's weapons manufacture. Washington has been almost silent about the chemical weapons production of Damascus in comparison to the warnings issued to Tripoli about its construction of a chemical weapons facility in a Libyan mountain during 1995-1996.

A further rogue state criterion applies to Syria, given its participation in drug trafficking. Again, there is little indication that Washington diplomats care enough about this problem to let it interfere with the felt need to bring Assad into the "family of nations." This phrase stems from the Bush Administration's efforts to appease Saddam for the sake of gaining his support in the Arab-Israel peace process.

Because of the desire of Washington to engage Damascus in the peace process, there is a tendency to discount the Syrian threat. Successive administrations have engaged in bouts of wishful thinking. American officials have imagined that overlooking Syrian "delicts" will result in reciprocity, that ignoring Syrian participation in terrorism will produce concessions from Assad in the Arab-Israel peace process. Furthermore, accommodating Assad's preference to exercise suzerainty over Lebanon will supposedly lead him to reduce the flow of arms from Tehran to Hezbollah in Lebanon via Damascus. In order to get Assad to take part in the alignment against Saddam during the Gulf War, Washington ignored his move to integrate Lebanon into Greater Syria. It has been thought that not taking Assad to task for his housing of suicide bombers in Damascus will moderate Syria in the Golan Heights negotiations.

Assad does take risks by engaging in the Washington-led peace process. And he did participate in the American-led Gulf War coalition. But these risks are insufficient to justify letting him get away with opposing the United States in the Arab-Israel conflict zone. Washington should encourage Damascus to cease being a conduit for Iranian arms for Hezbollah in Lebanon and refrain from housing groups in Syria that commit acts of international terrorism. These three activities constitute a threat to the United States and its allies in the region.

By way of comparison between perceived threats to the United States from Tehran and Damascus, moreover, there is a legitimate dispute among analysts as to whether the pro-Israel community "invented" the Iranian threat.[31] No such dispute pertains to threat perception about Syria. There is an unchallenged consensus that there is danger from Damascus, but the threat is less than that from Tehran and Baghdad. Furthermore, the Iranian menace directly threatens American civilians and military personnel in the Gulf, who are major intrinsic interests of the United States. Iran is also a risk to other inherently valuable assets like Western petroleum products transiting the Gulf and other sea-lanes of communications. Although there are no comparable threats to American intrinsic interests from Syria in the late 1990s, the behavior of its government is a threat to U.S. interests in other areas.

Even though the evidence is strong that Syria is an outlaw state, American officials have been reluctant to name it among the other rogues. President Reagan gave a speech in 1985, in which he named Cuba, Iran, Libya, Nicaragua, and North Korea as being a part of a confederation of terrorist states. He called them outlaws that sought to undermine U.S. interests.[32] The Clinton Administration also provided a list of rogues and conveniently omitted Syria. President Clinton's Assistant to the President for National Security Affairs, Anthony Lake, wrote an article on backlash states that threatened to undermine global security. He listed by name only Iran, Iraq, Libya, and North Korea.[33] The failure of Lake to include Syria is indicative of the vapid policy Washington follows regarding Damascus.

Antiterrorism legislation bars American companies from doing business with countries on the State Department list of nations that support international terrorism. It names seven countries as sponsors of international terrorism, but only five are subject to comprehensive embargoes—Iran, Iraq, Libya, Cuba, and North Korea. Two states escaped sweeping trade embargo status: Syria and the Sudan. The Anti-Terrorism Act of 1996 permits financial dealings with Syria, if these transactions are found not to have an impact on any potential act of terrorism. Syria was subject to less restrictive terms in the 1996 Anti-Terrorism Act because the United States wanted to encourage its participation in the Arab-Israel peace process.

Despite Washington's interest in encouraging Damascus, there are intrinsic interests of the United States under threat from Syria. They include Syrian support for international terrorism and proliferation of weapons of mass destruction, chemical weapons in particular. With respect to terrorism, Syria has a long record. In 1979, the United States officially classified it as a state that supported international terrorism.[34]

Damascus provides safehaven and support for several groups that engage in international terrorism. Hamas, the Palestinian group responsible for suicide bombings in Israel, openly operates a political office in Damascus, where it maintains contacts with Iranian officials. Palestinian Islamic Jihad, which also has claimed responsibility for suicide attacks in Israel, has resident status in Syria.[35] Damascus also provides basing privileges to groups engaged in terrorism or refuge in Lebanon's Beka'a Valley, which is under the control of Syrian armed forces. These groups include Hamas, the Popular Front for the Liberation of Palestine–General Command, the Palestinian Islamic Jihad, and the Japanese Red Army.

Under the authority of Section Six of the Export Administration Act, the State Department established the terrorism list. On it are countries that provide state sponsorship of international terrorism.[36] Once a country is on the list, it cannot be removed without meeting certain requirements, including a presidential determination and advance notification to Congress. States on this list, such as Syria, have trade controls levied against them.

In 1986, Washington expanded economic sanctions against Damascus to include aircraft, aircraft parts, and computers of U.S.-origin or equipment containing such components and technologies. This action was in response to evidence indicating Syrian involvement in the effort to bomb an Israeli passenger airplane at London's Heathrow Airport. Under the 1986 sanctions, Syria is ineligible for the Export Enhancement Program and the Commodity Credit Corporation Program in all agricultural products. The Export-Import Bank suspended its programs in Syria.[37]

In short, American sanctions against Syria include bans on economic assistance and military sales, controls on dual-use equipment that could support terrorism or military activities, and prohibitions on U.S. government support for multilateral economic assistance. The Anti-Terrorism and Arms Export Act of 1989 triggers most of the sanctions against Syria, given its membership on the terrorism list.

Damascus denies charges of supporting terrorism and narcotics trafficking. On terrorism, it claims to use its influence with organizations like Hezbollah—the Party of God—to limit outbreaks of violence on the border between Lebanon and Israel. Also, since 1991, Damascus has actively worked to secure the release of Western hostages held in Lebanon and has removed restrictions on travel by Syrian Jews.[38]

Assad denies claims that Syria is even involved in terrorism. During an October 1994 joint press conference with President Clinton in Damascus, Assad asserted Syria's innocence. "I said in these [peace process] discussions to the American senior officers whom I asked then to mention for me one incident in which Syria has committed a terrorist action, and he was helpless. He was not able to mention one single incident in which Syria supported terrorism."[39] If Assad's statement is true regarding an American diplomat's inability to document Syrian involvement in terrorism, then Washington has not done a good job communicating with Damascus.

Syria also constitutes a threat to the United States through its complicity in international narcotics trafficking. The Foreign Assistance Act of 1961 requires the State Department to publish annually the International Narcotics Control Strategy Report. And section 2346(a) of the Foreign Assistance Act of 1961 requires the termination of U.S. foreign aid to countries implicated in this report.[40] Syria has been a mainstay on the list since the early 1980s, and it appears in the 1995 report, which describes how Syrian military and security personnel personally profited from the drug trade in 1994. It goes on to show how Syrian military protection for drug traffickers persisted in 1994, despite official claims to the contrary.

Syria also engaged in controlled deliveries of narcotics with individuals in Jordan and Lebanon.[41] Moreover, Syria serves as a transit country for Lebanese and Turkish refined cocaine going to Europe and heroin and hashish bound for regional and Western markets.[42] As a result of Syrian complicity in drug trafficking, there is no bilateral narcotics agreement between Washington and Damascus, and Syria receives no U.S. foreign assistance.[43]

Unlike the denials of involvement in terrorism, Damascus does not deny that there is serious international narcotics trafficking in areas under its control. But it does renounce any official assistance or involvement in drug trafficking. Syria also boasts that it is party to the 1988 United Nations Single Convention on Narcotics and its 1972 protocol. In February 1994, Damascus hosted the thirtieth session of a UN Sub-Commission on Illicit Drug Traffic in the Near and Middle East. In addition, Syria publicly reiterated its willingness to pursue all information regarding the possible production of narcotics in Lebanon and Syria. Other important developments include: supposed implementation of stiff drug laws passed in 1993 and joint Syrian and Lebanese eradication efforts in the Beka'a Valley of Lebanon that Syria claims have reduced opium production. Damascus also asserts that there was an increase in the reported number of drug seizures and destruction of drug crops in Lebanon during 1994.[44]

There are political differences over how to handle Syrian complicity in the drug trade. The Clinton State Department lobbied to waive Syria's inclusion on the list of states that do not work hard to stop the drug trade. Officials wanted to remove Damascus from the list as a reward for Syrian participation in the Middle East peace process. Representatives on Capitol Hill strongly objected to the prospective elimination of Syria from the list and threatened to denounce the Clinton Administration for compensating Syria.[45] In opposition to the State Department were not only members of Congress, but also officials of the Drug Enforcement Administration, who contended, with good reason, that Syria had not acted strongly enough to stop the opium trade.[46]

Terrorism and drug trafficking are threats to American intrinsic interests. Syria also poses a danger to U.S. strategic interests. These include the credibility of the U.S. threat to use military force; the American resolve to remain engaged in the world; and the U.S. commitment to defend its friends against its foes.[47] To the extent that Damascus stands up to Washington, it challenges U.S. credibility, resolve, and commitments.

One means by which Damascus confronts Washington is through the provision of safehavens to terrorists who attack American citizens and individuals from allied countries. Subsidizing terrorists is equivalent to state-sponsored terrorism. But the threat to American strategic interests from Damascus is not as great as from Tehran. Not only does Iran target American citizens, it also directs terrorism against the Iranian political opposition at home and abroad. To the extent that the domestic opposition derives from Iranians who were associated with the Shah's regime and thus tarred by the American brush, Tehran's attacks are threats to the strategic interests of the United States.

Given Syria's involvement in terrorism and complicity in the drug trade, the question remains what is the best approach for the United States if it wants to end these dangers? Washington's strategy is to retain sanctions until Damascus ceases its support for terrorism. But what is the best way to maintain pressure on Syria? Two approaches are available: public denunciations and private diplomacy. Washington has given too much attention to private discussions and not enough to public denunciations.

On the one hand, the State Department's Office for Counterterrorism and the Bureau for International Narcotics and Law Enforcement Affairs follow a public policy of describing Syrian misbehavior. On the other hand, the Department's Near Eastern Bureau is less harsh publicly in its depiction of Syria. Robert Pelletreau, Assistant Secretary of State for Near Eastern and South Asian Affairs, even failed to mention Syria when he discussed American interests to suppress terrorism and the spread of weapons of mass destruction. Although the secretary acknowledges the need "for containing rogue regimes in Iran, Iraq, and Libya," he does not include Syria in his list.[48] What kind of signal does failure to name Syria send to Assad? That it is acceptable to help terrorists, engage in a search for weapons of mass destruction, and take part in drug trafficking.

## CLINTON ADMINISTRATION AND SYRIA

The Clinton Administration's approach to Syria reflects the dilemma that faced its predecessors as well. In addition to Clinton's supplications at the Presidential palace in Damascus in October 1994, Secretary of State Warren Christopher made over 20 trips to Syria during the 1992-1996 period. These visits indicate the Clinton Administration's preference to accommodate Assad. But Christopher's retention of Damascus on Washington's list of nations that support international terrorism also shows its inclination to contain Syria. The administration seeks both to engage and contain Syria. As in the past, a central puzzle arises for the United States with respect to Syria: why would the Clinton Administration engage in negotiations with Damascus, despite its participation in international terrorism, proliferation of chemical weapons, and drug trafficking?

An answer to this puzzle lies in the reference point Washington sets for the Middle East.[49] The administration desires peace between Damascus and Jerusalem more than cessation of Syria's terrorism, proliferation, and trafficking. The Clinton Administration fears losing Syria's participation in the peace process more than it values termination of rogue state activity.[50] The United States was willing to take major risks in order to avoid the loss of Syria in the peace process. Hence, Clinton was willing to risk his prestige when he met with Assad in 1994. Because that summit meeting violated the U.S. position of refraining to appear too close diplomatically to states that subsidize groups sponsoring terrorism, it was risky to hold the summit.

## SCENARIOS

Whether the United States pursues a posture of embracing or containing Syria depends in part on scenarios that develop between Damascus and Jerusalem. The possibilities are: peace; no-peace, no-war; and war. If Washington would like to facilitate a peace scenario, then the approach of Moshe Maoz seems to be most relevant. He suggests that Assad has made a strategic commitment to peace; hence, Washington should test the validity of his pledge. Not doing so would leave open the possibility of a deterioration of the situation and make the other two scenarios likely.

### Peace

A peace scenario stems from the assumptions that both Israel and Syria have made strategic commitments toward a settlement. In this respect, Ze'ev Schiff, a leading Israeli political-military analyst, wrote a seminal essay on the relation of peace to security. Schiff said, "If peace with Syria is the strategic goal toward which Israel is driving, and if the Syrian decision to make peace with Israel and end the conflict is indeed a strategic concept—as President Assad said in Geneva—then the chance for peace is very great."[51]

Schiff's assumption is that commitments by Damascus and Jerusalem are necessary but not sufficient conditions for success of the peace process. The missing ingredient is the American role. The U.S. approach has been like that of a host at a cocktail party, serving the food and drinks but not interfering too much in the conversation among the partygoers. In order to facilitate the peace process between Israel and Syria, however, a more active role on the part of Washington might be required. But an active role need not focus on Damascus.

Ignoring Assad and making progress on the withdrawal of most of the Israeli military from Hebron may have resulted in a Syrian démarche to resume negotiations with Israel during December 1996. Indirect pressure on Syria via progress on the Palestinian front helps to avoid slippage in the journey toward peace on the northern front.[52]

## No-Peace, No-War

Neither peace nor war was the approach adopted by Assad from 1974 to 1991. At that time, there was stalemate in negotiations between Israel and Syria, yet war did not occur. From the 1974 disengagement accord between Israel and Syria brokered by Henry Kissinger until the commencement of the Madrid talks in 1991, there was a freeze in Israel's relations with Syria. This period was a time during which both sides "muddled through." Damascus did not choose military action, however, to unfreeze the political stalemate. Rather, Syria chose to wait for a change in the strategic situation, which occurred with the end of the Cold War and the hot war in the Gulf.

At the turn of the century, Assad may calculate that a middle-ground approach is the best means of keeping the pot boiling without falling into the hot water of a war with Israel. In this regard, he could achieve the following objectives. He could extract from Israel a high price that could include Israeli recognition of the Syrian presence in Lebanon, disrupt the process of rapprochement between Israel and the Arab states as well as the Palestinians, and drive a wedge between Israel and the United States. In addition, he might lay the groundwork for the renewal of future negotiations under more promising conditions; for example, after the next elections in Israel.[53]

In the no-peace, no-war scenario, Syria could continue its practice of brinkmanship and tacit support of terrorist groups. Doing so enhances its bargaining position vis-à-vis Israel. Also, attacks against Israel by Syrian surrogates help keep the Golan Heights item on the agenda of the peace process. In the American-led negotiations, Israel has stopped most negotiations with Syria. The initial impetus for the cessation was due to a series of suicide bombings. Because of the role of Palestinians in the bombings and the timetable of the Oslo accords of 1993, the Israeli-Palestinian dimension has received more attention than issues concerning Syria. The closer Israel and the Palestinian Authority come to normalizing relations, however, the worse Assad's bargaining position would be when the talks resume between Jerusalem and Damascus. Although Syria needs to keep the pot boiling, it has to be careful not to let the peace process proceed too far without its active participation.

## War

In the absence of diplomatic progress on the Syrian front due to Assad's perception that this is the best course of action to get the peace process moving, the parties could head down the slippery slope to war. Assume the persistence of the policy of Israel as a "peace for peace" approach rather than "land for peace," as envisioned in UN Security Council Resolutions 242 and 338. In this event, Ze'ev Maoz believes that the government might as well prepare the country for war in the not-too-distant future.[54] The likelihood of an accord on terms that Assad could accept are lower without the magic of diplomatic momentum.

In the context of stalemate on the Syrian front, Ze'ev Maoz reasons that Assad would face two inter-Arab scenarios, each creating incentives for war. According to the first, the peace process on the Palestinian track would continue, and the Arab world would maintain its rapprochement with Israel. In this scenario, there would be a significant risk of perpetuating Israel's rule over the Golan Heights. A Syrian attack on Israel would pose a dilemma for the Arab Nation. In the best case for Damascus, it would receive military and/or economic support from several Arab states. In the worst case for Damascus, it would still have Arab political support, which manifests itself as pressure on Washington to move the negotiations with Israel forward.

According to the second scenario of Ze'ev Maoz, there would be a radical change in Israel's relations with Arab states because of a stalemate on the Palestinian track and Jordanian disappointment with the dividends of its peace with Israel. In this event, a war with Israel could restore Syria to its position as a leader in the peace process— thus bringing the Palestinians, and even the Jordanians, in line behind the Syrian position. In both scenarios, an inability to ignite the peace process through a military initiative against Israel could exacerbate Assad's domestic political problems.

Yet another possibility stems from the fact that Syrian frustration over the internal political situation might increase to the point where Assad is willing to bear additional risks. The area in which Syria has the capability of causing genuine psychological damage to Israel is to attack its heartland with missiles.[55] Damascus has emphasized massive procurement of missiles in order to balance Jerusalem's air superiority. Syria has over 300 ballistic missiles, including the Scud-C, whose range is more than 500 kilometers. Damascus has even developed an ability to manufacture this missile independently. Syria manufactures these missiles in underground installations that Damascus built with the assistance of China, Iran, and North Korea.[56]

Recall the four themes that cut across *Rogue Regimes:* threat perception, opportunities, politics, and policies. For Syria, bureaucratic and domestic politics are not important elements in the American policy process. Given similar perceptions of threat and opportunity between the United States and its allies, it is comparatively easy to fashion policies to change Assad's behavior or to punish him for misbehavior. The allies are of little consequence in determining Washington's policy of continued sanctions against Damascus. There is little indication of opportunities foregone as a result of maintaining sanctions against Syria. But with respect to the debate about the nature of threats in the international system, the United States does not perceive Syria as equivalent to the former Soviet threat.

## CHAPTER SIX

# NORTH KOREA:
# CONTAIN AND EMBRACE

## MANIPULATOR OF CRISIS
## OR VICTIM OF CIRCUMSTANCE

AT ISSUE IS WHETHER NORTH KOREA is a "crisis creator," on the one hand, or a "victim of circumstance," on the other. Pyongyang has a history of creating political crises. The regime, however, may be on its last throes of existence as its economic situation spins out of control. To the extent that Pyongyang is a manipulator of political/military crises, then it should be contained; to the degree that it is a potential casualty on its economic deathbed, then it needs to be embraced with humanitarian assistance.

Pyongyang as a crisis manipulator is a more or less rational actor looking for windows of opportunity through which to jump. These openings need to be closed with deterrent threats by status quo powers like the United States and its allies in northeast Asia. The containment/deterrence strategy Washington has employed against Pyongyang since the end of the Korean War assumes that the regime is capable of approximately rational action. In other words, when confronted with greater expected losses than anticipated gains, North Korea should be able to make a simple calculation and refrain from attacking South Korea.

In contrast to North Korea as a rational actor, the regime as a member of the walking wounded may not be deterrable. Pyongyang lives in an environment not of its own making and, in effect, resides in a windowless basement of fear. In this respect, Washington and its allies may wish to provide aid and comfort to heal the diseased body lest it become a corpse. They need to reassure the body politic of North Korea that the United States means no harm. In so doing, the United States averts the tragedy of a paranoid North Korea: acting out in acute desperation, factions within the regime would behave like victims that lash out at perceived adversaries.

The threat strategy Washington has used against Pyongyang in the aftermath of the Korean War is irrelevant against a divided regime motivated more by fear than gain. There are no windows to be closed to deter by threat of punishment and few gates to be locked to deter by denial. The military elites in Pyongyang worry about losses over which they have scant control. And when losses are the focal point of decision making, actors have a hard time making simple calculations necessary to be deterred.

Two camps come to mind regarding explanations of North Korea's behavior. The first sees Pyongyang as a unitary actor in control of its own destiny. It invents emergencies as a routine part of a rational negotiating strategy.[1] "Talk to me; I may go nuclear," was the diplomatic marker laid down by Pyongyang during the early 1990s.[2] "Feed me, or I'll kill you," is the North Korean outcry of the late 1990s.[3] Pyongyang has polished a sophisticated diplomatic game of bluff. Threaten, receive rewards; then promise, procrastinate, provoke, and pause in anticipation of further appeasement from the powers.[4] Cite floods, feign famine, and place the West on a guilt trip in order to squeeze concessions that would not otherwise be forthcoming.

The second camp frames North Korea as a divided nation whose destiny is in the hands of forces outside the regime's control. North Korea is fated to be a failed state torn asunder by rival factions. Humanitarian predicaments are the circumstances that force the elites to make choices not of their own making. "Feed me before I die and infect your friends," is the moan of the moment. "Prop me up before I fall and bring down your friends," is the lamentation of the lame. But as North Korea teeters on the brink of falling, this relic of a bygone era may be even more dangerous than in Cold War times.

There is historical precedent for empires and nation states to be healthy while youthful and infirm in old age. But because the North and the South are about the same age—about a half-century-old—and Seoul is healthy, longevity is not the explanation for the deterioration of North Korea.[5] Perhaps what ails the nation is the same malady that afflicted other Communist states at the close of the twentieth century. Because there was no private sector to do the job, these states disintegrated when unable to feed and clothe noncomplacent populations. Contrast the collapse of the Soviet Empire and the coherence of China, a Communist nation in the midst of economic reforms and growth.

On the one hand, a Velcro-like blame clings to those in power when famine derives from the politics of defective distribution: the political system falls under the burden of its own bankrupt policies. On the other hand, a Teflon-like immunity shields politicians when famine stems from the economics of scarcity. The USSR fell apart when its politicians could not survive the consequences of an economic system unable to support its population. The Soviet parent who fathered North Korea in 1948 as a child of the Cold War has gone out of business and filed for a "Chapter Eleven"–type bankruptcy.

Irrespective of whether the government is in control or the society is in free fall, the neighbors may wish to ensure that the political outcomes do not jeopardize their own national interests. When the sick man of Europe—the Ottoman Empire—began to collapse, the Great Powers during the nineteenth century propped it up. Their goal was to keep each other from decimating the Ottoman corpse in a feeding frenzy. By keeping the empire together, the Great Powers avoided conflict over the distribution of spoils. The Powers on the eve of the twenty-first century also see a need to hold up a falling North Korean regime. Fortunately, a Dr. Kevorkian-like assisted suicide is not an option: the patient is in a state of severe denial and unwilling to confront death.[6]

## QUESTIONS AND PRELIMINARY ANSWERS

As the North Korean regime proceeds down a slippery slope, either by choice or by circumstance, three questions arise. The first requires explanations of the past; the second demands scenarios of the future; and the third calls for plans for the present. The past, the future, and the present march in that order for good reason. If we can explain the past and project the future, we can formulate effective policies for the present.

Question One. Why has North Korea engaged in brinkmanship with the United States, and what are the prospects for a continuation of this pattern? Answer: Pyongyang went to the brink when it was healthy. One of its goals was to compel Washington to negotiate directly, without including South Korea. The government in the North used "crisis as an opportunity" for diplomatic engagement with Washington.[7] While this pattern dominated prior interactions, it may not last.

As floods and famine vanquish the North, the regime is not able to control its future as it controlled its past. Because North Korea deserves the label of "Sick Man of Asia," it is not able to pursue a more or less rational course of action to use crisis as an occasion for diplomatic success. In short, North Korea has used crisis as an opportunity for gaining concessions, but may not be able to continue to use this strategy in the future.

Question Two. Under what conditions will North Korea implode from within and/or explode across international borders? Answer: massive starvation exacerbated by natural disasters, such as floods, could result in an implosion of civil society in North Korea. As a result, civilians would run for their lives. They could flee over land and via the Yalu River into China, escape by sea to Japan, or dare to run the gauntlet of the "militarized" Demilitarized Zone (DMZ) between the Koreas.[8] Starvation also might prompt a military invasion of the South by dissident elements in Pyongyang. Like Samson's destruction of the Philistines' temple, North Korea could bring down others as it falls. Doing so would constitute a severe threat to regional security. In summary, floods and famine may result in national implosion and/or international explosion. But collapse seems more likely than invasion: North Korea's economic situation has worsened more than the political/military environment for the regime.

Question Three. If implosion is more likely than explosion in the midterm, what policy packages should the United States pursue in the short term? Washington's four options are: to contain (deter) North

Korea, to embrace the Pyongyang regime, to contain and embrace it, or to gradually withdraw from the Korean peninsula.[9]

## A POLITICAL AVIARY

A consideration of the past, future, and present warrants a framework for analysis. As a first step in its construction, consider the metaphor of a "political aviary." In the bureaucratic politics of Washington, policy analysts act as if they were in a birdhouse—a virtual international political preserve comprised of hawks and doves. Owls from outside the Washington zoo provide critiques relevant to both sets of policy analysts.[10]

Hawks assume that Pyongyang is in command of its own destiny. Doves presume that North Korea is sliding away into an abyss and dragging others with it. And owls explain the past and project the future in order to discover whether the regime was or will be in command or out of control.

Indeed, owls can strengthen the hand of either hawks or doves, once analysis is complete. On the one side, if owls find the leaders in Pyongyang manipulating crises, this reinforces the position of hawks in the bureaucracy. On the other side, if owls discover that circumstances manipulate the leadership, this conclusion gives doves the upper hand.

Given their assumption that the government in power is responsible for its own actions, hawks prefer containment or deterrence. In light of their presumption that situations have the potential to spin out of hand, doves split between accommodation and withdrawal. And their theory-inebriated counterparts in the academic community, the owls, are willing to accept a variety of policy packages, including a mix of containing and embracing.[11]

Hawks also would allow North Korea to collapse on its own without any assistance from the West. They would permit a hard landing for the regime, irrespective of costs. Because hawks assume that problems in North Korea are intractable, they are willing to refrain from intervention. If pressed to intervene, they would condition assistance to Pyongyang on its implementation of economic reforms.

The bottom line, however, is that hawks follow a policy of using threats to contain, while making humanitarian assistance to the North conditional on economic reforms that could doom the regime.

Doves wish for a soft landing for North Korea. They worry about the risks of a hard landing. They prefer a policy of unconditional assurance and humanitarian rewards. Additionally, doves hope for a happy ending at best or a muddling through at the least. They perceive the problems of Pyongyang to be tractable: incremental economic reforms could produce a peaceful transition and subsequent reunification of the peninsula. While doves would like to see economic reforms, they would not use food as a weapon to force compliance.

Following a further clarification of the hawks-doves-owls framework, there is in this chapter a discussion of ideals and interests in American policy, followed by a treatment of United States–North Korean relations. This historical analysis feeds into a specification of war and peace scenarios for the future. Finally, the chapter addresses policy packages available to the Clinton Administration in light of rival perspectives, ideals and interests, prior history, and alternative futures.

## THE WAR FOR WASHINGTON

### Hawks: Deterrence and Coercion

Hawks favor policies designed to deter and coerce. They assume that leaders can accurately calculate the balance between gains and losses, equally weigh losses relative to gains, and act to maximize expected gain and minimize expected loss. From this perspective, these leaders are "rational calculators" who rarely believe they make errors. According to hawks, disastrous outcomes like wars are due to a vacuum of power and/or an absence of commitment. Wars result from the actions of power-hungry, "error-free," cold-hearted mercenaries who are not held in constant check by capability and commitment.

In the context of avoiding military conflict on the Korean Peninsula, hawks see the proximate cause of a future war as one-sided weakness. This imbalance tempts an adversary, such as the regime in Pyongyang, to exploit an advantage. The classic example of such exploitation is the case of Munich. It symbolizes the failed British and French attempt to appease Nazi Germany. The two allies sold out Czechoslovakia in 1938, as a way of "buying off" Hitler—but he did not "stay bought." Hitler continued to engage in aggression against his neighbors.

To avoid another Korean War conducted by a modern-day Hitler, hawks suggest a policy of "peace through strength." Paradoxically, a demonstrated will to use force is one way of achieving peace. According to hawks, leaders of threatened states will be deterred from going to war if they perceive the expected costs to be greater than the anticipated gains from fighting. Accordingly, they place a high premium on relative capability and credible threats, irrespective of costs—escalation.

Through the eyes of hawks, an aim of the United States is to make sure that North Korea perceives the costs of war to outweigh the gains. Also, the North should realize that the odds of losing are higher than the chances of success. The United States cannot assume that Pyongyang understands this calculus. In order for the North to be deterred from launching an attack, Washington needs to make it very clear that the risks of going to war exceed the foreseen gains. Issuing credible threats to the regime's leaders is a surefire way to bolster deterrence and coerce successfully.

According to the hawks, it was understandable that North Korea launched a war of aggression against South Korea in 1950. Why? There was an "interest vacuum" and a "commitment void." The United States failed to make clear its interests in protecting the South and its commitment to do so.[12] As a part of an overall containment policy, hawks would announce U.S. commitments to friend and foe alike and not worry about the destabilizing effects that might occur as a result of reinforcing deterrence.

To illustrate the idea of announcing commitments, consider an incident regarding Taiwan that occurred in 1997. The speaker of the U.S. House of Representatives, Newt Gingrich, went to China. He explicitly warned the leadership that Washington would defend Taipei if Beijing attacked. The speaker said that the United States should avoid the kind of situation that led to the Korean War, when ambiguity in the American commitment to defend South Korea provided an incentive for the North to attack.[13] The speaker is clearly a hawk. But what kind? Because in the case of Taiwan he focuses on deterring rather than coercing, Gingrich is a "deterrent hawk" rather than a "compellent hawk."

## Doves: Unintended Escalation

The upside of explicit commitments is to reinforce deterrence; the downside of making commitments clear-cut is to provoke escalation: there is a risk that those abroad and at home may read too much into an unambiguous commitment. Such misperception may lead to unintended escalation. Commitments that are too precise may send the wrong signal to multiple audiences. Pledges to support a friend against a foe may inadvertently prompt that friend to take undesired or unforeseen action; the foe then can use this action as a rationale to take military steps against that friend.

American reluctance to incite the pro-independence movement in Taiwan serves as a prime example of a policy of "strategic ambiguity."[14] If Taipei were to affirm its independence, that would be a pretext for Beijing to take military action. Hence, U.S. policy is consciously ambiguous: it implies an American commitment to defend Taiwan without provoking Beijing. Unlike hawks, doves are inclined to focus on such downside risks of policies that reinforce deterrence.

Doves presume that threats to deter and coerce often provoke an already agitated leader to retaliate. This process drags all parties into an unwanted conflict. If there were disastrous outcomes—for example, war—it would not be due to an interest vacuum or an absence of commitment. According to the doves, disaster results from the actions of fear-driven, mistake-ridden, risk-prone paranoids.

For doves, the main cause of a future war on the Korean Peninsula would be the destabilizing consequence of mutual efforts to reinforce deterrence: American threats for deterrence would actually provoke an imperiled state like North Korea to risk preemptive attacks or preventive wars.[15]

On the one hand, preemption is a response to an immediate crisis situation: mutually escalating fears and threats place a premium on offensive action. On the other hand, preventive war involves longer-term premeditated behavior on the part of one antagonist: before a situation deteriorates even further, the threatened nation would rather risk war. In this respect, a goal of preventive war is to forestall a change in the overall balance of power. Doves are concerned with both decreasing incentives for preemptive strikes and reducing provocation for preventive wars.

The doves claim that the lesson of the First World War—reassure at all costs—is applicable to North Korea. Prior to the outbreak of World War I, Dual Alliance members (Germany and Austria-Hungary) and Triple Entente allies (England, France, and Russia) failed to reassure one another. As a result, the alliance members saw efforts to reinforce deterrence as attempts to gain advantage. The principal European powers misjudged how their mobilization schemes would interact. Each feared that delay would allow their enemy to gain a decisive tactical advantage. They felt there was no choice but to escalate in order to avoid losing the advantage of going on the offense. This perceptual security dilemma resulted in provocation and unintended war.

With respect to preventive war, doves hold that leaders may decide to make war to avoid war. Leaders of endangered nations may risk war now to avoid a sure defeat later. An illustration of a preventive war is the attack by Israel on Egypt in the 1956 Sinai Campaign. Because of an arms race between Iraq and Egypt, Cairo began to acquire Soviet-bloc arms. Although they were ostensibly intended for use against Baghdad, Cairo's arms could have been employed against Tel Aviv. Hence, in return, Israel purchased arms from France. To avoid a situation where Egypt could start a war later that Israel could not win, it decided to attack before the situation worsened.[16]

To avoid preventive wars, doves suggest conciliation and accommodation to reassure threatened nations. Following the lead of doves, Cairo should have reassured Tel Aviv that Egypt's arms buildup was directed at Iraq, not Israel. But given the animosity between the Arab states and Israel, reassurance was not a realistic option for Egypt. Cairo could not reassure Tel Aviv without being criticized by Baghdad, Amman, and Damascus. In addition, Israel would not have believed Egypt's reassurance.

Just as the Middle East offers precedents for illustrating processes that lead to preventive wars, so does the Far East. Like Israel in the

1950s, North Korea in the 1990s may feel itself to be an "endangered species." Perceiving a growing disparity between themselves and South Korea, the rulers in Pyongyang may have incentives to launch a preventive war. In this regard, incentives for prevention and preemption may coincide. A perception in the present that it is better to fight now instead of allowing the situation to degenerate even further could converge with a perceived loss of control in a short-term crisis.

Were Pyongyang to launch a preemptive attack on Seoul, an incentive for this action might be a perception that it had no choice but to strike first in a crisis. This "crisis instability" could result from the vulnerability of Pyongyang's weapons systems to a first strike by Seoul. Furthermore, were North Korea to launch a preventive war against the South, it might be due to its perception that Pyongyang was on the losing side of a long-term trend in a changing balance of power.

## Hawks: Deterrent versus Compellent

Hawks split along a passive-active line of deterrence and coercion. Both groups advocate action; the issue is in the application. Deterrent hawks prefer a policy of threats to rewards; they seek to discourage action not yet taken. Deterrence can be achieved with a more passive approach, while compellence requires a more active policy. Compellent hawks advocate a conventional hard-line policy of threats over rewards; they want a target to cease taking an action or to undo an action already taken.[17]

With respect to North Korea, there is little distinction between deterrent and compellent hawks in practice. Deterrent hawks abound: they suggest a policy of threats to prevent North Korea from acquiring weapons of mass destruction. Compellent hawks exist only in principle: they would suggest a policy of threats to coerce North Korea to cease pursuing its nuclear weapons program or to dismantle it. And if rewards are in the policy package, hawks would link the rewards to evidence that Pyongyang has been rehabilitated from its naughty nuclear ways.

In other words, deterrent hawks advocate a linkage policy: any carrots should be tied to a change in North Korea's behavior. Conditional humanitarian assistance would be a carrot to be earned by proper behavior, such as agreeing to negotiate with South Korea. Instead of requiring linkage, however, the Clinton Administration has tolerated Pyongyang's reluctance to deal directly with Seoul.

The administration proposed that North Korea enter four-power negotiations involving Beijing, Pyongyang, Seoul, and Washington. When North Korea refused to come to the four-sided table, the administration continued with its humanitarian assistance.[18] This approach of providing unconditional assistance drives hawks up the trees of Washington's aviary. Indeed, hawks claim that Pyongyang requests food aid to keep the entire population from starving while its military continues to operate and absorb the limited resources of the country.[19]

Hawks assume that Pyongyang's goal of a separate peace with the United States, to the exclusion of Seoul, is a consequence of American weakness, saying in effect that U.S. diplomatic flexibility encourages North Korean belligerence.[20] The Heritage Foundation in Washington is a home for deterrent hawks, dubbed here as "Heritage hawks."

Heritage hawks argue that the strategy of North Korea is the deliberate destruction of the existing armistice structure that ended the Korean War. The goal is to convince the United States to sign a bilateral peace treaty with the North. Pyongyang desires "to cut Seoul out of the loop," for example, to exclude South Korea from a military settlement and facilitate the withdrawal of American forces from Korea. The Clinton Administration insists that the United States will not agree to such a deal; nevertheless, it implies that such a deal might be possible because of a willingness of Washington to engage in separate diplomatic discussions. Any Pyongyang-Washington talks imply a bilateral treaty. That is, when the United States negotiates with North Korea without the presence of the South, there is an implication that a separate deal might be acceptable.

Because the United States and its allies fought the Korean War under the UN flag, Washington should not be involved in negotiations with Pyongyang on its own. There should be multilateral talks followed by a replacement of the existing armistice structure with a peace treaty negotiated and signed by the North and South Korean governments. The State Department should announce that the United States will never consider a bilateral peace treaty with the North. That statement should recall for all parties that in the Reconciliation Agreement ratified by the governments of the North and South in 1992, the two sides pledged to negotiate a North-South peace agreement. Heritage hawks believe that the Clinton Administration's policies have failed to protect U.S. national interests in the Koreas. One primary interest is reduction of military tension along the DMZ. In order to achieve the objective of tension reduction along the borders, hawks advocate a series of interrelated moves.

The United States should condemn the North's behavior and reiterate to friend and foe alike a commitment to the defense of Seoul. In this respect, Washington should reinforce American ground troops in South Korea with radar aircraft and temporarily deploy one additional aircraft carrier to the Seventh Fleet in the Pacific. The bottom line is this: to deter the North from undertaking aggression against the South, Washington needs to augment American combat forces in the Korean Peninsula.

When hawks split along an active/passive dimension, the issue is whether to deter or coerce. Similarly, doves divide into two camps. The focus of doves is not whether to deter or coerce; their emphasis is on short-term and midterm consequences of deterrence and coercion.

## Doves: Libertarians versus Activists

Just as the Heritage Foundation typifies deterrent hawks, the Cato Institute exemplifies one wing of doves. Cato doves are of the "libertarian" variety. They are generally unwilling to take actions to avert conflicts. These doves place their faith in the long-term balance of political and economic power to avoid unwanted escalation.

Cato doves are coming into vogue during the post–Cold War era. Because the threat is less, it is more "politically correct" to be a libertarian than during Cold War days. Cato doves are the laissez-faire analysts of the policy process. They rely on the political-military balance of power among the parties and the magic of the economic marketplace to take care of a given situation. If there is an imbalance in favor of the status quo powers, they can take risks for peace. Similarly, a favorable balance of power for challengers allows them to have enhanced degrees of freedom vis-à-vis status quo powers.

To illustrate the libertarian position, consider an actual confrontation between a Cato dove and an unabashed hawk on an American television talk show. After Iraq had invaded Kuwait, I had the honor of making a guest appearance on *The Oprah Winfrey Show,* August 16, 1990.[21] My role was to defend the Bush Administration's hawkish decision to deploy hundreds of thousands of combat troops to Saudi Arabia. A former colleague of mine from the Reagan White House, Doug Bandow, represented the Cato Institute. He took it upon himself to criticize the American deployment in the Gulf. Bandow's argument was that the natural operation of the marketplace would cancel out the negative effects to the United States of the Iraqi possession of Kuwaiti oil. According to Bandow, it does not matter who owns the oil; what counts is the nature of the market for it. In order for oil to have value, it must eventually flow into international markets. Once there, its price is a consequence of economic supply and demand, not political ownership. In light of the operation of the oil market, Iraq's invasion of Kuwait was of little consequence to American consumers and thus was not a threat to American national interests, according to Bandow's logic.

I disagreed with Bandow. The Iraqi invasion of Kuwait was a threat to the U.S. national interest. The United States had made a commitment to the defense of Kuwait during the Iran-Iraq War. To allow Iraq to seize Kuwait would be a blow to American credibility and signal a lack of U.S. resolve. I paraphrased President Kennedy's statement that the United States had to honor its commitments. As the leader of the free world, Washington had to be prepared to go anywhere, to defend any friend against any foe, so that the light of liberty could survive. This broad strategic argument contrasted sharply with Bandow's narrow economic perspective. Of course, my strategic argument carried the day. (But who can recall losing a debate described by oneself!)

The Bandow libertarian position on the Gulf bears close resemblance to the Cato argument about the Korean Peninsula. Narrow economic cost-benefit calculations are at the core for both regions. The libertarian approach sees a South Korea that has twice the population of the North, an economy over ten times the size, and hence a Seoul that has the capability to match Pyongyang in defense spending.[22] Additionally, there is an imbalance of diplomatic clout in favor of Seoul and its allies over Pyongyang. With the possible exception of China, North Korea has no allies as such. Because South Korea can take care of itself, it should do so—such is the libertarian bottom line. Although

Seoul's economy is extremely strong in comparison to Pyongyang's, it may not be strong enough to handle the rush of refugees if and when North Korea implodes.

Regarding the political-military situation on the Korean Peninsula, the Cato doves favor accommodation between Washington and Pyongyang. The reasoning: embracing North Korea with economic incentives would reduce its motivations to harm its neighbors.

Additionally, Cato views the North as less of a threat in the post–Cold War era. And in the absence of a global Soviet threat, libertarians maintain that the American defense of South Korea loses its connection to U.S. security. With the lessening of the danger from the North, moreover, the rationale for Washington to defend Seoul is even less compelling.[23]

These libertarians suggest the following policy package for the United States. Washington should withdraw all American forces from South Korea over a four-year period, offer to transfer to Seoul whatever conventional armaments it desires to purchase, and announce an intention to terminate the United States–South Korea mutual defense treaty by the end of the twentieth century.

Also, libertarians prefer to continue improving relations with Pyongyang. One way of doing so is to meet the obligations Washington assumed under the 1994 Agreed Framework with Pyongyang, under which North Korea was to receive two new light-water nuclear reactors, heavy fuel, liaison offices with the United States, and a reduction in American economic sanctions. Other ways to foster enhanced relations include mediation of territorial disputes between the South and North, expansion of South Korean security cooperation with Japan, and participation of Seoul in regional security organizations.[24]

In contrast to the libertarian position, activist doves prefer to avoid preemptive strikes and preventive wars, regardless of the cost. They favor a policy of accommodation, irrespective of motivation. Libertarian doves advocate a hands-off approach, despite the risks of inaction.

Activist doves would agree to provide economic benefits to North Korea and to enhance political relations with its government, in the absence of any improvement in relations between Pyongyang and Seoul.

Activist doves are few and far between in Washington. During the Cold War, there was an "open hunting season" on activist doves. Only in the post–Cold War era has it been legitimate to argue this viewpoint. Even now, however, they are similar to an endangered species. Activist doves would assure, embrace, accommodate, and even appease North Korea. They would make promises to gain the confidence of the regime in Pyongyang. They would include North Korea into a regional alliance system and would reconcile past differences with Pyongyang. And in the worst case, they would appease the North Korean regime by buying it off. Doves of an activist feather would also lift economic sanctions on North Korea and provide humanitarian relief for its starving people. They would continue aiding Pyongyang, irrespective of the fact that doing so rescues that noncompliant regime from collapse.

Consider a policy problem to illustrate linkage. At issue was whether the Clinton Administration should provide about $25 million in unconditional food aid. The administration decided to do so. And during the spring of 1997, the *Galveston Bay*, an American-flagged ship, carried its first load of humanitarian assistance to North Korea. Doves ask, "If the people of a faraway country are starving, does the United States have a moral obligation to feed them?"[25] Activist doves would answer in the affirmative. Their ethical principle: "Ought implies can, and can implies should." That is, the United States ought to do good because it has the capability to do so. This self-imposed moral obligation is an inevitable consequence of the doves' vision of "America the good," versus the hawks' vision of "America the brave."

Indeed, because the obligation is moral, it is unconditional. Critics of the dovish approach advocate linking American humanitarian assistance to the North Korean diplomatic position: Washington should condition its supplies to Pyongyang's participation in multilateral talks, which would include Seoul. In answer to this proposed linkage, however, the State Department announced that the United States does not link food aid to peace talks.[26] In effect, the Clinton Administration assumes that floods and famine in North Korea are equivalent to similar events in friendly countries like England, Israel, and Mexico.

American hawks emphasize threats to North Korea over assistance to Pyongyang. Libertarian doves would provide assistance only as a transition toward withdrawal from the Korean Peninsula, while activist doves would give aid to North Korea regardless of its behavior.

## Hawks and Doves: Rational "Roosters"?

At first glance, it appears that both hawks and doves share in common an assumption that nations act rationally in their decisions to make war or peace. Both believe that leaders are capable of perceiving threat credibility, imbalance of power arrayed against them, and the likely consequences of their defensive actions. Do they simply "roost" on the same rational branch and argue about the best place on which to sit?[27] No, they do not dwell on the same branch. Because they divide over where on the branch threats cease to deter and begin to provoke, hawks and doves make different assumptions about rationality.

Hawks have more faith in rational action than do doves. Hawks do not even raise the prospect that threats can provoke. When doves ponder the circumstances in which deterrent threats become provocative threats, they imply that misperception is an explanation for the slide from deterrence to provocation. Those who would categorize hawks and doves together presume that perception is not a problem between them. But in fact, perception is at the core of the difference between them.

Hawks and doves focus on the balance of power between challengers and status quo powers. For hawks, imbalance in favor of the status quo actor should facilitate deterrence. For doves, a projection of imbalance in the long term may provoke a preventive war in the short term by the nation on the losing side of the trend.

Hawks follow the precepts of comprehensive rationality more than doves. Both, however, presume that the behavior of a target actor is more a result of the external environment than its internal nature. That is, they take a "billiard ball" approach: nations are like balls that ricochet off one another, driven by some hidden hand holding the cue stick of their national fate. Behavior is a consequence of the actions of others, not the result of attributes of the target actor.

The billiard ball approach ignores the characteristics of people. In this view, it is unnecessary to inquire into their incentives, motivations, and fears; it is enough to assume that people are more or less rational, and would avoid punishments and seek rewards from the external environment. This approach, in effect, "black boxes" the attributes of individuals: it conveniently sets aside human characteristics in order to make inferences about how a stimulus like a threat brings about a response, such as compliant behavior.

## Owls: Misperception and Loss of Control

In contrast to hawks and doves, owls take issue with the billiard ball approach. Not only do owls consider external incentives for behavior, they also look within the "black boxes" of individuals. Owls regard threat, reward, and prior reinforcement as candidate explanations for misperception and loss of control. They also take into account attributes of the actors, such as their risk-taking propensity. Owls believe that behavior is a consequence of the policies of an external, status quo power *and* the internal nature of a challenger. In this respect, owls attribute both compliant and roguish behavior to internal predisposition as well as prior reinforcements or punishments from the external environment.

Irrespective of risks, hawks suggest threats and doves favor rewards.[28] Owls, however, prefer either, neither, or both. An owlish approach recognizes that there are two ideal types of leaders: 1) power-hungry, error-free, cold-hearted mercenaries; and 2) fear-driven, mistake-ridden, risk-prone paranoids.[29] For owls, disastrous outcomes are due to a lack of knowledge. Owls might recommend policies of punishment, reward or both, as well as a hands-off approach, depending upon the attributes of the challenger.

Hawks and doves care little about the internal factors driving the actions of the North Korean regime. They explain Pyongyang's roguish behavior as due to the absence, or presence, of threats from Washington and Seoul. In contrast, owls would examine the internal nature of Kim Jong-Il's regime, seek to discover his motivations, hopes, and fears, and then from all of these, develop a suitable policy to influence the regime's actions.

Hawks make the most comprehensive set of assumptions about rationality, while doves make fewer, and owls make the least. Indeed, owls explicitly take into account the inability of some leaders to think rationally. In particular, owls focus on misperception as a constraint on decision making. They do not roost in the tree of rational decision making. Owls depend upon the tree of knowledge to underpin their policy recommendations: they nest on the limb of life rather than the assumed branch of rational action. In short, hawks see the proximate cause of war to be weakness; doves attribute war to provocation, while owls stress perceived loss of control among a package of internal and external factors.

Owls understand that national leaders are people with problems that cut across time and space. One set of issues concerns how humans value their possessions. They do not want to lose what they already have, and if given the chance, would like to possess what they desire. But if the world actually operated this simply, scholars would be out of a job. There are factors that cloud human decision making, namely emotions and motives. Owls accept the fact that emotions are almost impossible to control, and those of policy-makers are no exception.

The bottom line for owls is: people fear losses more than they covet gains. Owls contend that when the prospect of losing approaches, people become frantic to avoid deprivation. Situations become fuzzy, and claustrophobia reigns. When leaders are desirous, they become cautious; when leaders are fearful, they run risks.[30] Threats are effective when directed at cautious challengers; threats are ineffective when targeted against risk-takers. Hence, the owls' principle: accommodate those fearful of losing; confront those desirous of gaining. In contrast, hawks and doves are less concerned than owls with the risk-taking propensity of challengers.

World War II is the hawks' paradigm: confront the Hitlers of the world to deter their future aggressions. World War I and the Sinai Campaign are banner cases for doves: reassure the threatened and so avoid preemptive strikes and preventive wars. Both world wars are the consummate situations for owls: know thine adversary's fears and hopes.

## MISPERCEPTION IN THE
## POLICY PROCESS OF PYONGYANG

If misperception dominates decision making in North Korea, the regime may see no other alternative but war. If the dictators in Pyongyang misperceive American efforts to reinforce deterrence as attempts to gain advantage in an offensive war, they are likely to choose suicidal military action. Also, if perceived loss of control characterizes the leadership, such fears may force them to choose self-destructive war.

Owls would seek to ascertain whether the leaders in Pyongyang are capable of rational analysis. To the degree that they are, these leaders can be deterred and coerced; to the extent that they are not, Pyongyang can neither be deterred nor coerced. If the North Korean elite is on the low end of a "rheostat of rationality," then the leadership is liable to miscalculate the risk and expected gain of warfare.

In connection with threat perception, hawks magnify threats and rely too much on force as a means of conflict resolution. Doves underestimate dangers and overemphasize diplomacy. Owls seek valid estimations of threat and may advocate a balance of force and diplomacy.

On the one hand, hawks and doves suggest feasible policy recommendations. Their policies may be ineffective, because they disregard the psychology of decision making, but the particular appeal of hawks and doves in the policy process is that their analyses make use of simplifying assumptions about rationality. Presumptions of hawks and doves nest well with policy options.

On the other hand, owls, with their devotion to the richness of human behavior, may offer more valid explanations; yet these may be of little use in policy making. Hence, owls are likely to be theoretically valid but pragmatically bankrupt.[31]

In addition to the political aviary metaphor, another way of analyzing the case of North Korea is to inquire as to the aims of U.S. policy. To what extent are the goals retributive, rehabilitative, and idealistic? Also, to what degree are U.S. interests strategic and intrinsic in nature? The next section on the purposes of American policy addresses these two questions.

## THE PURPOSES OF AMERICAN POLICY

### Retribution and Rehabilitation

While post–Cold War optimists choose rehabilitation of Pyongyang, it was the Cold War pessimists who opted for a policy of retribution toward this floundering regime. In the past, the United States sought to punish the illegitimate government in the north, with little regard for changing its behavior. By contrast, the Clinton Administration leans toward a change in the behavior of the government, not the regime itself. Hence, Washington implicitly accepts its legitimacy. If Pyongyang plays the accommodation game with Washington, it is conceivable that a full range of conciliatory measures may fall into the laps of power-holders of the North.

If the main purpose of the sanctions is to oppose a regime or to right a wrong, retributive justice is at work. Retributive sanctions act in a punitive manner to change a regime, not its behavior. Rehabilitative sanctions, however, are implemented in response to a particular transgression. American sanctions imposed on North Korea in 1950 were mainly retributive. They demonstrated opposition to the North Korean Communist regime. The sanctions sought to punish North Korea and were targeted generally at the regime rather than its behavior.

Consider sanctions imposed on North Korea ostensibly on the grounds of its participation in terrorism. Although the sanctions are in response to a particular provocation, they derive from a retributive justice motivation. Despite the fact that North Korea has not engaged in any act of terrorism for nearly a decade and has repeatedly indicated its opposition to such activity, the United States still categorizes the regime as a sponsor of terrorism. As such, the sanctions may seek to punish North Korea, focusing on the U.S. government's broad opposition to the Communist regime, instead of on what remains of a former terrorist policy.

Pyongyang plays on Washington's anxiety. The Clinton Administration fears implosion of North Korea, with its population flooding across the border toward both China and South Korea. The administration also worries about military explosion by the armed forces of the North against the South. This anxiety is so pervasive that Washington is willing to take huge risks to give peace a chance, so to speak. Given these concerns, Washington underestimates the threat from North Korea, engages in a flight of wishful thinking, and concludes with a sunny scenario with a happy ending.

But there is a risk in discounting the threat: the regime may misuse American assistance. In preparation for an invasion of the South, Pyongyang could employ U.S aid to prop itself up instead of feeding its starving population. This humanitarian relief could unintentionally prolong the inevitable collapse of the regime. What line to take against North Korea can be understood in the context of a description of the nature of that regime in relation to American ideals and interests in the region.

## Ideals

In the first phase of the post–Cold War era, Washington perceived North Korea as a rogue elephant substitute for the slain Soviet bear. But this perception may change if evidence continues to mount that the elephant is more fearful than gainful in nature. Meanwhile, North Korea is unique among the rogue states of the world because of its self-inflicted isolation.[32] The unequivocal American support for North Korea's enemy to the south intensifies the separation.

One school of thought that wishes to embrace Kim Jong-Il assumes that he is not deterrable, but may be amenable to assurance and persuasion. But because he believes that the United States is determined to undermine his regime no matter what he does, Kim Jong-Il may be comparatively immune even to reassuring statements. He is a vulnerable leader motivated by need, rather than an opportunity-driven aggressor motivated by greed. Irrespective of which school provides the most valid explanation of Kim Jong-Il's behavior, reassurance must take into account his acute sense of vulnerability.

In contrast to the fear-based explanation, another school accounts for North Korea's behavior with the assumption that Kim Jong-Il is a would-be aggressor. Although he probably is a mixture of an opportunity-driven Machiavellian and a need-based paranoid, the Machiavellian part dominates. His decision to go to war with South Korea would partly be a matter of being provoked, but mostly his own opportunism would explain his choice to invade. At issue is the relative validity of these competing schools that seek to explain the same behavior: noncompliance.

Consistent with North Korea's intended isolation from foreign influences is a philosophy of self-sufficiency—*Juche*.[33] An emphasis on self-sacrifice and hard work manifests itself through the "Drink No Soup Movement." This so-called movement is a bizarre campaign by Pyongyang to keep factory workers from having too frequent a number of rest-room breaks. The goal is to keep the workers on the production lines rather than in the toilets!

The Drink No Soup Movement illustrates the gap between Washington and Pyongyang. At its core are differences concerning ideals and interests. Both governments believe strongly in conflicting ideals and see their interests in direct opposition to one another. Were Alexis de Tocqueville to visit North Korea, he would likely write about the strong links between values and policy. But while de Tocqueville attributed idealistic standards in America to widespread political discourse, such debate is absent in North Korea. Its values derive from a firm commitment to its *Juche* ideology. Just as America prides itself on committing blood and treasure in the defense of its allies, North Korea prides itself in defending itself against all outside influences.

## Strategic Interests

In addition to differences in ideals, there is a profound split between the United States and North Korea in perceived strategic and intrinsic interests. A strategic interest is one that is valuable because it allows for achievement of other ends: reputation, credibility, and alliances permit realization of objectives like deterrence and coercion. An intrinsic interest is one that is valuable in and of itself like lives, oil, and industry. Goals and interests are interrelated. Interests are the driving force behind goals.

A particular kind of strategic interest for deterrent purposes is a commitment to an ally. The North Korean case has become a metaphor for the failure to do so. Consider how Dean Acheson, Secretary of State prior to the outbreak of the Korean War, publicly stated that the U.S. defense perimeter in the Pacific ran from the Aleutians to the Philippines, including Japan and the Ryukyu Islands.[34] He tacitly excluded South Korea from the defense perimeter. The lesson for the future was to refrain from such explicit statements of inclusion or exclusion.

As a superpower, the United States has a strategic interest in making sure that Washington is the place where negotiations take place, and that the United States remains unchallenged. A perception of control and invincibility is the glue that holds together the American deterrent system. To the extent that Pyongyang stands up to Washington, there is a challenge to U.S. credibility, resolve, and commitments. When nations like North Korea confront Washington's resolve, the likelihood of deterrence failure elsewhere increases.

Regarding the Clinton Administration's definition of interests, consider a speech to the National Press Club in July of 1995, by former Secretary of State Warren Christopher. He outlined U.S. goals toward East Asia.[35] The first strategic goal is to maintain and strengthen U.S. alliances with Japan, South Korea, Australia, the Philippines, and Thailand. The second strategic objective is to engage former Cold War adversaries in the region. The third strategic aim is to build a regional system that maintains economic growth, facilitates integration, and insures long-term stability. The fourth goal is intrinsic—to support democracy and human rights, which serve U.S. ideals as well as interests.

In addition to the goals outlined by Christopher, there is another overriding one that is both strategic and intrinsic: nuclear nonproliferation. Assistant Secretary of Defense for International Security Affairs Joseph Nye specified that the U.S. aim was to stem the threat of proliferation of weapons of mass destruction and their means of delivery.[36]

The U.S. strategic interests regarding North Korea are related to objectives for Asia as a whole. Washington has an interest in continuing the flow of goods in the world market at prices that are consistent with the economic growth of the industrialized democracies. With the end of the Cold War, the regional menace from North Korea was a good substitute for the Soviet threat.

## Intrinsic Interests

American leaders also believe that North Korea threatens intrinsic interests: American civilians and military personnel in northeast Asia and American military personnel near the DMZ. Pyongyang is also seen as a danger to American citizens in general via its support for international terrorism, even though North Korea has renounced its support in this regard.[37]

In the context of the rival perspectives of hawks, doves, and owls, as well as the discussion of ideals and interests, consider the relationship between Pyongyang and Washington across three broad cases: the Korean War at mid-century, a nuclear crisis of the mid-1990s, and a set of humanitarian crises at the close of the century.

# FROM CONVENTIONAL WAR
# TO NUCLEAR AND HUMANITARIAN CRISES[38]

A brief overview of the early history of the American–North Korean relationship sets the stage for a discussion of the lessons of the Korean case. That history, moreover, establishes a framework for viewing Pyongyang's nuclear weapons development.[39]

American-North Korean relations have been on a roller coaster of ups and downs. The "down times" of confrontation drove the "up times" of negotiations. A first phase in the 1950s consisted of the Korean War followed by protracted negotiations. A second period between the 1960s and the 1980s included small-scale incidents that did not escalate into full-blown military action because of crisis diplomacy. A third phase in the 1990s saw Washington and Pyongyang go to the nuclear brink only to be pulled back by creative diplomacy.[40]

And as the twentieth century closes, a fourth phase opens. This stage finds crisis as an unexpected consequence of flood and famine. Instead of the pattern of Pyongyang inducing a crisis as an opportunity to squeeze Washington, the new model reverses the process. Just as North Korea used crises as an occasion to obtain concessions from the United States, Washington might be able to employ humanitarian crises to pressure Pyongyang to make concessions to Seoul. In other words, these new crises are an opportunity for Western humanitarian diplomacy. Explicit linkage of crises to concessions, however, might be counterproductive.

While the upside of humanitarian crises may be to provide an opening for diplomacy, the downside could be to increase the likelihood for implosion of North Korea's society and/or military explosion across the DMZ. But before turning to floods, food, and fuel, consider briefly the early period in the relationship between North Korea and the United States.

## Korean War: Lessons Learned

In 1948, Moscow established a new Communist state in North Korea; Washington replied with a South Korea aligned with the West.[41] Though the United States played an important role in the region, Washington considered South Korea to be of only secondary strategic interest. Of primary concern were Japan and Formosa. As a result, the United States hoped to keep only a short-term tactical force in the Korean Peninsula, but to deploy strategic forces for a longer term in or near Japan and Formosa. Neither Moscow nor Washington expected to occupy the Korean Peninsula for an indefinite period of time. The division of the peninsula into two countries was to have been part of an interim trusteeship prior to a general election.

Tensions rose during the early 1950s, with two opposing ideologies rising between "brotherly" nation-states. Hostilities broke out on June 25, 1950: North Korean troops attacked South Korea. Prior to that assault, Secretary of State Acheson had publicly announced that the United States would support Seoul through the United Nations. But Pyongyang may not have interpreted Washington's commitment to signal military intervention to save Seoul in the event of an attack from the North. However, in apparent contradiction to the U.S. pledge to take any aggression against the South to the United Nations, the State Department omitted South Korea from a list of countries that were a part of the U.S. defense perimeter in East Asia. But the Secretary of State was not alone in excluding South Korea from the defense perimeter.

The U.S. Joint Chiefs of Staff also considered South Korea to be of minor strategic value in terms of another general war. Because its fate would be decided in other theaters of war, Korea lacked strategic significance for the global pattern of U.S. security. In other words, the Truman Administration considered South Korea to be of minor importance in and of itself and significant only to the extent that it was a part of a war with the USSR. Not only did the Chiefs consider South Korea to be of secondary value, they believed it was a strategic liability.[42]

A Cold War idea that Washington had to oppose what Moscow favored had not yet taken root. Indeed, the Korean War was a threshold event precisely because it established the Cold War principle that neither superpower could afford to lose land to the other or to its proxies.

But another of Washington's allies in Asia had already been defeated in the civil war in China during 1949, when the Chinese Nationalists lost their foothold on the mainland and fled to Formosa. Hence, when the Korean War came on the heels of the defeat of America's Chinese allies, the two events reinforced the interdependency of commitments and the connection between national security and domestic politics.

The United States intervened to protect South Korea because of a convergence of perceived threats to international security and the domestic political security of American presidents. As stated above, the danger from the North Korean invasion of the South had been underestimated because of a focus on the global threat, rather than the regional menace of Communism. On top of the reformulated national security assessment that the Korean Peninsula had regional value as well as global utility, there was the significance of Asia to American domestic politics. During the 1950s, China, Korea, and Indochina became hot-button political issues that Republicans could use to slam Democrats.

President Truman had already made a controversial decision to evade the American commitment to the Chinese Nationalists. Once the Communists had defeated the Nationalists in their civil war, Asian national security affairs became a domestic political liability for Truman. He was hammered incessantly with questions about "Who lost China?" The clear answer was that the Democrats had lost China. Consequently, they had a huge image problem. The Democrats were seen as soft on Communism. Even to raise the question was equivalent to political homicide.[43]

Having already been charged with losing China, the Truman Administration could hardly afford to accept the responsibility of having also lost Korea. After the defeat in China and the war in Korea, the Democratic administration was more willing to help the French in Indochina.[44] Thereafter, successive administrations upped the ante. The net effect of these expanding commitments was the Vietnam War.[45] Domestic political danger of inaction in foreign affairs was a motivation for actions abroad that inadvertently spiraled out of control.

With respect to lessons learned, two sets of principles emerged from the 1950s in general and the Korean War in particular. They concern threat and opportunity as well as politics and policies. With respect to the first set, North Korea uses threat in a crisis as an opportunity for diplomacy. In the phases of the American–North Korean relationship, Pyongyang was the initiator during the mid–twentieth century. It created crises in order to control outcomes involving the United States.

But as the twenty-first century opens, North Korea is losing the capability of initiation; rather, events such as floods and famine are creating chaos instead of control. Because it is not as easy for North Korea to use threats for diplomatic gain, there is an opportunity for Washington to be the diplomatic initiator.

Another aspect of the threat/opportunity nexus consists of perception. In the mid-1950s, the Truman Administration misperceived the regional threat as it focused on the global danger. Yet in defining the threat, the geographical frame of reference was crucial. Because it underestimated the regional threat, Washington omitted Seoul from the American defense perimeter.[46]

This omission then led Pyongyang to miscalculate the depth of the American commitment to South Korea. The Korean War was a defining moment in the expansion of America's security perspective. Perceived regional threats from the "Pyongyangs of the world" then took their positions alongside the global menace from Moscow.

A further aspect of the threat/opportunity relationship involves unanticipated consequences of success. The United States succeeded in establishing South Korea as an independent state. Washington perceived independence for the South under its tutelage as an opportunity to gain a strategic foothold in Asia along the Soviet and Chinese borders. But in setting up this presence, Washington failed to include Seoul in its regional defense perimeter. As a result, North Korea seized this exclusion as an opportunity to attack the South. In other words, Pyongyang saw a window of opportunity to reunite the country under Kim Il Sung.

The bottom-line lesson is that the United States should bring its commitments in line with its obligations. In setting up South Korea, the United States took on an implicit obligation to protect it. But by excluding South Korea from its defense perimeter in Asia, Washington created a gap between obligation and commitment.

The second set of lessons deriving from the American–North Korean relationship consists of politics and policies. Politics divide into domestic and bureaucratic aspects. On the domestic side, the loss of land in Asia made national security policies into domestic political priorities. Consequently, decisionmakers need to be aware of the political costs of both inaction and action in foreign affairs. On the bureaucratic side, the 1950s found hawks and doves at odds as usual.

The Truman Administration's initial hands-off policy regarding South Korea was in line with the globalist, libertarian dove policy-making schema. Policy analysts in that administration advocated a laissez faire approach to the regional threat that North Korea posed to the South and emphasized instead the global threat from the Soviet Union. The Truman analysts relied on the global balance of power to take care of regional threats. In the 1950s, the balance of power worldwide was the focus of what was, in effect, a libertarian approach. But the administration failed to pay attention to the strategic consequences of the regional balance.

Another consequence of the Korean War for politics and policies was to change from the bankrupt libertarian dove approach to a hawkish policy. Doves "flew south" in the bureaucratic war for Washington as the North Korean troops marched south into Seoul. From then on, hawks dominated the U.S. national security decision-making process. In short, hawks presided in the bureaucratic politics of Washington in response to aggression from Pyongyang against

Seoul and because Korea had become a controversial topic in American politics generally.

## Nuclear Crisis: Lessons Learned

Following the war in the 1950s, North Korea maintained a large standing army, while the United States continued to deploy troops along the border between the North and the South. On top of these large conventional forces facing one another, the pursuit of nuclear weapons by North Korea created a crisis for the United States and its allies in the region.

Tensions reemerged on the Korean Peninsula in 1984. Intelligence indicated that Pyongyang was pursuing an active program of nuclear weapons development. With the construction of a nuclear power reactor in Yongbyon during the early 1980s, North Korea began to acquire a capability to produce weapons-grade plutonium.[47] In 1985, North Korea joined the Non-Proliferation Treaty (NPT). It officially revealed the existence of the Yongbyon plant.

During 1990, North Korea had a demonstrated capacity to separate plutonium. Doing so indicated that Pyongyang had taken a major step in the direction of nuclear weapons construction. And three years later, North Korea revealed plans to withdraw from the NPT.[48] And although Pyongyang did not officially do so, it created a crisis that resulted in negotiations during 1994. At that time, Pyongyang temporarily ceased operations at the Yongbyon plant to allow for the removal of weapons-grade material. A conservative estimation of the yield potential of the fuel was 7-14 kilograms of plutonium, enough to build one or two nuclear weapons.[49]

The North had claimed that it had withdrawn from the NPT and was hence not bound by International Atomic Energy Agency (IAEA) inspections. But Washington did not accept Pyongyang's claim, holding that North Korea remained a member of the NPT and was subject to its rules. Later in 1994, Pyongyang suspended its nuclear program after signing an accord with Washington, the Agreed Framework.[50]

Two years after signing the Agreed Framework, Secretary of Defense William Perry commented on the accord.[51] He said that the United States reached the agreement with a mixed policy that combined threats with promises; that is, coercive diplomacy. The United States and its allies linked threats to impose economic sanctions with promises of commercial nuclear power.

Perry and other defenders of the accord held that both sides had something to gain from the 1994 Framework. On the one side, it would allow North Korea to acquire two new 1000-megawatt light-water reactors and heavy oil for heating and electricity to suffice until the West built the first reactor. These actions would result from a $4 billion deal over a ten-year period. On the other side, Pyongyang would agree to cease all activities at its nuclear weapons–producing gas-graphite reactors, adhere to the NPT, and allow inspections of suspect nuclear facilities.

Critics contend that Washington should have obtained more from Pyongyang in return for exchanging diplomatic liaison offices and supplying North Korea with fuel oil for dismantling its plutonium-generating reactors. Detractors of the accord hold that the United States was too eager to cut a deal with North Korea. These same critics assume that the regime in North Korea is on the verge of collapse and that the Framework Agreement breathed new life into a dying regime.[52]

In connection with lessons learned, the nuclear crisis of the 1990s reinforced principles from the 1950s concerning threat and opportunity as well as politics and policies. North Korea seized upon the nuclear threat as an opportunity to create a crisis, because the issue was so salient to the United States. Pyongyang accomplished one of its main objectives—bilateral negotiations with the United States.

But contrary to North Korea's hope for institutionalizing its bilateral relationship with the United States, Washington was able to create a multilateral organization in solving its nuclear crisis with Pyongyang. The Korean Economic Development Organization (KEDO) is a multinational organization of American, Japanese, and South Korean officials. Their countries created KEDO in order to carry out the Agreed Framework, and it has become an effective interlocutor with North Korea on nuclear-related issues.[53] Therefore, what is the lesson for threat and opportunity? Namely, that a threatening nuclear crisis became a diplomatic opportunity for the three allies to work together.

A related lesson involves the nexus of politics and policies. Third parties like the United States enter alliances to protect weaker parties like

South Korea. In the politics of alliance management, however, there are times in which the protector has to negotiate policies with the challenger and not just with the protected. In such a case, however, it is crucial to include the protected in the talks. In spite of excluding South Korea in some of the bilateral negotiations with the North, though, it was possible to make diplomatic progress on Korean problems while maintaining an international consensus among Seoul, Tokyo, and Washington.[54]

## Humanitarian Crises: Lessons Learned

Using the threat of a nuclear crisis to manipulate the West was supposed to be consistent with the North Korea's philosophy of self-sufficiency—*Juche*. But even the nuclear issue produced a multilateral mechanism in the form of KEDO, an organization that further decreased North Korea's self-imposed isolation. Humanitarian crises involving floods and food in North Korea may effect a similar outcome. There is no institutionalized international tool for managing economic crisis and political instability for North Korea. One result of international involvement in addressing humanitarian issues, however, is that it is likely to decrease North Korea's freedom of action and integrate it within the family of nations more than it intended.

As background for examining humanitarian crises concerning North Korea, consider its economic situation. North Korea has a population, estimated in 1995, at about 24 million people. The average population density is over 500 people per square mile. There has been a rapid influx of North Koreans from the countryside to the cities. Over 60 percent of the population is urban. The annual national budget in the late 1980s was about $16 billion. During the mid-1990s, North Korea's economy declined four years in a row. The decrease was as much as 25 percent between 1989 and 1993. The North's external debt was over $10 billion at the beginning of 1994. Its debt is equal to approximately one half of its annual GDP, which is only about $22 billion. The GDP per capita of North Korea is less than $1,000. In contrast to the North, South Korea's GDP is $424 billion, with a per capita value of almost $10,000.[55]

Floods occurred in North Korea in August 1995, and the food situation there immediately worsened. That summer Pyongyang had already negotiated grain deals with Seoul and Tokyo for over 600,000 tons of rice, and by the fall, there was a sea change in Pyongyang's relationship with the outside world. North Korea requested international assistance for the first time in its almost half century of existence, an event that jettisoned its philosophy of *Juche*. During 1996, the North confronted another grain shortfall of about a million tons. Additionally, a dearth of fertilizer reinforced a premature harvest in that year, worsening the food shortages. Without outside help, the food scarcity would become a famine.

During the spring of 1997, the United Nations World Food Programme stated that North Korea needed about 1.3 million tons of food to avoid a famine, and requested them from the international community. The UN agency also announced that North Korea sought direct donations of about one million tons. For two years in a row, North Korea had to ask for food assistance, suggesting an erosion of its philosophy of *Juche*.[56]

At issue in the humanitarian crisis confronting North Korea is what should be the mechanism by which to address it. Based on the lesson learned from the nuclear crisis, multilateral rather than bilateral approaches are the most effective route. A bilateral approach from the South would give rise to political differences both between the two and within each country about the propriety of the assistance. Similarly, a bilateral solution with the United States in the lead could lead to misperceptions on the part of North Korea as to Washington's intent. The bottom line is that the food crisis is not only a threat to the economic security and political instability of the North, but also an opportunity for the international community to insert itself into the politics and policies of the Pyongyang regime.[57]

On the basis of this journey from war to crisis, consider future scenarios and alternative policy packages by hawks and doves. Although owls prefer to analyze the past and the present, their portraits of future states of affairs also are instructive.

## SCENARIOS[58]

Policy-planning hawks and doves expect North Korea to experience one of four scenarios. First is explosion—a desperate bid by Pyongyang to unify the peninsula by force. A second is implosion—an economic and political collapse that would fuel a mass exodus of refugees into China, Japan, and South Korea. A third is a happy ending—diplomatic concessions from North Korea in return for Western food and investment, which might reverse its economic deterioration and maintain the regime in Pyongyang, and result in peaceful reunification. And a fourth is "muddling through," or the continuation of the status quo with minor adjustments.

Hawks would continue to contain North Korea, irrespective of whether such containment exacerbates tendencies toward implosion.[59] They argue that power-hungry, error-free, cold-hearted mercenaries would take advantage of humanitarian aid. Therefore, credible strength and effective force must be available to deter a cool-minded Machiavellian leadership from attacking. One problem with this approach of letting North Korea collapse is that it could result in a civil war among factions in the North, in which nuclear fuel becomes a bargaining chip in the struggle for succession, while the collapse itself could provoke intervention by third parties in a crisis that spins out of control.

Indeed, doves would argue that containment and threats toward a fear-driven, mistake-ridden, risk-prone paranoid would bring about unintended disaster: an explosion by factions within North Korea across the border against the South. In contrast, embracing the fearful will bring about a peaceful resolution, avoiding both implosion and explosion. Humanitarian food aid for flood victims and starving civilians are an option to help Pyongyang avoid implosion while quelling its fears of Western control. In fact, doves are not concerned about where food relief is allocated. Even if aid is diverted to the military, at least the military will not have an incentive to march southward for food relief for themselves, or so the doves argue.

Because owls are not a direct part of the policy-making process, they have the time and temperament to analyze each situation individually. They would assess whether or not the North Korean leadership is comprised of the power-hungry or fear-driven, which would let owls know whether leaders are working from a window of opportunity or a basement of fear. But in the context of a North Korea that is very secretive with respect to information, it is hardly likely that owls would be able to gather the data necessary to perform their analyses.

According to owls, North Korean mercenaries would perceive an embrace by the United States as a window of opportunity to explode against the South. In other words, mercenaries are cold-blooded opportunists who jump at occasions to take advantage of enemies. Owls reason further that if North Korean leaders are fearful, they could misperceive deterrent threats as provocations that would warrant lashing out and escaping the basement of fear. Analytic owls, by refraining from the policy-making process and integrating different situational ideas, are able to come up with mixed policy packages, such as a combination of embracing and containing, which could lead to scenarios of both explosion and implosion.

## Explosion

Though both hawks and doves have different opinions as to how explosion might come about, they are in agreement as to the consequences. If Pyongyang explodes, it could start a war with a salvo of 170mm shells from its 240 howitzer batteries along the 38th Parallel. The North Korean army would then make a southward charge using all the means at its disposal. Methods would include land and sea forces, especially submarine units. The goal of the quick strike would be a fait accompli.[60] However, the purpose of the assault would not be the military conquest of South Korea and forced unification of the peninsula, but rather Pyongyang's seizure of Seoul as a diplomatic bargaining chip to play during the peace talks.

If Pyongyang pursues Soviet military doctrine, an assault on the South would include an artillery shower followed by a lightning attack. South Korea's half-million-plus army along with about 37,000 American armed forces deployed along the DMZ would be overwhelmed by North Korea's one-million man army. American counteraction would include stealth attacks by the hard-to-detect B-2 and F-117 warplanes. The tactical aim would be to cut off the eyes and ears of Pyongyang by destroying its command, control, and intelligence. Such a strategy would demolish railroads and bridges, followed by direct American engagement by helicopter, such as the infamous Apache.

During an invasion by the North, there would be an evacuation of all American citizens, as well as those from Japan, Canada, and Great Britain. During a tense period in 1994, this American evacuation plan was 24-72 hours away from initiation. Doves maintain that explosion would be a result of a hard-line approach that provokes North Korea into a desperate preemptive strike or preventive war. Without provocation, doves believe that quelling Pyongyang's fears would avoid an explosion against Seoul. Hawks hold that explosion would be a result of a soft-line approach by Washington. A policy of accommodation might have too many undesirable consequences for hawks. Therefore, the only option for hawks is containment. As the nuclear crisis gives way to humanitarian crisis, however, the likelihood of military confrontation decreases relative to that of implosion.

## Implosion and Unification

If the North Korean regime did little to avert the collapse of its society and government structures, unification with the South could be a result. But Seoul strongly opposes unification because of its economic costs, which might amount to about $1 trillion.[61]

Both Hawks and doves consider the possibility that North Korea may just collapse into a vacuum of power. They agree on how an implosion scenario would evolve. The scenario begins with food shortages, famine, and natural disasters. If there were a deterioration of the economic situation, there could be an escalation of the flow of refugees from the North to the South, with only half the food necessary to feed the population available.

If the regime in Pyongyang collapses, Seoul has a contingency plan to handle the influx of refugees from the North. South Korea would establish "counter-brainwashing centers" where refugees would be deprogrammed of Communist beliefs acquired over a lifetime. But with unification costs so large, Seoul has not budgeted for this contingency.

The implosion scenario has two facets. One is that the refugees from the Pyongyang region will automatically turn to the South, beginning the long walk to a land of milk and honey. The other aspect is that villagers from the countryside will not know where to turn. They have been programmed to believe that North Korea has been better off than the rest of the world. They have also been led to believe that China has always been and will continue to be North Korea's only ally. Hence, it is likely that these uninformed rural refugees will turn northwest toward the Yalu River.

In addition to Seoul, Washington has also engaged in contingency planning based upon the implosion scenario. The American military has geared up to be the lead department in the government for implosion planning. Rather than preparing to fight, moreover, the Pentagon proposes to head up a large international relief effort on the Korean Peninsula. At issue is what to do when large numbers of hungry refugees begin flowing out of North Korea via land and sea— by foot and by boat.

One of Washington's main priorities is to limit the American ground combat involvement inside North Korea. In this connection, the UN would assume a major role in the relief operation, while ground-based military personnel would come from South Korea and other nations. The United States would confine itself to long-range transportation, large-scale communications, and international coordination. One reason for minimizing the American involvement would be to avoid a situation in which North Korean troops, uninformed about the American role in a humanitarian relief effort, might open fire on U.S. personnel and equipment operating within North Korea.[62]

Activist doves argue that continued application of sanctions without food relief would exacerbate the humanitarian crisis and provoke remnants of the North Korean armed forces either to fight among themselves or launch a preemptive strike against South Korea. Libertarian doves contend that an implosion is inevitable. But instead of attributing collapse to a hard-line policy, Cato doves would promote a hands-off approach, perhaps even a withdrawal of the 37,000 American troops from the DMZ. Why should the United State waste resources to prop up a falling regime? According to libertarian doves, Washington should not. Without international aid to keep it alive, Pyongyang will eventually crumble. Libertarian doves advocate a hands-off approach, regardless of the risks of inaction. What they neglect to realize, however, is that withdrawal not only reduces threat credibility, but should the North explode into the South, Washington would take the blame.

## Happy Ending—A Soft Landing

A happy-ending scenario implies that North Korea will reform its Cold War Communist economy, increase its economic output, and engage in international trade with other nations, irrespective of ideology. But such reforms would challenge the existence of North Korea as a Communist state. Also, economic reform by North Korea would imply détente with the South, a political realignment that would take considerable negotiation to put into effect.

A negotiated reunification of the Korean Peninsula without war or disintegration of North Korea is indeed a sunny scenario. While Heritage hawks and Cato doves agree that propping up a failing regime would be futile, activist doves have a different vision. They would provide assistance in order to avoid preemptive strikes and preventive war and appease Pyongyang to avoid confrontation. The international community would give assistance in proportion to diplomatic concessions, even at the risk of propping up the regime. Pursuit of such a politically risky policy is why activist doves are few and far between in Washington. One reason this scenario would be the least painful is that it hinges on shaky assumptions regarding North Korea and other nations in Asia.

The first supposition is that Pyongyang will be persuaded into compliance and thus consent to a normalizing of ties. But this presumption has been shown to be false in the past. The second assumption of the soft landing scenario is that other Asian countries, including China, Japan, and Taiwan, will see their interests coinciding and will act in concert. In fact, though, a reunified Korean Peninsula may not be in the perceived interests of these three countries. Economically, they may not want to see Seoul, already a fierce competitor, become even stronger years after unification. Politically, these same countries would feel uneasy with a fast growing, militarily strong Korea.

Should policy toward North Korea be based on the happy-ending scenario, owls would be quick to point out a motivated bias. They would state that activist doves see what they want to see—a North Korea that would comply if the United States would only let them. But in so thinking, activist doves would be ignoring the many contradicting facts that make the happy-ending scenario unlikely.

## Muddling Through

With the explosion scenario becoming an unlikely possibility, the two main possibilities are happy ending and collapse. But in between reform and collapse lies "muddling through."[63] China, Japan, and Russia, as well as South Korea, might all desire muddling through in contrast to implosion, which is more likely than reform. In the context of a North Korea that neither reforms nor collapses, there would be less of a threat to the United States and its allies than other contingencies. But just as we should guard against the soft-landing scenario because it is so desirable, so we should be wary of the muddling through scenario. Minimizing a threat is a bias in information processing that often stems from the tendency to see what we desire to see, a bias that raises the issue of threat perception.

## THREAT PERCEPTION AND POLICY PACKAGES

In contrast to hawks and doves, an aspect of the owl's approach to the evaluation of policies is to inquire as to the nature of threat perception. At issue concerning threat perception is how people see each other as threatening. Such a question requires an explanation of why individuals validly perceive or misperceive threats. Thus, why does the United States view North Korea as a hazard, and why does Pyongyang see Washington as a danger? While some actors discern threats as intended, others misperceive the same actions and experience threat misperception.

Recall from Chapter Six the discussion of American-Cuban threat perception: Washington and Havana misperceive peril because of biased information processing. When the Clinton Administration views Pyongyang, moreover, there may also be a misperception of threat. But there are differences between the two cases.

Unlike its overestimation of the danger from Castro's Havana, the administration may be underestimating the menace from Kim Jong-Il's regime in Pyongyang. Prior administrations tended to magnify the risk from North Korea. During the Cold War, conventional wisdom rewarded North Korean bashing. It bolstered both domestic political fortunes and national deterrence. Magnification of menace was a motivated bias that brought handsome dividends to politicians and diplomats alike.[64] Washington decisionmakers benefited at home and abroad from hostility toward Pyongyang. Overestimation of threat was strengthened by an unmotivated historical bias against communism.

From about 1950 to 1975, the political landscape was riddled with East-West confrontations. This was a time of tensions between the United States and Asian communist states. Accordingly, American politicians stood to gain a political bounce in the polls for standing up to communists in general and to China and North Korea in particular. When U.S. leaders saw both what they *wanted* to see and what they *expected* to see, they magnified the threat posed by North Korea. But in the post–Cold War era, there is less incentive to play the anticommunist card.

According to the reasoning of those who accuse the Pentagon of threat magnification, however, there is a difference between national interests and those of departments within the U.S. government. For example, critics of the Department of Defense argue that it needs a pretext to defend its budget. But it is nonsense to imagine that the Pentagon created a North Korean threat out of thin air just to serve its bureaucratic needs. Yet with the Cold War over, Michael Klare makes the case that the Pentagon indeed magnified a threat from rogue states in general.[65]

The post–Cold War age finds different dispositions operating in American-North Korean relations. As a result, there is a tendency to minimize the threat because of these inclinations. In terms of motivated bias, the Clinton Administration sees benefits in a happy-ending scenario to the Korean conflict. These include a lower U.S. defense budget that allows for higher domestic spending, good economic relations with China, and enhanced security at lower costs for allies like South Korea and Japan. In other words, the administration sees a comparatively benign North Korea, because doing so serves these three goals. In addition, unmotivated biases regarding communism reinforce Washington's threat underestimation. After the fall of the Berlin Wall, communists simply do not look as threatening as they once did. Hence, if Washington expects to see a less menacing Pyongyang, presto! North Korea is less threatening!

But the dispositions do not always move in the same direction or imply a similar course of action. One reason why U.S. policy toward North Korea continues unchanged after the Cold War has ended is that there is a clash among American biases. As stated above, motivated bias causes underestimation of threat. Such a minimal danger is consistent with an approach of embracing North Korea.

Some unmotivated biases operate at cross-purposes to each other. Due to the historical image of Kim Il Sung as one of the lesser communist enemies of Asia, there was an unmotivated bias that associated him with "evil." Thus, there is a tendency by the American public to perceive his son, Kim Jong-Il, in the same light. Such perception is a drag on the policy process. As a result of the anchoring effect of this unmotivated bias, a shift of American policy from containment to accommodation is difficult. In short, motivated bias rewards a change toward accommodation, but an unmotivated bias reinforces the tendency for containment. As a result of this conflict, American policy remains the same.

Just as American policy resists change, so does North Korea's policy defy alteration. Kim Jong-Il has a motivated bias that causes him to underestimate the American threat. His dire economic situation impels him to see less danger in associating with the enemy; consequently, he does so as a means to acquire food assistance, flood relief, and other humanitarian aid.

Kim Jong-Il also has a motivated bias that causes him to overestimate the American hazard. Because of the domestic political benefits for standing up to the United States, he augments the threat from Washington. And his recollection of the bad old days of the Cold War propels him toward a policy of confrontation. In other words, a historical image of American leaders as enemies pushes Kim Jong-Il to view their behavior as aggressive, without interpreting that behavior on its own merits. Dictators facing potential internal challengers may be pleased to have an external threat with which to divert the attention of the population. The American embargo is an external threat that enables the North Korean leadership to maintain a tight grip on the country.

Owls would suggest dealing out sticks when punishment is warranted. They would distinguish situations where a tough response is called for from those in which it is appropriate to provide humanitarian relief. Pyongyang needs to learn that sending a submarine full of spies into Seoul's territory is unacceptable. In this situation, owls would opt to teach the lesson with a forceful reply.

But owls would also acknowledge the fact that Pyongyang is afraid and faltering. As a result of floods and a famine that has wiped out most of their agriculture, North Koreans have been eating only about one bowl of rice per day. Owls would point to evidence that the mass starvation includes 100,000 deaths just in one year and a whole generation shrinking in height. Also, Pyongyang has been involved with a "dance of defecting diplomats," where top officials have escaped to neighboring countries. Owls take all of these factors into consideration and would couple a policy of embracement to quell the regime's fears and one of containment to deter when warranted.[66]

A combination policy not only addresses individual scenarios of implosion and explosion, but also deals with the possibility that both may happen at the same time. Pyongyang may start to implode and, with a last gasp of air, explode toward Seoul. In the event of the mixed contingency of implosion and explosion, owls would say, deal with the aggression of explosion with an iron fist, but deal with Pyongyang's collapse with a soft hug.

President Clinton shares a sense of optimism with the libertarians. His administration, however, parts ways over the balance of diplomatic carrots over economic and military sticks. Both would provide rewards, but the Clinton Administration takes an owlish approach to include carrots and sticks. Critics of the administration, however, would argue that rewards dominate punishments. However, given the history of North Korea and its present rogue status, it is puzzling that the administration believes that Pyongyang can be influenced by a policy of alleviating punishments and augmenting rewards. Despite its faults, the administration pursues a mixed policy toward the peninsula that is about right in its application.

The mixed approach of the Clinton Administration is a shift away from the approach of the Cold War years. The original American sanctions approach was pessimistic and overestimated the threat from the North. Pyongyang, after all, was a child of the Cold War, and its behavior would change only with the fall of the regime and reunification of the Korean Peninsula under the sovereignty of Seoul. Initial American sanctions sought to destabilize the North Korean regime because of its invasion of South Korea. On top of the Korean War came other egregious conduct, including seizure of an American intelligence vessel and construction of nuclear facilities with a capacity for producing weapons-grade plutonium.

U.S. policy toward North Korea is neither too pessimistic nor too optimistic regarding the estimated threat from the North. Because of the end of the Cold War, Pyongyang's behavior is ripe for change, according to the doves. The Clinton Policy assumes that the post–Cold War era is an opportune time for the regime to mend its naughty ways. The administration also assumes that the ruling clique acts more from a basement of fear than a window of opportunity. Three factors justify this optimistic perspective: an end of the international welfare safety net afforded by the Cold War; the death of a long-time dictator and his replacement by an unsteady hand at the helm; and a series of natural disasters. These three make Pyongyang more vulnerable to reason and reward. Rewards are more effective than punishment of a noncomplying or a frightened North Korea. Additional penalties might frighten it into making counterproductive choices, according to the optimists.

But, according to the owls, the Clinton Administration approach makes sense only if the North Korean regime is driven more by fear than by opportunity. Otherwise, post–Cold War optimists in Washington may lead the United States down a slippery slope to assure, embrace, accommodate, and perhaps even appease the oppressors in Pyongyang.

Whether the United States pursues a posture of embracing or containing North Korea depends in part on scenarios that develop between Pyongyang and Seoul. The option of a military withdrawal by the United States is a nonstarter. With the memories of prior failures and fallen countries due to American inaction, successive administrations have been cautious about the Korean Peninsula. In order to avoid the possibility of being blamed for inaction when disaster strikes, it would be less risky politically to retain the American troop deployment in Korea even in the event of war than to withdraw prior to an attack. If the United States were to withdraw the 37,000 troops from around the DMZ, and the North attacked, the administration in office would receive a well-deserved domestic political blow. This fear of a political loss brands the military withdrawal policy as political suicide.

Cold War hawks criticized the Truman Administration for implicitly excluding South Korea from the American defense perimeter. Post–Cold War hawks would condemn a withdrawal option as a military weakness that provides a window of opportunity for the North either to launch a new Korean War or to collapse as a society. In this respect, military withdrawal and allowing North Korea to collapse are both nonstarters.

## THREAT, OPPORTUNITY, POLITICS, AND POLICY

Recall the four themes that cut across *Rogue Regimes:* threat perception, opportunities, politics, and policies. In the case of Cuba, American threat perception is a result of national security, alliance politics, ideals, ethnic politics, and economic benefits. The main elements of United States threat perception regarding North Korea, however, are national security and alliance politics. In the Cuban case, ethnicity triumphs over economics because of the convergence of ideals and politics. But for North Korea, national security trumps domestic politics.

Korean-Americans are neither as numerous nor as influential as are supporters of Israel in the United States. Korean-Americans also are not as significant a factor in East-Asian policy making as Cuban-Americans are concerning the Caribbean. In the bureaucratic politics of Washington, moreover, hard-liners have dominated the policy process. As a result, ideas about bureaucratic politics are of little import in explaining decision making about North Korea.

Nor are alliance politics of great consequence regarding North Korea. There are, however, disputes among Seoul, Tokyo, and Washington over how to approach Pyongyang. The United States is more willing than Japan and South Korea to be accommodative with the North. But the allies agree more than they disagree. Consequently, it is comparatively easy to create joint policies to change the regime's behavior or punish it for misbehavior. And there is little indication of economic opportunities foregone as a result of maintaining a high threat perception toward North Korea. Economic changes, however, are turning former military belligerents into "tigers" in Asia. If political developments in Pyongyang permit, the Korean Peninsula as a whole may fall prey to the pull of a global economy and turn into a tiger itself.

Returning to the main issue that opened this chapter—whether North Korea is a crisis creator or victim of circumstance—Pyongyang does have a history of making crises, but the regime is on its last legs. The days in which Pyongyang could be in command of crises of its own conception are over. As long as it has large military forces, however, containment needs to be maintained, though it could be phased out in proportion to disarmament of the regime. North Korea is a potential casualty on a deathbed of its own making but is unable to arrest the aging process and economic deterioration. The bottom line is that military forces of North Korea need to be contained, but its population should be embraced with humanitarian assistance.

## CHAPTER SEVEN

# ROGUE REGIMES, CONTRACTORS, AND FREELANCERS

## ROUNDING UP THE USUAL SUSPECTS

*Casablanca* actor Claude Rains in his role of Captain Louis Renault had a standard operating procedure for confronting trouble: he would simply "round up the usual suspects" for interrogation. Once their faces appeared in the lineup, all was well at Rick's American Cafe.

The bombings of two American embassies in Africa, during August 1998, appear to be a mystery crying out for a Captain Renault. But, in fact, there were no "usual suspects" in the bombing investigation. Upon examination, western intelligence found that new suspects had emerged to threaten the allies and Japan. The new threats are freelance individuals. Although they may collude with rogue states like Iraq, freelancers often act on their own while taking advantage of failed states like Afghanistan.

Three assumptions underlying this chapter are that rogue regimes are identifiable as threats, groups that engage in terrorism are discernible dangers, and that the growth of freelance terrorists and proliferators of weapons of mass destruction (WMD) is a perceptible hazard. An alternative perspective is that this book imagines or at least overestimates the rogue state threat. Labeling groups and individuals as "rogues," or "freelance terrorists," demonizes them and forgoes an occasion to promote desirable norms of international conduct.

According to this critical viewpoint, simply by using the term "rogue regimes," this book paints a hostile picture that might become a self–fulfilling prophecy. One variant of the critique labels the present approach as "rogue rage."[1] But as willful violators of the international rules of the road, state sponsors of terrorism, groups that agree to carry out terrorist deeds for states, and freelance terrorists all deserve punishment. Is it unreasonable to fear the potential and actual ability of hostile states to inflict mass destruction? Not only is it judicious to fear such a prospect, it also is prudent to take preemptive or preventive actions that limit damage or deter the use of WMD.

In treating the nature of American post–Cold War threat assessment, the present study contrasts sharply with the critical approach. The alternative outlook argues that the Pentagon manufactured a rogue state threat.[2] That approach claims that the U.S. policy of containment of the USSR shifted to containment of rogue states simply to maintain approximate levels of defense spending in the post–Cold War days.

This book differs with these critics in its assumption that rogue regimes are a threat. Because they engage in terrorism and the proliferation of WMD, it is reasonable to presume that formal groups—those with a defined membership—engaged in similar activities also constitute a danger. Finally, if freelancers partake in terrorism and proliferation, they also are a hazard to international peace and security.

At issue is who should act as the Paul Revere of the global village to call attention to new threats on the horizon. The traditional view of the academic community is that scholars should only create and disseminate knowledge but leave the task of value judgment regarding threat assessment to the policy community.

The approach here is to work at the intersection of theory and policy. In this regard, this book seeks to inform, making explicit value judgments concerning policies that control terrorism and proliferation. Explaining why rogue states and freelance individuals fail to comply with deterrent and coercive attempts contributes to the policy process regarding threat perception.

## THREATS ACROSS LEVELS

This chapter discusses threats across levels of analysis. It introduces the concept of levels, presents one approach of the U.S. government to them, and provides a categorization preferred by this study. The levels are global, state, group, and individual.[3] The politics of charismatic personalities and risk–taking propensity cut across the levels. Such politics have the least impact at the global level and the most effect at the group and individual level.

In view of these levels, the main research inquiry in this chapter is why groups and individuals seek WMD and engage in terrorism. Prior chapters asked similar queries regarding regimes. Again, the primary theoretical source for addressing these questions is prospect theory. The working hypothesis is that aversion to loss explains the propensity to take risks, which in turn increases as one moves down from the global to the individual levels.

## Introduction to the Levels

At a global level, caution was the name of the game as the two superpowers sought to consolidate their gains. Because each was generally in a domain of gain, they were risk–averse, and mutual deterrence held. Crises occurred when either actor shifted to a domain of loss and began to challenge the status quo. The East–West struggle between the Soviet Union and the United States for the most part was a cautious stalemate.

Meanwhile, risk–taking abounded in the indirect confrontations via regional surrogates. In comparison with the superpowers, surrogates acted as if they were in a domain of loss. With the end of the Cold War, there is enhanced risk–taking by regional actors in their efforts to secure WMD and partake in state–sponsored terrorism.

At the group level, there are attacks by subnational organizations against each other, nation–states, and individuals. At the individual level, freelancers pose a unique type of threat. As they move unhindered across borders, searching for WMD and conducting terrorist operations, it is difficult to cope with the risk–taking of freelancers. In comparison with the global and state levels, risk–acceptance is highest at the group and individual levels.

*Global Level.* During the Cold War, the Soviet Union was the main threat to the West. The danger from Moscow consisted of a nuclear attack, a conventional force assault, as well as subversion and military action by Soviet surrogates. But the Kremlin took few risks in direct confrontations with Washington and displaced dangers to regional surrogates—for example—in the form of state–sponsored subversion. Angola, Cuba, and North Vietnam were among the Soviet substitutes in the global East–West struggle with the allies.

The implosion of the Soviet Union and collapse of communism resulted in an increase in the unauthorized flow of armaments from the southern republics of the former USSR to, for example, adjacent oil–rich states like Iran. Another consequence of the dissolution is that former Soviet surrogates had an opportunity to subvert their neighbors without guidelines from Moscow.

As the threat shifts from the global level of the Cold War to regional states, and from formal groups to individuals, there also is less emphasis on nuclear dangers in contrast to chemical and biological hazards. While states pursue nuclear armaments, formal groups are more likely to seek biological and chemical systems.

In relation to other WMD, nuclear weapons are lethal, costly, difficult to acquire, and easy to detect. In contrast, biological armaments are as lethal, are much less costly, easier to acquire, and more difficult to detect. A quantity of 100 kilograms of anthrax, which is fewer than Iraq had produced in the 1990s, could kill up to 3 million people if dispersed under optimal conditions. By contrast, a hydrogen bomb with a yield of 1 million tons of TNT could kill between 600,000 and 2 million people.[4] The technology and expertise needed for constructing nuclear weapons, moreover, is more complex than what it takes to create chemical and biological armaments.

Formal groups that practice terrorism may want to obtain chemical and biological weapons because of their high lethality and low cost. It is not very difficult to create a comparatively primitive biological weapon capable of killing thousands of people.

Technical expertise for constructing WMD abounds because of emigration from the former Soviet Union. Russian scientists and technicians trained in WMD constitute one group of particular relevance to proliferation dangers. As Russia liquidates its supply of WMD, former Soviet scientists and technicians are finding work in the West but also in states along the periphery of the former USSR.

Consider the defection of Dr. Kanatjan Alibekov from the former Soviet Union. He was the First Deputy Director of Biopreparat—the Kremlin's 1988 to 1992 biological weapons program. Alibekov defected and moved to Washington in 1992. But what if he had defected to Iran, Iraq, or Libya? Were Alibekov to abscond to one of these nations, the country would be in a good position to construct biological weapons. And if he were to provide advice to groups or freelancers that practice international terrorism, they would be much more dangerous with such expertise.

One incentive for formal groups to seek biological and chemical arms is the abundance of soft targets, such as metropolitan areas, administrative and commercial buildings, stadiums, and shopping malls in western states. According to Alibekov, such places would be very vulnerable to biological terrorist attack.[5]

Another reason why terrorist groups are motivated to acquire biological and chemical weapons concerns the asymmetry in their relationship to a target state. If a terrorist group uses chemical and biological weapons against a state, the victimized regime would find it difficult to respond in kind. Even though terrorist groups may have employed WMD against that state, it would be unlikely for a state to use WMD against a small group of terrorists.[6] And even if legitimacy issues were bypassed, locating a terrorist group within a failed state like Afghanistan would be problematic.

Another set of reasons why third world nations sought WMD is their strategic situation. To make up for the strategic weight lost with the dissolution of the USSR, regimes have an incentive to overcompensate for that difference. Iraq, Libya, and Syria assume that their own WMD might make up for the loss of Soviet deterrent capability vis-à-vis the United States. [7]

By similar logic, third world nations partake in state–sponsored terrorism in order to make up for their weakness in conventional military capability in contrast to that of the United States. Not only did former Soviet allies in the third world seek WMD and take part in state–sponsored terrorism, but one of them—Iraq—opted for the use of brute force. During 1990, Iraq invaded Kuwait with Soviet–made weapons.

With respect to terrorism, Baghdad also contracted with terrorists to conduct Iraq's business abroad.[8] Indeed, those who worked for the intelligence services of governments like Iraq and Libya are precursors of a later era of freelancers, who generally work on their own.

*State Level.* While in the process of pursuing its own interests in Africa, Libya sometimes acted as if it were a Soviet surrogate. During the late 1970s, Moscow agreed to train about a thousand Libyan soldiers per year. Additionally, the Soviet Union stationed military advisors in Tripoli, and the Kremlin supplied the Libyan regime with modern offensive military equipment.[9] And what acts did Libya perform in exchange for Soviet training, advice, and equipment?

Recall Tripoli's misdeeds from Chapter Four. During 1980, Libya deployed its ground combat forces, helicopters, and aircraft to Chad. In coordination with Moscow, Havana and Berlin sent military advisors to help Libya. Tripoli employed long–range, Soviet–built aircraft in bombing raids against Chad. Indeed, Qadhafi also sent his military across the border into the Sudan. With initial Soviet support, the Libyan invasion of Chad and its raids into the Sudan were accompanied by the subversion of regimes throughout Africa.

*Formal Group Level.* In addition to encouraging states like Libya to act as surrogates, Moscow facilitated group–sponsored terrorism. The USSR supported Ahmed Jibril of the Popular Front for the Liberation of Palestine–General Command (PFLP–GC). Moscow provided Jibril with equipment and gave him a residence in Sofia Bulgaria. He took regular deliveries of Soviet–bloc military equipment such as machine guns, Katyusha rockets, night–sight field glasses, and electronic range finders.[10]

And what terrorist acts did the PFLP–GC perform in exchange for Soviet military training and equipment? In late 1978, the PFLP–GC decided to disrupt the Camp David peace negotiations. Jibril's associates loaded 42 Katyusha rockets and four tons of dynamite on a Greek steamer en route to Eilat Israel. Had the Israeli Army not intercepted the ship, the dynamite might have detonated and slowed down progress toward an accord between Egypt and Israel.[11]

Another motive that drove formal groups to engage in the terrorist enterprise was to gain recognition for their cause. The more outrageous the act of terrorism, the more publicity a group attained for its cause.[12]

*Individual Level.* In addition to the formal group level, there is the individual level. Because individual terrorists pose a threat to Americans abroad and at home, the United States Federal Bureau of Investigation (FBI) monitors activities that might suggest complicity in international terrorism, especially across groups and individuals.

## U.S. Federal Bureau of Investigation and Levels of Analysis

The FBI divides international terrorism into three categories: state sponsors, formalized groups, and loosely affiliated radical extremists—termed freelancers here. The first hazard includes state–sponsored terrorism by Iran, Iraq, Syria, and Libya—some of the rogue regimes presented in this book.

Nonstate groups constitute a second type of terrorist danger for the FBI. They include Palestinian entities like the Popular Front for the Liberation of Palestine–General Command as well as the Lebanese Hezballah (Party of God), and the Egyptian Al–Gama'a Al–Islamiyya (The Islamic Group).

The FBI's third terrorist category is a set of loosely affiliated international radical extremists. They include Ramzi Ahmed Yousef and others convicted in the February 1993 bombing of the World Trade Center in New York City. The FBI contends that these "extremists" are neither surrogates of nor strongly influenced by any one nation. According to the Bureau, they have the ability to tap into a variety of official and private resource bases in order to facilitate terrorist acts against U.S. interests.

In short, one official U.S. government classification posits state sponsors, formalized groups, and international extremists. This scheme is a useful point of departure for developing the framework used here: state sponsors, contractors, and freelancers. Including a role for charismatic personality and a risk–taking propensity in the conduct of terrorist activities across levels might strengthen the FBI classification.

## FRAMEWORK FOR ANALYSIS

The politics of charisma and risk–taking, state sponsorship of international terrorism, the use of contractors by states, and freelancers make up four elements of a framework for analysis.

*The Politics of Charisma and Risk–taking.* Charisma and risk–taking are two sides of a coin in the first element of the framework. A common assumption is that the more charismatic rulers see themselves in a domain of loss, the more they engage in risky behavior. Charismatic leaders appear at all levels of analysis—global/regional, state, group, and individual. System–level attributes, such as the overall balance of power, characterize the global level. Personality characteristics like charisma have the least impact at the global/regional level and greatest effect at the group/individual level.

The charismatic leaders in this book are politicians who excite their public and command compliance via the force of their personalities. Their authority is religious, revolutionary, and/or nationalistic.[13] Charismatic rulers make policy based on their deep emotions, and they are willing to take great risks.

During the Cold War, superpowers on the world stage were like members of a guild who adhered to a script and played by the rules. The post–Cold War age cast a new threat onto the international scene. The playbill consisted of charismatic actors who emphatically threw scripts aside. These new players acted as if they were part of an improv troupe that improvises to such an extent that rules have little meaning.

Previous chapters introduced well–known charismatic leaders, such as Saddam Hussein. Although apparently all–powerful, even

Saddam has to operate within limits. These include the United Nations Special Commission [on Iraq], an anti–Saddam western coalition, Islamic faith, the Arab nation, and the Iraqi State. Although outside the mainstream in the post–Gulf War era, Saddam still has to play by some rules of the game.

Following state–based rulers operating under multiple constraints, a new cast of characters shot their way onto the world stage during the post–Gulf War era—freelance terrorists. Performing at the group and individual level in borderless arenas, freelancers have fewer constraints than leaders who operate at the global/regional and state levels. And in comparison with rulers of states, freelancers have the greatest propensity to take risks.

*State Sponsors.* The category of state–sponsored terrorism is a second element in the framework. Middle Eastern states that sponsor terrorism fuel American perception that the area is a hotbed of hazards.

In the Middle West of America, there is a race for the political center because that is where the votes are. In the Middle East, there is a race for the political extremes because that is where the souls lie. In the center of America, secular states are part and parcel of the political landscape. In the region of the Near East, sacred and failed states are on the rise. If one were cultivating terrorism as a plant, the area between the Nile Valley and the Fertile Crescent might be a fruitful garden.

For these reasons, Americans have the mental image of the Middle East as an incubator for terrorist attacks. Consequently, if residents of the Middle West were pressed to identify who was responsible for a violent assault against American civilians, two images might come to mind. As stated in Chapter One, the first image is of an evil–looking domineering man in a green military suit. Cartoonists might portray him as plotting corrupt actions against the occupants of the Land of the Free. Qadhafi and Saddam fit this picture. The second figure is of a sinister–looking, thickly bearded man in a *thawb* (male dress) with a *kuuffiyya* (male headdress), who masterminds hostile deeds against overseas U.S. assets as well as innocent American citizens. Ayatollah Khomeni is the archetype of this person.

These stereotypes of Middle Eastern leaders loom large because of the way that a few rulers have left their marks on the world. Ruthless and calculating, these men behave according to rules that sponsor terrorism—politically motivated violence against innocent civilians. Leaders like the Ayatollahs of Iran, Assad, Qadhafi, and Saddam deserve rage because they rule states that sponsor international terrorism. Moreover, their personalities all share one trait—a drive for power in a fear–based milieu. Accordingly, these men are not afraid to carry out policy through risky means.

Khomeni, Saddam, Qadhafi, and Hafez–al Assad are all guilty of using bullying tactics in order to keep political power. They use such means not only against citizens of their own countries but also against international enemies. A motivation for domestic power shapes their policy toward the West. Indeed, attracting western enemies abroad is one way to maintain power at home.

For fear of western retaliation, leaders of rogue regimes need "plausible deniability," the capacity to deny that they are the source of a terrorist deed. Consequently, the name of the game is "outsourcing." State leaders provide contracts to nonstate groups to carry out terrorist deeds. These groups become contractors of terrorism because they are less susceptible to retaliation.

*Contractors.* A second category of charismatic leaders includes persons to whom the rogue state leaders make requests. Notable terrorist contractors are Palestinian leaders George Habash of the Popular Front for the Liberation of Palestine (PFLP), Abu Nidal of the Fatah Revolutionary Council, and Abu Abbas of the Palestine Liberation Front.

History has passed by the likes of Habash, Abu Nidal, and Abu Abbas. Once revolutionaries, some of them are retired or politically dead. At one time, these men were advocates of hijackings and other terrorist attacks as a means of pursuing political objectives. Although they worked with state sponsorship, these men did not have the limitation of ruling a state. Being so unfettered, group leaders are often more risk–acceptant than heads of states. While leaders of formal groups can take risky actions, it would be foolhardy for rulers of states to be so risk–acceptant.

In contrast to state–confined rulers, Palestinian group leaders often operated from a domain of loss. Lacking the resources of a sovereign Palestinian entity and denied such a state by western imperialism and political Zionism, they were willing to run great risks.[14]

George Habash and Ahmed Jibril were two notable risk takers. During December 1967, Habash established the PFLP with Jibril. As a result of Israel's defeat of Egypt in 1967, there was a political vacuum in the Arab nation. Palestinian groups emerged to fill the void. In contrast to Jibril, Habash had good relations with the Baath leadership of Syria. Indeed the Baath entered into a contractual relationship with Habash by funding his organization. When he sought approval from Damascus to take the risky step of launching raids on Israel from Syrian territory, Damascus imprisoned him. At that time, Syria helped Ahmed Jibril form his own Palestinian group.

Besides Habash, another contractor willing to run great risks was Abu Nidal. By 1969, Abu Nidal had become a leader within the ranks of the PLO and was posted in Khartoum, Sudan. But in 1970, he transferred to Baghdad and became an agent of Iraq's intelligence service. Under contract with Baghdad, Abu Nidal seized the Embassy of Saudi Arabia in Paris during 1973. Subsequently, Iraqi officials admitted that they had contracted with Abu Nidal to seize Saudi hostages.

A year later, the PLO distanced itself from Abu Nidal. He was too close to his hosts in Baghdad. But pushing Abu Nidal away from the PLO simply resulted in moving closer to his state sponsor—Iraq. As a full–fledged Iraqi agent, he set up his own formal group, the Fatah Revolutionary Council (FRC). Under Iraqi contract, Abu Nidal sought to assassinate PLO diplomats abroad.

During 1983, Washington and Amman persuaded Baghdad to oust Abu Nidal from Iraq. Just as Abu Nidal worked under contract for Iraq, he just as easily accepted orders from Syria. Damascus was in the process of outsourcing tasks to Palestinian groups for the purpose of coercing the PLO and Amman. But because President Assad of Syria considered Abu Nidal as a mere contractor, the relationship that Abu Nidal had with Damascus deteriorated.

After a few years in Syria, Washington and London persuaded Damascus to distance itself from Abu Nidal. Subsequently, Abu Nidal transferred his corporate headquarters to Tripoli. Landing on his feet again, Abu Nidal received contracts from Libya to launch attacks on the "enemies of his friends." Cairo and Washington were prominent opponents of Tripoli.

Iraq has a history of outsourcing to the FRC. When Baghdad wanted to cause trouble between Israel and Syria, Iraq turned to Abu Nidal. Iraqi intelligence agents provided training for his hit squads. With technical assistance and financial aid from Baghdad, he organized an almost fatal assassination attempt of Shlomo Argov—Israel's Ambassador to London.[15] The Iraqi motive to assassinate Argov in 1982 was to provoke an Israeli invasion of Lebanon. Baghdad's goal was to destroy the armed Palestinian movement in Lebanon, oust Arafat from leadership of the PLO, and weaken Syria's influence in the Palestinian movement.[16]

In addition to George Habash and Abu Nidal, another contract terrorist is Mohammed Abbas, a.k.a., Abu Abbas, the leader of the Palestinian Liberation Front (PLF). During 1977, the PLF split from Habash's PFLP–GC. In a sense, Abu Abbas may be something of a cross between Habash and Abu Nidal.[17]

Under the pay of state sponsors of international terrorism—Iraq, Libya, and Syria—contractors George Habash, Abu Nidal, and Abu Abbas are a good segue to freelancers.

*Freelancers.* A third element in the framework for analysis is the category of freelancer. They are the most likely to run great risks in order to avoid large losses. While the FBI considers freelancers as completely independent of states, these individuals operate within nations and may collude with other rogue regimes.

One prominent freelancer is Sheik Omar Abdul Rahman. He is a militant Egyptian cleric who is serving a life sentence in the United States. In October 1995, a Federal Court convicted Rahman of complicity in the World Trade Center bombing and of leading a "war of urban terrorism" against the United States. It found him guilty in a plot to bomb New York City landmarks, among them the United Nations. Even after being sentenced to life in prison without parole, the sheik continued to profess his innocence and affirmed that, "America will fall."[18]

Sheik Rahman began operating out of the popular revolutionary mosques of Egypt, preaching Holy War against the country's secular regime. The Egyptian government tried Rahman for inspiring the 1981 assassination of President Anwar el–Sadat, but the courts acquitted the cleric.[19]

In 1990, by virtue of an antiquated computer system and a friend working in the American Embassy in Khartoum, Rahman breezed through United States customs on a tourist visa, even though the State Department had his name on a list of banned terrorists.[20] Before his U.S. incarceration, Rahman called for the creation of an Islamic theocracy in Egypt and prompted followers to engage in acts of terrorism.[21]

Sheik Rahman has a fierce hatred of American foreign policy and what he calls the "immorality of western life."[22] Following in the tradition of those risk–acceptant charismatic leaders who came before him, Rahman has attracted a following of young Muslims. He found an audience among frustrated young men who regard the secular governments in the Middle East as hopelessly corrupt and resent U.S. support for them. The sheik's most activist followers are often intelligent and idealistic, university educated, but poor "because they haven't been able to make it."[23]

Besides Rahman, the Federal Court convicted nine codefendants of conspiring to wage a war of urban terrorism against the United States. The codefendants included the reputed mastermind of the World Trade Center bombing, Ramzi Ahmed Yousef. Other governments captured and extradited or rendered to U.S. authorities some of Yousef's associates.[24]

During the late 1990s, Yousef had the distinction of occupying a "suite" in the highest–Federal security prison in the United States— Florence Colorado.[25] In January 1998, calling then 29-year–old Yousef "an apostle of evil," U.S. District Judge Kevin Thomas Duffy sentenced him to 240 years in prison and recommended that he be kept in solitary confinement for the rest of his life.[26] Yousef has remained silent about what nation or cause he serves or who has bankrolled his extensive travels. He hinted at the existence of a terrorist network, but he has refused to give Federal agents details about his bombs.[27] Following the Trade Center bombing, some members of the FBI expressed the belief that Iraq had been behind the attack, but they were unable to substantiate their feeling of Iraqi involvement.[28]

Yousef received training in Afghanistan shortly after the Central Intelligence Agency–backed Mujahedin had driven the Soviet Army from the country in 1989.[29] Yousef's electrical engineering vocation served him well: He specialized in improvising bombs that evaded airport security. He also made a lethal art of converting Casio digital watches into timing switches, using light bulb filaments to ignite cotton soaked in nitroglycerine explosive.[30] By 1991, Yousef had moved to the Philippines and joined the Islamist extremist group, Abu Sayyaf.[31]

Like Rahman, Yousef used trickery to gain access to the United States. On September 1, 1992, Yousef arrived in America on a false Iraqi passport and asked for political asylum. Fooling American authorities, he claimed to be a victim of the Gulf War who had been beaten by Iraqi soldiers because they had suspected he worked for Kuwaiti resistance.[32]

According to statements made by another convicted bomber to investigators in Yousef's trial, he repeatedly traded disguises and changed identities. After the 1993 World Trade Center Bombing, Yousef "embarked on an audacious terrorist marathon around the globe," according to Federal officials.[33]

Like other freelancers, Yousef was difficult to track down after the World Trade Center bombing because he was not based in a single country. First, while staying in Pakistan, Yousef allegedly joined an effort to assassinate Prime Minister Benazir Bhutto. Then, from Bangkok Thailand, fingerprints linked him to an attempt to blow up the Israeli Embassy.[34]

By sheer accident, Yousef was captured by the authorities. On January 6, 1995, a fire broke out in an apartment in Manila because he and two associates were building bombs. Neighbors called the police, who arrived and arrested Yousef's companions. Yousef escaped and fled to Pakistan but left behind a laptop computer that contained details of the bombing plot and a lengthy list of contacts. This information helped authorities locate and arrest him in Pakistan.

During his 1996 trial for plotting to bomb 12 U.S. airliners, Yousef was described by the former coordinator of counterterrorism for the State Department as, "ingenious, diabolical, and ruthless." The coordinator further characterized Yousef as part of a new breed of terrorists and a unique threat: "Ramzi Yousef is unique because of his technique. And, while I don't want to glorify him, he is something of a genius bomber."[35]

Another freelancer is Osama bin Laden. Perhaps because he is not accountable to a nation, bin Laden is even more risk–acceptant than the previous group of contractors. His main organization, al–Qa'ida, may not be as disciplined or sophisticated as the state–sponsored groups that attacked the United States in the past, such as the Libyan–backed Palestinian organization of Abu Nidal. But this very lack of discipline may be a source of risk–taking that is even more dangerous than the Palestinian contractors.

Who is Osama bin Laden? He is the prototype of a new breed of terrorist, a private entrepreneur who puts modern enterprise at the service of a worldwide network. Because he lacks a government and is not a head of state, bin Laden's charisma has to carry the day. Indeed, he is the type of charismatic leader who can attract a growing clientele of followers.

Bin Laden's mission is to wage a Holy War. In fact, he calls his group the Islamic Front for Holy War against Jews and Crusaders. It consists mainly of Afghan Arabs and Muslims from outside Afghanistan, mostly from Egypt, Saudi Arabia, and North Africa. Their common bond is having fought against the Soviets in Afghanistan.[36]

To compensate for the resources he lacks as a freelancer, bin Laden works within an international terrorist network. His group formed a coalition with the Egyptian Islamic Jihad and the Egyptian Gama'at— the group responsible for attacks on foreign tourists in Egypt. The Muslim Brotherhood, Palestinian Hamas, and Lebanese Hezbollah also have cooperated with bin Laden.[37]

The bin Laden family fortune is about $5 billion, some $300 million of which belongs to bin Laden. The Central Intelligence Agency estimates that he conceals most of his income in various foreign accounts. He spreads those accounts among dozens of apparently legitimate front organizations in the United States and abroad.

Bin Laden's investments include companies involved in property management, maritime transport, and aircraft rental. His investments include construction and agricultural projects in the Sudan and commercial activities in Somalia, Switzerland, and Luxembourg. Swiss lawyers manage bin Laden's European interests. This procedure makes his financial dealings and support of terrorism difficult to trace.

Bin Laden used his inheritance to become the principal source of funding and direction for al–Qa'ida, the military base, and a multinational terrorist organization. With members from various nations, the organization has a worldwide presence. Senior leaders in his group are also top–level leaders in other associations, including those designated by the U.S. State Department as "foreign terrorist organizations." These include the Egyptian al–Gama'at al–Islamiyya and the Egyptian al–Jihad.

Al–Qa'ida would like to radicalize existing Islamic groups and create Islamic ones. It supports Muslim fighters in Afghanistan, Bosnia, Chechnya, Tajikistan, Somalia, Yemen, and Kosovo. It also trains members of terrorist organizations from such diverse nations as the Philippines, Algeria, and Eritrea.

In addition to waging war against Jews and Christians, bin Laden issued three fatwahs—religious rulings—calling upon Muslims to take up arms against the United States. Terminating the deployment of American troops in Saudi Arabia is one of his main priorities at the close of the 1990s.

Bin Laden operated in the Sudan between 1991 and 1996, until Washington pressured that country to compel him to relocate. While in the Sudan, he may have been the spiritual leader of the car bomb that blew up the Saudi National Guard training base in Riyadh.

Subsequently, bin Laden left Saudi Arabia and moved his headquarters to Afghanistan to fight against the Soviets in 1979. During the 1980s, he sponsored and led some Arabs who fought in Afghanistan against the Soviets. In the mid–1980s, moreover, he co–founded the Maktab al–Khidamat (MAK) or the Services Office. Its goal was to provide personnel and money to the Afghan resistance in Peshawar, Pakistan. Along with a Palestinian Muslim Brotherhood leader, Abdallah Azzam, bin Laden founded recruitment centers around the world—including Egypt, Pakistan, Saudi Arabia, and the United States. They recruited, protected, and transported persons from over 50 countries to Afghanistan in order to fight Soviets forces.

Bin Laden split from Azzam in the late 1980s in order to extend his campaign to all corners of the globe. Bin Laden formed a new organization in 1988, al–Qa'ida. After Azzam was killed by a car bomb in late 1989, the MAK split and the extremist faction combined with bin Laden's organization. Bin Laden then returned to work in his family's Saudi–based construction business after the Soviets withdrew from Afghanistan in the late 1980s. Bin Laden, however, retained his organization in support of opposition movements in Saudi Arabia and Yemen. Following victory over Soviet forces in Afghanistan, bin Laden ran the Jihad Committee. It included the Egyptian Islamic Group, Jihad Organization in Yemen, the Pakistani al–Hadith group, Lebanese Partisans League, Libyan Islamic Group, Bayt al–Imam Group in Jordan, and the Islamic Group in Algeria. The Jihad Committee runs the Islamic Information Observatory Center in London. It organizes media activity for these associations, as well as the Advisory and Reformation Body that also has a bureau in London.

In 1991, bin Laden relocated to the Sudan. In 1994, moreover, Riyadh stripped him of his Saudi citizenship after Algeria, Saudi Arabia, and Yemen accused him of supporting subversive groups. Although the Afghan war had ended, al–Qa'ida remained an important organization. It included Mujahedin fighters of many nationalities, who had previously fought with bin Laden. Many of these combat veterans remained loyal to and continued working with bin Laden through the late 1990s.

In May 1996, Khartoum expelled bin Laden under Saudi pressure, U.S. insistence, and the threat of UN sanctions. After Sudan's alleged complicity in the attempted assassination of Egyptian President Hosni Mubarak in Ethiopia, pressure mounted for Khartoum to oust bin Laden.

As might be expected of a freelancer, bin Laden left the Sudan and returned to Afghanistan. There, his support for and participation in radical activities continued. The ouster from the Sudan exacerbated his domain of loss frame of reference, and he became even more risk–acceptant than he was before the expulsion.

Because bin Laden fought with the Mujahedin, he had less freedom in Afghanistan when it fell to the Taliban. During the days of the Mujahedin in Afghanistan, bin Laden moved around Kabul with ease. He subsequently resided in Taliban–held Jalalabad with about 50 of his family members and bodyguards. A few months after his arrival in Afghanistan, the Taliban gained control over both Jalalabad and Kabul. They then launched a campaign against the Afghan Arabs, of whom bin Laden was one.

Despite this campaign, the Taliban rejected a U.S. proposal to turn bin Laden over to Washington in return for international recognition and Afghanistan's seat in international organizations during February 1997. But also in early 1997, at least two large bombs detonated in Jalalabad. There were attempts to assassinate bin Laden, including a March 1997 explosion that destroyed a police station, killing more than 50 and wounding some 150 persons. Bin Laden subsequently moved to Kandahar from his Jalalabad stronghold due to concern for his personal safety. Given this description of bin Laden the man, consider what he has accomplished.

Washington suspects bin Laden of being responsible for the 1996 bomb attacks on American service personnel in Dhahran Saudi Arabia. There is evidence to implicate bin Laden in other terrorist attacks: December 1992, hotel bombings in Yemen against U.S. service en route to Somalia; June 1993, failed assassination of Jordan's Crown Prince Abdullah; June 1995, attempted assassination of Egyptian President Hosni Mubarak; November 1995, truck bombing that killed five U.S. servicemen in Riyadh Saudi Arabia; November 1995, bombing of Egypt's embassy in Pakistan that killed 17 people; February 1993, bombing of the World Trade Center that killed six people and injured hundreds; January 1995, attempt to assassinate the Pope in the Philippines.[38]

But the most celebrated incidents with which the world associates bin Laden are the bombings of U.S. embassies in Africa during August 1998.[39] In retaliation Washington launched cruise missiles against his installations in Afghanistan and against an alleged "dual use" pharmaceutical plant in the Sudan—El Shifa. It would be "dual use" if the plant had the capacity to produce both military and civilian products.

Hard evidence that El Shifa was a source of precursors for chemical weapons mainly comes from a soil sample that contained a chemical substance known as "EMPTA." Because the sample was taken from the vicinity of the plant and EMPTA can be converted into VX nerve gas, American intelligence inferred an intention to produce chemical weapons.

Supplementing hard intelligence was circumstantial evidence. If one followed the money trail with respect to the plant in Khartoum, a "usual suspect" might surface—Saddam Hussein. Because of international inspectors in Iraq, Saddam is no longer able to create chemical weapons with impunity. The United Nations Special Commission [on Iraq] had tests conducted on artillery shell fragments found in Iraq and discovered traces of VX on those shell casings.[40] Suspected of having violated prohibitions regarding WMD, Baghdad has a motivation to outsource production of VX nerve agent to the Khartoum plant.

Western intelligence agencies first noticed the El Shifa plant because there was a high level of security provided by the Sudanese Army during its construction. Because of visits to Baghdad by officials of the El Shifa plant, U.S. intelligence inferred a possible link between Khartoum and Baghdad to construct chemical weapons.[41] Additionally, contacts between the owners of the plant and members of Egyptian Islamic Jihad, a terrorist organization with ties to Osama bin Laden, suggest that the facility might be a source of chemical weapons production.

During the late 1990s, the Sudan had an impetus to acquire chemical weapons. The regime would have benefited from such weapons in a civil war fought against rebels supplied by Washington. Khartoum also had not signed the chemical weapons convention. In the past the regime had given refuge to terrorists, such as Osama bin Laden himself.

But there is an alternative interpretation of the activities at the Khartoum plant. A feud between Sudanese businessmen might explain allegations that the El Shifa plant was a source of chemical weapons production. The owner of the plant was Salah Idris, and Mubarak Al Mahdi was one of his opponents. Indeed, Al Mahdi was one of the sources of intelligence that the plant owned by Idris produced VX nerve agent.[42] In other words, a feud between two Sudanese entrepreneurs is an alternative explanation to an inference that the plant was a dual use facility. The El Shifa plant might be just a pharmaceutical facility mistaken to be a chemical weapons plant.

In short, the plant in Khartoum produced items of medicinal value for export, but it also may have been a source of chemical weapons production. If it were the case that Iraqi financing supported such a plant in Khartoum, an assumption of hostile intent would be prudent. The evidence seems to be stronger that El Shifa engaged in chemical weapons production, and that it had links with bin Laden and his associates.

Bin Laden is a good illustration of the freelancer who may become a major threat against the West in the area of proliferation and terrorism. Because bin Laden is such a prototype, it is appropriate to close the book with the above discussion about him.

This chapter discusses threats across levels of analysis. It introduces those levels, the FBI's approach, and a classification consisting of state–sponsors, contractors, and freelancers. In view of these levels, the main issue is why groups and individuals seek WMD and engage in terrorism.

In general, those who see themselves in a domain of loss are willing to run great risks to avoid losses. In particular, entities studied here wish to make up for the strategic weight lost when the Soviet Union dissolved. It is reasonable to chose WMD and terrorism in light of a lack of conventional military capability in relation to the United States.

## The New Challenge

During the Cold War, the fact of "mutual assured destruction" contributed to stable deterrence. Risk–averse superpowers were the norm. Threats of second strike retaliation contributed to mutual deterrence. In the wake of formal groups that colluded with state sponsors of terrorism, risk–acceptance increased, and new threats appeared on the horizon. With the rise of charismatic risk–acceptant freelancers who are able to capture a large following with their religious convictions, the threats increased again.

When the usual suspects were a global superpower, rogue regimes that sponsored international terrorism, or groups that contracted with such regimes, traditional tools of national security were sufficient. With the dissolution of the USSR, decline of state sponsored terrorism, and rise of freelancers, threats and military force need to be supplemented with international criminal justice procedures—police work within the global village.

# APPENDIX TO CHAPTER 7:

## SELECTED BACKGROUND INFORMATION OF FOREIGN TERRORIST ORGANIZATIONS[43]

### ABU NIDAL ORGANIZATION (ANO)

A.k.a.: Fatah Revolutionary Council, Arab Revolutionary Council, Arab Revolutionary Brigades, Black September, and Revolutionary Organization of Socialist Muslims

• DESCRIPTION

International terrorist organization led by Sabri al–Banna. Split from PLO in 1974. Made up of various functional committees, including political, military, and financial.

• ACTIVITIES

Has carried out terrorist attacks in 20 countries, killing or injuring almost 900 persons. Targets include the United States, the United Kingdom, France, Israel, moderate Palestinians, the PLO, and various Arab countries. Major attacks included the Rome and Vienna airports in December 1985, the Neve Shalom synagogue in Istanbul, the Pan Am Flight 73 hijacking in Karachi in September 1986, and the City of Poros day–excursion ship attack in July 1988 in Greece. Suspected of assassinating PLO deputy chief Abu Iyad and PLO security chief Abu Hul in Tunis in January 1991. ANO assassinated a Jordanian diplomat in Lebanon in January 1994 and has been linked to the killing of the PLO representative there. Has not attacked western targets since the late 1980s.

• STRENGTH

Several hundred plus militia in Lebanon and overseas support structure.

• LOCATION/AREA OF OPERATION

Headquartered in Libya with a presence in Lebanon in the Al Biqa' (Bekaa Valley) and also several Palestinian refugee camps in coastal areas of Lebanon. Also has a presence in Sudan. Has demonstrated ability to operate over wide area, including the Middle East, Asia, and Europe.

• EXTERNAL AID

Has received considerable support, including safehaven, training, logistic assistance, and financial aid from Iraq and Syria (until 1987); continues to receive aid from Libya, in addition to close support for selected operations.

## AL–GAMA'AT AL–ISLAMIYYA
## (ISLAMIC GROUP, IG)

• DESCRIPTION

An indigenous Egyptian Islamic extremist group active since the late 1970s; appears to be loosely organized with no single readily identifiable operational leader. Shaykh Umar Abd al–Rahman is the preeminent spiritual leader. Goal is to overthrow the government of President Hosni Mubarak and replace it with an Islamic state.

• ACTIVITIES

Armed attacks against Egyptian security and other government officials, Coptic Christians, and Egyptian opponents of Islamic extremism. The group also has launched attacks on tourists in Egypt since 1992. Al–Gama'at claimed responsibility for the attempt in June 1995 to assassinate President Hosni Mubarak in Addis Ababa, Ethiopia.

• STRENGTH

Not known, but probably several thousand hardcore members and another several thousand sympathizers.

• LOCATION/AREA OF OPERATION

Operates mainly in the Al Minya, Asyut, and Qina Governorates of southern Egypt. It also appears to have support in Cairo, Alexandria, and other urban locations, particularly among unemployed graduates and students.

• EXTERNAL AID

Not known. Egyptian Government believes that Iran, Sudan, and Afghan militant Islamic groups support the group HAMAS (Islamic Resistance Movement).

• DESCRIPTION

HAMAS was formed in late 1987 as an outgrowth of the Palestinian branch of the Muslim Brotherhood. Various elements of HAMAS have used both political and violent means, including terrorism, to pursue the goal of establishing an Islamic Palestinian state in place of Israel. HAMAS is loosely structured, with some elements working openly through mosques and social service institutions to recruit members, raise money, organize activities, and distribute propaganda. Militant elements of HAMAS, operating clandestinely, have advocated and used violence to advance their goals. HAMAS's strength is concentrated in the Gaza Strip and a few areas of the West Bank. It also has engaged in peaceful political activity, such as running candidates in West Bank Chamber of Commerce elections.

• ACTIVITIES

HAMAS activists, especially those in the Izz el–Din al–Qassem Forces, have conducted many attacks against Israeli civilian and military targets, suspected Palestinian collaborators, and Fatah rivals.

• STRENGTH

Unknown number of hardcore members; tens of thousands of supporters and sympathizers.

• LOCATION/AREA OF OPERATION

Primarily the occupied territories, Israel, and Jordan.

• EXTERNAL AID

Receives funding from Palestinian expatriates, Iran, and private benefactors in Saudi Arabia and other moderate Arab states. Some fundraising and propaganda activity take place in western Europe and North America.

## HEZBALLAH (PARTY OF GOD)

a.k.a.: Islamic Jihad, Revolutionary Justice Organization, Organization of the Oppressed on Earth, and Islamic Jihad for the Liberation of Palestine

• DESCRIPTION

Radical Shia group formed in Lebanon; dedicated to creation of Iranian–style Islamic republic in Lebanon and removal of all non–Islamic influences from area. Strongly anti–West and anti–Israel. Closely allied with, and often directed by, Iran, but may have conducted rogue operations that were not approved by Tehran.

• ACTIVITIES

Known or suspected to have been involved in numerous anti–U.S. terrorist attacks, including the suicide truck bombing of the U.S. Embassy and U.S. Marine barracks in Beirut in October 1983 and the U.S. Embassy annex in Beirut in September 1984. Elements of the group were responsible for the kidnapping and detention of U.S. and other western hostages in Lebanon. The group also attacked the Israeli Embassy in Argentina in 1992.

• STRENGTH

Several thousand.

• LOCATION/AREA OF OPERATION

Operates in the Bekaa Valley, the southern suburbs of Beirut, and southern Lebanon. Has established cells in Europe, Africa, South America, North America, and elsewhere.

• EXTERNAL AID
Receives substantial amounts of financial, training, weapons, explosives, political, diplomatic, and organizational aid from Iran.

## PALESTINE LIBERATION FRONT (PLF)

• DESCRIPTION
Terrorist group that broke away from the PFLP–GC in mid–1970s. Later split again into pro–PLO, pro–Syrian, and pro–Libyan factions. Pro–PLO faction led by Muhammad Abbas (Abu Abbas), who became member of PLO Executive Committee in 1984 but left it in 1991.

• ACTIVITIES
The Abu Abbas–led faction has carried out attacks against Israel. Abbas's group was also responsible for the attack in 1985 on the cruise ship Achille Lauro and the murder of U.S. citizen Leon Klinghoffer. A warrant for Abu Abbas's arrest is outstanding in Italy.

• STRENGTH
At least 50.

• LOCATION/AREA OF OPERATION
PLO faction based in Tunisia until Achille Lauro attack. Based in Iraq.

• EXTERNAL AID
Receives logistic and military support mainly from PLO, but also from Libya and Iraq.

## POPULAR FRONT FOR THE LIBERATION OF PALESTINE (PFLP)

• DESCRIPTION
Marxist–Leninist group founded in 1967 by George Habash as a member of the PLO. Advocates a Pan–Arab revolution. Opposes the Declaration of Principles signed in 1993 and has suspended participation in the PLO.

• ACTIVITIES
The PFLP has committed numerous international terrorist attacks during the 1970s. Since 1978 PFLP has carried out numerous attacks against Israeli or moderate Arab targets, including the killing of a settler and her son in December 1996.

- STRENGTH
Some 800.

- LOCATION/AREA OF OPERATION
Syria, Lebanon, Israel, and the occupied territories.

- EXTERNAL AID
Receives most of its financial and military assistance from Syria and Libya.

## POPULAR FRONT FOR THE LIBERATION OF PALESTINE–GENERAL COMMAND (PFLP–GC)

- DESCRIPTION
Split from the PFLP in 1968, claiming that it wanted to focus more on fighting and less on politics. Violently opposed to Arafat's PLO. Led by Ahmad Jibril, a former captain in the Syrian Army. Closely allied with, supported by, and probably directed by Syria.

- ACTIVITIES
Has carried out numerous cross–border terrorist attacks into Israel using unusual means, such as hot–air balloons and motorized hang gliders.

- STRENGTH
Several hundred.

- LOCATION/AREA OF OPERATION
Headquartered in Damascus, bases in Lebanon, and cells in Europe.

- EXTERNAL AID
Receives logistic and military support from Syria, its chief sponsor; financial support from Libya; safehaven in Syria. Receives support also from Iran.

## DEMOCRATIC FRONT FOR THE LIBERATION OF PALESTINE (DFLP).

- DESCRIPTION
Marxist group that split from the PFLP in 1969. Believes Palestinian national goals can be achieved only through revolution of the masses. Opposes the Declaration of Principles (DOP) signed in 1993. In early 1980s, occupied political stance midway between Arafat and the rejectionists. Split into two factions in 1991, one pro–Arafat of the Palestine Liberation Organization, and another more hardline faction headed by Nayif Hawatmah, which suspended participation in the PLO.

- ACTIVITIES

In the 1970s, carried out numerous small bombings and minor assaults and some more spectacular operations in Israel and the occupied territories, concentrating on Israeli targets. Involved only in border raids since 1988, but continues to oppose Israel–PLO peace agreements.

- STRENGTH

Estimated at 500 (total for both factions).

- LOCATION/AREA OF OPERATION

Syria, Lebanon, and the Israeli–occupied territories; attacks have taken place entirely in Israel and the occupied territories.

- EXTERNAL AID

Receives financial and military aid from Syria and Libya.

# NOTES

## Preface

1. Primary criteria for inclusion in *Rogue Regimes* are: large conventional military forces, international terrorism, and weapons of mass destruction. A secondary criterion is appearance on the State Department's *Patterns of Global Terrorism,* a list released annually by the Office of the Coordinator for Counterterrorism. Although Cuba fails to meet the main criteria, Havana appears on the terrorism list. The Sudan is a nation on State's list, but it fails to make *Rogue Regimes* because it is the proxy of another state, Iran, which does appear on the State list and is included here.

2. Nuclear Proliferation Prevention Act of 1994, Part B, sec. 221(a); Title II of the Omnibus Export Administration Act of 1994.

3. Regarding means for delivery of weapons of mass destruction, over 30 non-NATO countries have ballistic missiles. Five of our rogue states have missile programs: Iran, Iraq, Libya, Syria, and North Korea possess ballistic missiles. And North Korea has assisted Iran's missile program. And with respect to the missile threat, the Office of the Secretary of Defense states that "The theater threat to our allies and U.S. forces deployed abroad is real and growing. . . . Besides Iraq, we know that thousands of short-range missiles are deployed today with hundreds of launchers in as many as thirty different countries—some of these countries are quite hostile to the United States." Paul Kaminski, "Ballistic Missile Defense Programs," Prepared Statement of the Under Secretary of Defense for Acquisition and Technology to the Military Research and Development Subcommittee, House National Security Committee, in *Defense Issues,* vol. 12, Number 14, March 6, 1997. Available online at:

   http://www.dtic.dla.mil/defenselink/pubs/di97/di1214.html

   A related statement of the missile threat holds that, *"Within ten years, it is possible that every southern European capital will be within range of ballistic missiles based in North Africa or the Levant."* [Italics in original.] The area in question or missile envelope includes the eastern Mediterranean and its hinterlands, including Syria, Iraq, and Iran. See Ian Lesser and Ashley Tellis, *Strategic Exposure: Proliferation Around the Mediterranean* (Santa Monica, CA: The RAND Corporation, 1996), 32.

4. In a bet of one million dollars, a rational actor desires gain as much as it fears loss. Approximately rational actors weigh gain and loss about equally. An actor lower on a "rheostat of rationality" fears loss more than it desires the gain.

## Chapter One

1. The section *Times to Relive* contains dates that reflect the case studies in the chapters that follow: Iran, Iraq, Libya, Syria, and North Korea. As a result, the dates are not in chronological order. Chapter One gives a brief overview of each leader, and the chapters on each country provide details on that person, including references to the literature.

2. Is Assad "rational?" In addition to the definition of rationality in endnote 4 to the Preface, rationality assumes that Assad would be able to acquire information to make decisions without the distorting effects of biases, belief systems, or other preconceptions to cloud his judgment. The fact that Assad commits brutal acts is not relevant to his degree of rationality. Chapter Five revisits the issue of Assad's rationality.

3. For information on the destruction of the Syrian city of Hama, see Thomas Friedman, *From Beirut to Jerusalem* (New York: Farrar Straus Giroux, 1989). President Assad ordered tank and artillery fire to level the ancient city of Hama in 1982, resulting in thousands of casualties. Raymond Tanter, *Who's at the Helm?* (Boulder: Westview Press, 1990), 75.

4. The Muslim Brotherhood is an Islamic Organization that promotes a "purified" Islamic state, a position that places it opposite the secular Ba'ath Party that rules Syria. For decades, the Muslim Brothers clashed with the Ba'athists. These clashes escalated from fistfights on playgrounds to terrorism on the streets of Damascus and other Syrian cities. After a 1963 coup that put the Ba'ath Party in power, the Muslim Brotherhood went underground in various places, including Hama. For information about the Muslim Brotherhood, see Daniel Diller, ed., *The Middle East* (Washington, D.C.: Congressional Quarterly, Inc., 1994), 348.

5. For evidence of the complicity of Colonel Qadhafi in the destruction of Pan Am 103, see Steve Emerson and Brian Duffy, *Fall of Pan Am 103: Inside the Lockerbie Investigation* (New York: Putnam, 1990). For information about terrorism in general, see:
   http://www.emergency.com/panam103.htm
   ENN Archives, August 1993. (ENN is the EmergencyNet News Service.)

6. Regarding Libyan involvement in plots to assassinate Anwar Sadat of Egypt, beginning in the summer of 1977, see John Cooley, *Libyan Sandstorm* (London: Sidgwick & Jackson, 1983), 118-22. After the discovery of the early plots, Egyptian and Libyan border forces skirmished for four days, resulting in several dozen casualties on both sides.

7. Christopher Ogden, "Inside Kim Jong-Il's Brain; 'Baffling Outsiders Is What I Do Best'" *Time* 148, no. 15 (October 7, 1996).

8. Kevin Sullivan, "Congressman Finds 'Severe Famine' in North Korea," Washington Post, April 9, 1997, sec. A,24.

9. Anna Vania Song researched the personalities of the rogue leaders. She discovered that there was a great deal more written about some than others. There was an abundance of material about President Saddam Hussein because of the Gulf War, and there was a dearth of information about President Rafsanjani or the Ayatollah Khameni. Perhaps this difference

reflects the perceived magnitude of the events with which these leaders have been associated. There is more information on the Ayatollah Khomeni than on his successors. Because Khomeni succeeded the Shah in post-revolutionary Iran, there was considerable demand for information about him and interest in him as a person. Khomeni, however, discouraged inquires into his personal life.

10. Thekla Fischer, "The Currency of Coercion: For Washington and Tehran" (master's thesis, University of Michigan, Ann Arbor, 1996), 15.

11. Daniel Brumberg, "Khomeini's Legacy: Islamic Rule and Islamic Justice," in *Spokesmen for the Despised: Fundamentalist Leaders of the Middle East,* R. Scott Appleby, ed. (Chicago: University of Chicago Press, 1997), 21.

12. Amir Taheri, *The Spirit of Allah: Khomeni and the Islamic Revolution* (London: Hutchinson & Co., 1985).

13. Mostafa suddenly died in October 1977. Brumberg, "Khomeni's Legacy: Islamic Rule and Islamic Justice," 38. Also see Mark Gasiorowski, *U.S. Foreign Policy and the Shah: Building a Client State in Iran* (Ithaca: Cornell University Press, 1991), 216.

14. Fischer, "The Currency of Coercion," 50-56.

15. Diller, ed., *The Middle East,* 225.

16. Because the term "fundamentalist" also applies to Christians, it is advisable to use the word "Islamist" to depict radical Islam. See Graham Fuller and Ian Lesser, *A Sense of Siege: The Geopolitics of Islam and the West* (Boulder: Westview Press, 1995), 2.

17. Judith Miller, *God Has Ninety-Nine Names* (New York: Simon & Schuster, 1996), 460. See also Patrick Clawson, "Iran's Challenge to the West: How, When, and Why?" *Washington Institute Policy Papers,* no. 33, 1993.

18. Judith Miller and Laurie Mylroie, *Saddam Hussein and the Crisis in the Gulf* (New York: Random House, 1990), 24.

19. Ibid., 36.

20. Ibid., 37.

21. For example, Michael Corleone killed his younger brother, Fredo, for betraying the family.

22. For a description of Saddam's harsh childhood, see Efraim Karsh and Inari Rautsi, *Saddam Hussein: A Political Biography* (New York: The Free Press, 1991), and Miller and Mylroie, *Saddam Hussein,* 25-28.

23. In 1988, Baghdad "initiated a campaign to break Kurdish resistance. This campaign drew international condemnation, in part because of strong evidence that the Iraqi army used poison gas against Kurdish villages and camps in northern Iraq." Diller, ed., The Middle East, 237.

　　　An opponent of Saddam Hussein, Samir al-Khalil, wrote an unauthorized biography discussing Saddam's tendency toward violence. Saddam's generation (those born around 1937) were " . . . the children of violence for whom violence has become a way of life." Samir al-Khalil, *The Republic of Fear: The Inside Story of Saddam's Iraq* (New York: Pantheon Books, 1989), xviii.

24. Janice Gross Stein, "Deterrence and Compellence in the Gulf: A Failed or an Impossible Task?" *International Security* 17 (Fall 1992): 147-79. Stein takes

the position that Saddam's motivation was fear more than gain in his decision to order the invasion of Kuwait. An alternative explanation in Chapter Three of the present volume is that gain more than fear motivated Saddam to invade Kuwait.

25. Contrary to some of the other rogue leaders, Qadhafi grew up in a stable family. But his grandfather's murder greatly disturbed his family's stability and collective outlook toward the West. For more on Qadhafi's background see Mohamed El-Khawas, *Qaddafi: His Ideology in Theory and Practice* (Brattleboro: Amana Books, 1986).

26. People cannot be held responsible for actions they cannot control. "Insane" people cannot control their actions; therefore, they should not be punished for actions beyond their control.

27. Friedman, *From Beirut to Jerusalem*, 95.

28. "'Whenever a person is tortured,' the student testified to Amnesty, 'he is ordered to strip naked. Inside the room there is an electric apparatus, a Russian tool for ripping out fingernails, pincers, and scissors for plucking flesh and an apparatus called the Black Slave, on which they force the torture victim to sit. When switched on, a very hot and sharp metal skewer enters the rear, burning its way until it reaches the intestines, then returns only to be reinserted.'" Friedman, *From Beirut to Jerusalem*, 80.

29. "Shaykh Ali Bayanuni of the Islamic Front claims the Syrian government killed 20,000 civilians and lost 10,000 itself in the Hama incident (*Le Matin*, March 22, 1982, translation in Foreign Broadcast Information Service). Diplomatic observers are quoted as believing that 5,000-13,000 lives were lost (*Christian Science Monitor*, April 1, 1992)." Cited in endnote 6 of John Devlin, "Syrian Policy" in *The Middle East Since Camp David*, Robert Freedman, ed. (Boulder: Westview Press, 1984), 123-42; 141.

30. Patrick Seale, *Asad of Syria: The Struggle for the Middle East* (London: I.B. Tauris & Co Ltd., 1988).

31. The American view of nationalism differs from that of the Middle East. In the Middle West, national identity and citizenship are one and the same. In the Middle East, national identity has been molded by ethnic conflicts among peoples within the same nation. Though several groups may share citizenship, they may not share the same national identity. Therefore, a ruling class may not see other groups as citizens but as national rivals.

32. Syria occupies a portion of Lebanon, while Israel controls a small southern section of Lebanon near the Israeli border. Syria's large military presence in Lebanon casts a shadow on Lebanese politics. And if the troops are not enough to compel, Assad uses force to quell political opposition.

33. Friedman, *From Beirut to Jerusalem*, 104.

34. Institute for South-North Korea Studies, *The True Story of Kim Jong-Il* (Seoul, 1985). According to an American scholar at the United States Institute of Peace, the Korean media regularly use that institute as a source for information concerning South–North Korean relations. The inference here, then, is that this institute is as good a source about North Korea as the Korean media itself. Telephone interview by Anna Song with Scott Snyder, July 30, 1997, Ann Arbor, MI/Washington, D.C.

The literature on the Koreas produced by either North or South is a mixture of propaganda with less analysis than would be found in Western sources about the peninsula. One institute on which the present analysis relies is the Institute for South–North Korea Studies. Because it is in Seoul, the practice is to seek validation from non-Korean sources concerning controversial inferences.

35. Institute for South-North Korea Studies, *The True Story of Kim Jong-Il*, 59-60.

36. According to one source, Kim Il-Sung also used these pleasure groups. The Institute for South-North Korea Studies states that both father and son justify the use of pleasure groups with the claim that being the nation's supreme leader creates an overwhelming amount of stress. " . . . therefore, their mental and physical stress must be given an outlet." Institute for South-North Korea Studies, *The True Story of Kim Jong-Il*, 87-88.

37. Max Weber, a political leadership theorist, believed that there were three types of leadership, among them, charismatic. A charismatic leader portrays the image of having some type of divinity. Through this illusion of divinity, the leader can then motivate the people.

38. See The Institute of North Korean Studies, *The Red Dynasty* (Seoul: The Institute of North Korean Studies, 1982).

39. *The True Story of Kim Jong-Il*, 7-9, 20-21.

40. For the record, elephant herds generally consist of a cluster of females with their young daughters. Male elephants usually travel on their own or with a pair of youthful males. They chase the females from the herd for the purpose of mating with them. The use of the rogue elephant metaphor, however, does not imply that the United States chases rogue nations out of global herds for the purpose of "embracing" them!

41. "Embrace" is a process of forming an alignment, "accommodation" a procedure of compromising with a bargaining partner on issues but not principles, and "appeasement" a method of buying off potential antagonists at the sacrifice of principles. "Containment" is an effort to isolate, for example, through the imposition of economic sanctions. "Confrontation" is a process of issuing threats that may imply military action. Individuals who favor embrace, accommodation, and appeasement should guard against the underestimation of threats; and people who prefer to contain and confront should be careful of overestimation of threats. In particular, appeasement as a set of beliefs about how to deal with challengers is an unmotivated bias. It distorts threat perception and predisposes individuals to choose embrace and accommodation rather than containment and confrontation of rogue states.

42. Chinese characters for danger and opportunity are wei and chi, which together mean crisis.

43. Robert Jervis, Richard Ned Lebow, and Janice Gross Stein, eds., *Psychology and Deterrence* (Baltimore: Johns Hopkins University Press, 1985), 1-12.

44. Gary Clyde Hufbauer, Jeffrey J. Schott, and Kimberly Ann Elliot conducted a study that defined economic sanctions as the deliberate, government-

inspired withdrawal—or threat of withdrawal—of customary trade or financial relations. See their *Economic Sanctions Reconsidered: History and Current Policy* (Washington, D.C.: Institute for International Economics, 1985).

45. The United Nations Security Council imposes multilateral sanctions when there is a consensus among the permanent members: China, France, Russia, the United Kingdom, and the United States. In addition to Europe, the anti-sanctions school includes Great Powers in Asia like China and Japan.

46. The United States took two unilateral measures, the Cuban Liberty and Democratic Solidarity (Helms-Burton) Act and the Iran and Libya Sanctions Act. In anticipation of their passage, the European Union stated that if the U.S. Government wishes further measures to be implemented by the international community, it should introduce them for discussion in the relevant international body, such as the United Nations. See "European Commission Reacts to U.S. Announcement on Cuba," *European Union News*, no. 43/96 (July 16, 1996) and "EU Reacts to Iran/Libya Legislation," *European Union News*, no. 44/96 (July 23, 1996).

47. A German foundation representative in Washington gave a succinct summary of the different approaches between Europe and the United States regarding how to treat Third World states thought to be engaged in terrorism and proliferation of weapons of mass destruction. First, because détente worked to diffuse tensions during the Cold War, it can have similar effects against so-called rogue states as well. Second, Europeans have a long tradition in the practice of classical diplomacy. This tradition entails having diplomatic relations and conducting negotiations with countries with which there are profound differences: "Talk, talk, talk, is better than fight, fight, fight!" Hence, punitive measures like sanctions and the use of force should occur only after diplomacy has been tried and found wanting. Americans, however, are likely to incorporate force and diplomacy together. Third, there is the factor of economic interdependence between Europe and the Third World states like Libya. Europeans are far more dependent on Middle Eastern/North African oil and trade than the United States. As a result, preservation and furtherance of those ties is much more critical to them.

48. Although Europe is mostly a unitary actor in opposition to politically motivated trade restraints, there are differences among states. British Prime Minister Margaret Thatcher acted like an American idealist instead of like a European realist. Even the French may consider sanctions when the threat is small, the action is symbolic, and their domestic constituency is supportive.

49. Although the American business sector opposes political restraints on trade, many firms lobby on behalf of protectionist measures that benefit their particular sector. Of concern here, however, are only political trade restraints, not economic protectionism.

50. Businesses on both sides of the Atlantic are opposed to the imposition of political trade restraints. Mobil Oil, "Sanctions: The Last Resort," *New York Times*, February 15, 1996, sec. A, 15. Mobil Oil runs a series of advertise-

ments opposite the editorial page of the *New York Times* and other national newspapers.

51. In the fierce competition between the U.S.-based Boeing Corporation and Europe's Airbus Industrie over aircraft sales to China, Boeing had delivered 252 planes, while Airbus delivered only 25, by 1996. In reaction to tension between the United States and China over trade and human rights, however, China subsequently delayed renewed ordering from Boeing and pursued options with Airbus. Jeff Cole, Joseph Kahn, Craig S. Smith, and Douglas Lavin, "China Snubs Boeing Again in a Jet Deal," *Wall Street Journal,* April 12, 1996, sec. A, 3.

52. In 1996, I joined a Council on Foreign Relations study group on economic sanctions. Former White House aide Richard Haass, the head of the study group, stated, "Sanctions—ranging from cutting off aid to shutting down all trade and financing—offer U.S. policymakers and members of Congress an attractive compromise between doing nothing and sending in the Marines." Richard Haass, "Sanctions—With Care," *The Washington Post,* 27 July 1997, sec. C, 9. Available online:

    http://www.washingtonpost.com/wp-srv/WPlate/1997-07/27/1211-072797-idx.html#TOP

    See also Richard Haass, *Intervention: The Use of American Military Force in the Post–Cold War World* (Washington, D.C.: Carnegie Endowment for International Peace, 1994), regarding economic sanctions and the Gulf War and *The Reluctant Sheriff: The United States after the Cold War* (Washington, D.C.: Council on Foreign Relations, 1997).

53. During the Bush Administration, John Bolton was an assistant secretary at the State Department and in 1996 he was President of the National Policy Forum, a Republican study organization. John Bolton, "Appeasement As a Way of Life," *New York Times,* July 28, 1996, sec. E, 13.

54. In Nigeria, Royal/Dutch Shell has large-scale investments and backs the government at the risk of incurring the wrath of worldwide environmental and human rights groups. Paul Lewis, "Nigeria's Deadly Oil War: Shell Defends Its Record," *New York Times,* February 13, 1996, sec. A, 1.

55. As the world's ninth largest oil producer, Nigeria supplied about 600,000 barrels a day to the United States, about 8 percent of total U.S. oil imports during the mid-1990s. And Nigeria earned over $10 billion a year in oil revenues during this period. These funds account for some 90 percent of Nigeria's foreign export earnings and approximately 80 percent of its government revenues. Hence, Glenn Frankel concludes that an international embargo would have caused Nigeria immediate economic pain. Glenn Frankel, "Nigeria Mixes Oil and Money," *Washington Post,* November 24, 1996, sec. C, 1.

56. "We honestly don't believe a unilateral oil embargo against Nigeria would accomplish much except to further concentrate power and wealth in the hands of a few," said David Miller, the Corporate Council on Africa's executive director, as cited in Frankel, "Nigeria Mixes Oil and Money."

57. Neal Sher, "Comprehensive U.S. Sanctions Against Iran: A Plan For Action," in *A Report to AIPAC's Executive Council* (March 20, 1995), and Jim

Hoagland, "Money Does Talk," *Washington Post,* February 8, 1996, sec. A, 1, 12.

58. Richard Ellings, *Embargoes and World Power—Lessons from American Foreign Policy* (Boulder: Westview Press, 1985), 126.

59. In this regard, Richard Ellings finds that, "With eroding leverage, the once preeminent state finds weakening capacity to administer sanctions on a multilateral basis. . . . [Sanctions] indicate a residual will to lead, but a diminished capacity to do so." Ellings, *Embargoes and World Power—Lessons from American Foreign Policy,* 124.

60. Margaret Doxey, a leading scholar on economic warfare, finds that it is hard to achieve international accord on the definition of the situation that requires collective action. Margaret Doxey, *Economic Sanctions and International Enforcement* (London: Royal Institute of International Affairs, 1980), 80-81.

61. Retribution derives from the Latin *re + tribuo,* literally "to pay back." The unqualified noun, "retribution," refers solely to a deliberate return of evil for evil. M. Henberg, *Retribution: Evil for Evil in Ethics, Law, and Literature* (Philadelphia: Temple University Press, 1990), 18.

62. Richard Kim Nosily, "International Sanctions As International Punishment," *International Organization* (Spring 1989): 315, and Miroslav Nincic and Peter Wallenstein, *Dilemmas of Economic Coercion—Sanctions in World Politics* (New York: Praeger Special Studies, 1983), 20.

63. "They [the American people] were more conversant with the notions of rights and the principles of true freedom than the greater part of their European contemporaries." Alexis de Tocqueville, *Democracy in America,* trans. Henry Reeve, rev. Francis Bowen, ed. Phillips Bradley (New York: Modern Library, 1981), 31.

64. Extraterritoriality is the implementation of one nation's laws in other countries or the application of one state's laws to the firms from other nations. See Chapter Two, endnote 4, for an extended discussion of the Iran and Libya Sanctions Act and the concept of extraterritoriality.

65. In addition to the Spector-Wolf Bill, Senator Spencer Abraham (Rep.-Michigan) introduced a similar bill targeted at China. His *China Sanctions and Human Rights Advancement Act* would prohibit the granting of U.S. visas to Chinese Government officials who work in entities involved in the implementation and enforcement of China's law and directives on religious practices. The legislation requires an annual report by the president on whether there has been improvement in China's policy of religious toleration and in its overall human rights record. Congress, Senate, *The China Sanctions and Human Rights Advancement Act of 1997,* 105th Cong., 1st sess., S. 810.Available online:
http://www.access.gpo.gov/su_docs/aces/aaces002.html

66. Gerald Seib, "Clinton is Squeezed in Middle on Religious Persecution," *Wall Street Journal,* July 7, 1997, sec. A, 16.

67. "Let every nation know . . . whether it wishes us well or ill . . . that we shall pay any price, bear any burden, meet any hardship, support any friend, oppose any foe, to assure the survival and the success of liberty. This much

we pledge. . .and more." President, Speech, "Inaugural Address of President John F. Kennedy, January 20, 1961."Available online: http://users.southeast.net/~cheryl/speech.html

68. Sanctions regimes are norms that specify acceptable behavior. A United Nations Security Council resolution that mandates international sanctions is a sanctions regime.

69. Retributive sanctions serve as a tool to achieve catharsis. From Greek drama through Sigmund Freud, catharsis symbolizes an emotional release, relieving tension. In this respect, applying punishment by retributive sanctions always makes one feel good.

70. In defiance of American hegemony in the Caribbean, the Soviet Union had placed in Cuba nuclear missiles capable of striking the United States. President Kennedy demanded the immediate withdrawal of those missiles and sent American battleships to quarantine the island-nation. Soviet Premier Khrushchev consented to the withdrawal of the missiles under the condition that the United States not invade Cuba. This agreement precluded American military action, yet permitted economic sanctions. Thereafter, the economic embargo was the main tool that Washington directed against Havana. See Aleksandr Fursendo and Timothy Naftali, *One Hell of a Gamble: Khrushchev, Castro, and Kennedy, 1958-1964* (New York: W.W. Norton & Company, 1997).

71. Elliot Aronson, Timothy Wilson, and Robin Akert, *Social Psychology: The Heart and the Mind* (New York: Harper Collins, 1994).

72. Richard Ned Lebow, "Windows of Opportunity: Do States Jump Through Them?" *International Security* 9, no. 1 (Summer 1984): 150.

73. Prior to the Franco-Russian Alliance of 1891, a "mobilization-gap" existed between the Germans and the Russians. Both due to better physical infrastructure and to more efficient military command and control, Germany could mobilize its forces considerably faster. After 1891, however, the gap closed, as Germany had to account for faster French mobilization. Hence Germany developed the Schlieffen Plan. The strategy was to deal with France's faster mobilization potential by a series of lightning strikes, and then to turn to the slower Russians. See Lebow, "Windows of Opportunity: Do States Jump Through Them?" *International Security* 9, no. 1 (Summer 1984), 160-8.

74. Deterrence is a process of inducing a potential challenger not to take an action; coercion aims at getting an actor to take an action or undo something already in place. Sanctions may be both deterrent and coercive in nature. Alexander George and Richard Smoke, *Deterrence in American Foreign Policy* (New York: Columbia University Press, 1974); Alexander George, David Hall, and William Simons, *The Limits of Coercive Diplomacy* (Boston: Little Brown, 1971).

75. "Window of opportunity" refers to situations anticipated by classical deterrence: leaders are value maximizers who are deterrable, given the right combination of capability and resolve. "Basement of fear" highlights the failure of classical deterrence theory to explain "irrational" decisions. Prospect theory not only supports classical deterrence when explaining

opportunistic behavior, but also accounts for paranoid behavior, which classical theory ignores. Political psychologists who study deterrence theory find that states often are very cautious: they refrain from jumping through windows of opportunity when classical theory would expect them to act.

See also Lebow, "Window of Opportunity": 147-86; Robert Jervis, "Introduction," in Robert Jervis, Lebow, and Janice Gross Stein, eds., *Psychology and Deterrence*, 1-12.

76. In addition to the State Department, others concerned with sanctions include the Department of the Treasury's Office of Foreign Assets Control (OFAC). It administers and enforces economic and trade sanctions against targeted states, terrorism-sponsoring organizations, and international narcotics traffickers. Its mission statement declares that OFAC acts under presidential wartime and national emergency powers, as well as on the basis of authority granted by specific legislation. OFAC imposes controls on transactions and freezes foreign assets under U.S. jurisdiction. Some of the sanctions OFAC administers stem from United Nations and other international mandates; hence, they are multilateral in scope and involve close cooperation with allied governments. Available online:

    http://www.ustreas.gov/treasury/services/fac/fac.html

77. Assad has assumed the position of a proxy warrior in the conflicts between his neighbors and Israel, exploiting all parties involved to his exclusive benefit. Assad accomplishes his feats of *Realpolitik* by simply outsmarting the competition. By forcing both the United States and Israel to return time and again despite broken promises, Hezbollah rockets, and current Israeli politics, Assad emerges as a winner. He is "a rogue of the first order—but a rogue far more subtle and inconspicuous than his peers." A.M. Rosenthal, "The Winner in Lebanon," *New York Times,* April 16, 1996, sec. A, 13.

78. Department of State, *International Narcotics Control Strategy Report* (Washington, D.C.: Government Printing Office, 1996). Also available online:

    http://www.state.gov/www/global/narcotics_law/1996_
    narc_report/index.html

79. In his February 28, 1997 determination, Clinton denied certification to Colombia and five other countries. He decided that "it is in the vital national interest of the United States" to certify three "major illicit drug producing and/or transit countries," Belize, Lebanon, and Pakistan. See Office of the Press Secretary, The White House, Memorandum for the Secretary of State: "Certification for Major Narcotics Producing and Transit Countries" (Washington, D.C.), 28 February 1997. Available online:

    http://www.usembassy.org.uk/drugs3.html

80. "American sources estimate that during 1996 Lebanon exported approximately 60 tons of heroin and 100 tons of marijuana, with a total value of more than $12 billion. It is reasonable to assume that the Syrians pocketed a significant percentage of this sum, probably more than $1 billion." Ron Ben Yishai, *Yediot Ahronot,* June 6, 1997, sec. A, 4-7.

81. Although Colombia does not warrant a chapter in this study, it does merit further elaboration in an endnote. The Colombian drug cartels are responsible for about 80 percent of the cocaine and 30 percent of the heroin

entering the United States. These operations produced more than 700 metric tons of cocaine in 1994, yielding over $7 billion in U.S. sales alone. (Jesse Helms, "The Challenge of Colombia," *Wall Street Journal*, March 4, 1996, sec. A, 14). As a result of such shipments, narco-corruption is a threat to U.S. interests. But such a threat is only one aspect of a multidimensional relationship between Colombia and the United States. Along with Colombia, Iran also failed to be certified as working on the drug problem, yet it is a subject of this study. In contrast to Bogota, Washington seeks to isolate Tehran as a pariah.

## Chapter Two

1. For a critique of balance of power principles such as "The enemy of my enemy is my friend" as applied to Iran, Iraq, and the United States, see Bruce Jentleson, *With Friends Like These: Reagan, Bush, and Saddam, 1982-1990* (New York: W. W . Norton, 1994), 15 ff.

2. The Clinton Administration rejects the Reagan-Bush policy of building up either Iran or Iraq to counter the threat from the other and favors a policy of "dual containment." Anthony Lake, "Confronting Backlash States," *Foreign Affairs* 73, no. 2 (March/April 1994): 48-51.

   A grand debate rages regarding dual containment. On the one side is the Clinton Administration as represented by Anthony Lake. On the other side are two former national security advisors and a former assistant secretary of state: Zbigniew Brzezinski, Brent Scowcroft, and Richard Murphy, "Differentiated Containment," *Foreign Affairs* 76, no. 3 (May/June 1997), 20. They dismiss dual containment as "more a slogan than a strategy."

3. A structural security dilemma is a situation in which the security of each state requires the insecurity of others. A perceptual security dilemma occurs when decisionmakers overrate the advantages of the offensive or the hostility of others. Jack Snyder, "Saving Face for the Sake of Deterrence," in Robert Jervis, Richard Lebow, and Janice Gross Stein, eds., *Psychology and Deterrence*, (Baltimore: Johns Hopkins University Press, 1985), 155.

4. The Iran and Libya Sanctions Act seeks to deny both countries the ability to support international terrorism and to fund the development and acquisition of weapons of mass destruction. The Act limits their ability to explore, extract, refine, or transport petroleum resources by pipeline. If foreign persons (people or firms) invest more than $40 million, they are subject to U.S. penalties. The act does not require the president to sanction foreign persons, but it allows the president to do so. Furthermore, mandatory sanctions are also applicable against companies that violate the UN Security Council trade sanctions against Libya. Available online:
   `http://thomas.loc.gov/cgi-bin/bdquery/L?d104:./`
   `list/bd/d104sh.1st:493`

5. Allison Mitchell, "Clinton Signs Bill Against Investing in Iran and Libya," *New York Times*, August 6, 1996, sec. A, 1.

6. Reuters, "Perry: Iran May Be Suspect in Saudi Bombing," August 3, 1996.

7. National Public Radio interview by Martha Raddatz with Secretary of Defense William Perry, August 2, 1996, Washington, D.C. Available online: http://www.npr.org/plweb-cgi/fastweb?getdoc+npr+ npr+ 8729+15+wAAA+August%262,1996

8. See William Safire, "October Surprises," *New York Times* August 15, 1996, sec. A, 19. With respect to the possibility of an Iranian connection, Safire reports that Clinton Administration national security officials secretly tipped the presidential campaign of Bob Dole about the likelihood of a punitive strike against Iran if the evidence of Iranian involvement were compelling.

9. Reuters, "U.S. Defense Secretary Clarifies Iran Comments," August 3, 1996.

10. Youssef Ibrahim, "Saudi Rebels Tied to June Bombing," *New York Times,* August 15, 1996, sec. A, 1, 6.

11. Reuters, "Iran's Spiritual Leader Lashes Out at U.S. Claim of Saudi Bomb Link," August 3, 1997.

12. During 1997, the United States maintained a robust military presence in the gulf region: about 25,000 military personnel, 100 aircraft, 25 ships, as well as prepositioned equipment for at least one heavy armored division. There should be about two divisions by the end of the year 2000. U.S. forces could be used against either Iraq or Iran. Tehran perceives American economic warfare and the U.S. military presence in the Gulf as a threat. Therefore, Iran's perception of a high American threat is not unreasonable.

13. See Joshua Epstein, *Strategy & Force Planning: The Case of the Persian Gulf* (Washington, D.C.: Brookings Institution, 1987), 2-6, for an analysis of a Soviet assault on the oil fields of Khuzestan Province, Iran's principal oil region. Such an attack was the central planning contingency for the Gulf region within the Pentagon during most of the Cold War. A Soviet invasion of Iran would have required some 15 armored division equivalents as well as approximately 700 aircraft. This force could have reached Tehran in about 45 days.

   The Pentagon assumed that a Soviet intervention in Iran could have been conducted under the cover of a peacekeeping role in the event of an Iranian civil war. And there might have been direct attacks on oil facilities by guerrillas as a part of a larger war. In addition, this scenario included attacks on oil sea-lines of communications, such as mining, submarine, or air assaults on tankers. The result might have been Soviet control of the Strait of Hormuz. Office of the Assistant Secretary of Defense for Program Analysis and Evaluation: "Capabilities for Limited Contingencies in the Persian Gulf," unclassified summary, (Washington, D.C.: 1979).

14. Jentleson, *With Friends Like These,* 15.

15. Politics, interests, and values may lead to biases in information processing. All three can result in misperceptions and provide incentives to magnify threats. Motivated biases are those that distort perceptions because individuals see what they want to see. Unmotivated biases distort perceptions because people see what they expect to see. Bureaucratic and domestic politics are sources of motivated biases affecting American decisionmakers in their overestimation of the Iranian threat. For a discussion of biases and

threat perception, see Robert Jervis, "Perceiving and Coping with Threat," in Jervis, Lebow, and Stein, eds., *Psychology and Deterrence*, 18-27.

16. I attended the Atlanta briefing along with Richard Allen, William Casey, Joseph Chourba, Daniel Graham, Fred Ikle, Jack Kemp, and Michael Pillsbury. After Reagan's victory in November, some of us served in his Administration. They included Allen as National Security Advisor; Casey as Director of Central Intelligence; Graham as advisor to the President on the Strategic Defense Initiative; Ikle as Under Secretary of Defense/Policy; Kemp as a member of the House of Representatives and later Secretary of Housing and Urban Development in the Bush Administration. And I became co-chair of the Middle East Task Force for the Reagan-Bush Campaign, senior staff member of the National Security Council at the White House, and then personal representative of the Secretary of Defense at security talks in Europe.

17. Some members of the advisory group thought that the Soviets also had options across different regions. In the event that conflict in the Middle East expanded to a NATO–Warsaw Pact war in Europe, Soviet armed forces could engage in selective attacks in Asia against American forces capable of attacking Soviet land-based forces. And Soviet forces could conduct operations to prevent reinforcement and supply of NATO-Europe from the Pacific.

18. Iranian militants seized 52 Americans at the U.S. embassy in Tehran on November 4, 1979, held them for 445 days, and released them on January 20, 1981, the day Reagan replaced Carter as President. Following the seizure of the embassy, Washington blocked the assets of the government of Iran in the United States or in overseas branches of U.S banks. Washington took that action on November 14, 1979, based on the legal authority of the International Emergency Economic Powers Act. Under the Iranian Assets Control Regulations (Title 31 Part 535 of the U.S. Code of Federal Regulations), Washington froze some $12 billion in Iranian government assets. The Carter Administration expanded the assets freeze into a full-scale trade embargo. It remained in effect until Iran and the United States signed the Algiers Accord on January 19, 1981. Office of Foreign Assets Control, "What You Need to Know About U.S. Sanctions: An Overview of O.F.A.C. Regulations Involving Sanctions Against Iran," Washington, D.C.: Department of the Treasury, August 22, 1996.

19. Regarding the politics of the hostage crisis, see Gary Sick, *October Surprise: America's Hostages in Iran and the Election of Ronald Reagan* (New York: Random House Times Books, 1992), 12, and Barbara Honegger, *October Surprise* (New York: Tudor, 1989). Sick was a member of the National Security Council staff and the principal White House aide for dealing with Iranian affairs in the Carter Administration. He and I overlapped on the Council staff during 1981. Sick concluded that elements within the U.S. government worked with members of the Reagan-Bush campaign to delay release of the hostages in order to influence the outcome of the November 1980 election in Reagan's favor. As a member of the Reagan campaign team, I saw no evidence to sustain Sick's allegations.

20. Briefings of nonincumbent presidential candidates are a traditional means of minimizing statements by challengers that could jeopardize national security. With respect to the Wexford briefing, here is the way one former intelligence officer describes the meeting that followed our prebrief.

> Before the election, candidate Reagan received only one intelligence briefing . . . D.C.I. [Director of Central Intelligence] Adm. Stansfield Turner, accompanied by three senior Agency officers, represented CIA . . . Participants in that first briefing remember it as "a circus." The living room of the Middleburg home where the session was held was like a chaotic movie set with chairs scattered more or less randomly about the room and people constantly coming and going. The Governor was an engaging host, but in the impossible setting it was extraordinarily difficult to make effective use of the briefing aids and other materials that Turner had brought with him. Throughout the meeting, which went on for approximately one hour, the CIA participants had the feeling that the Reagan camp had accepted the briefing simply because it had been offered and they had to do it. There was no evidence that anyone had the expectation that the Governor would engage in an in-depth review of the substantive issues.
>
> Even in these awkward circumstances there was some serious discussion of developments in the Middle East, the agreed focus of the session. Turner discussed the petroleum aspects of the issue and the conflicts between Iran and Iraq and in Afghanistan. National Intelligence Officer for the Middle East Robert Ames briefed on the internal politics of Saudi Arabia and Iran. Richard Lehman, from the National Intelligence Council, elaborated on the impact of the Iran-Iraq war on the region and on the Soviet role.

John Helgerson, *Getting to Know the President: CIA Briefings of Presidential Candidates 1952-1992*, (Washington, D.C.: Center for the Study of Intelligence, Central Intelligence Agency). Available online: http://www.oD.C.i.gov/csi/books/briefing/index.htm

21. I attended the Reagan prebriefing. In attendance were vice-presidential candidate George Bush; former Secretary of State Henry Kissinger; General Alexander Haig, former Nixon deputy National Security Advisor who subsequently became Reagan's Secretary of State. Also included were Admiral Thomas Moorer, former Chairman Joint Chiefs of Staff; Edwin Meese III, who later became Reagan's Attorney General; and Richard Allen, who subsequently became the President's National Security Advisor. In addition, there was Robert Neumann, former Ambassador to Saudi Arabia and co-chair with me of the Middle East Task Force of the Reagan-Bush campaign.

22. Gary Sick named Reagan campaign advisers to be part of a network of informants throughout the government. They were to alert the campaign about hostage developments. According to Sick, they included, Henry

Kissinger, Alexander Haig, Thomas Moorer, and Robert Neumann. See Sick, *October Surprise*, 23, 27, 35, 101.

23. Personal recollection of author from the "prebrief" that prepared presidential candidate Reagan to receive a briefing from the Director of Central Intelligence, October 4, 1980, Virginia, at the Wexford Estate.

24. T. N. Kaul, *The Kissinger Years: Indo-American Relations* (New Delhi: Arnold-Heinemann, 1980), 2.

25. Michael Lynch, "The Next Oil Crisis," *Technology Review* 90, no. 9, Massachusetts Institute of Technology Alumni Association (November 1987): 38.

26. On September 22, 1980, Iraq launched an attack against Iran's southwestern province of Khuzestan. Baghdad falsely assumed that the mainly Arab population of Khuzestan, a large Iranian minority, would rise up in arms against their rulers from Tehran.

27. My assessment was that the Reagan advisers leaned toward Iraq. In contrast, Sick asserts that the Reagan-Bush campaign wanted to come to terms with Tehran on the hostages, even at the expense of entering into an arms-supply relationship with Iran. Sick, *October Surprise*, 143. My inference derives from first-hand experience.

28. See "Case Four: A Jordanian-Syrian Alliance—the Eastern Front," Anthony Cordesman, *Perilous Prospects: The Peace Process and the Arab-Israeli Military Balance* (Boulder: Westview Press, 1996).

29. See also Sick, *October Surprise*, 108, for his assessment of Israel's doctrine of the periphery. With respect to Israel's relations with Iran, moreover, Sick (p. 65) found that the hostage crisis and Iran's vulnerability to Iraq in their war gave Israel an occasion to reopen its ties with the Islamic Republic of Iran. Tehran was desperate for supply parts for its American-origin arms in October 1980, the first month of the Iran-Iraq War.

30. From about 1965 to 1975, Iran and Israel may have trained and supplied arms to Kurdish rebels in Iraq.

31. Congressman Toby Roth (Rep.-Wisconsin), "New Iranian-Libyan Sanctions Will Only Hurt U.S.," *Wall Street Journal,* August 6, 1996, sec. A, 14. A Roth staff aide, who had the action on the Iran and Libya Sanctions Act, explained why Roth wrote in opposition to a law for which he voted. "Along with 414 other members in a unanimous vote, no Member wanted to be on the wrong side of an issue concerning Iran and Libya." Telephone interview with Raymond Tanter, Ann Arbor, MI, August 19, 1996.

32. While engaging in rhetoric of confrontation, Jerusalem also has provided arms to Tehran. The goal is to form alignments with non-Arab Muslim states like Iran and Turkey, which are on the periphery of the Arab-Israel conflict zone.

33. Despite negligible amounts of oil, Israel has a per capita income higher than that of Saudi Arabia's. Israel: population, 5.4 million (July 1995 est.); GDP, $80.1 billion (1995 est.); $15,500 per capita GDP (1995 est.). Saudi Arabia: population, 19.4 million (July 1996 est.); GDP, $189.3 billion (1995 est.); $10,100 per capita GDP (1995 est.). Central Intelligence Agency, "Israel and Saudi Arabia," in *World Factbook 1996* (Washington, D.C.: U.S. Govern-

ment, 1997). Available online:

http://www.odci.gov/cia/publications/pubs.html

With respect to American economic aid and military assistance to Israel, it receives $3.2 billion dollars annually. Dividing that figure by the 1995 population of 5.4 million yields U.S. aid per capita to Israel of roughly $500. Subtracting that $500 per head from Israel's GDP per capita of $15,500 amounts to $15,000, which is still $4,900 greater than the Saudi Arabian figure of $10,100. The bottom line is that it is false to state that Israel's wealth derives mainly from American assistance.

The per capita income of Saudi Arabia has declined by about 50 percent during the 10 years from the mid-1980s: the population has about doubled while the GDP growth rate has remained essentially flat. And 54 percent of the population is under the age of 24. Finally, Saudi Arabia had 12 years of budget deficits during this period, and the Kingdom paid $120 billion for the cost of the war with Iraq. See also Douglas Jehl, "A Tutorial for Young Saudis On Ways to Toil for Money," *New York Times*, November 21, 1996, sec. A, 1, 4. He cites a Petroleum Finance Company chart to show real per capita GNP for Saudi Arabia just above $8,000 a year for 1996.

34. The good news is that the traditional Arab-Israel conflict, as one of wars between nation-states, is coming rapidly to a close. The bad news is that a new set of conflicts between secular governments and religious radicals vying for political control is emerging. The last decades of the twentieth century no longer experience a bipolar conflict between Israel and the Arab bloc. Rather, Israel focuses on specific threats, such as from Iran or Hezbollah in Lebanon. Because of the changing nature of the threat, Israel now enjoys relative state security. Individuals, however, may be personally less secure as a result of an increase in the rate of suicide bombings and other attacks against Israelis.

35. Hedrick Smith, *The Power Game* (New York: Random House, 1988), 216-31.

36. Christine Helms, "Washington Gains Moral High Ground on Iran, But Leaves US Business High-And-Dry," *Energy Compass Weekend Review* (May 5, 1995): 11-12.

37. Ibid.

38. The chairman of the Petroleum Finance Company said, "Washington must reexamine its strategy toward Iran, the largest and most stable country in the region. Whether we like it or not, Iran's Gulf neighbors must work with it. Besides, our attempt to isolate Iran lacks credibility with European and Asian governments." J. Robinson West, "How to Avert a New Oil Crisis," *New York Times*, November 30, 1996, sec. A, 19.

39. Menas' Associates, "US-Iran: Bad Feelings Made Worse," *Iran Focus Economy and Business* (1995): 1.

40. Mobil Oil, "Sanctions: The Last Resort," *New York Times*, February 15, 1996, sec. A, 15, paid advertisement.

41. John Lichtblau, "Oil Markets and Economic Sanctions," *Petroleum Industry Research Foundation* (April 29, 1996): 2. An ally of the Petroleum Industry Research Foundation is the U.S. Council for International Business, whose Washington representative is Joseph Gavin III.

42. Robert Mosbacher, speech delivered at the "Iran in Transition" Conference, (May 1, 1996); Brent Scowcroft, speech delivered at the "Iran in Transition" Conference, (May 2, 1996).

43. Michael Klare, *Rogue States and Nuclear Outlaws* (New York: Hill and Wang, 1995).

44. Klare, *Rogue States,* 10.

45. Klare, *Rogue States,* 219-20.

46. Klare, *Rogue States,* 24-28.

47. The Cuban Liberty and Democratic Solidarity Act of 1996 (Helms-Burton) made permanent the 34-year-old economic embargo that previously had to be renewed by a president each year. The act gave U.S. citizens the right to sue foreign companies that trafficked in property these people formerly owned in Cuba and denied U.S. visas to foreigners who derive benefits from confiscated property. The act also provided a three-month grace period for foreign companies to dispose of or pay for confiscated property. The act remains in effect until a president determines that a democratically elected government is in Cuba, presumably without Fidel Castro or his brother Raul. Available online:
    `http://thomas.loc.gov/cgi-bin/bdquery/L?d104:./list/bd/d104sh.`
    `lst:169`

48. A comprehensive rational process sets logically exhaustive goals, searches across a full range of alternatives, and specifies consequences of options in terms of cost, benefit, and likelihood of success. In light of such a process, a rational choice is one that promises to yield the highest expected gain or the lowest expected loss. Leaders need not be fully rational to be held accountable for their actions. It is enough that they have "bounded rationality" to hold them responsible. Limited rationality is less demanding of people. In contrast to comprehensive rationality, bounded rational individuals need only search across some goals, specify fewer options, make fewer calculations, and make less than optimal choices. See Janice Stein and Raymond Tanter, *Rational Decisionmaking* (Columbus: Ohio State University Press, 1980).

49. During November 1979, Carter took action against Iran. He prevented the export of $300 million in U.S.-origin military equipment to Iran, deported Iranian students living illegally in the United States, ended all crude-oil imports from Iran, and froze Iran's assets in the United States. See Gary Sick, *All Fall Down* (New York: Random House, 1985), for an analysis of Carter's approach to Iran. In the Carter Administration, Sick had responsibility for Iran as a Special Assistant to the President for National Security Affairs.

50. The memoirs of Zbigniew Brzezinski, Carter's National Security Affairs Advisor, describe the period between the fall of the Shah and rise of the Ayatollah. "Khomeni's return to Tehran created in effect a situation in which two governments were competing for power, with growing turmoil in the streets and with increasing signs of demoralization within the Army." Zbigniew Brzezinski, *Power and Principle* (New York: Farrar Straus Giroux, 1983), 389-90.

51. President Reagan took action against Tehran in response to Iranian-sponsored terrorism and assaults on Gulf shipping. He banned most Iranian imports: " . . . no goods or services of Iranian origin may be imported into the United States. . . ." Excluded were petroleum products from Iran refined from Iranian oil by a third party. Office of the Federal Register, "Prohibiting Imports from Iran, Executive Order 12613," October 29, 1987. Reagan imposed sanctions under the legal authority of the International Security and Development Cooperation Act, which gave rise to the Iranian Transactions Regulations (Title 31 Part 560 of the U.S. Code of Federal Regulations). Office of Foreign Assets Control, "What You Need to Know About U.S. Economic Sanctions."

52. An indication that retribution plays a role in a sanctions policy is whether the stated goal is to change a regime's behavior—rehabilitation—but an unstated aim is to overthrow that regime. There is nothing that some regimes can do that would warrant a lifting of sanctions. At issue is the existence of the regime, not its behavior. But, it is illegitimate and perhaps illegal under international law to interfere in the domestic affairs of member states of the United Nations. Explicitly calling for revolution in a sovereign state is not an acceptable practice in the affairs of nations.

53. President Clinton issued Executive Order 12957, which was effective on March 16, 1995. And on May 8, 1995, he signed Executive Order 12959, which further tightened sanctions on Iran. The statutory authority was the International Emergency Economic Powers Act and the International Security and Development Cooperation Act. Office of Foreign Assets Control, "What You Need to Know About U.S. Economic Sanctions." Available online:

    http://www.ustreas.gov/treasury/services/fac/fac.html

    Clinton prohibited American oil firms like Conoco from engaging in commercial transactions with Iran without an export license.

54. Deterrence by denial seeks to gain compliance by reducing the capability of a prospective challenger; deterrence by threat of punishment endeavors to gain compliance by targeting a challenger's motivation and intention.

55. Patrick Clawson, "The Impacts of U.S. Sanctions on Iran," Unpublished Paper Prepared for the Council on Foreign Relations Economic Sanctions Study Group (January 1997), 9.

56. Clawson, "The Impacts of U.S. Sanctions on Iran," states that during the first year of the Iran and Libyan Sanctions Act, American sanctions reduced Iran's foreign exchange receipts by $2 billion, or ten percent of its foreign exchange receipts.

57. While the same threatened interests may have both intrinsic and strategic aspects, the analysis here treats them as analytically distinct. For a further discussion of intrinsic interests and strategic interests, see Janice Stein, "The View From Cairo," in Jervis, Lebow, and Stein, eds., *Psychology and Deterrence,* 38-39.

58. During 1996, about 40,000 Americans worked in Saudi Arabia, the world's leading oil producer. The U.S. military presence in the Kingdom was some 5,000 personnel.

59. In order to prevent Saddam's forces from attacking the Kurds, the Coalition created another zone over northern Iraq for Operation Provide Comfort. During the post–Gulf War era, the Coalition aircraft operated out of Incirlik air facility in Turkey.

60. In making alliance commitments, the United States assumes the responsibility to defend its allies primarily from American foes. If Washington pledged to defend its friends against their foes, the United States would invariably become involved in fighting its own friends.

61. Department of State Office of the Coordinator for Counterterrorism, *Patterns of Global Terrorism*, released annually.

62. A centrist Israeli newspaper, *Ma'ariv*, first reported the meetings in Tehran on July 1, 1996.

63. Hezbollah, or Party of God, began after the 1982 war between Israel and the Palestine Liberation Organization in Lebanon. Iran sent Revolutionary Guards to assist in the establishment of revolutionary groups in Lebanon. Hezbollah uses southern Lebanon as a platform for launching attacks on northern Israel. Goals of Hezbollah include: establishment of an Islamic Republic of Lebanon, complete destruction of Israel, and Islamic rule over Jerusalem. It also calls Israel "Little Satan."

64. "Iran remains the premier state sponsor of international terrorism and is deeply involved in the planning and execution of terrorist acts both by its own agents and by surrogate groups. This year [1995] Tehran escalated its assassination campaign against dissidents living abroad; there were seven confirmed Iranian murders of dissidents in 1995, compared with four in 1994." Department of State, Office of the Coordinator for Counterterrorism, *1995 Patterns of Global Terrorism* (Washington, D.C.: April, 1996), Available online:

    http://www.usis.usemb.se/terror/rpt1995/TERSST.HTM#Iran

65. "Since 1989 [to February 1996], Iran has murdered at least 48 regime opponents abroad, provided up to $100 million annually to the Lebanese Hizballah—a group responsible for the killing of over 250 Americans—and refused to repeal the religious judgment condemning British author Salman Rushdie to death." John Deutch, "Worldwide Threat Assessment Brief to the Senate Select Committee on Intelligence," Washington, D.C.: Public Affairs Staff, Central Intelligence Agency, February 22, 1996.

66. Douglas Frantz, "Looking to History, Crash Investigators Compile a Short List of Jetliner Terrorists," *New York Times*, August 24, 1996, sec. A, 11. With respect to the threat against Iranian dissidents in Pakistan, see Department of State, Office of the Coordinator for Counterterrorism, *1993 Patterns of Global Terrorism* (Washington, D.C.: Government Printing Office, April 1994). Also available online: http://www.hri.org/docs/USSD-Terror/93/asian.html

67. Hamas is the dominant, radical group in Gaza and the West Bank of the Jordan River. Hamas wants to establish Islamic Palestine from the Mediterranean Sea to the Jordan. It challenges Fatah, the mainstream Palestinian group, for leadership of the Palestinians. Hamas defines itself as the Palestinian branch of the Muslim Brotherhood that began in Egypt. Cairo

accuses the Brothers of seeking to destabilize Egypt. Hamas stands for total rejection of the Arab-Israel peace process. For an explication of the difference between radical Islamists and mainstream Islam, see Graham Fuller and Ian Lesser, *A Sense of Siege* (Boulder: Westview Press, 1995), 4-6.

68. Palestinian rejectionists formed the Popular Front for the Liberation of Palestine-General Command (PFLP-GC) in 1968. Led by Ahmed Jabril, it emphasizes a military strategy in the struggle against Israel. Sponsored by Libya and Syria, the PFLP-GC may have been involved in the downing of Pan Am 103 over Lockerbie Scotland in December 1988. For an overview of Palestine Liberation Organization factions, see Daniel Diller, ed., *The Middle East* (Washington: Congressional Quarterly, 1991), 28-29.

69. Frantz, "Looking to History."

70. *1993 Patterns of Global Terrorism* (Washington, D.C.: April, 1994). Available online:

    http://www.hri.org/docs/USSD-Terror/93/midleeast.html#Algeria

71. James Risen, "Administration Defends Bosnian Arms Policy," *Los Angeles Times,* April 24, 1996, sec. A.

72. In September 1991, the international community decided to impose a UN arms embargo on the former Yugoslavia (Security Council Resolution 713). The goal was to stabilize the situation among the former republics. But the embargo left the Serbs with an unfair advantage vis-à-vis other republics, such as Bosnia. The weaponry from Tito's Yugoslav army remained with Serbia and their Bosnian Serb allies. In early April 1994, Croatian President Franjo Tudjman approached the Zagreb-based American Ambassador Peter Galbraith. The question was whether the United States would object to Croatia acting as a transshipment point for Iranian arms en route to Muslim Bosnia. The United States gave a green light when President Clinton instructed Galbraith to inform Tudjman that the ambassador had "no instructions." Washington, in effect, traded the risk of Iranian penetration into the heart of Europe with Revolutionary Guards for the benefit of keeping the Bosnian Muslim regime afloat. For a further explication of the Iranian connection in arms transshipments to Bosnia, see Kristin McLean "Washington's Green Light to Tehran for Arms to Sarajevo via Zagreb?" Unpublished Paper Prepared for Political Science 472, the University of Michigan, (Spring 1996). Available online:

    http://www-personal.umich.edu/~rtanter/S96PS472_Papers

73. The Director of Central Intelligence testified that Iran may be devoting up to $1 billion a year on its nuclear program. U.S. Senate. Committee on Governmental Affairs. *Proliferation Threats of the 1990's* Hearing, 24 February 1993. Available online:

    http://web.lexis-nexis.com/cis/retrieve/document/s_witness.
    html?_form=s_witness.hmtl&_mode=FULL&_results=
    G{H^*KO!WAD!UUB$M[SWAD$UUB$AV!DUB]!BD!ABC$E$]DU]AB]DU$U&_
    library=LEGIS&_file=CISINX&_firstdoc=1&_reldoc=8&_
    citesper= 25&_maxdocs=9&_md5=11dd2eed24de20c90964f99c4a095e6b

    See also Mark Skootsky, "U.S. Nuclear Policy Toward Iran," Unpublished Paper (June 1, 1995). Available online:

http://xpress.studby.uio.no/toofan/public_html/persian/usiran.
html

74. Iran's chemical weapons program is already the largest in the Third World, claims Michael Eisenstadt. In a paper delivered to the Washington Institute for Near East Studies, he said that Iran can produce several hundred tons of chemical agent a year and may have produced as much as 2,000 tons of agent to date.

And with respect to biological weapons, Iran is thought to be able to deploy them and disseminate them via terrorist saboteurs, or spray tanks on aircraft or ships, although more advanced means of dissemination—by unmanned aircraft or missiles for instance—may currently be beyond its means. Rick Marshall, "Iranian Military Power Assessed," USIA, March 13, 1996. Available online:

gopher://198.80.36.82:70/OR6423641-6427508-range/archives/
1996/pdq.96

75. See Lenore Martin, "Patterns of Regional Conflict and U.S. Gulf Policy," in William Olson, ed., *US Strategic Interests in the Gulf Region,* (Boulder: Westview Press, 1987), 9-10.

76. Although Nixon receives sole credit for the doctrine, Henry Kissinger provided the intellectual basis. In his memoirs, Kissinger writes, "We remain willing to participate, but we can not supply all the . . . resources. The initiative has to move increasingly into that region." To Kissinger's surprise, Nixon readily accepted the idea of relying less on the United States and more on regional allies. Henry Kissinger, *White House Years* (Boston: Little Brown, 1979), 222-25. See also George Lenczowski, *American Presidents and the Middle East* (Durham: Duke University Press, 1990), 116-17.

77. The Backfire bomber has an unrefueled combat radius of 2,486 miles or 4,000 kilometers. It can perform various tasks, such as nuclear strikes, conventional attacks, antiship strikes, and reconnaissance. U.S. Department of Defense, *Soviet Military Power: 1987,* 6th ed. (Washington, D.C.: U.S. Government Printing Office, March 1987), 36-37.

78. In his State of the Union Address on January 23, 1980, President Carter said the following. "An attempt by any outside force to gain control of the Persian Gulf region will be regarded as an assault on the vital interests of the United States of America, and such an assault will be repelled by any means necessary, including military force." "The State of the Union, January 23, 1980," *Public Papers of the Presidents of the United States: Jimmy Carter 1980-1981: Book 1, January 1 to May 23, 1980* (Washington, D.C.: U.S. Government Printing Office, 1982), 197.

79. After the invasion of Afghanistan in 1979, Soviet military forces in the Southern Theater of Military Operations conducted a command post exercise simulating an invasion of Iran. This exercise set off alarm bells in the White House and transformed President Carter from one who sought accommodation with Moscow to a leader who accepted the possibility of a Soviet-American confrontation over Iran.

80. President Reagan stated, "We wanted to keep the Soviets out of the region as well as prevent the radical, anti-American Iranian revolution from

spreading to Saudi Arabia, with all the implications that could have for our economy. To put it simply, I didn't want Saudi Arabia to become another Iran," *Ronald Reagan, An American Life: The Autobiography* (New York: Simon & Schuster, 1990), 411.

81.  A former Reagan cabinet member claimed, "That 1981-82 period was pretty grim for Iraq, and we were worried about the imbalance in the war with Iran." By 1982, American agencies used Jordan as a transshipment point for U.S.-origin helicopters en route to Iraq. Alan Friedman, *Spider's Web: The Secret History of How the White House Illegally Armed Iraq* (New York: Bantam, 1993), 17.

82.  President Bush ignored Saddam Hussein's human rights violations in order to slant American policy toward Iraq. On January 17, 1990, he signed a waiver voiding a prohibition against providing Export-Import Bank financing. In doing so, he paved the way for Baghdad to acquire equipment that it otherwise could not afford. Friedman, *Spider's Web,* 157.

83.  After Iraq invaded Kuwait on August 2, 1990, there was a National Security Council meeting the next day at the White House. General Colin Powell asked President Bush, "'Should we think about laying down a line in the sand concerning Saudi Arabia?' Bush thought for a moment, then said, 'yes, we should.'" Colin Powell, *My American Journey* (New York: Random House, 1995), 462-63.

84.  On May 18, 1993, Martin Indyk, Special Assistant to the President for Near Eastern and South Asian Affairs at the National Security Council, gave a speech. He addressed the Washington Institute for Near East Policy. It was the first statement by the Clinton Administration of the dual containment doctrine. Indyk described the threat from Iran in terms of international terrorism and opposition to the Arab-Israel peace process. Tehran opposed the peace process by supporting groups like Hamas and Hezbollah. Iran also subverted friendly Arab regimes and directed a military buildup at the Arab Gulf states. In addition to opposition to the peace process, Tehran has made a concerted effort to obtain weapons of mass destruction. See Washington Institute for Near East Policy, "Special Report: Clinton Administration Policy Toward the Middle East," *Policy Watch* (May 21, 1993). See also Anthony Cordesman and Ahmed Hashim, *Iran: Dilemmas of Dual Containment* (Boulder: Westview Press, 1996).

85.  Assistant to the President on National Security Affairs Anthony Lake described the logic of dual containment. The Clinton Administration's strategy toward Iran and Iraq began with the assumption that both regimes pursued policies hostile to American interests. The Administration rejected the Reagan-Bush policy of building up one to counter the other, in favor of a policy of dual containment. Lake, "Confronting Backlash States."

86.  Paul Jabber, "Introduction: Western Interests and Gulf Stability," in *Great Power Interests in the Persian Gulf* (New York: Council on Foreign Relations, 1989), 2.

87.  See also F. Gregory Gause III, "The Illogic of Dual Containment," *Foreign Affairs* 73, no. 2 (March/April 1994): 60.

88. Steven Lee Meyers, "U.S. Calls Alert As Iraqis Strike a Kurd Enclave," *New York Times,* September 1, 1996, sec. A, 1, 7; Chris Hedges, "Safehaven for Iraqi Kurds Has a History of Violence," *New York Times,* September 1, 1996, sec. A, 7.

89. For a description of Secretary of State George Shultz's approach to terrorism, see Shultz, *Turmoil and Triumph: My Years as Secretary of State,* (New York: Scribner's, 1993), 643-88.

90. The Export Administration Act of 1979 seeks to limit the military capability of a foreign state to sponsor international terrorism. The act contains a list of exports subject to national security controls. These include dual-use items that can be used for both civilian and military applications. Additional laws relevant to anti-terrorism are Section 620 (a) of the Foreign Assistance Act. It prohibits American financial assistance under that act as well under the Agricultural Trade Development Act, the Peace Corps Act, or the Export-Import Bank Act to any country designated by the secretary of state to be a supporter of international terrorism. The Arms Export Control Act contains prohibitions regarding international terrorism. One restriction requires that decisions to approve an export take into account whether that item would be used in support of international terrorism.

91. The act applies to both a "United States person" and "any person." Thus, it applies to foreign firms trading with or investing in Iran or Libya.

92. "While the EU [European Union] may share some of the objectives underlying such laws, it opposes the extraterritorial application of domestic legislation as a matter of principle, insofar as it purports to force persons present in—and companies incorporated in—the EU to follow U.S. laws or policies outside of the U.S." European Commission, *Report on United States Barriers to Trade and Investments* (Brussels: European Union, May 1996), 3. Available online:

    http://europa.eu.int/en/comm/dgoi/eu-us.htm

    The European Commission acts as the "guardian" of the EU treaties to ensure that European legislation is applied correctly. The European Union (Brussels: 1995-97). Available online:

    http://europa.eu.int/en/comm/c9500/comm9500.html

93. Both Iran-Libya and the Cuban Act are secondary boycotts. A primary boycott bans direct trade between a boycotter and a proscribed nation. A secondary boycott informs third countries that if they trade with the proscribed nation, there will be penalties; for example, a ban on trading with the boycotting country. And a tertiary boycott informs other states that if they trade with nations in violation of the secondary boycott, there will be sanctions; for example, a ban on trading with the boycotter. For the standard legal definitions of primary and secondary boycotts as applied to union management relations, see Henry Black, *Black's Law dictionary,* 6th ed., (St. Paul: West Publishing, 1991), 1190, 1351.

    See endnote 46 for the contents of the Cuban Liberty and Democratic Solidarity Act.

94. Clawson, "The Impacts of U.S. Sanctions on Iran," 10.

95. As defined in Chapter One, extraterritoriality is the implementation of one nation's laws in other countries or the application of one state's laws to the firms from other nations.

96. Personal interview with University of Michigan Professor of Law Jose Alvarez by Brian Clune, August 8, 1997, Ann Arbor, MI.

But a prominent international law firm in Washington, Fried, Frank, Harris, Shriver & Jacobson, states, "Although Helms-Burton is, at least arguably, not strictly extraterritorial in its application, it is correctly perceived as having the equivalent effect (i.e., imposing the dictates of U.S. law on persons who are not U.S. nationals or residents whose proscribed conduct occurs outside the U.S.)."

The bottom line, however, is, "Helms-Burton, the Iran and Libya Sanctions Act and the substantial body of other U.S. laws with extraterritorial effect make it probable that U.S. and foreign law will come into conflict." David Birenbaum, Jay Kraemer, and William Taft, IV, "The War of the Laws: Coping With Helms-Burton, the Iran-Libya Sanctions and Beyond," Unpublished Paper Prepared for the Client Memoranda Archives (Washington, D.C.: Fried, Frank, Harris, Shriver & Jacobson) July 31, 1996. Available online:

http://www.ffhsj.com/firmpage/cmemos/0086223.htm#32

97. Section 821 of the Foreign Relations Authorization Act of 1994 imposes sanctions on persons engaging in export activities that contribute to proliferation. Available online:

http://thomas.loc.gov/cgi-bin/query/6?c103:./temp/~c103fjIp::

The Arms Export Control Act authorizes a president to control the import and the export of defense articles and services. Available online:

http://samsara.law.cwru.edu/aeca.html

Formed in 1987, the Missile Technology Control Regime (MTCR) has a membership of 28 nations. Its aim is to restrict the proliferation of missiles, unmanned air vehicles, and related technology for those systems capable of carrying a 500 kilogram payload at least 300 kilometers, as well as systems intended for the delivery of weapons of mass destruction. Available online:

http://www.usis-israel.org.il/publish/press/security/archive/november/ds11118.htm

98. The primary boycott banned direct Arab trade with Israel. The secondary boycott prohibited any non-Arab country from trading with Israel. And the tertiary boycott forbade companies from dealing with persons on the secondary boycott list.

99. European Commission, "EU Reacts to Iran/Libya Legislation."

100. Article XXI of the GATT states: "Nothing in this agreement shall be construed . . . to prevent any contracting party from taking any action . . . it considers necessary for the protection of its essential security interests . . . ." Available online:

gopher://gopher.law.cornell.edu:70/00/foreign/fletcher/BH209.txt

101. European Commission, "EU Reacts to Iran/Libya Legislation."

102. One of the pioneers who called for a rethinking of American policy towards Iran is Geoffrey Kemp. See his *Control of the Middle East Arms Race* (Washington, D.C.: Carnegie Endowment for International Peace, 1991). See also his co-edited volume, *Arms Control and Weapons Proliferation in the Middle East and South Asia*, (New York: St. Martin's Press, 1992). Especially relevant is Kemp's *Forever Enemies? American Policy and the Islamic Republic of Iran* (Washington, D.C.: Carnegie Endowment for International Peace, 1994) and his co-edited volume with Janice Gross Stein, *Powder Keg in the Middle East: The Struggle for Gulf Security* (Lanham MD: Rowman & Littlefield, 1995).

103. " . . . dual containment cannot provide a sustainable basis for U.S. policy in the Persian Gulf. A more nuanced and differentiated approach to the region is in order, one in tune with America's longer-term interests." Zbigniew Brzezinski, Brent Scowcroft, and Richard Murphy, "Differentiated Containment," *Foreign Affairs*, 76, no. 3 (May/June 1997): 20-30; 29. See also their book, *Differentiated Containment: U.S. Policy Toward Iran and Iraq* (New York: Council on Foreign Relations, 1997).

104. A former Member of President Bush's National Security Council staff, Richard Haass, also makes a case for a change in American policy toward Iran. He concurs with the Clinton Administration that the United States should express a willingness to use force if there is incontrovertible indication of Iranian sponsorship of terrorism against the United States or the allies. Going beyond the Administration's policy, Haass suggests that Washington ask its European and Asian allies to join in a "critical dialogue" with Tehran. The allies should make it clear that it would be unacceptable for a military move by Iran against Iraq. For its part in the dialogue, the United States could offer a temporary suspension of that part of the Iran and Libya Sanctions Act that penalizes others for doing business with Iran. See Richard Haass, "The United States and Iraq: A Strategy for the Long Haul," Washington, D.C.: The Brookings Institution, *Policy Brief* no. 7, 1996. Available online:
http://www.brook.edu/fp/polbrief/polbrf7.htm

105. For evidence of Iran's acquisition of weapons of mass destruction see Yoav Limor, "Within Two Years, Iran Will Have Missiles Capable of Hitting Israel," *Ma'ariv*, 25 June 1997, sec. A, 10.

106. Department of State, Office of the Coordinator for Counterterrorism, *1995 Patterns of Global Terrorism* (Washington, D.C.: April, 1996). Available online:
http://www.usis.usemb.se/terror/rpt1995/index.html

107. Iran reduced the number of terror incidents in Europe during 1995 and targeted mainly Iranian nationals. But Tehran did not entirely relinquish its practice of European-based terrorism.

Chapter Three

1. Eric D. K. Melby, "Iraq," in Richard Haass, ed., *Economic Sanctions and American Diplomacy,* (Washington D.C.: Brookings Institution Press, 1998), 107–8.

2. Steven Erlanger, "U.S. to Give Up Arms Inspections for Curbing Iraq," *New York Times,* 8 November 1998, 1.

3. "If sanctions and international inspections were to end, the Central Intelligence Agency estimates, Iraq could produce enough fissile material for an atomic bomb in five to seven years." Also, the Central Intelligence Agency estimates that if UNSCOM were to stop monitoring Iraq's activities, the chemical and biological programs could be reactivated, "almost immediately." Jessica Stern, *The Ultimate Terrorists* (Cambridge MA: Harvard University Press, 1999), 123–25.

4. UN Security Council Resolution 687 of April 3, 1991 requires destruction or dismantlement of Iraq's weapons of mass destruction. The Security Council decided to authorize the destruction, removal, or rendering harmless all chemical and biological weapons, stocks of agents, related subsystems, and components in Iraq. Also to be destroyed or dismantled were all ballistic missiles with a range greater than 150 kilometers and related major parts and repair and production facilities. Furthermore, it decided to prohibit Iraq from acquiring or developing nuclear weapons, nuclear–weapons–usable material, any subsystems or components. Finally, the Council banned Iraq from conducting research on weapons of mass destruction. United Nations Security Council Resolution 687. Available online:

    http://www3.sympatico.ca/aal/private/un/UN-0687.txt

5. In games like football, hockey, and soccer, there are goal posts that are in fixed positions. When players cross these boundaries with the ball or puck, they expect to score a goal and thus to win a reward. However, if the officials move the posts every time the players are about to cross them, that would be an unfair change in the rules of the game. Saddam Hussein accuses the United States of changing the rules every time Iraq approaches compliance.

6. "Assurance" is a way of making promises in order to enhance confidence. In order to reduce fear, misunderstanding, and insecurity, assurance suggests that individuals try to communicate to adversaries their benign intentions.

7. Janice Gross Stein, "Deterrence and Compellence in the Gulf: A Failed or an Impossible Task?" *International Security* 17 (Fall 1992): 147–79. Also see her "Threat Based Strategies of Conflict Management: Why Did They Fail in the Gulf?" in Stanley Renshon, ed., *The Political Psychology of the Gulf War* (Pittsburgh: University of Pittsburgh Press, 1993), 121–53.

    For a general overview of Saddam Hussein's activities from the perspective of an opponent, see Samir al-Khalil, *The Republic of Fear: The Inside Story of Saddam's Iraq* (New York: Pantheon, 1989).

8. But assurance is also unlikely to result in compliance, because of misperception. One explanation of misperception is "top–down processing" of information: "Top" is a metaphor that explains how the human mind biases perception; "down" is a metaphor that symbolizes how mental biases influence incoming information. In top–down processing, people use

existing beliefs and schema to make shortcut judgments in processing information. "Bottom–up" processing occurs when people encounter information, and their assessment is comparatively unbiased by belief systems. Bottom–up is less likely to bias perception than top–down, because people gather information from the environment with less reference to their beliefs. With respect to Saddam, the assumption here is that his misperceptions stem from top–down processing of information about the United States.

9. Richard Straus, *Middle East Policy Survey* (Washington D.C., November 25, 1998): 1–2.

10. Stein, "Deterrence and Compellence," notes that King Hussein of Jordan believed Saddam to be embittered because Gulf leaders seemed indifferent to Iraq's sacrifice of blood and treasure to protect the Arab Gulf against the Persian enemy.

11. John M. Goshko and Thomas W. Lippman, "Iraq Blocks U.S. Arms Inspectors; Incident Is Second in 4 Days," *Washington Post*, November 3, 1997, A1. Available online:
   http://washingtonpost.com/wp-srv/inatl/longterm/iraq/timeline/110397.htm

12. Consider the statements of the Republican opposition leaders who show a consensus in support of military action against Iraq. Former Speaker of the House of Representatives Newt Gingrich said that Iraq needs "to abide by the rules, and we should be prepared to take whatever steps are necessary to enforce those rules." Goshko and Lippman, "Iraq Blocks U.S. Arms Inspectors." Senate Majority Leader Trent Lott added his weight to the consensus by saying that the weapons inspectors "were very close to finding some more dangerous weapons, and I think we're going to have to take whatever actions are necessary" to ensure that the inspections are carried out.

13. Bruce Jentleson, *With Friends Like These: Reagan, Bush, and Saddam, 1982–1990* (New York: W. W. Norton, 1994), 41.

14. Saddam Hussein sees himself as a modern–day Nebuchadnezzar, the Babylonian conqueror of Jerusalem during the sixth century B.C.

15. With respect to Sir Percy Cox's role in drawing the borders of Iraq, see Emory Bogle, *The Modern Middle East: From Imperialism to Freedom, 1800–1958* (Upper Saddle River, NJ: Prentice Hall, 1996), 221.

16. "The foreigner entered their lands, and Western colonialism divided and established weak states ruled by families that offered him services that facilitated his mission. The colonialists, to ensure their petroleum interest set up those disfigured petroleum states. Through this, they kept the wealth away from the masses of this nation." Saddam Hussein, quoted in the *New York Times*, August 11, 1990, A6.

17. Frontline, "The Gulf War," (Alexandria, VA: Public Broadcasting Service, 1997). Available online:
   http://www.pbs.org/wgbh/pages/frontline/teach/gulfguide/gwtimeline.html

18. Tomahawk cruise missiles cost about $1.3 million each, have a payload of 1,000 pounds, have a subsonic speed of 760 miles per hour, have a range of up to 1,500 miles, can fly at low levels—100 to 300 feet—and can be fired as an antiship or as a land–attack weapon. They fly at low altitudes, have

low heat emissions, and thus they are difficult to detect by infrared devices or by radar. Compared to the 297 cruise missiles fired during Desert Shield/ Storm, the 47 cruise missiles launched against Iraq during September 1996 had a minor effect on Iraqi military installations. For information about the attributes and performance characteristics of cruise missiles, see Norman Friedman, *Desert Victory: The War for Kuwait* (Annapolis, MD: Naval Institute Press, 1991), and Thomas Keaney and Eliot Cohen, *Gulf War Airpower Survey Summary Report* (Washington, D.C.: Office of the Secretary of the Air Force, 1993).

19. Because people see what they expect to see, the anticipation that Iraq is a threat may result in an overestimation of that threat. This pattern is an unmotivated bias that distorts threat perception.

20. Statement by Republican presidential candidate Robert Dole, Salt Lake City, Utah, Reuters, September 3, 1996.

21. The government of Turkey placed constraints on use of its air space for conduct of offensive operations in northern Iraq. The Erbakan government in Ankara was concerned that the Iranian–backed Patriotic Union of Kurdistan in northern Iraq supported the Kurdish Workers Party, an anti–Turkish terrorist movement. Another Kurdish faction, the Kurdish Democratic Party, invited Saddam Hussein into northern Iraq. That group was locked in battle with the Patriotic Union of Kurdistan. The two factions vied for political control of the region and over the income from oil smuggled across the borders.

    "Nobody is happy with the situation in Kurdistan," lamented Saad Bazzaz, a former aide to Saddam Hussein who defected to Jordan. "As long as the two sides fight each other and the Iranians gain influence, nobody is happy with what is going on there. So Saddam figured this is a suitable minute to catch." Ethan Bronner (reporting from Amman, Jordan), "Iraq's Limited Move Was Carefully Timed," *Boston Globe,* September 2, 1996.

22. "Within the very core of his power base he found rot so he needed to do something as a prestige booster," Amatzia Bar–Am, a specialist on Iraq at Israel's Haifa University was quoted as saying in Bronner, "Iraq's Limited Move."

    On the opportunity side, moreover, the move against the Kurds also gave Saddam an occasion to settle scores with Iraqi officers. He had sent some of his military north in 1991 to put down postwar unrest, but some defected to the Kurdish side.

23. Because of that revolution, the United States had a motivated bias to underestimate the Iraqi threat: In a search for allies against Iran, the United States overlooked Iraq's misdeeds with a bout of wishful thinking. That is, Washington saw what it wanted to see—an Iraq that was more a friend than it was an enemy.

24. As stated in Chapter Two on Iran, misperceptions stem from the distorting effects of biases. Politics can bias observation and thus may provide motivation to increase or decrease threat perception. Motivated biases are those that distort perceptions because individuals see what they want to see. Unmotivated biases distort perceptions because people see what they expect

to see. Bureaucratic and domestic politics are sources of motivated biases affecting American decisionmakers to overestimate the Iraqi threat. For a discussion of biases and threat perception, see Robert Jervis, "Perceiving and Coping with Threat," in Robert Jervis, Richard Ned Lebow, and Janice Gross Stein, eds., *Psychology and Deterrence*, (Baltimore: The Johns Hopkins Press, 1985), 1-12.

25. Upon concluding that Baghdad had been circumventing U.S. export control laws, Fairbanks formally ended his relationship with the Iraqis, with whom he had been associated since the mid–1980s. While at the State Department, Fairbanks had been in charge of administering Operation Staunch, the U.S. attempt to stop the sale of arms to Iran. Richard Straus, ed., *Middle East Policy Survey*, no. 246 (April 13, 1990).

26. The following nations appeared on the State Department list of countries that sponsor international terrorism: Cuba, Iran, Iraq, Libya, North Korea, Sudan, and Syria. Sudan is the only country on that list not included in the hardback copy of this book. Department of State Office of the Coordinator for Counterterrorism, *1995 Patterns of Global Terrorism* (Washington, D.C.: April, 1996). Available online: http://www.usis.usemb.se/terror/rpt1995/TERSST.HTM#Iraq

27. The failed Prevention of Genocide Act of 1988 would have prohibited American imports of Iraqi oil, dual–use technology exports to Iraq, and credits to Baghdad from the Commodity Credit Corporation and the Export–Import Bank. The senior Middle East analyst at AIPAC confirmed that the organization did not work as hard against Iraq in the 1980s as it worked against Iran in the mid–1990s. Keith Weissman, Senior Middle East Analyst, American–Israel Public Affairs Committee, telephone interview by Raymond Tanter, January 10, 1997, Ann Arbor, MI.

28. The U.S. policy of containing both Iran and Iraq—dual containment—began officially with the Clinton Administration. AIPAC, however, had opposed both countries without the imprimatur of the concept of dual containment.

29. Albert Wohlstetter, *Interests and Power in the Persian Gulf* (Los Angeles: Pan Heuristics, 1980).

30. Albert Wohlstetter, personal interview by Raymond Tanter, July 31, 1980, Washington, D.C. See also Robert Bartley, "A Wohlstetter Life," *Wall Street Journal,* January 13, 1997, A16, regarding the impact of his work on strategic thinking in general as well as with respect to the Gulf in particular.

31. Office of the Assistant Secretary of Defense, Program Analysis and Evaluation, *Capabilities for Limited Contingencies in the Persian Gulf* (Washington, D.C.: Unpublished paper, June 1979).

32. Note that as of June 1979, the assumption was that Iraq would be on the Soviet side and Iran on the American side. Also, the Pentagon study assumed Iranian cooperation with the United States in the defense of Iran.

33. Howard Teicher and Gayle Radley Teicher, *Twin Pillars to Desert Storm* (New York: William Morrow, 1993), 61. Teicher asserts that Richard Haass, who became President Bush's top Middle East official on the National Security Council staff, also favored a tilt toward Iraq, as did Brzezinski, Howard

Teicher, and Oliver North. He replaced me on the National Security Council staff in September 1982.

34. Wohlstetter, personal interview by Raymond Tanter, July 31, 1980, Washington, D.C.

35. On December 12, 1981, the USSR made a move against Solidarity by ordering the government of Poland to launch a crackdown.

36. Following Iranian–inspired riots at Mecca in Saudi Arabia on November 20, 1979, Riyadh moved closer to Baghdad. The Saudis defended their approach to Iraq because of a felt need to balance the growing threat from Iran.

37. As momentous a decision as it was to remove Iraq from the list of states that supported international terrorism, there was little evidence of interagency consideration of the pros and cons for doing so. As a member of the National Security Council staff, I had access to classified information about such a decision, but I could not locate the origins of the decision to remove Iraq nor the paper trail that justified removal.

38. In the 1990s, the State Department divided the Bureau of Near Eastern and South Asian Affairs into two units: the Bureau of Near Eastern Affairs and the Bureau of South Asian Affairs.

39. Representative Henry Gonzalez (Dem., New Mexico), reprinted part of NSD 26 in the *Congressional Record* for July 7, 1992: H6012.

40. Steven Spiegel, *The Other Arab–Israeli Conflict* (Chicago: University of Chicago Press, 1985), 5, 16 ff.

41. Officials within the Carter Pentagon also debated whether to tilt toward Iraq. As a young analyst in the Office of the Assistant Security of Defense, International Security Affairs, Howard Teicher wrote a paper on Iraq in 1979. Because this paper opposed the dominant mindset that favored accommodation with Iraq, it was a nonstarter at the Department of Defense and had virtually no impact within the national security bureaucracy. And by March 1984, even Teicher had come around to the view that the United States "had no choice but to work with Iraq in the short term to protect America's vital interests in the Gulf." (Teicher and Teicher, *Twin Pillars to Desert Storm*, 59–71, 303–4. In November 1984, there was a normalization of relations between Washington and Baghdad.

42. Richard Perle, American Enterprise Institute, telephone interview by Raymond Tanter, January 27, 1997, Ann Arbor, MI. During 1983–1984, Perle and I were colleagues. As personal representative of the Secretary of Defense to arms control and security talks in Vienna, Helsinki, Stockholm, and Madrid, I reported to the secretary via Under Secretary of Defense/Policy Fred Ikle. The assistant secretaries for International Security Affairs and for International Security Policy were line officials under the authority of Ikle.

43. Michael Klare, *Rogue States and Nuclear Outlaws* (New York: Hill and Wang, 1995), 37.

44. Tensions between Cairo and Baghdad reflect the traditional conflict between leaders of the Nile Valley and those from Mesopotamia—ancient Iraq—over the Fertile Crescent, including Greater Syria. This area includes present–day Lebanon and Syria as well as ancient Palestine.

45. Robert McFarlane, *Special Trust* (New York: Cadell & Davis, 1994), 310–11.
This memo gave birth to the idea that Iran was of such importance to the
United States that it would be worthwhile to seek an opening to Tehran,
even using the secret sale of American arms to effect such an opening.

46. While the same threatened interests may have both intrinsic and strategic
aspects, the analysis here treats them as analytically distinct. For a further
discussion of intrinsic interests and strategic interests, see Stein, "The View
from Cairo," in Jervis, Lebow, and Stein, eds., *Psychology and Deterrence*, 38–
39.

47. It is irrelevant that Iraq has a diminished capacity to threaten intrinsic and
strategic interests. What matters is the image of the enemy held by American
leaders. After the invasion of Kuwait, occupants of the Oval Office perceived
Iraq as an "evil" nation. This perception constitutes an unmotivated bias
that associates Baghdad with malice, irrespective of its behavior at a given
time. Because of the invasion, American presidents perceive Iraq's conduct
as malicious, without evaluating that behavior on its own merits.

48. John Deutch, Director of Central Intelligence, "Worldwide Threat Assessment Brief to the Senate Select Committee on Intelligence" (Washington,
D.C.: Public Affairs Staff, Central Intelligence Agency, February 22, 1996),
3. Available online:
`http://www.odci.gov/cia/public_affairs/speeches/archives/1996/`
`dci_speech_022296.html`

49. Department of State Office of the Coordinator for Counterterrorism, *1993
Patterns of Global Terrorism* (Washington, D.C.: April 1994). The following
states appeared on the State Department terrorist list for 1995: Cuba, Iran,
Iraq, Libya, North Korea, Sudan, and Syria. Sudan is the only country on
that list not included in the hardback copy of *Rogue Regimes*.

50. Baghdad continued its war of attrition on UN and humanitarian targets in
northern Iraq aimed at driving the foreign presence out of the area and
depriving the Kurdish population of relief supplies. Baghdad ordered the
assault of UN and relief workers. Iraqi agents threw bombs and grenades at
civilian residences and vehicles; and they placed bombs on UN trucks
loaded with relief supplies. During September 1993, agents of Baghdad
destroyed a UN truck carrying 12 tons of medical supplies with a bomb
attached to the fuel tank. The explosion injured the truck driver and 12
civilians.

51. "Iraq continues to provide haven and training facilities for several terrorist
clients. Abu Abbas' Palestine Liberation Front (PLF) maintains its headquarters in Baghdad. The Abu Nidal organization (ANO) continues to have
an office in Baghdad. The Arab Liberation Front (ALF), headquartered in
Baghdad, continues to receive funding from Saddam's regime. Iraq also
continues to host the former head of the now–defunct 15 May organization,
Abu Ibrahim, who masterminded several bombings of U.S. aircraft. A
terrorist group opposed to the current Iranian regime, the Mojahedin–e
Khalq (MEK), still is based in Iraq and has carried out several violent attacks
in Iran from bases in Iraq." Department of State, *1995 Patterns of Global
Terrorism*. Available online:
`http://www.usis.usemb.se/terror/rpt1995/TERSST.HTM#Iraq`

52. UN Security Council Resolution 686, March 2, 1991, available online:
    http://www3.sympatico.ca/aal/private/un/UN-0686.txt
53. Deutch, "Worldwide Threat," 3. In violation of the Nuclear Non–Prolifera-
    tion Treaty, Iraq almost developed a functional nuclear device shortly before
    the Gulf War. The International Atomic Energy Agency, however, estimates
    that it has terminated potentially dangerous nuclear weapon projects in
    Iraq. Although Iraq has continued intense weapons research to solve
    problems that inhibited its early nuclear program, basically most of Iraq's
    pre–Gulf War nuclear facilities and equipment have been eliminated or
    converted to purposes that are not banned by UN resolutions.
54. Airpower advocates wanted coalition forces to strike deep into Iraq to
    destroy the command and control structure of Saddam's war machine as well
    as infrastructure and air–defense networks. In addition to attacks on Iraq,
    air war proponents anticipated the following results with respect to Kuwait:
    Iraq's army in Kuwait might be effectively destroyed. The reoccupation of
    Kuwait would be met with minimal resistance; U.S. ground forces could be
    held in reserve as a "cocked fist." And there might be the "near–certain"
    achievement of the American objective to liberate Kuwait with minimal
    casualties. Colonel John Warden (U.S. Air Force), classified briefing to
    Defense Secretary Richard Cheney on the expected results of the air
    campaign against Iraqi forces, December 11, 1990. See Michael Gordon and
    Bernard Trainor, *The Generals' War: The Inside Story of the Conflict in the Gulf*
    (Boston: Little, Brown, 1995), 178.
55. In contrast to the air war advocates, Powell stressed the need for airpower
    in conjunction with a ground force buildup. He held that an air war alone
    would leave the initiative to Saddam Hussein, a policy that conflicted with
    basic army doctrine of taking and holding the initiative. To give the
    Coalition time to deploy its forces, Powell favored a strategy of sanctions
    against Iraq. See Bob Woodward, *The Commanders* (New York: Simon &
    Schuster, 1991), 342–43.

    In Powell's own words, "Many experts, amateurs and others in this
    town believe that [the defeat of the Iraqi army in Kuwait] can be accom-
    plished by such things as surgical airstrikes or perhaps a sustained airstrike.
    Such strategies are designed to hope to win, they are not designed to win."
    General Colin Powell, testimony before the Senate Armed Services Commit-
    tee, December 3, 1990. U.S. Senate, Committee on Armed Services. *Crisis in
    the Persian Gulf Region: U.S. Policy Options and Implications* Hearing,
    December 3, 1990. Available online:
    http://web.lexis-nexis.com/cis/retrieve/document/s_witness.ht-
    ml?_form=s_witness.html&_mode=FULL&_results=G
    {H^*KO!WA]!UUB$M[SWA]$UUZ$AV!ZZUW!AZ!ABA$AA$]DU]
    AWUWV$U&_library=LEGIS&_file=CISINX&_firstdoc=1&_reldoc=
    3&_citesper=25&_maxdocs=11&_md5=2097e593dd15aff00d6ad0e0fab5b9
    9c
    See also Harry Summers, Jr, *On Strategy II: A Critical Analysis of the Gulf War*
    (New York: Bantam Doubleday Dell, 1992), 192–93.
56. Caspar Weinberger, *Fighting for Peace* (New York: Warner, 1990), 442.
    Powell called Weinberger's rules "a practical guide." Colin Powell, *My
    American Journey* (New York: Random House, 1995), 303.

57. Powell, *My American Journey*, 480. Backing up General Powell's version of history is Secretary of State James Baker. In his memoirs, Secretary Baker recalls an October 1990 meeting with Chairman Powell that produced a consensus both in favor of a more aggressive military policy and a diplomatic approach that included sanctions. The goal was to drive the Iraqi armed forces out of Kuwait. Secretary Baker supports General Powell's emphasis on combining force and diplomacy, as opposed to being a sanctions–only advocate. James Baker, *The Politics of Diplomacy: Revolution, War and Peace, 1989–1992* (New York: G.P. Putnam Sons, 1995), 277, 301–2.

58. Chapter Two discusses dual containment, balance of power, and differentiated containment. See Zbigniew Brzezinski, Brent Scowcroft, and Richard Murphy, "Differentiated Containment," *Foreign Affairs* 76, no. 3 (May/June 1997): 20–30. In addition to these three authors, another critic of dual containment is Richard Haass. He said, "The policy of 'dual containment' of Iraq and Iran gave us a slogan when what we needed was a strategy and sustained efforts to implement it." See Richard Haass, "The United States and Iraq: A Strategy for the Long Haul," *Policy Brief*, no. 7 (1996). Available online:
    http://www.brook.edu/fp/polbrief/polbrf7.htm

59. Bahrain, Kuwait, Oman, the United Arab Emirates, Saudi Arabia, and Qatar make up the six–member Gulf Cooperation Council (GCC). This section on threat perceptions draws on the research of Phebe Marr. See Marr, "Differing Threat Perceptions," *U.S.–GCC Security Relations*, I, no. 39 (August 1995). Available online:
    http://www.ndu.edu/ndu/inss/strforum/forum39.html
    See also Marr, *The Modern History of Iraq* (Boulder CO: Westview, 1985).

60. "Most GCC states see Iran, not Iraq, as the long–term threat (a position closer to that of the United States), and do not want Iraq weakened as a balance against Iran (a position more at variance with the United States). This position is particularly strong at the foot of the Gulf, where the UAE and Oman worry about the long–term intentions of Iran." Marr, "Differing Threat Perceptions."

61. But even if there were American diplomatic moves in the direction of a relaxation of tensions with Iraq, Washington needs to remain on guard as long as Saddam is in power and Baghdad retains its military capabilities. "If Iraq continues to be a threat—and there is every indication that it will be—the [United States] needs to maintain a robust force posture in the Gulf for the foreseeable future." Marr, "Differing Threat Perceptions."

62. Daniel Diller, ed., *The Middle East* (Washington, D.C.: Congressional Quarterly, 1991), 392.

63. The Gulf states lie along the Arabian shore of the Gulf. They include Bahrain, Kuwait, and Qatar as well as the seven former Trucial States of Abu Dhabi, Ajman, Dubayy, Al Fujayrah, R'as al Khaymah, Ash Shariqah, and Umm al Qaywayn, which constitute the United Arab Emirates.

64. Richard Straus, "Outlook," *Middle East Policy Survey* (Washington, D.C., December 16, 1997): 2.

65. With respect to the scenario of a resumption of a Kurdish civil war, Richard Haass states, "Saddam is a serial prober; at some point he will turn on his new Kurdish friends, in the process triggering a large flow of refugees in the direction of the Turkish border." Haass, "The United States and Iraq: A Strategy for the Long Haul."

66. Gregory Milne, "The Disintegration of Iraq and the Consequences for the Middle East," Unpublished paper submitted for a seminar at the University of Michigan, Winter 1998. See the Milne paper for a discussion of implications of a breakup of Iraq for Israel and Syria.
   Available online:
   http://www-personal.umich.edu/~rtanter/W98PS353498PAPERS/
   MILNE.GREG.TITLE.HTML

67. Kemal Kirisci and Gareth Winrow, *The Kurdish Question and Turkey*, (London: Frank Cass, 1997), 161–67.

68. Following the 1978–1979 Iranian revolution, claims by Iran's spiritual rulers that Basra was unfairly taken from Shiite Muslim Iran by the Western powers gained added significance. After World War I, Iraq has ruled a large Shiite population as well as Najaf and Karbala—two of the holiest cities in the Shiite faith.

69. UN Security Resolution 986 of April 14, 1995, authorizes states to permit the import of petroleum and petroleum products originating in Iraq. This resolution is an exception to the sanctions levied on Iraq by the United Nations for its 1990 invasion of Kuwait in 1990. The purpose of permitting the exception is to allow Iraq to import medicine, health supplies, foodstuffs, and materials for essential civilian needs. Iraq may sell up to $1 billion worth of oil every 90 days. United Nations Security Council Resolution 986, available online:
   http://www3.sympatico.ca/aal/private/un/UN-0986.txt

## Chapter Four

1. The President signed the Iran and Libya Sanctions Act of 1996 on August 5. It passed the House by 415 to zero and the senate by voice vote. Available online:
   http://thomas.loc.gov/cgi-bin/bdquery/L?d104:./list/bd/
   d104sh.lst:493

2. In contrast to accommodation, dual containment is an effort to isolate two countries at the same time; for example, Iran and Iraq.

3. Chapter Two discusses dual containment, balance of power, and differentiated containment. See Zbigniew Brzezinski, Brent Scowcroft, and Richard Murphy, "Differentiated Containment," *Foreign Affairs* 76, no. 3 (May/June 1997): 20-30.

4. Ariel Sharon, speech prepared for a conference at the Institute for Strategic Studies, Tel Aviv University, December 14, 1981, in *Foreign Broadcast Information Service*, (December 18, 1981). See also Raymond Tanter, *Who's at the Helm? Lessons of Lebanon* (Boulder: Westview Press, 1990), 56-58.

5. Ariel Sharon, December 14, 1981, in *Foreign Broadcast Information Service,* (18 December 1981).

6. Sadat was worried that Qadhafi was attempting to develop a nuclear weapons capability. During the summer of 1981, an American diplomatic envoy, Robert McFarlane, assured Sadat that the Reagan Administration stood by its promise to prevent Qadhafi and the Soviets from gaining further advantages in the Middle East. Howard Teicher and Gayle Teicher, *Twin Pillars to Desert Storm* (New York: William Morrow, 1993), 137-39.

7. Richard Straus, "After the AWACS—Constructing a Middle East Policy with Limited Resources," *Middle East Policy Survey,* no. 42 (October 23, 1981).

8. For a general discussion of political coalitions within the Arab world, see Malcolm Kerr, *The Arab Cold War: Gamal Abd al-Nasir and His rivals, 1958-1970,* 3d ed. (London: Oxford University Press, 1971).

9. Ilich Ramirez Sanchez, commonly known as "Carlos the Jackal," is one of the best known "revolutionary terrorists." He reportedly has worked under contract for Qadhafi of Libya, Saddam Hussein of Iraq, Assad of Syria, and Fidel Castro of Cuba. "Perhaps the only international terrorist of greater repute is Abu Nidal (Sabri Banna)." On October 10, 1994, the government of the Sudan arrested Carlos and handed him over to French authorities.

   Amal or the "Shi'ite Movement of Hope," an organization based in Lebanon, serves as the Shi'ite voice within the Arab world. Clark Staten, "Carlos Captured; Revolutionary Terrorist," *Emergency Net News Service,* October 10, 1994. Available online:
   http://205.243.133.2/carlos-j.htm

10. While the same threatened interests may have both intrinsic and strategic aspects, the analysis here treats them as analytically distinct.

11. Security Council Resolution 731 is available online:
    gopher://gopher.undp.org:70/00/undocs/scd/scouncil/s92/6

12. Security Council Resolution 748 is available online:
    gopher://gopher.undp.org:70/00/undocs/scd/scouncil/s92/23

13. Security Council Resolution 883 is available online:
    gopher://gopher.undp.org:70/00/undocs/scd/scouncil/s93/883

14. Department of State, Office of the Coordinator for Counterterrorism, *1995 Patterns of Global Terrorism* (Washington, D.C.: April, 1996). Available online:
    http://www.usis.usemb.se/terror/rpt1995/TERSST.HTM#Libya

15. Department of State, *1995 Patterns of Global Terrorism.*

16. Regarding the plant at Rabta see Associated Press, "Perry: U.S. Won't allow Libya Chemical Weapons Plant to be Built," Ismailiya, Egypt (April 3, 1996). With respect to the use of chemical weapons by Iran and Iraq in their 1980-1988 war see Anthony Cordesman, *The Iran-Iraq War and Western Security 1984-87: Strategic Implications and Policy Options* (London: Jane's, 1987). And in connection with Baghdad's use of poison gas against its own citizens the Department of State reported, " . . . a number of Iraqi oppositionists in northern Iraq were poisoned by thallium." *1995 Patterns of Global Terrorism.* Available online:
    http://www.usis.usemb.se/terror/rpt1995/TERSST.HTM#Iraq

17. Barbara Balaj, "Germany and Libya," in "The Federal Republic of Germany and the Middle East" (Ph.D. dissertation, George Washington University, 1997), 59 ff.

18. The Geneva Protocol of 1925 banned the use in war of asphyxiating, poisonous, or other gases and of bacteriological methods of warfare. See Major International Instruments on Disarmament and Related Issues, "Protocol for the Prohibition of the Use in War of Asphyxiating, Poisonous or Other Gases, and of Bacteriological Methods of Warfare," June 17, 1925. Available online:

    http://www.unog.ch/frames/disarm/distreat/warfare.htm

19. Thomas Wiegele, *The Clandestine Building of Libya's Chemical Weapons Factory* (Carbondale: Southern Illinois University Press, 1992), 28.

20. "Journalists' Visit to Libyan Plant Leaves Its Purpose Unclear," *Washington Post*, January 8, 1989, sec. A, 24.

21. In March of 1990, a fire supposedly decimated the Rabta facility. According to *TIME* magazine, the CIA later reported that the fire was a strategic "hoax" to ward off U.S. attack. "In 1990 Gadaffi shut down the Rabta plant after Washington threatened to attack it with warplanes and publicly identified European companies that had provided equipment. But U.S. satellites soon discovered that Rabta's equipment had been moved and stored in underground bunkers a mile away." Douglas Waller, "Target Gaddafi, Again," *TIME*, April 1, 1996.

22. One senior Defense Department official told the *Middle East Policy Survey* in 1981 that the United States was "taking new initiatives" regarding Libya. Other well-informed officials said that the Joint Chiefs of Staff repeatedly vetoed civilian suggestions to conduct military planning against Qadhafi on the grounds of "insufficient resources." Therefore, while there was agreement between State and Defense on the need to "get tough" with Qadhafi, there was no consensus on what practical measures could be taken. In this regard, consider the president's public rejection of an economic boycott of Libya. One unhappy U.S. official commented that a boycott would be "bad for business." The rejection forced State Department officials to come up with alternative plans, including repatriation of U.S. citizens in Libya. Richard Straus, ed., "After the AWACS," *Middle East Policy Survey*.

23. Secretary of State Alexander Haig received hard-line recommendations about Libya from the Policy Planning Staff (S/P) and the Bureau of Politico-Military Affairs, State's "functional" bureaus. (In the 1990s, the Department changed the name of PM to Political-Military Affairs.) S/P and PM called for additional measures to demonstrate the seriousness and consistency of U.S. policy. The State Department's Near Eastern and European bureaus opposed the hard line of maximum economic sanctions. The European bureau was particularly adamant. It argued that imposing sanctions on Libya would have exacerbated relations with European countries during the Polish crisis and after Qadhafi's decision to withdraw his troops from Chad. Richard Straus, ed., *Middle East Policy Survey*, no. 49 (February 12, 1982).

24. Washington had demanded that Tripoli refrain from conducting subversive operations in neighboring countries and cease its state sponsorship of

international terrorism. Verbal assurances that Libya had ceased its operations were welcome but unnecessary. United States intelligence had its own
ways of knowing when Libyan operations had terminated. Reportedly,
American intelligence could intercept Libyan military communications.

25. Expressing uncertainty over U.S. policy objectives and impatience with the
administration's year-long debate over Libya, one Arab diplomat summed
up a lot of Washington thinking: "If you're going to do something, do it,
don't just talk about it." "The Next Move Against Libya," *Middle East Policy
Survey*, no. 49 (February 12, 1982).
Other press commentary was also critical of the delay. "After months
of well-publicized indecision, President Reagan has resolved to stop American oil trade with Libya," in "A Mere Gesture Again," *New York Times*,
March 7, 1982, editorial page.

26. Personal recollection of author from service as one of the action officers for
Libya at the White House, 1981-1982.

27. To illustrate bureaucracy in action, consider the way some meetings occur.
I asked the secretary to Acting National Security Advisor Nance to call a
meeting in the White House Situation Room on Libya. "Who asked for this
meeting?" she replied. I said, "Bud McFarlane at State asked Geoffrey Kemp
in my office at the National Security Council staff to ask Paul Wolfowitz at
State to ask me to ask Bud Nance at the White House!" She replied, "OK."
Outside the beltway of bureaucracy in Washington, such statements are
meaningless. But within, they indicate the cover-your-flank mentality of
bureaucrats who desire to share the risk of responsibility.

28. In a meeting I attended on December 30, 1981 with White House Counsel
Edwin Meese, Secretary of Defense Caspar Weinberger recommended the
beginning of more stringent measures against Libya, such as a total trade
embargo. He felt that the withdrawal of American citizens was a prudent
step but was of marginal economic significance.

29. On March 25, 1982, the departments of Defense and Commerce came out
in favor of applying export controls to prevent a French firm from exporting
General Electric rotors to the USSR. There was a contract between General
Electric and Alsthom Alantique that New York law governed. The contract
required that Alsthom comply with all future export control regulations.
This type of restriction is common for licenses from American firms to
foreign manufacturers. In accepting the restriction, the French firm was
aware that sales to the USSR were subject to future prohibition.

30. Legal authorities for potential action against Libya included the Trade
Expansion Act (Section 232b), Export Administration Act, and the International Emergency Economic Powers Act, in conjunction with the National
Emergency Act. Either 232b of the Trade Expansion Act or International
Emergency Economic Powers Act could have been used to effect an oil
embargo. The Export Administration Act could have been employed to
effect a broad but not total ban on exports to Libya. Only IEEPA, however,
could have been used for a total export embargo or transaction controls,
including those to bring about a withdrawal of American citizens. There was
a constitutional issue raised by restriction on travel implicit in an order for

mandatory withdrawal of American citizens. But if the withdrawal were ordered under IEEPA in conjunction with other mandated measures taken under the act, that action would have blurred the constitutional issue.

31. Under the Export Administration Act, Commerce has responsibility with the Department of State to report on export controls, which terminate annually in December. The Export Administration Act has a list of controls. Libya was on the State Department's list of state sponsors of international terrorism, while State had removed Iraq. The Department determined that Iraq's improved record warranted removal, but the real reason was to justify the transfer of dual-use equipment to Iraq in its war against Iran. See Chapter Three on Iraq.

32. Some State Department insiders warned that a decision by the administration might not have been imminent. They pointed out that following the "disappearance" of the "hit team," President Reagan might have been reluctant to approve further sanctions without further provocation from Libya. "The Next Move Against Libya," *Middle East Policy Survey.*

33. On the bureaucratic politics of arms control in the Reagan Administration, see Strobe Talbott, *Deadly Gambits: The Reagan Administration and the Stalemate in Nuclear Arms Control* (New York: Vintage, 1984). For bureaucratic warfare on Middle East policy making, see Tanter, *Who's at the Helm?*

34. For a general overview of the Wilson case see Joseph Goulden with Alexander Raffio, *The Death Merchant: The Rise and Fall of Edwin P. Wilson* (New York: Simon & Schuster, 1984).

35. Saudi Arabia launched an investigation with the assistance of the FBI to discover whether its own dissidents or foreign powers, such as Iran and Syria, were responsible for a bombing of the Saudi National Guard installation in Riyadh, on November 13, 1995. There was also an attack on June 25, 1996, of an air facility in Dhahran that the Gulf War coalition air forces used for monitoring Iraq's compliance with the terms of the cease-fire. Those assaults were the first political attacks against the American military in Saudi Arabia. The Kingdom convicted four dissidents and beheaded them for the 1995 bombing. One motive for a subsequent assault on the Dhahran air base was to avenge this beheading. The CIA helped train some of the Saudi dissidents in order to fight in the Afghanistan war against the Soviets, and they had also fought alongside Bosnia's Muslim-led army against Bosnian Serbs.

36. *The Nation* (February 6, 1989): 153-54.

37. Personal recollection of author from service as one of the action officers for Libya at the White House, 1981-1982.

38. Personal recollection of author from service as one of the action officers for Libya at the White House, 1981-1982.

39. Working with the Dominican Republic, CIA and FBI agents managed to lure Wilson out of Zurich, Switzerland. Arriving at Santo Domingo, Dominican officials declared Wilson's travel papers to be faulty and compelled him to board an aircraft for New York. FBI agents arrested him after he deplaned. Goulden with Raffio, *The Death Merchant,* 382-91.

40. David Johnston, "Reno Says Saudis Did Not Cooperate in Bombing Inquiry," *New York Times,* January 24, 1997, A1, A6.

41. One Administration critic of an oil embargo caustically asked, "Consistency of U.S. policy? What is consistent about lifting the grain embargo when the Soviet Union is still in Afghanistan and imposing an oil embargo on Libya when it is getting out of Chad?" The implicit assumption behind the query was that the Reagan Administration was not consistent in its handling of similar cases. "The Next Move Against Libya," *Middle East Policy Survey.*

42. Department of Treasury, Office of Foreign Assets Control, "Libya." Available online:
    http://www.ustreas.gov/treasury/services/fac/fac.html

43. "In 1985 Abu Nidal, a terrorist leader who had defected from the mainstream of the PLO, moved his base of operations from Syria to Libya. In December 1985 members of his group attacked the check-in counters of El Al airlines at the Rome and Vienna airports with automatic weapons and hand grenades . . . On January 7, 1986, Reagan announced that there was 'irrefutable evidence' that Libya had sponsored the Palestinian terrorists . . . He ended all economic activity between the United States and Libya and ordered all American citizens to leave Libya." Daniel Diller, ed., *The Middle East* (Washington, D.C.: Congressional Quarterly, 1991), 82.

44. Gideon Rose, "Sanctions Against Libya," Unpublished Paper prepared for the Council on Foreign Relations (January 1997), 23.

45. Suleiman Bengharsa, "Sanctions in the Middle East: The Libya Case," Unpublished Paper prepared for the conference on Sanctions and the Middle East: Political Rationale and Economic Impact, cosponsored by the Middle East Institute and the Petroleum Industry Research Foundation (April 22, 1996), 2.

46. Bengharsa, "Sanctions in the Middle East," 3.

47. "Libya: Life in Qadhafi's Shadow," *EIU Business Middle East,* October 1, 1994, as quoted in Rose, "Sanctions Against Libya," 31.

48. George Gedda, "US May Tighten Sudan Sanctions," Associated Press, February 17, 1997.

49. Gedda, "US May Tighten Sudan Sanctions."

50. Associated Press, "White House Blasts Trip by Farrakhan As 'Thugfest,'" February 27, 1996. Available online: http//www.sltrib.com/96/FEB/27/twr/02314317 htm

   Acknowledgements to Brandi Weaver for her assistance in locating the above citation. See "Libya, the United States, and Louis Farrakhan," Unpublished Paper prepared for Political Science 472, the University of Michigan (Fall, 1996). The Weaver paper is available online:
   http://www-personal.umich.edu/~rtanter/

51. Associated Press, "White House Blasts Trip by Farrakhan As 'Thugfest.'"

52. Additionally, the State Department's spokesperson Glyn Davies said, "We don't view Muammar Qadhafi as somebody who is trustworthy and we can deal with. That is why many years ago an embargo was enacted against Libya. The most egregious example of Qadhafi's support for terrorism, of course, was the bombing of Pan Am 103." U.S. State Department Directory,

Office of the Spokesman, daily press briefing, Wednesday, August 28, 1996. Available online:

gopher://dosfan.lib.uic.edu/

53. Associated Press, "White House Blasts Trip by Farrakhan As 'Thugfest.'"

54. Associated Press, "White House Blasts Trip by Farrakhan As 'Thugfest.'"

55. Tommy Baer, "The Farrakhan Divide," *B'nai B'rith News*, April 4, 1995. Available online:

http://bnaibrith.org/pr/farrakha.html

56. "We are not content to hear from present Iranian officials words without deeds, rather they must fulfill their non-negotiable commitments at the forefront of which are the release of Iraqi POW's and the return of Iraqi possessions including civilian and military aircraft which were transferred to Iran with their approval before and during the glorious Um Al-Ma'rik (The Mother of All Battles) and entrusted with them." Saddam Hussein, "President Saddam Hussein's [1997] Speech on the 9th Anniversary of (The Great Victory Day) marking the end of the war with Iran." Available online: http://southmovement.alphalink.com.au/countries/Iraq/victory1.htm

57. Institute for National Strategic Studies, *Strategic Assessments 1996: Elements of U.S. Power*, "Limited Military Intervention," (Washington, D.C.: National Defense University, 1996). Available online:

http://www.ndu.edu/ndu/inss/sa96/sa96ch13.html

58. Teicher and Teicher, *Twin Pillars to Desert Storm*, 347.

59. Edward Wakin contends that Qadhafi is sidelined in Arab-Israel relations, and that he is not even a significant player. Edward Wakin, *Contemporary Political Leaders of the Middle East* (New York: Facts on File, 1996).

60. Teicher and Teicher, 340-47.

61. Teicher and Teicher, 340-47.

62. Associated Press, "Perry: U.S. Won't Allow Libya Chemical Weapons Plant to be Built," Ismailiya, Egypt, April 3, 1996.

63. In contrast to the case studies of Iran, Iraq, Syria, Cuba, and North Korea, the Libya chapter contains only one scenario—renewed military activity. Happy ending or muddling through scenarios are highly unlikely, given the incentives on each side for limited military activity.

## Chapter Five

1. Syria is very much a unitary actor. Despite the existence of some institutions that mirror those of a democratic government, its political system places almost absolute authority in the hands of President Hafez al-Assad and a small group of national security advisors. Assad makes the primary decisions on foreign policy, national defense, and the economy. The Syrian legislature is a parliament in name only. It does not initiate laws but only passes judgment on legislation proposed by the executive branch. See Daniel Diller, ed., *The Middle East* (Washington, D.C.: Congressional Quarterly, 1991), 352.

2. Greater Syria includes Syria, Jordan, Lebanon, Israel, the West Bank, the Gaza Strip, and a portion of Turkey.

3. Thanks to John Post, Steve Hessler, and Anna Vania Song for research on the personality of President Hafez al-Assad.

4. "Like any one-man dictatorship, Syria is dominated by its ruler. President Assad unilaterally issues the country's laws and makes most of the life-and-death decisions affecting the . . . Syrians he rules." Daniel Pipes, "Is Damascus Ready for Peace?" *Foreign Affairs* 70, no. 4 (Fall 1991): 36.

5. Some 90 percent of Syria's population of almost 15 million are Muslim. Of these, about 74 percent are Sunni Muslim, and the remaining 16 percent are Alawite, Shiite, Druze, and other sects. Assad, as well as the majority of his ruling military and political apparatus, are from the minority Alawites sect. Central Intelligence Agency, *World Factbook 1993* (Washington, D.C.: U.S. Government Printing Office, 1994.) The Alawites are an offshoot of Shiite Islam, in contrast to the orthodox Sunni Muslim sect, which constitutes the majority of the Arab world.

6. Pipes, "Is Damascus Ready for Peace?"

7. "Economically Syria has been stalled for years in the grip of socialism, cronyism, and huge military expenditures. Inept policies have produced an annual inflation rate of some 50 percent, a grossly overvalued Syrian lira and debts of some $6 billion to the West and $9 billion to the USSR. Although 30 percent of the work force is engaged in agriculture, grain has to be imported. Cities routinely experience electricity shortfalls, and ordinary items such as toilet paper are unavailable for long stretches of time." Pipes, "Is Damascus Ready for Peace?": 39.

8. According to Moshe Ma'oz, Assad's efforts to align with Egypt were in order to prevent an Egyptian unilateral agreement with Israel. During the October 1974 Arab summit meeting in Rabat, Assad organized Arab support to disapprove any unilateral agreements between Egypt and Israel that would exclude Israel's withdrawal from the Golan Heights. Moshe Maoz, *Assad, The Sphinx of Damascus: A Political Biography* (New York: Weidenfeld & Nicholson, 1988), 110-11.

9. Moshe Maoz, *Assad,* and Pipes, "Is Damascus Ready for Peace,": 50. See also Moshe Maoz, *Middle Eastern Politics* (New York: St. Martin's Press, 1996), and Patrick Seale, *Assad of Syria: The Struggle for the Middle East* (Berkeley: University of California Press, 1989).

10. Moshe Maoz is a professor of Middle Eastern Studies and Director of the Truman Institute for Middle Eastern studies at the Hebrew Institute of Jerusalem. See Maoz, *Assad, The Sphinx of Damascus: A Political Biography* (New York: Weldenfeld & Nicholson, 1988), *Middle Eastern Politics* (New York: St. Martin's Press, 1996), and *Syria and Israel: From War to Peacemaking* (New York: Oxford University Press, 1995).

11. Daniel Pipes is the editor of the Middle East Quarterly.

12. Some of these changes included Soviet opposition to Assad's central strategic doctrine. That is, the Soviet Union urged Assad to seek a diplomatic solution to the Arab-Israel conflict. It would "provide Syria with the means to deter Israel from attacking, but [it would] not support any Syrian attempt to launch war." Alasdair Drysdale and Raymond Hinnebusch, *Syria and the Middle East Peace Process* (New York: Council on Foreign Relations

Press, 1991), 165-67. See also Judith Miller, *God Has Ninety-Nine Names* (New York: Simon & Schuster, 1996), 310-15.

13. See Moshe Maoz, *Syria and Israel: From War to Peacemaking* (New York: Oxford University Press, 1995).

14. Why would Assad be willing to take a great chance regarding his hold on power to avoid losing the Golan Heights to Israel? Prospect theory suggests an answer. It holds that individuals are risk-averse concerning gains and risk-acceptant regarding losses: they fear losses more than they desire gains and hence are more willing to take chances to avoid losses than to secure gains. Losing a million dollars is more painful than a corresponding gain is coveted. Individuals choose risky alternatives when they frame choice as avoiding losses rather than obtaining gains.

15. During the Cold War, Soviet decisionmakers were willing to run high military risks to avoid domestic political losses. Retreat would have harmed the prospects for the ruling coalition to retain power. See Dennis Ross, "Risk Aversion in Soviet Decisionmaking," in J. Valenta and William Potter, eds., *Soviet Decisionmaking for National Security* (Boston: Allen & Unwin, 1984), 237-51.

16. In the field of cognitive psychology, prospect theory defines a reference point as a threshold value above which individuals perceive gains and below which they see losses. See Jack Levy, "An Introduction to Prospect Theory," in Barbara Farnham, ed., *Avoiding Losses/Taking Risks: Prospect Theory and International Conflict* (Ann Arbor: University of Michigan Press, 1994), 7-22, and Robert Jervis, in Farnham, *op. cit.,* "Political Implications of Loss Aversion," 23-40.

    The assumption here is that Assad frames prior Syrian possession of the Golan Heights as his reference point for negotiations. Outcomes falling below that point are losses. Hence, Assad perceives the status quo—Israeli control over the Golan with the application of Israeli law there—as a severe loss. He could opt for a risky gamble that might return the situation to the former status quo, that is, undisputed Syrian sovereignty over the Golan.

    For the Pipes view of how some Arab leaders frame their problems and fears, see Daniel Pipes, *The Hidden Hand: Middle East Fears of Conspiracy* (New York: St. Martin's Press, 1996).

17. For a description of approaches to value conflict with special reference to denial of trade-offs, see Alexander George, *Presidential Decision Making in Foreign Policy* (Boulder: Westview Press, 1980), 28 ff.

18. *Hatzofeh,* January 7, 1997. *Hatzofeh* is an Israeli newspaper of the National Religious Party.

19. Prospect theory supports the Maoz approach better than the Pipes perspective, because it accounts for Assad's risk-taking behavior.

20. I served at the White House from April 1981 to September 1982 as a senior staffer with the National Security Council and reported to the Assistant to the President for National Security Affairs, Richard Allen. He went on administrative leave on November 29, 1981, and William Clark assumed his office on January 5, 1982. For an elaboration of the role of Lebanon in the

battle over whether to embrace or contain Syria, see Raymond Tanter, *Who's at the Helm? Lessons of Lebanon* (Boulder: Westview Press, 1990), 73 ff.

21. During the Reagan years in the 1980s, there was a gap between arms quantity, in which Arab confrontation states came out on top, and quality, in which the balance favored Israel. Consider the significance of the July 1980 projected Arab-Israel conflict balance for 1980-1985. Since the 1973 war against Egypt and Syria, Israel had continued to increase its margin of military superiority. Hence, it could exercise a wide range of military options and was capable of decisively defeating its Arab opponents on any or all fronts. Without Egypt, the Arab confrontation states were reduced to Syria, and perhaps Jordan, with Iraq as a main source of expeditionary forces against Israel.

  Personal recollection of author from having attended a meeting at the White House on November 19, 1981.

22. During the Clinton era of the 1990s, Syria had some 4,500 tanks, about 4,000 armored personnel carriers, and more than 4,000 artillery pieces. The Syrian air force had 511 combat fighter planes and approximately 120 combat helicopters. Syria had more weapons systems than did Israel in all categories of consequence. An analysis of these data makes it clear that in practice, the qualitative gap in Israel's favor held from the Reagan to Clinton administrations. Most of the Syrian military equipment was relatively outdated. Since the Gulf War, the Israel Defense Forces had invested more than $10 billion in equipment and absorbed advanced American tanks and combat helicopters.

  Additionally, Syria invested about $2 billion in military procurement. The weapons systems that the Syrian military absorbed originated in the Eastern bloc. Even the more advanced Eastern bloc armaments, however, were of a lower quality than their Western counterparts. Of all of Syria's combat planes, only around 11 percent may be considered advanced (MiG-29s and Sukhoi-27s), in contrast to a larger proportion of the Israeli air force combat planes. Reuven Pedhatzur, "A New Balance of Terror," *Ha'aretz*, August 15, 1996, sec. B, 1.

23. Before 1967, Syria had harassed Israeli farmers in their Hula Valley settlements. Damascus had undermined Israel's economic development plans and attempts to divert the sources of the Jordan River. These sources were in Syrian territory. Following the 1967 war, the situation was reversed. After Israel captured the Golan Heights, the Syrians were the ones who felt threatened. Their capital, Damascus, is only about 60 kilometers from Israel's front lines, and there is little difficulty in bringing Damascus into range of Israel's artillery. Moreover, Syria perceives the presence of Israel's army in southern Lebanon as a reminder of what occurred in 1982, when Israeli forces advanced in the Beka'a Valley of Lebanon and positioned themselves so as to outflank Syrian forces protecting Damascus.

  Personal recollection of author from service as one of the action officers for Syria at the White House, 1981-1982.

24. On June 12, 1969, the Israeli military governor for the Golan Heights applied Israel's military law to the area. The authority of the governor to act

in 1969 derived from the Geneva Convention regarding the occupation of territory seized in fighting. In contrast to his action as a military commander of occupied territory, the July 1968 administrative order that annexed East Jerusalem to West Jerusalem was pursuant to an act of Israel's parliament—the Knesset. Similarly, the de facto annexation of the Golan Heights was an act of the Knesset.

25. Dennis Ross was a member of the Policy Planning Staff of Secretary of State Alexander Haig during the Reagan Administration in 1981, head of that office in the Bush Administration during 1989, and President Clinton's special envoy to the Middle East. He wrote about the Assad regime while he was between tours of government service. Ross held that the regime would be constrained internationally by internal factors that would continue to absorb its attention, energy, and resources. These domestic problems were likely to limit Assad's coercive potential in the rest of the region. Moreover, Assad has demonstrated a willingness to accept tacit or indirect international constraints on his freedom of action if he believes that there is an internal danger. Dennis Ross, "Middle East Policy Planning for the Second Reagan Term," *Policy Papers*, no. 1 (Washington, D.C.: Washington Institute for Near East Policy, 1985): 10-12. The Ross paper not only reflected his awareness of domestic constraints on Assad, it also could be used as a justification for a proactive policy of initiating covert actions to destabilize Syria.

26. Irrespective of how the crisis might be used in Washington, one question was whether or not Israel had actually annexed the Golan or just applied its laws to that area. The Israeli desk officer at the State Department told me, "You may now need an Israeli postage stamp to mail a letter from the Golan, but otherwise there were no legal changes in its status!"

27. In the midst of the Golan Heights crisis between Israel and Syria, bureaucratic infighting seemed to decrease among United States departments and agencies concerned with the issue. This apparent lull was deceptive. Reagan's first National Security Advisor, Richard Allen, went on administrative leave. Admiral Nance had taken over as National Security Advisor. And the military assistant to the president, Admiral John Poindexter, had moved up to be Nance's deputy. Poindexter called me to discuss whether the State Department had been cooperative in the Golan issue. I answered, "Absolutely." He asked, "Why?" I answered, "State is using us to achieve their bureaucratic objectives." Poindexter replied, "Yes, to get rid of Allen, they're making sure that the National Security Council staff looks good!" Press reports appeared in weekly magazines describing how National Security Council staffers were pleased with the way that Nance and Poindexter had been processing the paperwork in the absence of Allen.

    Personal recollection of conversation with Poindexter by author in the White House Situation Room.

28. During meetings in Israel, Begin took the position that the United States government had punished Israel at least three times in three months. First, after Israel's bombing of Iraq's nuclear facilities in June, shipments of F-16s were suspended. Second, after the bombing of the PLO command center in

Beirut in July, shipments of F-15s were suspended. Third, after Israel applied its laws to the Golan, Washington suspended implementation of the Memorandum of Understanding (MOU) between Jerusalem and Washington. Begin said that he refused to let the MOU become a hostage for the United States to secure major concessions on Lebanon or on the peace process. He said, "Jews have lived for 3,700 years without an MOU and can live another 3,700 more without one!"

Personal recollection of remarks made by Begin, from author's service as one of the action officers for Israel at the White House, 1981-1982.

29. In relation to Israel's de facto annexation of the Golan Heights, there is an Arab proverb: "I against my brothers. I and my brothers against my cousins. I and my cousins against the world." Israel's actions rallied support for Syria even among those Arab states that were adversaries of the regime in Damascus. This proverb calls attention to the felt need for cohesion when the Arab nation as a whole is under attack by non-Arab forces.

30. The Golan Heights crisis was of great importance to Washington because it threatened American policy goals for the Middle East. At the regional level during the Cold War, southwest Asia was a focal point of contention. United States policy included prevention of the spread of Soviet influence, elimination of the Soviet presence in Afghanistan, and deterrence or defeat of the USSR and/or its proxy or other radical intervention throughout the region. Goals also included preservation of stability and security of friendly states. In November 1979, the United States perceived large-scale Soviet arms transfers to Ethiopia, Iraq, and Syria as a threat to American friends and allies in the region. Israel's annexation of the Golan Heights provided a further bridge for the USSR into Syria.

31. Michael Klare, *Rogue States and Nuclear Outlaws* (New York: Hill and Wang, 1995).

32. U.S. Department of State, "Address by President Reagan Before the American Bar Association," *Current Policy*, no. 721 (July 8, 1985).

33. Anthony Lake, "Confronting Backlash States," *Foreign Affairs* 73, no. 2 (March/April 1994): 45-46.

34. In Title 22, Section 2656f(d) of the United States Code, there is a definition of terrorism: premeditated, politically motivated violence perpetrated against noncombatant targets by subnational groups or agents, usually intended to influence an audience.

35. U.S. Congress, Committee on International Relations, *Syria: Peace Partner or Rogue Regime* Hearing, 104th Cong., 2nd sess., 25 July 1996. Testimony of Ambassador Philip Wilcox. Available online via Congressional Information Service's Congressional Compass.

36. Department of State, Office of the Coordinator for Counterterrorism, *1994 Patterns of Global Terrorism* (Washington, D.C.: Government Printing Office, April 1995).

37. Department of State Bureau of Economic and Business Affairs, *Syria: 1994 Country Report on Economic Policy and Trade Practices* (Washington, D.C.: Government Printing Office, 1995).

38. Department of State Bureau of Public Affairs, *Background Notes: Syria* (Washington, D.C.: Government Printing Office, November 1994).

39. White House, Office of the Press Secretary, "Remarks at a Press Conference by President Clinton and President Asad on October 27, 1994," in the Great Hall of the Presidential Palace in Damascus, Syria.

40. The Foreign Assistance Act of 1961 requires that the State Department issue on an annual basis the *International Narcotics Control Strategy Report*. The act also mandates that the president identify a list of the major drug-producing and transit countries as defined by law. Syria has been on the narcotics list since its armed forces moved into Lebanon in large numbers during the 1980s. Damascus appears on the 1997 list of major drug producing and transit countries. See Department of State, Bureau for International Narcotics and Law Enforcement Affairs, *International Narcotics Control Strategy Report*, "Syria," March 1997. Available online: http://www.usis.usemb.se/drugs/Africa/syria.htm

41. Department of State Bureau for International Narcotics and Law Enforcement Affairs, *International Narcotics Strategy Report* (Washington, D.C.: U.S. Government Printing Office, March 1995).

42. Central Intelligence Agency, *World Factbook 1993*.

43. Department of State Bureau for International Narcotics and Law Enforcement Affairs, *International Narcotics Strategy Report* (Washington, D.C.: U.S. Government Printing Office, March 1995). But Syrian participation in the drug trade may be a rational decision, because it allows Damascus to regain some losses due to the cost of American sanctions.

44. There is some confirmation for the Syrian claim to have worked to control the drug trade. One report indicates that illicit opium and cannabis cultivation in Lebanon is less due to strict enforcement and highly effective continued eradication efforts by joint Lebanese-Syrian authorities. Bureau for International Narcotics and Law Enforcement, *International Narcotics Control Strategy Report* (Washington, D.C.: March 1996).

45. There was a May 7, 1996 letter sent to Secretary of State Warren Christopher from Representative Michael Forbes (Rep.-New York). Twenty-nine other members signed the letter. It concerned Washington's role in the Israeli-Syrian talks. The letter referred to reports that the Clinton Administration might be prepared to provide significant monetary, diplomatic, and security benefits to Syria in exchange for a peace agreement with Israel. The letter suggested that because of Syrian support for terrorism, it would be inappropriate to remove Damascus from the list of terrorist nations, even if the administration believed that it would further the peace process with Israel. Available online: http://www.covesoft.com/afsi/forbes/forbes.htm

46. Thomas Lipman, "State Department Back on Effort to Court Syria," *Washington Post*, March 31, 1994, sec. A, 1.; Steve Greenhouse, "State Department Steps Back on Effort to Court Syria," *New York Times*, April 1, 1994.

47. In making alliance commitments, the United States assumes responsibility to defend its allies primarily from U.S. foes. If the United States pledged to

defend its friends against their foes, Washington would invariably become involved in fighting its own friends.

48. Robert Pelletreau, "U.S. Policy Toward the Middle East: Steering a Steady Course," address by the Assistant Secretary of State before the Chautauqua Institution, Chautauqua, N.Y. (August 21, 1996).

49. A reference point is a threshold, such as the status quo, below which are perceived losses.

50. The State Department under Warren Christopher shifted its primary goal or reference point regarding Syria from condemnation and isolation of state sponsors of terrorism to viewing Damascus as an integral part of the peace process with Jerusalem, a "key to completing the circle of peace." See Charles Lane, "A Man of Good Intentions: St. Chris on the Road to Damascus," New Republic (July 29, 1996).

51. Ze'ev Schiff, "The Necessary Security Conditions for Peace with Syria," Ha'aretz, January 21, 1994, sec. B, 5.

52. In an editorial in the Israeli newspaper Hatzofeh, on December 29, 1996, there was a report that Damascus had sent a message via Paris of an interest in resuming talks with Israel. The editors speculated that Assad may have felt that he was liable to miss the train if he continued his delaying policy vis-à-vis the negotiations, while the Israeli-Palestinian negotiations were moving forward.

53. Ephraim Kam, "Warning of War Before Its Time," Ma'ariv, August 29, 1996, sec. B, 2.

54. Ze'ev Maoz, "The Probability That Syria Will Go to War Increasing Considerably," Ha'aretz, August 18, 1996, sec. B, 3.

55. Syria has developed a military capability to strike at the Israeli rear, at population centers, and at other targets. And during the summer of 1996, Damascus ordered test firing of the Scud-C missile. But Israeli security specialists did not view these tests as cause for concern. Soviet doctrine required such tests to be held at the end of annual training exercises by Syrian ground to ground missile brigades. See Danny Leshem, "Between the Missile and the Katyusha," Yediot Aharonot, August 22, 1996, sec. B, 3.

However, "The Syrians estimate that Israel has no effective response to a missile attack on it. Damascus' intention: to deter Israel for the next few years, until the 'arrow' missile becomes operational. Thus Syria will be able to carry out a limited military operation to revive the peace process. Over the last months fortified launch sites have been built, and the development of chemical warheads accelerated. Experiments with VX gas failed. Israel torpedoed Syrian missile deal with China by diplomatic means." See Ron Ben-Yishai, "Syrian Missiles—The Primary Strategic Threat to Israel," Yediot Ahronot, June 22, 1997, sec. A, 8-9.

56. See Aaron Lerner, "Review of Syria's Missile Strategy and Iraqi Biological Weapons?" October 23, 1996. Available online:
http://www.torget.se/users/g/GaNdAlF/Vapen1.html
And Eitan Rabin, "Iran Developing Missile with Range of 1,300 Kilometers," Ha'aretz, July 13, 1997, sec. A, 2.

## Chapter Six

1. Scott Snyder, "North Korean Crises and American Choices: Managing U.S. Policy Toward the Korean Peninsula," Unpublished Paper presented at the 1997 International Studies Association Convention, panel entitled "Crisis Forecasting on North Korea: Myth and Reality," Toronto, Canada (March 19, 1997; updated May 1, 1997), 8. See also, Snyder, "A Framework for Achieving Reconciliation on the Korean Peninsula," *Asian Survey* (August 1995): 35, 699-710.

2. "North Korea literally has a gun at our [the United States] head even as it begs for relief." See Robert Manning and James Przystup, "Feed Me Or I'll Kill You," *Washington Post,* February 20, 1997, sec. A, 23.

3. "Pyongyang should be given the choice of keeping its gun or its tin cup. But to allow it to have both is sheer folly." Manning and Przystup, "Feed Me Or I'll Kill You."

4. Karen Elliott House, "Let North Korea Collapse," *Wall Street Journal,* February 21, 1997, sec. A, 14. See also Bruce Cumings, "Divided Korea: United Future?" *Headline Series* 306 (Spring 1994): 25-28.

5. Following the post–World War II Soviet military occupation of the northern portion of the Korean Peninsula, the USSR established the state of North Korea in 1948. In the same year, the occupying forces of the United States established South Korea.

6. People in the North Korean countryside are starving, underweight and "rapidly descending into the hell of a severe famine," according to Representative Tony Hall (Dem.-Ohio). He completed a three-day visit to North Korea in April 1997. "Evidence of slow starvation on a massive scale was plain wherever we made an effort to look," Hall said. He added that conditions had deteriorated significantly since he had made a similar visit in August 1996. The member of Congress said he was allowed unlimited access to villages north of Pyongyang, where few outsiders are permitted. Hall told how he had met an elderly woman making soup from year-old cabbage leaves; he visited an unheated hospital with no medicine that was so cold that he could see his own breath. He saw underweight children. Many of them had become orphans when their mothers died from malnutrition. Kevin Sullivan, "Congressman Finds 'Severe Famine' in North Korea," *Washington Post,* April 9, 1997, sec. A, 24.

7. For an explication of crisis as an opportunity for bureaucratic warfare, see Raymond Tanter, *Who's at the Helm? Lessons of Lebanon* (Boulder: Westview Press, 1990), 120-23.

8. North Korea borders China on the north and Russia on the northeast, the Sea of Japan on the east, South Korea on the south, and the Yellow Sea on the west. The Yalu River is North Korea's longest river, and it forms part of the border with China.

9. The third alternative explicitly calls for combining two options—contain *and* embrace. With about 37,000 in combat along the DMZ, Washington seeks to contain the regime in Pyongyang. By providing humanitarian assistance, Americans embrace North Koreans.

10. Graham Allison, Albert Carnesale, and Joseph Nye, *Hawks, Doves, and Owls* (New York: W. W. Norton, 1985), 206-22. In addition to these three, others have used the hawk-dove framework. A journalist, Jim Mann, adds "hummingbirds" to the classification. They are analysts who believe that North Korea has the strength to ride out floods and famine without extreme changes in their manner of operations. See Jim Mann, "Future of North Korea May Become Clinton's Biggest Foreign Policy Test," *Los Angeles Times*, December 30, 1996, sec. A, 5. Another adherent of the idea that North Korea can ride out its economic crisis is Marcus Noland, "Why North Korea Will Muddle Through," *Foreign Affairs* 76, no. 4 (July/August 1997): 105-19, 114.

    See also Fred Ikle, *Every War Must End* (New York: Columbia University Press, 1991), 60-61, for his analysis of hawks and doves. In contrast to Allison, Carnesale, and Nye, Ikle uses these terms to describe the struggle within a government for how a war should end. In answering the question, "Who are the traitors?," Ikle defines hawks as those who engage in treasonous adventurism instead of terminating the fighting: in search of peace with honor, they fight too much and too long. Doves are those who give aid and comfort to the enemy by retreating in the face of aggression: in a quest for peace at any cost, they would fight too little and for too short a time.

11. In addition to applying this framework to North Korea, a hawks-doves-owls classification is relevant to Iran, Iraq, Libya, Syria, and Cuba. But the framework is particularly suited to an analysis of the Korean Peninsula. Because of the higher likelihood of deterrence failure, unintended escalation, and loss of control due to misperception in Korea than in the other cases, this conceptual framework is of great heuristic value.

12. Thomas Schelling, *Arms and Influence* (New Haven: Yale University Press, 1996), 53-55. He discusses the relationship among interests, credible commitments, and capabilities.

13. Seth Faison, "Gingrich Warns China That U.S. Would Act If It Attacked Taiwan," *New York Times*, March 31, 1997, sec. A, 1, 5.

    Kenneth Lieberthal, a China scholar at the University of Michigan, said that Gingrich apparently would commit the United States to defending Taiwan, even if Taiwan took provocative steps. Such steps might include making unilateral statements that could be construed as declarations of independence. Patrick Tyler, "Unfazed by Gingrich, China Agrees With Some of What He Said," *New York Times*, April 2, 1997, sec. A, 4.

14. On the one hand, Taiwan and China make claims on each other. In this sense, neither is "independent." Even though the Nationalists fled the mainland because of the civil war in China, their successors in Taiwan have never given up their claim to represent the whole country. Their counterparts on the mainland claim that Taiwan is a part of China and that they are its sole representatives. On the other hand, both countries act as independent states. At issue is whether the pro-independence movement on Taiwan will induce the leadership to make an explicit break from the mainland.

15. Robert Harkavy, *Preemption and Two-Front Conventional Warfare* (Jerusalem: Leonard Davis Institute for International Relations, Hebrew University of

Jerusalem, Papers on Peace Problems, 1977), 8. Harkavy distinguishes between preemptive attack and preventive war. In preemption, the threatened actor places a premium on offensive action. But in prevention, that actor does not perceive striking the first blow as crucial. In a decision to launch a preventive war, "What *is* important is the forestalling of a change in the balance of power," *Op. cit.,* 7 [emphasis in original].

16. Edward Luttwak and Dan Horowitz, *The Israeli Army* (London: Allen Lane, 1975), 141.

17. Deterrence is a process of inducing a potential challenger not to take an action; coercion aims to get an actor to take an action or undo something already in place. Sanctions may be both deterrent and coercive in nature. Alexander George and Richard Smoke, *Deterrence in American Foreign Policy* (New York: Columbia University Press, 1974); Alexander George, David Hall, and William Simons, *The Limits of Coercive Diplomacy* (Boston: Little Brown, 1971).

18. During August 1997, however, four-power "talks about talks" began under the auspices of Columbia University in New York. Online Focus, "A Parched Land," August 5, 1997. Available online:
    http://www.pbs.org/newshour/bb/asia/july-dec97/korea_8-5.html

19. "And the chairman of the Joint Chiefs of Staff noted that, famine or no famine, the North Koreans were engaging in more military training than ever. 'If they are in such great difficulty, as they claim they are, and if they are in need of assistance,' asked Gen. John Shalikashvili, 'why are they spending their resources on this kind of military exercising? You have to ask yourself.'" Charles Krauthammer, "Why Feed a Mortal Enemy?" *Washington Post,* April 25, 1997, sec. A, 27.

20. "The North has chosen a bold and provocative course of action because the Clinton Administration's Korea policy is weak and misguided." Daryl M. Plunk, "Warning to North Korea: Stop Provocations and Talk with South Korea," *Backgrounder Update,* no. 273 (April 12, 1996, Foundation). See also Plunk, "Clinton's Korea Policy Falls Short: A Call to Congressional Action," *Backgrounder Update,* no. 236 (January 13, 1995), and "The Clinton Nuclear Deal with Pyongyang: Road Map to Progress or Dead End Street?" *Asian Studies Center Backgrounder,* no. 133 (November 4, 1994).

21. For a transcript of The Oprah Winfrey Show, "America Speaks Out on the Middle East Issue," number 1024, August 16, 1990, write to: Burrell's Transcripts, Box 7, Livingston, NJ, 07039 or call 1-800-777-TEXT (8398). In particular, see pages 13-14 of the transcript.

22. The approximate 1995 population of North Korea was 24 million. The estimate for South Korea was over 45 million. The GDP of South Korea in 1992 was about $270 billion, over ten times the size of the North Korean economy—estimated for 1995 at $21.5 billion. North Korea is one of the richer nations in Asia in terms of mineral resources. Major reserves include coal, iron ore, tungsten, and graphite. In contrast to North Korea, South Korea is poor in mineral resources. The main resources are coal (mostly anthracite), iron ore, and graphite. And there are reserves of natural gas offshore. See "North Korea" and "South Korea," *Microsoft Encarta 96*

*Encyclopedia*, 1993-1995 Microsoft Corporation. See also Central Intelligence Agency, "Korea, North," and "Korea, South," *World FactBook 1996* (Washington, D.C., 1997). Available online:
`http://www.odci.gov/cia/publications/nsolo/factbook/global.htm`

23. Doug Bandow and Ted Galen Carpenter are two leading advocates of cutting American ties with South Korea. See Doug Bandow, "A New Korea Policy for a Changed World," *Korean Journal of Defense Analysis* (Winter 1992); "North Korea and the Risks of Coercive Nonproliferation," Cato Institute Foreign Policy Briefing, no. 24 (May 4, 1993); *Tripwire: Korea and U.S. Foreign Policy in a Changed World* (Washington, D.C.: Cato Institute, 1996).

24. *Cato Handbook for Congress, 105th Congress*, "Weaning South Korea" (Washington, D.C.: Cato Institute, 1997), 485. Available online:
`http://www.frc.org/heritage/links/`

25. Krauthammer, "Why Feed a Mortal Enemy?"

26. "Indeed, State Department spokesman Nicholas Burns enunciated the more general principle: 'We believe countries ought to react to this [famine] the way they would to any other part of the world where there is a serious food crisis. All of us have a humanitarian imperative to help.'

   "'We don't want to link food aid to the peace talks, because we want to get the food to the people who need it quickly, without regard to politics and to international negotiations.'" Krauthammer, "Why Feed a Mortal Enemy?"

27. Allison, Carnesale, and Nye, *Hawks, Doves, and Owls*, 210.

28. Doves, however, do not always favor carrots. Doves divide into "activists" and "libertarians." Although activist doves perceive threats from adversaries, they would embrace rather than confront. Libertarian doves discern less of a threat and can justify less accommodation *and* less confrontation.

29. This bipolar classification obscures the overlap between the ideal types. One can envision power-hungry, mistake-ridden mercenaries as well as risk-prone, cold-hearted paranoids. In spite of the existence of these hybrid combinations, the assumption here is that they are exceptions rather than the rule.

30. In the field of psychology, prospect theory defines a reference point as a threshold value above which individuals perceive gains and below which they see losses. See Jack Levy, "An Introduction to Prospect Theory," in Barbara Farnham, ed., *Avoiding Losses/Taking Risks: Prospect Theory and International Conflict* (Ann Arbor: University of Michigan Press, 1994), 7-22, and Robert Jervis, in Farnham, *op. cit.*, "Political Implications of Loss Aversion," 23-40.

31. James Blight, "The New Psychology of War and Peace: A Book Review of Robert Jervis, Richard Ned Lebow, and Janice Gross Stein (with contributions by Patrick M. Morgan and Jack L. Snyder)," *International Security* 2, no. 3 (Winter 1986-87): 175-86. See also Raymond Tanter, "Psychology and Deterrence: A Book Review," *American Political Science Review* 82 (March 1988): 345-46.

32. Senator Craig Thomas, Chairman of the Senate Subcommittee on East Asian and Pacific Affairs, described North Korea as becoming increasingly iso-

lated, paranoid, and violent. He concluded that if any country has come to epitomize a rogue regime, it is North Korea. Senator Craig Thomas, "The United States-North Korea Agreed Framework," Senate Subcommittee on East Asian and Pacific Affairs, February 12, 1995. Available online: http://rs9.loc.gov/cgi.bin/query

33. For explications of *Juche*, see Chaouki Ajami, *Juche, Theory and Application* (Pyongyang: Foreign Languages Pub. House, 1978) and Kim Il Sung, *On Juche in Our Revolution* (New York: Weekly Guardian Associates, 1977).

34. Department of State, speech by Secretary of State Dean Acheson, Washington, D.C.: Government Printing Office, January 12, 1950.

35. Warren Christopher, "America's Strategy for a Peaceful and Prosperous Asia-Pacific," *Dispatch* [Magazine of the State Department], 6, (Summer, 1995): 591-94.

36. Joseph Nye, "Strategy for East Asia and U.S.-Japan Security Alliance," *Defense Issues*, 10, no. 35 ( March 29, 1995), 1.

While the same threatened interests may have both intrinsic and strategic aspects, the analysis here treats them as analytically distinct. For a further discussion of intrinsic and strategic interests, see Janice Stein, "The View From Cairo," in Robert Jervis, Richard Lebow, and Janice Gross Stein, eds., *Psychology and Deterrence* (Baltimore: Johns Hopkins University Press), 38-39.

37. Department of State, Office of the Coordinator for Counterterrorism, *1993 Patterns of Global Terrorism* (Washington, D.C.: Government Printing Office, April 1994). The following nations appeared on the State Department list of sponsors of international terrorism for 1995 (and 1996): Cuba, Iran, Iraq, Libya, North Korea, Sudan, and Syria. Sudan is the only country on that list not included in *Rogue Regimes*.

38. For an overview of scholarship on crisis decision making, see Michael Brecher, *Crises in World Politics: Theory and Reality,* 1st ed. (Oxford: Pergamon Press, 1993). Also see Michael Brecher, Jonathan Wilkenfeld, and Sheila Moser, *Crises in the Twentieth Century,* 1st ed. (New York: Pergamon Press, 1988); Michael Brecher and Patrick James, *Crisis and Change in World Politics* (Boulder: Westview Press, 1986).

39. In between the Korean War and the nuclear as well as humanitarian crises are several incidents of little relevance to the construction of scenarios and policy packages. These events include the North Korean seizure of the USS *Pueblo,* an electronic surveillance intelligence ship. See Michael Brecher and Jonathan Wilkenfeld, *A Study of Crisis* (Ann Arbor: University of Michigan Press, 1997), for a detailed historical account of such confrontations between the United States and North Korea.

40. Under the 1994 Agreed Framework between Pyongyang and Washington, North Korea agreed to contain spent fuel from its five-megawatt experimental reactor. Because such fuel could be used in nuclear weapons development, it was a source of confrontation between North Korea and the United States.

41. Moscow and Washington agreed to divide Korea at the 38th Parallel for the purpose of accepting the surrender of Japan's forces just prior to the

termination of World War II in the Pacific theater. But the United States and the USSR then employed their respective military presences to encourage friendly governments in their spheres of influence. Although Koreans in both the North and the South expressed hope for unification of the peninsula, they were unable to overcome their differences in the context of the Cold War. Hence, unification conferences during 1946 and 1947 ended without success. Then in 1947, Moscow and Washington began to set up separate governments. The United Nations adopted a resolution to hold general elections under its supervision. The USSR, however, declined to permit the UN to have access to North Korea. As a result, only the South Koreans held elections under UN supervision. The North's elections took place without widespread international acceptance of their legitimacy. Moscow had supported Kim Il Sung, a Communist who had led anti-Japanese irregulars in Manchuria. Likewise, Washington supported Syngman Rhee, a nationalist who also fought against the Japanese. In the South, Syngman Rhee won the election; in the North, Kim Il Sung emerged as Premier. The UN-monitored and American-sponsored elections in the South during 1948 resulted in the formation of the Republic of Korea in August of that year. A month later, the USSR set up the Democratic People's Republic of Korea (DPRK) in the north.

42. George and Smoke, *Deterrence in American Foreign Policy,* 145-46.

43. Regarding the question of "Who lost China?" Senator Joe McCarthy explained the loss as a product of a great conspiracy on a scale so immense as to dwarf any previous venture in history. He said, "It was not Chinese democracy under Mao that conquered China . . . as Acheson, [and others] contend. Soviet Russia conquered China and an important ally of the conquerors was this small left-wing element in our Department of State." Daniel Ellsberg, *Papers on the War* (New York: Simon & Schuster, 1972), 81. Ellsberg quotes McCarthy from the *Congressional Record,* January 25, 1949, 532-33.

44. A core concern within Indochina from the mid-1950s on was the developing Vietnam War. After the fall of China during its civil war and the Korean War, any American administration would be afraid of losing an Asian country to Communism. This fear trapped successive administrations in a basement of fear. The fear of loss to Communism explains why successive administrations were willing to expend blood and treasure without much hope of success. Such theoretical reasoning stems from prospect theory. See Farnham, ed., *Avoiding Losses/Taking Risks.*

45. Ellsberg explains the incremental commitments that eventuated in the Vietnam War as being a consequence of a succession of American presidents who feared the loss of land to communists on their watch. Because of the domestic costs associated with losing the war, presidents escalated without expectation of winning. In other words, they fought to avoid loss rather than to pursue gain. He calls this explanation the "stalemate machine," in contrast to a "quagmire" explanation. Ellsberg, *Papers on the War,* 42 ff.

An alternative explanation for why American became involved in the Vietnam War draws on the quagmire metaphor: "Each step in the deepening of the American commitment was reasonably regarded at the time as the last that would be necessary. Yet, in retrospect, each step led only to the next, until we find ourselves entrapped in that nightmare of American strategists, a land war in Asia." Arthur Schlesinger, Jr., *The Bitter Heritage: Vietnam and American Democracy, 1941-1966* (Boston: Houghton Mifflin, 1967), as cited in Ellsberg, *Papers on the War,* 49-50. Later, however, Schlesinger admitted that he had been mistaken in the suggestion that escalatory steps would be the last ones necessary. See Arthur Schlesinger, Jr., "Eyeless in Indochina," *New York Review of Books* (October 21, 1971).

46. In connection with threat perception, at issue is whether the underestimation of threat stemmed from a motivated or unmotivated bias. If the Truman Administration discounted the regional threat because doing so provided a benefit, doing so would be evidence of a motivated bias. Conversely, if it downplayed the menace because of expectations, that would suggest an unmotivated bias. In fact, the Truman Administration misperceived the North Korean regional threat because it expected to confront a Soviet global threat. Such misperceptions indicate that an unmotivated bias dominated decision making.

47. David Albright, "How Much Plutonium Does North Korea Have?" *Bulletin of the Atomic Scientists,* September/October 1994, 46.

48. John Fialka, "Asian Tinderbox," *Wall Street Journal,* September 3, 1993, sec. A, 1, 2.

49. David Albright, "How Much Plutonium Does North Korea Have?" 53.

50. According to the Clinton Administration, the Agreed Framework stops Pyongyang's nuclear program in its tracks. A special focus of the accord is to halt North Korea's separation of weapons-grade plutonium and all nuclear fuel-related facilities. The Agreement requires North Korea to resume full compliance with its obligations under the NPT and IAEA safeguards agreement. The Framework provides alternate energy in the form of heavy fuel to compensate for the projected loss of nuclear energy supplies. It anticipates formation of an international consortium to provide two proliferation-resistant light-water reactors to replace the more dangerous graphite-moderated facilities. In addition, the Agreement neutralizes the threat posed by the spent nuclear fuel already in North Korea by removing it for disposal in a third nation. The Agreed Framework requires dismantlement of North Korea's graphite-moderated reactors and begins a process of normalizing diplomatic and trade relations between Pyongyang and the rest of the world community in steps, as the parties implement the agreement. It also encourages restoration of a dialogue between North and South Korea, whose aim is "denuclearization" of the Korean Peninsula and, ultimately, establishment of a permanent mechanism of peace there. U.S. Congress, Committee on Armed Services United States, *Security Implications of the Nuclear Non-Proliferation Agreement with North Korea* Hearing, 104th Cong., 1st sess., 26 January 1995. Prepared statement by Honorable William Perry, Secretary of Defense, 15-16. Available online: http://web.lexis-nexis.com/cis/retrieve/document/s_witness. html?_form=s_witness.html&_mode=FULL&_results=G

{H^*KO!DUA!UUW$M[SDUA$UUC$AZ!WVZE!V!V$AA$]DAZDZ]
EZ$U&_library=news&_file=cngtst,fednew,poltrn,
polsum&_firstdoc=1&_reldoc=11&_citesper=25&_maxdocs=11
&_md5=32054202b33b83c0511ffc0ca76a1fc7

51. William Perry, "Fulfilling the Role of Preventive Defenses," U.S. Department of Defense Publications, Volume 11, Number 44, January 18, 1996. Available online:
http://www.dtic.dla.mil/defenselink/pubs/di95/di1144.html

52. Scott Snyder, "The North Korean Nuclear Challenge," Unpublished Paper for the U.S. Institute of Peace: Special Report (September 4, 1996).

53. Scott Snyder, "A Coming Crisis on the Korean Peninsula? The Food Crisis, Economic Decline, and Political Considerations," Unpublished Paper for the U.S. Institute of Peace: Special Report (September 17, 1996).

54. "In the summer of 1994, many [in Washington] feared that military measures might be required to halt the North Korean weapons program. The challenge at that time was coordinating policy with regional neighbors—Japan, South Korea, and the People's Republic of China—which were reluctant or unwilling to apply economic sanctions to prod North Korea toward full observance of the Nuclear Non-Proliferation Treaty." Snyder, "A Coming Crisis on the Korean Peninsula?"

55. Jon Leverenz and Brett Gover, eds., *The World*, (New York: Rand McNally, 1996), 103-4.

56. United Press International, "UN Seeks More Aid for North Korea," UN World Food Programme (UNWFP), May 6, 1997, available online:
http://biz.yahoo.com/upi/97/05/06/international_news/
norkorun_1.html

57. "An alternative might be a multilateral effort to provide food credits (perhaps with continuing monitored deliveries by UNWFP) in proportion to North Korean progress toward economic transparency and fundamental agricultural reforms. By dealing multilaterally with the food problem as a core structural issue in North Korea's economy rather than as a political issue, South Korea, the United States, and Japan might be able to help North Korea while simultaneously inducing it to take initial steps toward reform and integration with the global economy." Snyder, "A Coming Crisis on the Korean Peninsula?"

58. Three articles contributed to the different perspectives concerning the future of North Korea: House, "Let North Korea Collapse"; Kevin Sullivan, "Survival Instinct: Don't Bet the Collective on North Korea's Imminent Collapse," *Washington Post,* March 9, 1997, sec. C, 1; and Steve Glain, "The Endgame in North Korea: Regime Could Go With a Bang, a Whimper—Or a Handshake," *Wall Street Journal,* February 27, 1997, sec. A, 12.

59. See House, "Let North Korea Collapse."

60. See Caspar Weinberger, *The Next War* (Washington, D.C.: Regnery Publishing, 1996).

61. Marcus Noland, "Why North Korea Will Muddle Through."

62. Thomas Ricks and Steve Glain, "U.S. Gears Up for North Korean Collapse," *Wall Street Journal,* June 26, 1997, sec. A, 14.

63. Ricks and Glain, "U.S. Gears Up for North Korean Collapse."
64. Motivated bias is one that distorts threat perception because individuals see what they wish to notice; unmotivated bias operates when they view what they expect to observe.
65. "When U.S. strategists began looking for the 'Iraqs of the future,' most eyes in Washington turned to Korea—the last remaining Stalinist regime in Asia and a longtime foe of the United States." Michael Klare, *Rogue States and Nuclear Outlaws* (New York: Hill and Wang, 1995), 136.
66. "The nation's 24 million people are living off an average 150 grams of food per day, or about 12 spoonfuls—one-fifth the intake experts say is needed for a healthful diet. Children and elderly are dying at an increasing rate . . ." "CNN Gets Rare Glimpse of North Korea," CNN Interactive, August 13, 1997. Available online:

    http://www.cnn.com/WORLD/9708/13/korea.gallery/index.html

## Chapter Seven

1. Eric Herring, "Rogue Rage, Can We Prevent Mass Destruction?" Paper delivered at the Third Pan–European International Relations–International Studies Association Annual Conference, Vienna, 16–19 September 1998. Submitted for publication to a special issue of *Journal of Strategic Studies* on "Preventing the Use of Weapons of Mass Destruction," forthcoming 1999.
2. Michael Klare, *Rogue States and Nuclear Outlaws* (New York: Hill and Wang, 1995).
3. Also see the levels of analysis categories in Kenneth Waltz, *Man, the State, and War* (New York: Columbia University Press, 1959).
4. Jessica Stern, *The Ultimate Terrorists* (Cambridge MA: Harvard University Press, 1999), prepublication proofs, 3–4.
5. Interview with Dr. Kanatjan Alibekov, former First Deputy Director of Biopreparat, USSR. Public Broadcasting System, Frontline, October 11, 1998. Available online:

    http://www.pbs.org/wgbh/pages/frontline/shows/plague/
    interviews/
6. Interview with James Baker, former Secretary of State, Public Broadcasting System, Frontline, October 11, 1998. Available online:

    http://www.pbs.org/wgbh/pages/frontline/shows/plague/
    interviews/
7. Ian Lesser and Ashley Tellis, *Strategic Exposure: Proliferation around the Mediterranean* (Santa Monica California: Rand Corporation, 1996), 5–6.
8. For documentation, see the discussion and sources below under the topic heading of Contractors.
9. Claire Sterling, *The Terror Network: The Secret War of International Terrorism* (New York: Holt, Rinehart, and Winston, 1981), 268–269.
10. Sterling, *The Terror Network,* 272–285.
11. Sterling, *The Terror Network,* 280.
12. Bruce Hoffman, *Inside Terrorism* NY: Columbia University Press, 1998.

13. Also see R. Scott Appleby, "Introduction" in *Spokesmen for the Despised: Fundamentalist Leaders of the Middle East* R. Scott Appleby, ed. (Chicago: University of Chicago Press, 1997), 13, endnote omitted.
14. Appleby, *Spokesmen for the Despised.*
15. Raymond Tanter, *Who's at The Helm? Lessons of Lebanon* (Boulder: Westview Press, 1990), 94–96.
16. Tanter, *Who's at The Helm?*, 94–96.
17. Also see Charles M. Sennott, *Boston Globe*, 26 June 1998. Available online: http://cnn.com/WORLD/9605/10/abu.abbas/index.html
18. Office of the Coordinator for Counterterrorism, U.S. Department of State, *1995 Patterns of Global Terrorism*. Available online: http://www.usis.usemb.se/terror/rpt1995/TERINT.HTM
    Also see Frances McMorris, "Sheik Rahman is Given Sentence of Life Without Parole for 'Urban Terrorism,'" *Wall Street Journal*, 18 January 1996, sec. B, 5.
19. Alison Mitchell, "The Twin Towers: Sifting Through Mideast Politics In Ashes of World Trade Center—Sheik Rahman The Cleric Under Scrutiny," *New York Times*, 14 March 1993, sec. 1, 39.
20. Mitchell, *New York Times*, 39. The ease in which Sheik Rahman obtained an American visa mirrors a later case involving suspects involved in the bombing of U.S. embassies in Africa during 1998. In that case, the suspects carried false passports from Yemen.
21. Washington Post Staff Writers, "Experts Say Sheik Rahman Has Found Following Among Frustrated Muslims," *Washington Post*, 26 June 1993, sec. A, 14.
22. Mitchell, *New York Times*, 39.
23. Washington Post Writers, sec. A, 14.
24. Office of the Coordinator for Counterterrorism, U.S. Department of State, *1995 Patterns of Global Terrorism*. Available online: http://www.usis.usemb.se/terror/rpt1995/TERINT.HTM
25. "Center Bomber Sues Jailers," *The Dominion (Wellington)*, 21 September, 1998, 5.
26. Sharon Walsh, "Mastermind In N.Y. City Blast Faces Solitary Confinement," *Buffalo News*, 9 January 1998, sec. A, 4.
27. Christopher Wren, "A Terrorist, Not a Defense Lawyer," *New York Times*, 7 September 1996, sec. 1, 25.
28. Laurie Mylroie, "Who is Ramzi Yousef; What it Matters," *The National Interest*, Winter 1995–1996. Available at: http://www.fas.org/irp/world/iraq/956-tni.htm
29. David Kocienewski, "In Terror Trial: The Mastermind; An Enigmatic Personality Whose Mission Was to Punish America," *New York Times*, 6 September 1996, sec. B, 8.
30. Wren, *New York Times*, 25.
31. Edwin Angeles, who was Abu Sayyaf's second-in-command until 1995, said Yousef used the Philippines as a "launching pad" for terrorist attacks around the world. Kocienewski, *New York Times*, 8.
32. Kocienewski, *New York Times*, 8.
33. Kocienewski, *New York Times*, 8.

34. Kocienewski, *New York Times*, 8.
35. Wren, *New York Times*, 25.
36. Yael Shahar, "Osama Bin Laden: Marketing Terrorism," International Policy Institute for Counter Terrorism, 22 August 1998. Available online: http://www.ict.org.il/default.htm.
37. Shahar, International Policy Institute for Counter Terrorism. See the Appendix to this chapter for a description of some of these groups.
38. Shahar, International Policy Institute for Counter Terrorism.
39. A 238–count indictment against Osama bin Laden for the bombings of the U.S. embassies is available online:
    ```
    http://www.fbi.gov/fo/nyfo/prladen.htm
    http://www.usia.gov/current/news/topic/intrel/98110602.npo.
    html?/products/washfile/newsitem.shtml
    ```
40. Richard Straus, ed., *Middle East Policy Survey*, 30 September 1998, 2.
41. After the bombing of American Embassies in Africa during August 1998, Washington highlighted the role of freelance terrorists and launched cruise missile attacks against their bases in Afghanistan and a plant ostensibly used to produce WMD in the Sudan.

    But in a discussion of Iraq–Sudan connections, a specialist on Iraq—Laurie Mylroie—contends that the Clinton Administration focused too much on Osama Bin Laden and not enough on his ties to Iraq. She points to a widespread Iraqi intelligence presence in the Sudan as circumstantial evidence of a Baghdad–bin Laden link. *IRAQ NEWS*, August 24, 1998. Available online:
    ```
    sam11@erols.com
    ```
42. Daniel Pearl, "Strange Chemistry: How a Sudan Factory became the Target of U.S. Airstrikes," *Wall Street Journal*, 28 October 1998, sec. 1, 1, 11.
43. Excerpts from Office of the Coordinator for Counterterrorism, U.S. Department of State, *1996 Patterns of Global Terrorism*. Available online:
    ```
    http://www.state.gov/www/global/terrorism/1996Report/appb.html
    ```

# INDEX